T5-AVN-396

A SHORT HISTORY OF ENGLISH LAW

A SHORT

HISTORY OF ENGLISH LAW

FROM THE EARLIEST TIMES TO THE END OF THE YEAR 1911

BY

EDWARD JENKS, M.A., B.C.L.

OF THE MIDDLE TEMPLE, BARRISTER-AT-LAW

PRINCIPAL AND DIRECTOR OF LEGAL STUDIES OF THE LAW SOCIETY

BOSTON

LITTLE, BROWN, AND COMPANY

1912

Printers
S. J. Parkhill & Co., Boston, U.S.A.

TO

OLIVER WENDELL HOLMES

ASSOCIATE JUSTICE OF THE SUPREME COURT

OF THE UNITED STATES

FORMERLY CHIEF JUSTICE OF MASSACHUSETTS

AUTHOR OF "THE COMMON LAW"

THE AMERICAN EDITION OF THIS WORK

IS (WITH PERMISSION)

DEDICATED

PREFACE

About ten years ago, Messrs. Methuen & Co. approached the author with a proposal for a "History of English Law" in one volume. The interest aroused in a long-neglected subject by the brilliant work of the late Sir Fitzjames Stephen, of Sir Frederick Pollock, of Mr. Justice Holmes, and, above all, of the late Professor Maitland, to say nothing of others whose contributions, though more fragmentary, were profoundly interesting, had convinced most teachers of English Law that a rich field of educational effort awaited development. Unfortunately, the scale on which the writing of these authors was planned, rendered them unsuitable for the average student, whose time was limited; and it was felt that the subject could hardly take the place which it deserved in the ordinary training of the lawyer, till some more modest, but comprehensive, manual had appeared.

At the time when the approach referred to was made, the author's time was deeply pledged in other directions; and he doubted, also, whether the moment had then arrived at which the state of available knowledge rendered such a work possible. He therefore suggested an application to his friend Dr. Holdsworth.

As is well known, that application was not made in vain; and the world is to-day the richer by Dr. Holdsworth's three volumes. But, in the hands of Dr. Holdsworth, the work has proved to be something very different from what was at first contemplated; and the plan for a single volume has developed into a scheme of which the first three volumes bring us down only to the end of the sixteenth century.

Meanwhile, largely owing to the labours of Professor Maitland and other contributors to the noble series of volumes produced by the Selden Society, more material has become available; while the recent publication, the fruit of American enterprise, of the three volumes of *Select Essays in Anglo-American Legal History*, has further stimulated interest in the subject.

It seemed, therefore, to the author, that the time had at last arrived, at which Messrs. Methuen & Co.'s original idea might be realized; and he ventured to approach them with a suggestion for a revival of the plan. It was, of course, obviously due to Dr. Holdsworth that his concurrence should also be obtained. In both quarters the response was prompt and cordial; and Dr. Holdsworth, with great generosity, further offered to read the proof sheets of the intended work, and give the author the benefit of his criticism.

Thus the way seemed clear; and the present book is the result. As space was limited, the author has touched lightly upon that side of our legal history which has already been made the subject of adequate treatment, viz. the origin and development of the Courts, and the relations of the State towards its subjects. These can be found conveniently summarized in Professor Maitland's posthumously published *Constitutional History of England*, in the first volume of Dr. Holdsworth's *History of English Law*, and in Dr. Carter's *English Legal Institutions*, as well as in the many other useful treatises on Constitutional History. But with this exception, the present volume attempts to cover the whole field of English legal history, from the earliest times to the present day.

That this is a sufficiently ambitious attempt, no one can be better aware than the author. Though he has made no statement which he has not verified from original evidence, he has, naturally, availed himself to the full of the work of previous writers for the earlier part of his task. But, from the end of the sixteenth century, he has sailed over an almost uncharted sea; and his responsibility is great. He can only plead that he has kept a careful look-out, and that he has striven faithfully to sail the ship in the main current, without attempting to enter the bays and inlets, which to have explored would either have prolonged the voyage to an undue length, or have neglected the essential for the picturesque but less important.

One other word as to the plan of the book may be permitted. An American correspondent, whose reputation as a teacher and writer stands high, has urged upon the author the adoption of what is known as the "vertical" method of writing history, by which the development of each existing institution is separately traced from its origin to its present form. After long reflection, the author felt it impossible to adopt the plan proposed by this suggestion, because, in his view, it would either involve almost endless repetition, or it would obscure one of the most important lessons to be learnt from English legal history. For, if there is one truth which that history makes more clear than another, it is that the sharp division into distinct subjects which is so familiar a feature of a modern and highly complex system of law, finds no place in its early stages. Property, contract, tort, crime, even the apparently fundamental distinction between substantive law and procedure, are not recognized by primitive people. The germs of all these ideas may be detected in early law by the microscope of the expert; just as the future stem, tendrils, leaves, flowers, and fruit, may be detected in the seed of a plant. But one of the most valuable lessons to be learnt from the study of the growth of a native and independent system of law like the English, is an appreciation of the processes by which these specialized ideas have slowly detached themselves from those primitive notions of right and wrong which are the kernel of all systems of law. So the author has adhered to the old-fashioned plan; dividing his subject into historical periods, marked by events which seemed to him to be milestones on the ever-broadening path of legal development.

It remains only for the author to express his grateful thanks to those whose labours have rendered his task possible of achievement (if indeed it has been achieved), and to commit his work to the judgment of the public. To Dr. Holdsworth, who, as has been stated, has been kind enough to spare the time to read the proof sheets, his thanks are most especially due. It is needless to say that he has benefited greatly by Dr. Holdsworth's suggestions; and, where he has not been convinced by them, he has, doubtless, been wrong. As for the work, the author will be more than satisfied if his attempt encourages others to do better. He makes, of course, no claim to completeness; his hope is only that he has shown some sense of proportion, and an essential reverence for the truth, which will not be found without their uses. In a word, his aim has been to stimulate, not to satisfy.

LONDON, April, 1912.

CONTENTS

PERIOD I

BEFORE THE NORMAN CONQUEST

CHAPTER I

OLD ENGLISH LAW

PERIOD II

THE CONQUEST TO THE DEATH OF HENRY III

(1066–1272)

CHAPTER II

SOURCES OF THE COMMON LAW

CHAPTER III

FEUDALISM AND LAND LAW

CHAPTER IV

IMPROVED LEGAL PROCEDURE

CHAPTER V

THE LAW OF CHATTELS

PERIOD III

EDWARD I TO THE COMMONWEALTH

(1272–1660)

CHAPTER VI

THE TRIUMPH OF THE KING'S COURTS

CHAPTER VII

NEW INTERESTS IN LAND

CHAPTER VIII

RIGHTS AND METHODS OF ALIENATION

CHAPTER IX

THE LAW OF PERSONAL PROPERTY

CHAPTER X

CONTRACT AND TORT

CHAPTER XI

CRIMINAL LAW AND PROCEDURE

CHAPTER XII

CIVIL PROCEDURE IN THE LATER MIDDLE AGES

PERIOD IV

THE RESTORATION TO THE PRESENT DAY

(1660–1911)

CHAPTER XIII

MODERN AUTHORITIES AND THE LEGAL PROFESSION

CHAPTER XIV

REFORM BY EQUITY

CHAPTER XV

CHANGES IN LAND LAW

CHAPTER XVI

NEW FORMS OF PERSONAL PROPERTY

CHAPTER XVII

CONTRACT AND TORT IN MODERN LAW

CHAPTER XVIII

REFORM IN THE CRIMINAL LAW

CHAPTER XIX

MODERN CIVIL PROCEDURE

TABLE OF STATUTES

		PAGE
1708	7 Anne, c. 20 (Land Registry)	180, 256
1709	8 Anne, c. 18 (or 14) (Landlord and Tenant)	133, 207
	c. 21 (or 19) (Copyright)	130, 278
1717	4 Geo. I, c. 11 (Transportation)	337
1718	5 Geo. I, c. 19 (South Sea Company)	287
1719	6 Geo. I, c. 18 (Royal Exchange Assurance)	287
1724	11 Geo. I, c. 18 (Wills)	268
1725	12 Geo. I, c. 29 (Arrest on Mesne Process)	348
1729	2 Geo. II, c. 23 (Attorneys)	204
1730	4 Geo. II, c. 28 (Landlord and Tenant)	207, 240, 242
1731	4 Geo. II, c. 26 (Proceedings in English)	348
1732	5 Geo. II, c. 27 (Small Debts)	348
	c. 30 (Bankruptcy)	375
1733	7 Geo. II, c. 8 (Stock Jobbing)	288
1735	8 Geo. II, c. 6 (Land Registry)	256
	9 Geo. II, c. 36 (Charitable Uses)	207
1737	11 Geo. II, c. 19 (Distress for Rent)	207, 240
1750	23 Geo. II, c. 26 (Attorneys)	204
1752	25 Geo. II, c. 6 (Witnesses)	270
1753	26 Geo. II, c. 33 (Marriages)	303
1767	7 Geo. III, c. 48 (Companies)	288
1772	12 Geo. III, c. 20 (Pleading)	51
1773	13 Geo. III, c. 26 (Ships)	293
1774	14 Geo. III, c. 78 (Life Assurance)	207, 311
1779	19 Geo. III, c. 70 (Arrest on Mesne Process)	348
1786	26 Geo. III, c. 60 (Ships)	293
1787	27 Geo. III, c. 38 (Designs)	283
1792	32 Geo. III, c. 53 (Stipendiary Magistrates)	337
	c. 60 (Libel)	309
1794	34 Geo. III, c. 23 (Designs)	283
1799	39 Geo. III, c. 81 (Conspiracy)	315
1800	39 & 40 Geo. III, c. 106 (Conspiracy)	315
1801	41 Geo. III, c. 107 (Books)	279
	c. 109 (Inclosures)	264
1803	43 Geo. III, c. 46 (Payment into Court)	348
1807	47 Geo. III, St. II, c. 74 (Debts)	250
1809	49 Geo. III, c. 115 (Insolvent Debtors)	376
1813	53 Geo. III, c. 24 (Vice-Chancellor)	214
1814	54 Geo. III, c. 156 (Copyright)	279
1815	55 Geo. III, c. 192 (Will)	241
1816	56 Geo. III, c. 100 (*Habeas Corpus*)	335
1819	59 Geo. III, c. 46 (Trial by Battle)	43, 55, 156
1823	4 Geo. IV, c. 41 (Shipping)	293
1824	5 Geo. IV, c. 95 (Conspiracy)	316
	c. 26 (Bankruptcy)	375
1825	6 Geo. IV, c. 91 (Companies)	288
	c. 105 (Customs)	293
	c. 110 (Shipping)	293
	c. 129 (Conspiracy)	317
1827	7 & 8 Geo. IV, c. 28 (Benefit of Clergy)	157, 338
	c. 29 (Larceny)	339

TABLE OF CASES

ABBREVIATIONS

A.S.L.	"Anglo-Saxon Laws," including both the German versions of Liebermann and Schmidt (*Gesetze der Angelsachsen*) and Thorpe's *Ancient Laws and Institutes of England* (Record Series).
H.L.R.	*Harvard Law Review.*
L.Q.R.	*Law Quarterly Review.*
P. & M.	Pollock, Sir F., and Maitland, F. W. *The History of English Law Before the Time of Edward I*, 2d edn. (Cambridge University Press, 1898, 2 vols.).
S.S.	*Publications of the Selden Society* (London, Quaritch, 1887).

REPORTERS

A.C.	(Law Reports) Appeal Cases.
A. &. E.	Adolphus and Ellis.
Ambl.	Ambler.
Atk.	Atkyns.
B. & Ald.	Barnewall and Alderson.
B. & C.	Barnewall and Cresswell.
B. & S.	Best and Smith.
Beav.	Beavan.
Bing.	Bingham.
Bro. C.C.	Brown's Chancery Cases.
Bro. P.C.	Brown's Cases in Parliament.
Burr.	Burrow.
C.B.	Common Bench.
C.B. (N.S.)	Common Bench (New Series).
Cart.	Carthew.
Ch. Ca. or Cha. Ca.	Cases in Chancery.
Ch.D.	(Law Reports) Chancery Division.
Cl. & F.	Clark & Finnelly.
C.P.D.	(Law Reports) Common Pleas Division.
Cowp.	Cowper.
Cox,	Cox's Chancery Cases.
Cox, Cr. Ca.	Cox's Criminal Cases.
Cro. Car. / Cro. Eliz. / Cro. Jac.	Croke.
De G. M. & G.	De Gex, Macnaghten, and Gordon.
Doug.	Douglas.
Drew.	Drewry.
E. & B.	Ellis and Blackburn.
Ed.	Eden.
Eq. Ca. Ab.	Equity Cases Abridged.
Eq.	(Law Reports) Equity.
Exch.	Welsby, Hurlstone, and Gordon.
Freem. Cha.Ca.	Freeman's Chancery Cases.
H.L.C.	Clark's House of Lords Cases.
Hagg.	Haggard.
Hob.	Hobart.
Hutt.	Hutton.
Keb.	Keble.
L.J.K.B.	Law Journal, King's Bench.
L.R.	Law Reports.

L.R. Ch. App.	(Law Reports) Chancery Appeal Cases.
L.R.H.L.	(Law Reports) House of Lords.
L.R.Q.B.	(Law Reports) Queen's Bench.
Ld. Raym.	Lord Raymond.
Leon.	Leonard.
Lev.	Levinz.
M. & Cr.	Mylne and Craig.
M. & G.	Manning and Granger.
M. & S.	Maule and Selwyn.
M. & W.	Meeson and Welsby.
Macq.	Macqueen (Scotch Appeals).
Mer.	Merivale.
Mod.	Modern Reports.
My. & K.	Mylne and Keene.
P. Wms.	Peere Williams.
Plowd.	Plowden.
Pre. Cha.	Precedents in Chancery.
Q.B.D.	(Law Reports) Queen's Bench Division.
Rep.	Coke.
Rep. in Ch. / Rep. Ch.	Reports in Chancery.
Salk.	Salkeld.
Sch. &. Lef.	Schoales and Lefroy (Irish).
Sid.	Siderfin.
St. Tr.	State Trials.
Stra.	Strange.
T.L.R.	Times Law Reports.
T.R.	Durnford and East, Term Reports.
Toth.	Tothill.
Vent.	Ventris.
Vern.	Vernon.
Ves. Sr.	Vesey, Senior.
Wms. Sand.	Sanders (ed. Williams).
Y.B.	Year Books.

PERIOD I

BEFORE THE NORMAN CONQUEST

AUTHORITIES

Gesetze der Angelsachsen, ed. Liebermann (best).
" " ed. Schmidt.

Ancient Laws and Institutes of England, ed. Thorpe (Record Series).

Codex Diplomaticus Aevi Saxonici, ed. Kemble.

Diplomatarium Anglicum Aevi Saxonici, ed. Thorpe.

Handbook to Land Charters, Earle.

TEXT-BOOKS

Bigelow, M. M. *History of Procedure in England*, chapters v–x (Macmillan).

Holdsworth, W. S. *A History of English Law*, Vol. II, Book I (Methuen).

Maitland, F. W. *A Prologue to a History of English Law* (Select Essays in Anglo-American Legal History, I, 7–33).

Pollock, Sir F. *English Law Before the Norman Conquest* (Select Essays in Anglo-American Legal History, I, 88–107).

Pollock, Sir F., and Maitland, F. W. *The History of English Law Before the Time of Edward I*, Book I, chapters I and II (Cambridge Press).

A SHORT HISTORY OF ENGLISH LAW

CHAPTER I

OLD ENGLISH LAW

It is the glory of English Law, that its roots are sunk deep into the soil of national history; that it is the slow product of the age-long growth of the national life. A few words, therefore, albeit diffident and cautious, must be said in this book of that dim period in which the foundations of the national character were laid. As years go, it was a long period, lasting little less than six centuries. During those long years, English men lived and died, married and begot children, fought a good deal and brawled more, were converted from heathendom to a rather secular Christianity, built a few petty towns. But, for the most part, their lives were occupied with clearing and tilling a fertile and well-watered country, whose very fertility was a source of endless labour; for the English settlers found vast forests to be cleared before the soil would begin to yield corn or pasture. The record of those long years is in the smiling fields of modern England, whose remotest village seems, to the visitor accustomed to the rough farming of virgin lands, like the garden of some lordly pleasure-house. Some few chronicles of this dim time have survived to us. But of laws and institutes we have little; and that little is obscure and untrustworthy.

The Anglo-Saxon Laws

The so-called Anglo-Saxon Laws date from a well-recognized stage in the evolution of law. They reveal to us a patriarchal folk, living in isolated settlements, and leading lives regulated by immemorial custom. Whilst there are certain features common to all of them, showing us a society to some extent homogeneous, they differ in detail from one petty kingdom to another, almost from one village to another. Therefore, it is very hard to base any general statements upon them. More serious drawback still, the longer one studies them, the more one suspects that they deal rather with the novel and uncertain, than with the normal and undoubted rules of law. That is, after all, natural; for, among primitive people, the process of law-making, or law-declaring, is painful and laborious, only to be resorted to under severe pressure. Why trouble to record that which every village elder knows? Only when a disputed point has long caused bloodshed and disturbance, or when a successful invader (military or theological) insists on a change, is it necessary to draw up a code. That is practical sense; but it has its drawbacks for the student of legal history.

Their Character

Still, the student must be grateful for the Anglo-Saxon Laws. In some respects they are unique. Some of them are very archaic in character, pointing to a society not far removed from utter barbarism, whose women and slaves stand on the same footing as cattle and sheep. Most of them seem to have been drawn up in the vernacular; whereas the corresponding *Leges Barbarorum* of the Continental Germans were, almost invariably, recorded in Latin, probably by Italian scribes. Consequently, the old English laws are more likely to be true pictures of life than codes like the *Lex Salica*, which, as the famous "Malberg glosses" suggest, was translated by its compilers from an uncouth tongue which they failed to understand.[1]

Foreign Influences

A much-debated question stands at the threshold of our story. How far are we justified in assuming that our English law is of English origin? England was settled by other tribes before the English arrived. Those tribes had a civilization of their own. They were conquered by the Romans, who governed them for centuries. Those almost-prehistoric centuries were the golden age of Roman jurisprudence; before the oldest of the Anglo-Saxon codes was drawn up, Justinian's monumental *Corpus Juris* had been given to the world. When Edward Longshanks conquered the Welsh in the thirteenth century, his officials held an inquest which revealed a highly organized system of tribal land-ownership; and this system may (though that is by no means certain) have dated from very ancient British times, and once have prevailed throughout Britain. Once more, the Anglo-Saxon laws bear evident traces of ecclesiastical influence; Aethelbirht's code was drawn up "on St. Augustine's Day." Are we to suppose that nothing found its way into

[1] See the Notes in the synoptic edition of the *Lex Salica* by Hessels and Kern (Murray, 1880).

them from decrees of Councils and Synods; though the days of a refined Canon Law were yet to come?[1]

The Question Unsolved

Each branch of this enquiry is matter for specialists; and none can safely yet dogmatize. Only it may be pointed out, that a rough and ignorant people like the English, noted from of old for their sullen aloofness from the wider world, would not be very amenable to foreign influences; that they would hardly be likely to borrow much from the conquered Welsh, from an Emperor at Constantinople, or even from an Eastern Council. Such outside influences as did penetrate into primitive England came, probably, from household slaves, some of whom might be captives of superior education, from provincial versions of the Theodosian Code, or from the Penitentials of the mass priest. It is doubtful whether Justinian's legislation was generally known in Western Europe before the Norman Conquest.

People's Ranks

First we notice, that there is no 'equality before the law.' A man's rights depended, both on his social rank, and, in some cases at least, on the custom of his neighbourhood. In various apocryphal documents drawn up after the Norman Conquest,[2] we see clear traces of a **status system,** which, though it was giving way, long continued to dominate English society. The noble by birth (**eorl, ætheling, gesith**), natural product of pure patriarchal life, had almost disappeared. He survives in the older laws as protected by a special wergild; probably, if analogy is to be trusted, he was maintained by special gifts from his fellow tribesmen, entitled to feast at their houses and to be clothed with the finest produce of their looms. The **ceorl** is the typical farmer. If we call him 'free,' we import modern ideas into primitive society. Probably he was not free in the sense that he could throw up his calling and go where he liked; with equal probability he had no desire to do so. Probably he paid some tribute; so does the modern 'free citizen.' Certainly he was liable (or, should we say, entitled?) to military service. On the other hand, he had probably a substantial claim, by the mere fact of his birth, to a share in the land of his

[1] The oldest collection of Canons, that of Dionysius Exiguus, is also older than the oldest English code.

[2] *E.g.* the *Rectitudines Singularum Personarum* and the *De Veteri Consuetudine Promotionum*, both printed in the collections of Anglo-Saxon Laws.

village; and his life was protected by a wergild which was, almost certainly, payable to his kindred, and not, even towards the end of the period, to his lord.[1] Below the ceorl came a class whom we may fairly call 'unfree,' in the sense that they were treated more as property than as persons. Doubtless (as some of the names given them imply) they were not mere domestic slaves, herded together in their lord's house, but were allowed to occupy cottages and, probably, patches of land. But, in the period of which this chapter treats, they were marked off from the ceorl by the facts that they did not serve in the host, they had no place in the moot, and that violence to their persons, though it was punishable, brought them no personal compensation. The **mannbot** of the unfree went to his lord. The many names (**theow, esne, laet,** &c.) by which this class is described in the Anglo-Saxon Laws, seem to point, not merely to differences of race, but to differences of legal standing. Still, no conclusive solution of these problems has yet appeared.

The Thegn

Most important, for legal purposes, is the class of **thegns,** which, apparently unknown or little important in the earliest days, from the end of the ninth century rapidly acquired a prominent position. The origin of the thegn is matter for general and constitutional history. But it must be noticed that, from his earliest mention in the codes, he is specially marked by signs which rapidly become characteristic of later law. He is peculiarly connected with the royal service.[2] All thegns are servants, as their name implies;[3] but the "King's thegn" overshadow the others, and tend to exclude them finally from a class which is rapidly becoming of special importance. Service, with the thegns, at any rate with many of them, was peculiarly associated with land-holding; we shall probably not be wrong in identifying the thegn with the **landrica** or **land-hlaford**, who appears as an established institution from the time of Aethelstan, exercising jurisdiction in matter of purchases, collection of tithes, accusing of criminals, and other functions of local authority. Of his relation to land-ownership, something more must be said when we come to deal with that

[1] Liebermann, p. 393 (*Walreaf*). The lord may have had an additional claim against the murderer.

[2] The "king's thegn" is mentioned as early as the code of Wihtraed (20), attributed to the year 695 A.D.

[3] It is the modern German 'dienen' = 'to serve.'

subject. But we cannot here part from the thegn without noticing, that through him the rule of forfeiture for misbehaviour seems to have come into our law. The thegn who deems an unjust doom is to lose his thegnship.[1] It is a principle which can be widely applied.

In matters more strictly legal than the organization of society, we note at first, apparently, an almost entire absence of that exercise of State authority which, at the present day, is regarded as an essential of civilized life. This is specially remarkable in that branch of law which to us seems the peculiar province of the State, viz. the administration of justice. Nothing can be clearer than that, in the earlier part, at least, of the Early English period, the action of the State, or even of the local authorities, in this matter, was only invoked in rare cases, and with great reluctance.

The Feud

The oldest form of redress for injuries suffered is personal vengeance. In one sense it is, of course, illegal, because it is not regulated or formally sanctioned by the State; in another it is not, for there is, in the earliest days, no law against it. Moreover, whatever public opinion may then have existed regarded it with toleration, if not with actual approval. The first restriction comes with the feeling that indiscriminate vengeance is intolerable. The man who has been wounded by a chance arrow must not shoot at sight the first man he happens to meet. He must make some attempt to identify the aggressor. If the wound proves fatal, the relatives of the slain may avenge the victim. But they, too, must not slay indiscriminately; they must restrict their vengeance to the murderer, and his kindred, who may be supposed to be sheltering him.

Following the Trail

If an ox is stolen, there must be some attempt to track it; the trail must be followed until it leads to the stall of the thief. It is not permissible to seize the nearest beast to replace the loss. If the track leads to the thief's stall, but the stolen ox cannot be found, the pursuer may seize a beast belonging to the suspected thief, to compel the return of the stolen ox. But he may not make good his loss at the expense of his peaceful neighbour, who has done him no wrong.

Distress

There is abundant evidence in the Anglo-Saxon Laws, that

[1] A. S. L., Edgar, III, 3 (Andover)

the feud, the fresh pursuit, and the distress (**nam**) were perfectly familiar to the compilers of the codes. There is also evidence that the wiser members of the community, supported by the kings, were anxious to modify and, perhaps, ultimately to suppress them. Not only do there appear numerous attempts to restrict the feud to its narrowest limits — it is to be levied only against the actual wrong-doer and his harbourers, the right of sanctuary is to be respected, and on peace days hostilities are to cease. But the Laws aim continually and earnestly, with minute care, to persuade the aggrieved party to accept the blood fine or **wergild** in lieu of corporal revenge; at any rate if the wrong-doer does not attempt further violence, 'right' must be demanded of him before the ancient claim of vengeance is enforced.[1] So also, even if the stolen beast is tracked, the person with whom it is found must be given a chance of proving his innocence; he may have bought it in an open market before proper witnesses. And so the picturesque process of **intertiatio,** or **anefang,** is enjoined; after a formal claim has been made, the beast is lodged with a third person to await the issue of the dispute.[2] Only with the advent of a strong monarchy was it possible to stamp out the extra-judicial distress,[3] or at least to confine it to claims by a lord against his vassal. In later days, the process of *vée de nam* became one of the most important in the legal armoury; and the remedy of **replevin** curbed even the privileges of a lord.

Clearing Oath and Ordeal

What exactly happened if, as the result of these attempts to substitute legal procedure for self-help, the hot blood was cooled, and the parties made to swear the peace, it is very difficult to say. Mr. Bigelow,[4] arguing from the evidence of the next period, and founding himself on the very reasonable assumption that the Norman procedure took over a good deal of the pre-Norman, has attempted to construct a sort of general picture of a primitive English lawsuit. But the subject is beset with difficulties; for of contemporary evidence there is little or none, if we except the few forms of

[1] See especially Aelfred, 42; Aethelr. IV, 4 (London); Edmund, II, 1, 2 (London); all in A. S. L.

[2] Ine, 25, 1; 75; Aethelst. II, 9; Aethelr. II, 8. Apparently the native word does not appear in the Laws. This suggests that the process was of foreign origin.

[3] There is clear prohibition in the so-called Laws of William, 44 (A. S. L.). It may or may not represent pre-Conquest law.

[4] *History of Procedure in England*, Macmillan, 1880.

oath and the fragments of the ordeal ritual which survive.[1] Generally speaking, it may be said that the formal proceedings commenced with the pronouncement, by the elders of the moot, of a **doom** which specified the penalties for the alleged offence, and settled the very important question of the onus of proof, or, as it ought, perhaps, according to the ideas of the day to be called, the privilege of proof. And so we are not surprised to find that 'denial is ever stronger than claim';[2] for the 'proof' was not what we should understand by evidence at all, but merely a general denial of the accusation by the accused and his **oath-helpers**. Generally speaking, if the accused was of good character, and the circumstances were not overwhelmingly against him, a day was set for the performance of this ceremony; and, if it were successfully accomplished, with due number of helpers and due observance of technicalities, the accused was acquitted. But if the accused were 'tihtbysig,' *i.e.* of bad character, or if he had been taken red-handed, he was put to the severer test of the **ordeal**.

What happened in either case if the accused failed to clear himself, is also a matter of no little doubt. Probably he or his relatives paid, or gave security for, the proper wergild without further dispute. If he or they were still obstinate, or too poor, the feud which these proceedings had attempted to scotch, revived; and the injured party or his relatives, if sufficiently strong, exercised the ancient right of corporal vengeance. Even at the end of this period, the local moot seems to have had no executive power whatever; and the royal action, if it applied at all to private lawsuits, was confined to the simple step of compelling the accused to come before the moot in the first instance. To secure his re-appearance, it was necessary to take security from him; either by pledge (**wed**) or by bail (**borh**).

In all this process, the action of the State, *i.e.* the central government, was, as has been said, very small. But there are signs that, even in this remote Early English period, the royal officials were beginning to play a larger part in the administration of justice. They probably approached the matter, first from the side of revenue, then from that of police.

State Action

[1] A. S. L.; Liebermann, I, 396–429.
[2] A. S. L.; Aethelr. II, 9 (3).

From the days of Ine, at least, the ceorl who neglected his military service paid 'fyrdwite' to the King;[1] in the reign of Edward the Elder[2] we see traces of the 'oferhyrnes,' or special fine to the King for disobedience to the royal command, which was, apparently, often used to support the authority of the local moot in the adjustment of disputes.

Bootless Wrongs

But the claims of the King soon went still further. Doubtless the ordinary offence, even the violent offence, was looked upon, primarily, as a wrong to the party specially injured, and his kindred. Yet there are traces, in almost all primitive law, of peculiarly detested acts, which the community takes upon itself to punish by some form of communal vengeance. The interesting survival of the *darrocade,* described by Mr. Round,[3] in the communes of the twelfth century, may or may not be primitive; but it is clear that very primitive people draw a distinction between a merely festive murder or robbery, and an act aimed directly at the security of the community, such as tampering with strangers against the common interest, or putting a spell on the common fields. In its modern form of 'Lynch law,' the same interest still manifests itself where the State is weak. The vengeance of the community is, however, slow and unorganized. A great step is gained when the King takes its place. Not only are 'bôtleas' offences more promptly punished; but the list of them can be indefinitely extended. The change was clearly marked in England by the time of Cnut;[4] by the time of the Conquest the list of the 'King's rights' had greatly extended.[5] Thus the land saw the beginnings of a true criminal law. A man accused on such a charge had no right to the elaborate privileges which stood between the private accuser and his prey. Until the Assise of Clarendon, in the next period, introduced something like a true criminal procedure, he was lucky if he could obtain some simple and summary method of trial, probably by ordeal.[6] It was centuries before the person accused at the King's suit

[1] A. S. L.; Ine, 51. (Note the difference between the punishment of the gesith or thegn, and the ceorl.)

[2] Edward, II, 2 (1).

[3] *Feudal England*, pp. 552–562.

[4] A. S. L.; Cnut, II, 12.

[5] Leges Henrici (Primi), c. X (1) (A. S. L.; Liebermann, I, 556).

[6] Leges Henrici (Primi), c. XLVII, c. LX (17). This compilation probably represents the law as it was supposed to be at the time of the Conquest.

secured what would now be considered the elements of a fair trial.[1]

Property

It is only indirectly, and through unintentional hints, that we can detach from the heap of unsystematic 'dooms' which make up the Anglo-Saxon Laws, any hints of a law of property. The existence of ideas which will some day produce the notion of property, or at least of possession, is to be found in the recognition of theft as an offence, and in the reluctant allowance, under stringent safeguards, of the sale of cattle. It is clear that, in fact, many other articles, *e.g.* garments, armour, and weapons, and, presumably, threshed corn, and ale, were known to our pre-Conquest ancestors. But the fact that the word 'chattel' has survived as the inclusive legal term for all movable goods, points, not merely to the great importance of cattle in primitive times, but to the importance of the notion of sale or barter in generating the institution of property. Apparently, the Laws do not regard other goods as transferable; except, perhaps, for special purposes, such as the satisfaction of wergilds.[2] And, obviously, the man who was found with a beast bred in another man's stall was, *primâ facie*, a thief; if he wished to clear his character, he had to name the man from whom he bought it in open market, and this man must take up the burden of the charge, or fight the man who has 'vouched him to warranty.' In this process of vouching to warranty (*têam*), there was much that influenced the law of property in later days. In the oldest time, it was, primarily, a means of escaping a charge of theft.

Property in Land

Still more reticent are the Anglo-Saxon Laws in anything that relates to land-ownership. In one famous passage,[3] land, regarded as a subject of property, is divided into **boc-land** and **folc-land**. The division may or may not be exhaustive. A curiously unfounded theory, which was

[1] By the time of the Conquest, murder had, in theory, become one of the 'bôt-leas crimes.' But, so late as the year 1220, a survival of the old wergild system for homicide was recognized by the King's judges on the plea of local custom. (See *Bracton's Note-Book*, Vol. III, plea 1474.) But possibly the case was one of 'sudden affray.'

[2] It is clear that, on the Continent, the practice of satisfying wergilds by payment in kind was recognized early, *e.g.* in the *Lex Ribuaria* or code of the Ripuarian Franks (see the author's *Law and Politics in the Middle Ages*, pp. 198–9). There is, possibly, a trace of the practice in England in Edgar's *Ordinance of the Hundred* (8), printed among the A. S. L.

[3] A. S. L.; Edward, I, 2.

accepted for the best part of a century, identified it with the distinction between private and public ownership. The theory fell to pieces at the touch of Professor Vinogradoff;[1] and now, dark as the subject still is, it is generally accepted that Spelman was right[2] when he identified folc-land with the holding of the ordinary peasant. More recent researches have made it appear probable that this holding was a share allotted by local custom ('folc-riht') in the common fields of the township, probably not as a fixed, separate possession, but as a shifting interest. Boc-land, as its name implies, is 'land' which has been made the subject of a written charter, or 'boc'; and the few genuine charters of the period which profess to deal with alienation of land probably refer to this kind of ownership. It seems to have been specially connected with thegnship. The Rectitudines[3] speak of the thegn's 'boc-riht' in close connection with his land; and it is not unlikely that what the thegn really had was jurisdiction (*socn*) over a certain area, rather than what would now be called ownership. The ceorl's folc-land, on the contrary, was, probably, the land which he ploughed and reaped by ancient customary rule. Thus, the same acre of ground might be the folc-land of the ceorl and the boc-land of the thegn who was his lord. If so, it is clear that, even before the end of this period, a long step had been taken towards the establishment of that principle of **tenure** which to-day dominates our land law. For the thegn's right could hardly come, ultimately, from any one but the King; though it is possible that, even so early as the tenth century, a King's thegn might have had thegns under him. Apparently, folc-land could be alienated 'with shire witness.'[4] Boc-land might well be forfeited;[5] probably it could not be alienated without the permission of the donor. It was as much an office as property.

Finally, if it be asked whether, in this early period, there was anything which, without abuse of terms, may be called a Law of Contract, or a Law of Tort, it must be answered that, if we

[1] The famous article appeared in the *English Historical Review*, VIII, 1–17.

[2] *Feuds and Tenures*, caps. V, IX; *Antient Deeds and Charters*, in Posthumous Works (ed. 1723), pp. 12, 33, 233. Coke seems to have held the same view (*Compleate Copyholder*, s. IV).

[3] A. S. L.; Liebermann, I, 444.

[4] A. S. L.; Cnut, 79 (perhaps, however, the passage refers only to a disputed title).

[5] *Ib.* 77.

insist on modern distinctions, there was not. But if we are content to look for primitive practices which may afterwards give rise to these modern ideas, we shall not look entirely in vain. For in the practices of giving 'wed' (pledge), or security for the performance of some act, or 'borh' (bail), as surety for good conduct, we see undoubtedly the legal ancestors of the ancient contracts of pledge and guarantee. At first, it is probable, these practices were confined to the most urgent necessities of primitive law, viz. the submission to legal process and the maintenance of the peace. But we can hardly suppose King Alfred to have placed in the forefront of his secular code the supreme importance of 'holding one's wed'; unless the wed had covered a wider range of duty than the mere delivery of one's-self to justice. It is true that, along with breach of wed, Alfred classes breach of oath; but we know that, in later times, whatever the practice of the Church, the Courts of the State refused to punish the *læsio fidei* with a legal sanction. Of the very modern distinction which separates a breach of a promise from a 'wrong unconnected with contract,' there is in this period no trace. Scarcely, as we have seen, are men beginning to draw the much earlier distinction between offences which merely involve the offender in a family feud, and those which also draw down on him the wrath of the King, with its outlawry and forfeiture. Therefore the famous generalization of Sir Henry Maine hardly fits the facts of the Old English Law, if indeed of any primitive system. The 'penal law of ancient England' is not, 'to use the English technical word,' a 'law of Torts.'[1] It is a law which, with rare exceptions, recognizes merely the root idea of a *wrong;* it does not distinguish between crime, tort, and breach of contract. These sharp distinctions will come later on; but, even when they arrive, they will overlap in a way which points conclusively to their common origin. Even at the present day, one and the self-same act may be a crime, a breach of contract, and a tort.

Contract and Tort

[1] *Ancient Law* (ed. Pollock, 1906), p. 379.

PERIOD II

THE CONQUEST TO THE DEATH OF HENRY III

1066–1272

AUTHORITIES

Quadripartitus, ed. Liebermann (Halle, 1882).

Leges Henrici Primi, *Leges Willelmi*, *Leges Edwardi* (*Confessoris*) — Printed in the various editions of The Anglo-Saxon Laws (see Chap. I).

* *Corpus Juris Civilis.*

Digest ed. Mommsen; *Code* „ Krueger; *Institutes* „ „; *Novels* „ „ — (Berlin, 1904–8.)

* *Corpus Juris Canonici*, ed. Friedberg (Leipzig, 1879–1881).

Select Charters and Other Illustrations of English Constitutional History, ed. Stubbs (Oxford, 8th edition, 1905).

Red Book of the Exchequer, ed. Hall (Rolls Series, 3 vols. 1896).

Glanville, *Tractatus de Legibus et Consuetudinibus Angliæ*, ed. Rayner (1780, translation by Beames, 1821).

Bracton, *De Legibus et Consuetudinibus Angliæ* (Tottell, 1569).

Scargill-Bird, *Guide to the Various Classes of Documents Preserved in the Record Office* (3d edition, 1908).

TEXT-BOOKS

Brunner, H., *Sources of English Law* (Select Essays in Anglo-American Legal History, II, 7–52, trans.).

Holdsworth, W. S., *A History of English Law*, Vol. II, Bk. II, Pt. I, chapters I and II (Methuen).

Maitland, F. W., *Materials for the History of English Law* (Select Essays in Anglo-American Legal History, II, 53–95).

Pollock, Sir F., and Maitland, F. W., *The History of English Law Before the Time of Edward I*, Bk. I, chapters III–VI, Bk. II (all) (Cambridge Press).

Stubbs, William, *The History of the Canon Law in England* (Select Essays in Anglo-American Legal History, I, 248–288).

Thayer, J. B., *The Older Modes of Trial* (Select Essays in Anglo-American History, II, 367–402).

Vinogradoff, P., *Villainage in England* (Clarendon Press).
The Growth of the Manor (Sonnenschein).
English Society in the Eleventh Century (Clarendon Press).

* Of course, editions of the *Corpus Juris* are almost innumerable. Those named are good and easily accessible.

CHAPTER II

SOURCES OF THE COMMON LAW

WHATEVER else the Norman Conquest may or may not have done, it made the old haphazard state of legal affairs forever impossible. The natural desire of the conquerors to make the most of their new acquisition, the exceptional administrative and clerkly skill of the Normans, the introduction of Continental politics, the rapid growth of the country in wealth and civilization, soon proved the old customs to be inadequate. For some time, no one could tell what was going to take their place. In the end, there emerged a new national law; some of it based on immemorial native usage, some of it unconsciously imported from foreign literature, not a little imposed by the sheer command of a new and immensely stronger central government. The precise share attributable to each of these sources will, probably, never be ascertained. Here, at least, all that can be done, is, to give the reader some general idea of the materials which went to make up the common law.

A. The Lex Terrae

It was part of the policy of the Conqueror to persuade his new subjects that he was heir to the kingdom of Edward the Confessor by lawful succession. The fiction must have been almost too gross for belief, even in an unlettered age; but the motive which prompted it led William to promise respect for the 'law of the land,' *i.* . for the ancient customs of the people. The trouble was, that these customs differed from place to place and from class to class. No authoritative statement of them existed. As we have seen, the so-called 'Anglo-Saxon Laws' were fragmentary and unsystematic. The old moots had kept no records. There was no class of English legal experts, such as those jurisconsults of the Roman Empire who had reduced the usages of Republican Rome to order and method.

Not unnaturally, efforts were made to supply the gap. Various private compilations, one of them at least claiming (untruthfully) an official origin, appeared; and a few of them have survived. They throw comparatively little light on the subject; for their authors were utterly uncritical, by no means free from local and political bias, and totally devoid of literary skill.

Quadripartitus One of these compilations is known as the **Quadripartitus**, because (probably in imitation of the Roman Institutes) it starts with the announcement that it will comprise four books — the first containing a Latin translation of the old English Laws, the second certain contemporary documents, the third a treatise on status and pleading, the fourth a treatise on theft and its varieties. If it was ever completed, it must have been a curious production; but only the first two books have survived. The so-called 'English Laws' are a crudely modernized version of the dooms of Cnut, Alfred, Athelstan, Edward the Elder, Edmund, and Ethelred, in the order named. Some of them are mere titles or rubrics; others are translations more or less full. The second book begins with a few official documents attributed to Henry I, and helps us to date the compilation at about the year 1115; but it soon trails off into a wordy argument on the subject of investitures, with a special defence of Archbishop Gerard of York, who was, apparently, the compiler's patron.

Slightly later (probably about the year 1118) comes the compilation known as the **Laws of Henry I**, because it commences with a charter of that monarch. But it is principally occupied with a rather serious attempt, by a writer not well fitted for his task, to compile from a multitude of local customs, of the existence of which he had, somehow, become aware, a general statement of the principles of English law. The task, as has been hinted, was beyond the author's powers; he was no Bracton. But his work is not without value; though it can hardly be used safely by any but an expert.

Leges Henrici (Primi)

Passing by the two fragments known as *Instituta Cnuti* and the *Consiliatio Cnuti*, both, as their titles imply, based on the legislation of Cnut, as well as the forged Forest Laws scandalously foisted on the same monarch, we may notice, chiefly to distinguish it from the genuine legislation of the Conqueror, a work known in various editions as the **Laws of William the Conqueror, Leges Willelmi,** or **Leis**

Leges Willelmi

Willelme (or **Williame**). It seems, like its immediate predecessor (for it is attributed to the first half of the twelfth century) to have been an unofficial compilation by some one who had access to a collection of Old English dooms, and who was also more or less in touch with Norman and official usage. Apparently, it was compiled both in Latin and in Norman-French; hence it is sometimes spoken of as the 'bilingual code.' Its chief value is, perhaps, that it shows us a little of that feudalizing process which converted the old system of People's Ranks into the later system of tenure. At one point, the compiler seems about to tell us a good deal concerning this;[1] but, apparently, he found it too difficult a subject, and relapsed into a translation of Cnut's legislation, the general refuge of the compiler of the day.

Laws of Edward the Confessor

Finally, and perhaps the least trustworthy of all in this group of sources, we have the so-called **Laws of Edward the Confessor,** which profess to be an official collection, drawn up in 1070 from the mouths of local juries by wise and skilful officials. Had such an inquest ever really been taken, it would have been of priceless value. Unfortunately, there is no reason to suppose that it was; and, if it was, the result is certainly not to be found in the *Leges Edwardi*. In the opinion of good judges, this compilation is the least valuable of all the group, for historical purposes; though it seems to have been popular in its day.

B. Roman Law

Almost contemporaneously with William's descent on England, came the revival of the study of Roman Law in Western Europe. Beginning, naturally enough, in Italy, in the schools of Bologna and Pisa, it spread to Paris, and from Paris to Oxford. This time, it was not the barbaric versions of the Code of Theodosius which passed for Roman Law; but the great *Corpus Juris* of Justinian, published on the shores of the Bosphorus just before the final severance of the Eastern and Western Empires. As the command of a ruler, it had no force west of the Adriatic, save, perhaps, for some time, in the Exarchate of Ravenna, where the Byzantine Empire maintained a precarious

[1] *Leis Willelme* (Liebermann), 20–24.

footing for about a century and a half. It was as a revelation of the wisdom of the ancient world, not as the command of an imperial ruler, that the men of Western Europe received the Digest, Code, Institutes, and Novels, and began, with feverish haste, to apply their teaching to make good the yawning gaps in the barbaric laws of their native countries. Every ambitious youth studied eagerly the *Corpus Juris;* a knowledge of its contents gave him a sense of power almost intoxicating in its keenness. So fierce was the heat which radiated from this new enthusiasm, that the more conservative forces took alarm. In the year 1219, Pope Honorius III forbade the teaching of Roman Law in the schools of Paris, then, and for long after, under clerical sway. The pious Henry of England, in 1234, issued a similar ordinance concerning the schools of London (*i.e.* of St. Paul's). A still more effective antidote to the teaching of Vacarius at Oxford, was the later settlement of the professors of the Common Law in the Inns of Court, between the Palace of Westminster and the cathedral. Soon the cleric, sheltered beneath the coif which concealed his tonsure, was pleading and judging causes in the new royal courts of the Common Law. But we may be sure, even if we had no evidence, that he did not entirely forget the law which he had learned at Oxford or Cambridge, that, when the customs of the realm, faithfully searched, gave no answer to a new problem, he fell back on the Digest and the Code. The older view, that Bracton's great work was a mere attempt to pass off Roman Law as English, is no longer tenable; but Bracton's familiarity with Roman Law, and the channels through which he derived it, have been demonstrated by the hand of a master.[1] It is idle to suppose that such knowledge was not used; especially in the solution of those problems for which the ancient customs made no provision. But the point to be remembered is, that the influence of Roman Law became in England secret, and, as it were, illicit

Opposition to Roman Law

C. Canon Law

Quite otherwise was it with the Law of the Church. The famous ordinance of William the Conqueror, withdrawing

[1] *Bracton and Azo.* ed. Maitland (S. S. Vol. VIII, 1895).

spiritual pleas from the Court of the Hundred,[1] produced by, and co-operating with, that spirit of clerical separation which had become the settled policy of the Papacy, soon produced a hierarchy of Church courts — archidiaconal, episcopal, provincial. The business of these courts rapidly increased. They dealt with all matters which, by any exercise of clerical ingenuity, could be claimed as pertaining to the cure of souls. All matters in which a cleric was interested, all offences against the divine law, all claims of Church dues, all questions affecting matrimony (a sacrament of the Church), all disputes concerning the validity or meaning of wills (for these were usually made *in articulo mortis*), or the distribution of property given for pious uses — these and many other matters did the Church courts claim, in this and other lands, though by no means with invariable success. To solve the many problems thus arising, there had grown up, as a rival of the *Corpus Juris Civilis*, a *Corpus Juris Canonici*. The ancient collection of Dionysius Exiguus had been swelled by the forgeries of the so-called "**Isidore**" (ninth century), and by the **Decretum Gratiani** (c. 1140). Later on, these were followed by the collection of Papal decrees known as the **Decretales**, issued by Pope Gregory IX (1234), by the **Sext**, or sixth book, of Boniface VIII (1298), by the **Clementines** of Clement V (1317), and, finally, on the eve of the Reformation, by the **Extravagantes** (1500). It was formerly the orthodox view, that these collections had no inherent force in English ecclesiastical courts; but received only such courteous acknowledgment as was extended by the King's Courts to the masterpieces of Roman jurisprudence. Perhaps, indeed, the theory of the 'English Canon Law' was really a reflection of the attitude of the common lawyers towards the Romanists. Anyhow, it can no longer be held.[2] In matters properly cognizable by ecclesiastical courts, the Canon Law sanctioned by the Popes at Rome was binding on all persons in England — is, indeed, to a certain extent, still binding. As for the small English output of ecclesiastical legislation (the Canons of English Synods and Councils), it held a very subordinate place, recognized as of local operation only when the *Corpus Juris Canonici* was silent or not inconsistent.

[1] *Select Charters*, 85.

[2] The old theory is finally disposed of in the work entitled *Roman Canon Law in the Church of England*, published by Professor Maitland in 1898 (Methuen).

D. Charters and Concordats

It was inevitable, in spite of all their professions of peaceful inheritance, that the Norman kings should think, act, and even speak, as conquerors. The fight at Senlac, and the harrying of the north, were events not easily forgotten or misunderstood. William and his successors enjoyed immensely greater power than any of the older English kings. It was natural that their subjects should seek from them formal grants of rights, and recognitions of claims. The 'charter,' in this sense, is a striking feature of the period now under review.[1] The Conqueror himself, his son Henry, Henry's grandson Henry II, John, and John's son Henry III, all issued charters, professing to grant or yield disputed points on which the views of the nation differed from those of the King. For the most part, they deal rather with matters of public than of private law; though the distinction was not then recognized. Sometimes, in the later half of the period, when the royal power was less overwhelming, these documents take the form of agreements or 'concordats' between the King and his subjects. Such are the important **Constitutions of Clarendon** of 1164, the short-lived **Provisions of Oxford** (1258), the **Provisions of Westminster** of 1259 (afterwards embodied in the Statute of Marlborough of 1267); and even the earlier so-called 'statutes,' such as the Statute of Merton, of 1236, are really of this type. The true Parliamentary statute does not make its appearance until the next period. Most of the documents referred to under this head will be found in the useful *Select Charters* of the late Bishop Stubbs.

E. Official Practice

Lastly comes a source of which it is hardly possible to exaggerate the importance for this period. The striking feature of the Anglo-Norman system was the activity of the official. The clerks who followed in the train of the Conqueror swooped upon the neglected resources of England as a hawk upon its prey. Primarily, no doubt, their motives were not elevated. Men do not, as a rule, engage in an enterprise such as that of William with purely

[1] Of course the word 'charter' will cover any written document; especially if it professes to transfer rights. When the ordinary medieval conveyance was written, it was generally known as a 'charter.'

disinterested objects. Still, it is unquestionably true, that the Norman administrator contrasts honourably with the Norman baron in his treatment of the conquered country. And if there were, occasionally, glaring instances of corruption among the royal officials, it is evident also that the standard of ability and industry was, on the whole, admirably high. It will be convenient to group the mass of evidence which the Norman officials have left us, under three heads.

Assises

a. First come the formal regulations, known generally as **Assises,** which laid down general rules for the conduct of official business. Nominally, of course, these regulations were made by the King for the direction of his officials; in all probability they were, like Orders in Council at the present day, drawn up by the officials concerned, and issued with the royal approval. In theory, they did not profess to affect the conduct of the ordinary citizen; and, therefore, by a modern jurist, they would hardly be ranked as part of the general law. In practice, they had a substantial effect in that direction; because the royal officials, in their dealings with private persons, acted upon them, and took good care that they should control the course of business. Among the most famous are the **Assise of Clarendon** of the year 1166, which laid the foundations of modern criminal procedure; the **Grand Assise** and the **Assise of Novel Disseisin** of about the same date, neither of which survive in complete form, but the purport of which can be gathered from the forms of procedure to which they gave rise;[1] the **Assise of Northampton,** of 1176, a sort of second edition of the Assise of Clarendon; the **Assise of Arms,** of 1181, which is, however, concerned rather with public than with private law; and the **Assise of Woodstock,** of 1184, dealing with offences against the forest laws. All these (except the two which do not survive) will be found in Dr. Stubbs' *Select Charters.*

Records

b. The activity of the Norman officials showed itself nowhere more clearly than in the mass of records which began to accumulate in the royal offices soon after the Norman Conquest. So enormous was this mass, and so great the confusion into which it fell in later times, that, even

[1] So closely was this procedure connected with the Assises, that an action under it is usually, to the confusion of the student, also called an 'assise.' The name was even given to the jury which tried it, and, ultimately, to the court in which it was tried.

now, much remains to be done before its contents can be thoroughly classified and known. It is sufficient to mention such famous collections as Domesday Book, drawn up at the very end of the Conqueror's reign; the great rolls containing the **feet of fines** (*i.e.* the summary of the transactions effected by the judicial process known as a 'fine'), which begin with the reign of Richard I, and, after a short period of hesitation, run on for more than six centuries;[1] the **rotuli curiae regis,** or records of the King's Court, which, beginning in 1194, mark the definite establishment of new tribunals by throwing off the **De Banco rolls,** or records of the Court of Common Bench, in 1234, and the **Exchequer (plea) rolls** in 1268, till they themselves remain as the **Coram Rege rolls,** the records of the King's (or Upper) Bench.[2] Then, too, there are the returns made to the great **inquest of knights' fees,** in 1166, and to the **inquest of tenants in capite** in 1210.[3] More is to be learnt from these records of business than from formal statements of custom or law.

Text-Books

c. Finally, there survive from this period two text-books of first-class importance, both written by officials, and, therefore, in days which drew no sharp distinction between public and private capacity, probably treated as authoritative. These are the treatise attributed to **Glanville,** chief justiciar of Henry II, on the procedure of the then new royal tribunals, which may be dated about 1187; and the great work on the Laws and Customs of England, by Henry of **Bracton** or **Bratton,** Justice of the Court of King's Bench, and Archdeacon of Barnstaple, in the latter half of the reign of Henry III. Glanville's little book confines itself strictly to procedure; and its chief value is that it gives us, on the highest authority, the forms of that new writ-process which, as we shall see, was to revolutionize the administration of justice in England. Bracton's larger work, though it is likewise based on procedure, is much more; for it deals extensively also with what we should now call substantive law. Moreover, as has been hinted above, though it

[1] Certain extracts from these rolls have been published, *e.g.* by Sir T. D. Hardy (*Rotuli de Oblatis et Finibus*, Record Series). But these are not confined to the entries relating to the judicial conveyances which afterwards became so important.

[2] The first six years have been printed as *Rotuli Curiae Regis*, and abstracts from 1194 to 1324 as *Abbreviatio Placitorum;* both in the Record Series.

[3] Both these are printed in the Record Series edition of the *Red Book of the Exchequer;* the former at pp. 186–445, the latter at pp. 469–574.

was at one time under suspicion as a theoretical work, adapted from the Roman Law, its character has been triumphantly vindicated by the discovery, by Professor Vinogradoff, among the treasures of the British Museum, of the very materials from which it was composed. And these turn out to be notes of actual cases decided by the King's judges, made, in all probability, from the official records themselves, to which Bracton, as a judge, had special access. These materials have been edited, with masterly skill, by the late Professor Maitland, under the title of *Bracton's Note Book.*[1] Bracton seems not to have been able to resist the temptation of embellishing his work with flourishes which might impress his readers with his literary accomplishments; and so, as has been said, there is a good deal of Roman phraseology on the surface of his book. But the sub-soil will be found to be of native earth. A good modern edition of the text of Bracton is much to be desired. The pretentious issue in the Rolls Series cannot be trusted; and the sixteenth and seventeenth century editions are before the days of critical scholarship.

[1] Cambridge University Press, 3 vols., 1887.

CHAPTER III

FEUDALISM AND LAND LAW

IT is a lesson which cannot be too thoroughly learned, because without it an understanding of history is impossible, that distinctions which to us seem elementary were unrecognized in earlier stages of society. Every educated man now distinguishes clearly between government and property. No one supposes, for example, that the King can deal with the land on which London stands, in the way in which he can deal with Sandringham or any other of his private estates. And yet, in a sense, both 'belong' to him. At the present day, the difference is easily understood; and we find no difficulty in explaining it. We say that Sandringham is the King's property, but that London is only part of his dominions. The one he owns, the other he governs.

Such experienced administrators as the Norman officials must have realized the distinction in practice. They must have been aware that, except at the certain risk of revolution, the King could not attempt to treat the whole of England as his private possession. Other claims could not be denied. William's followers, including the officials themselves, wanted their share of the new conquest. Many of the English thegns had accepted William's authority on promises of good treatment. The Church expected to be rewarded for her support of the Norman claims. Finally, even the peasantry could not be treated as mere chattels; for the bulk of them were firmly rooted in the soil, and nothing could have been gained, while much would have been lost, by attempting to move them.

Nevertheless, William and his officials were quite determined not to ignore the obvious fact, that the country was his by the universally admitted right of conquest. Prudence might counsel him to reward his followers with gifts of good things, and to allow those English who had made their peace with him to remain undisturbed in enjoyment of their ancient rights. But, somehow or another, William meant to be a rich king instead of a poor duke; though he fixed a steady eye on the Danegeld and other items of the old revenue of his predecessors, he meant to have much more than that. Moreover, his career as Norman Duke had been made a burden to him by the independence of his vassals; just as he himself had been a thorn in the side of his nominal suzerain, the King at Paris. It was the business of his advisers to find a scheme which should bring him wealth, and, so far as possible, guarantee him against rebellion.

Tenure

The solution of the problem which William's advisers offered him was the application of the already recognized principle of lordship to the occupation of land. It is quite untrue to say, as is sometimes said, that in primitive times land is the only form of property which is of legal importance. The law of theft, for example, which clearly implies property in chattels, is much older than any land law; and not unnaturally. For, in primitive times, the trouble is, not to get land, but to find men willing to work it; whereas cattle, slaves, weapons, jewels, and other movables, are hard to come by, and jealously guarded. It is only when the growth of population begins to make land, especially land already cultivated, an object of desire, and when the accumulation of improvements has rendered men unwilling to leave the old homesteads, that land law becomes really important, and that eviction means ruin.

This stage had been reached by England, as well as other countries of Western Europe, by the eleventh century; and William's advisers determined to take advantage of the fact. Every man, noble and simple alike, should hold his land as a pledge of good behaviour. His duties, to King, lord, and neighbour, should be settled once and for all; and, if he failed in them, he should be turned out of his home and left to starve. It was a drastic scheme; but a conqueror holding a conquered country by the force of the sword cannot afford to be squeamish.

Domesday Book

The scheme is embodied in Domesday Book. Much of its details are, no doubt, obscure; it may well be that we shall never understand them fully. But one thing is clear. The universal formula: *A tenet de B*, expresses the new bond of society. The great noble, the tenant *in capite*, holds his many manors of the King; if he plots rebellion, or fails to account for the geld assessed on his manors, or neglects to render his due service, he loses his fief. So with his under vassals, down to the lord of a petty manor, the successor of the thegn 'who to the King's host five hides had.'

Knight Service

Villenage

Below him, again, comes the group of peasants who, and whose forefathers, from time immemorial, have ploughed and reaped the fields of the township within the manor. What precisely may be their duties towards their lord, and, through him, to the King who is lord paramount of all holdings, may take long to settle; Domesday concerns itself, in this respect, with little beyond the Danegeld. But when another great inquest is taken, nearly two hundred years after Domesday, we shall see that, during this long period, the manorial lord has gradually acquired rights to 'dues and services' from his peasants, which yield him a substantial income, and which have converted his office of lord into what we now understand by property. How exactly the process had worked, we do not know; though Professor Vinogradoff has told us much in his brilliant studies of the period.[1] At any rate, it seems that, as the result of that process, the ceorl of Saxon England had become, in a sense, an 'unfree man'; because a substantial part of his time had to be spent in labouring on his lord's domain, because he could not sell his land, or even desert it, without his lord's permission, because his rights as a land-holder were protected only by custom and his lord's court, not by the common law and the strong hand of the royal tribunals.

The Hundred Rolls

Outside this strictly feudal hierarchy, the Norman officials who framed our land law had to find places for two classes of persons who could not easily be fitted into the social pyramid. The first of these comprised the socagers, at first, apparently, few in number, but growing rapidly in later times, until they became, at least in importance, the foremost class of land-holders. Perhaps, originally, they were substantial ceorls who, because they kept clear of rebellion, could not be deprived of their lands, and who, because they were too wealthy, could not be treated as serfs. They were probably persuaded to go through some form of 'commendation,' or nominal surrender

Socage

[1] *Villainage in England* (1892); *The Growth of the Manor* (1905); *English Society in the Eleventh Century* (1908).

of their land to the King or other lord, from whom they received it back in terms which satisfied the principle of tenure, but left the tenant very free. It was not inconsistent with socage tenure that the tenant should render personal service to his lord; but such service must not be of a military character, for that was reserved for knightly tenure, nor must it be of a degrading character, such as that which too often bound the serf. On the other hand, it must be certain, not only in amount, but in time and mode of render; so that the socager may really be his own man. Socage service seems, in most cases, to have been early commuted for a fixed money rent; which, with the fall in the value of money which set in soon after the Norman Conquest, and continued for centuries, ceased to be worth collecting, and the socager became, as nearly as possible, an absolute owner of his land. The word 'socage' is an insoluble problem. Most speculators connect it with *socn* (jurisdiction); and it may be that attendance at his lord's court was almost the only badge of service by which a socager could be recognized as a tenant. Again, there seems no reason why the socager should not have had tenants of his own, for whom he might hold a court. But this would hardly distinguish him from those who held by knightly service.

Hardest of all was it to persuade the Church to accept the new doctrine of tenure. For one thing, the holder of Church lands was in a different position from that of the ordinary layman. If he was an individual, a bishop or a parish rector, he was rather what we should now call a 'trustee' than a beneficial owner. After his death, the land would go, not to his children, but to his successor. Over him was the power of the Church, which would take care that he did not dispoil the Church of her rights. But it was equally likely that the land would be claimed, not by an individual, but by a community or group of individuals, such as a monastery or a cathedral chapter, whose members might die, but which, as a community, went on forever, and which could not, without grave scandal, be dispossessed of its lands. Moreover, it could not be expected of the bishop, the rector, or the religious house, that he or it should render military service, or plough and reap a lord's domain. The growing recognition of the sanctity of the priesthood rendered it difficult for the King's officials to impose burdens upon the Church land.

Frankalmoign

And so we find recognized a fourth kind of tenure, viz. the tenure in *frankalmoign*, which is really not tenure at all, because there is no definite 'service' to be performed on pain of forfeiture, but which can, with some difficulty, be made to square, in theory, with the doctrine of tenure.

Naturally, the so-called 'tenure in frankalmoign' was exceedingly popular with those who were so fortunate as to hold land by it. Equally clear is it, that the royal judges and tax-collectors regarded it with dislike, as unprofitable to the royal power and revenue. It was never admitted that all the lands of the Church were frankalmoign. Where the possession was so ancient that all trace of its origin had been lost, as in the case of the ordinary parish glebe, or, perhaps, the chapter lands and those of the long established religious houses, the claim might be admitted; in other cases, it was for the claimant to prove that the land had been given to him or his predecessors in 'pure and free alms,' without any stipulation for definite service. If even a fixed number of masses had been promised, the land was not held in frankalmoign, but by 'divine service,' *i.e.* as a species of socage. The King won a great triumph when it was finally conceded that even the endowments of the bishops' sees were held by knight service,[1] not in frankalmoign; and that therefore the bishops sat as barons in the Council of the Magnates. It was also clear, that if a religious house acquired land which was held by the donor by knight service or socage, the land remained liable to distress for failure to render the services due from the donor; even though the latter had given the land to the monastery in 'free alms.'[2] The tenant in frankalmoign appeared to win his greatest victory when it was admitted, by the Constitutions of Clarendon,[3] that if an estate was really proved to be frankalmoign, it was beyond the jurisdiction of the royal courts — all that the latter could claim was the trial of the preliminary question whether such was in fact the case (*Assisa Utrum*). But, in this respect, as in others, the settlement of 1164 was not permanent; and, ultimately, the royal courts succeeded in ousting the Church courts from all pleas concerning land. Towards

[1] Constitutions of Clarendon, cap. XI (S.C. 139).

[2] These services were 'forinsec,' *i.e.* not rendered to the immediate lord. The under-tenant who had been forced to render them had a claim to indemnity against the 'mesne lord,' who ought to have satisfied them.

[3] Cap. IX (S.C. 139).

the end of the period, the Church sustained an even greater loss. The policy of Mortmain made it difficult for her to acquire lands at all. But the full development of that policy belongs to the next period.[1]

Incidents of Tenure

Upon the principle of tenure, thus applied to all ranks of society, the royal judges, and their imitators in the feudal courts, began to build up that elaborate superstructure which for six centuries attempted to express, with ever diminishing reality, the Englishman's notions of property in land. At bottom it was, in theory, a contract system; because, in theory, the terms of each holding were fixed by the original grant to the tenant himself, his ancestor or predecessor. In practice, these terms, at any rate in the absence of express stipulation, were settled by rules of ever increasing sharpness, which prescribed the 'incidents of tenure' in each case, *i.e.* those mutual rights and duties of lord and tenant which attached to the fact of their relationship. Some of these 'incidents' survive, at least in theory, to the present day, and are among the first things learnt by the student of real property law. Others have become legally or practically obsolete; but a brief mention of them can hardly be omitted from any account of the history of English law.

Common Law and Local Custom

One preliminary caution, of great importance, should be given. Tenures, as has been said, fall into two unequally divided classes — the free and the unfree. For the present purpose, the importance of the distinction lies in the fact, that the rules of the former were settled by the decisions of the royal courts, which held good throughout the realm; and that they were, therefore, with rare exceptions, uniform and universal. The tenant by knight service could not devise his land, at least directly, whether it lay in Northumberland or Essex. When the rules of inheritance once became settled, the eldest son of the socager succeeded to his father's land, whether it was in Gloucestershire or Devonshire; unless the land were subject to some well-recognized exception, such as that of gavelkind or burgage. But the tenant in villenage was governed, in respect of his holding, by the local custom, which differed from manor to manor; and, despite modern legislation,

[1] The first definite sign of the policy appears in the Charter of 1217, cap. 43 (S.C. 347). But the full principle is not enunciated till 1279 (7 Edw. I, st. II).

his successor, the copyholder, is, in the main, in the same position to-day. Even the fact that the King's courts at last, towards the end of the fifteenth century, began to protect the copyholder's rights, did not alter this state of things; for the royal judges, no longer enjoying the freedom of their predecessors of the twelfth and thirteenth centuries, deemed themselves bound by the manorial customs, save where, in rare cases, those customs were so opposed to all sense of fairness as to be held manifestly 'unreasonable.' Consequently, whilst knight service, socage, and, in so far as it was a tenure at all, frankalmoign, became 'common law tenures,' villenage, or, as it was later called, 'copyhold,' has always been treated as a 'local and customary tenure.' Nevertheless, though with many differences of detail, the local tenures were framed on the common law model; and so it is possible, with some reservations, to generalize about the incidents of all.

Fealty and Homage

Loyalty to one's lord was of the essence of the feudal tie of tenure; and it was symbolized in the oath of **fealty** exacted on the creation of all estates, save possibly, in frankalmoign. The form which it took at the beginning of the next period is given in a document attributed to the year 1323, and printed among the Statutes of the Realm.[1] It is a general promise to observe the terms of the relationship; and refusal to make it was, doubtless, treated as a renunciation of the tie. The ceremony of **homage** was rendered only to the lord of whom the tenant held his chief estate; possibly only when he held an estate of inheritance. It expressed a closer and more personal tie;[2] and comprised a special reservation of loyalty to the King.

Suit of Court

It was the symbol of lordly power to hold a court or assembly of vassals; and the tenant who refused to minister to his lord's pride by attending his summons was guilty of contempt, if not defiance, of his lord. Into the vast question of private jurisdiction in England, we cannot enter; it ceased to be of importance in free tenure after the royal courts were firmly established. But, for a similar reason, **suit of court** remained, and still remains, a liability of copyhold tenure.

The special importance of service was, as we have seen, that the nature of it determined the nature of the tenancy. Any

[1] 17 Edw. II (*Modus Faciendi Homagium et Fidelitatem*). [2] *Ibid.*

liability to military service stamped the holding as tenure *per militiam,* and so on. As is well known, it was a marked peculiarity of English tenure that all military service was rendered to the King alone, and could only be demanded by the King's writ. But when military service, like all other services, became commuted for a money rent ('scutage' or 'escuage'), it found its way into the pockets of the immediate lord, and was distinguished from other money rents only as entitling the lord to the specially profitable incidents of knight-service tenure.

Service

The most striking accompaniment of service is the right of the lord to seize the chattels on the tenement to enforce render of it. We have seen,[1] that this is a survival of a once universal process of self-help, which has been abolished in most other cases. In the period under review, it was not a complete remedy; for the lord could not sell the chattels distrained to satisfy his claim; as its name implies, 'distress' was merely a means of putting on pressure. But it was of peculiar value to the lord; for, to a certain extent, it made him indifferent to the personal character of his tenant. If the latter chose to 'sub-infeudate' the land to an under-tenant, the lord's remedy was not, in theory, affected. The service due to him was 'forinsec,' so far as the under-tenant was concerned. But it could be distrained for, all the same, because it attached to the land; and the remedy of the under-tenant whose beasts had been seized for his immediate lord's default was to pay the over-lord's claim, and deduct the amount from the 'intrinsec' service which he owed his immediate lord, or recover it by a Writ of Mesne. Thus 'rent-service,' as distinct from other rent charged on land, early acquired that peculiar security which it has never since entirely lost.

Distress

In addition to his regular and stipulated service, the tenant, as evidence of his loyalty, might be called upon to render occasional assistance, under the name of **aids,** to his lord in moments of urgency. As is well known, the number of these moments, and the calls which they made on the tenant's purse, were subjects of keen dispute. The former point, at least so far as the royal example was concerned, was settled by the well-known clause of the Great Charter;[2] the latter by

Aids and Reliefs

[1] *Ante,* p. 8

[2] Cap. XII (S.C. 298).

statute early in the next period.[1] The **relief** was payable on the succession of an heir to his ancestor's estate; and is interesting as a link in the obscure process by which the originally personal relationship between lord and vassal developed into a mere form of property. The tenant in villenage paid a 'fine on descent'; while his lord was also usually entitled, under a claim of 'heriot,' to seize the best beast or other chattel of the dead ancestor. The amount of the relief in knight service was fixed by the Great Charter;[2] in socage it was said, by a so-called statute of 1300,[3] that the tenant, on succeeding, paid two years' rent instead of relief. The fines paid by the heir in villenage were either 'arbitrary,' or fixed by the local custom.

Wardships and Marriages

The most oppressive incidents of tenure were the right of the lord to the custody of the person and estate of the infant heir of his deceased tenant, and to the disposal of such heir in marriage. Originating in the reasonable claim of the lord that his dues of service should not be lost by the inability of an infant to render them, and that an infant heiress should not, by marrying the lord's enemy, introduce a foe into his household, these incidents rapidly developed into means of extortion. The lord rendered no account, either of surplus rents or of the money received for his ward's hand. By an unfortunate wording of a clause in the Great Charter,[4] intended to control abuses, the claim of 'marraige' was actually extended beyond females to male heirs; and the two incidents continued, in theory at least, to disgrace the law, until they were abolished in 1660.[5] They were peculiar, apparently, to knight-service tenure; for in socage the guardian (not the lord, but the next-of-kin who could not inherit) was held strictly to account for all profits;[6] while there seems to be little trace of similar incidents in villenage.[7] Of course, they had no parallel in frankalmoign.

Whether or not the strict theory of tenure recognized the claim of the tenant's heir to succeed to his ancestor's estate, we may

[1] 3 Edw. I (1275) c. 36 (under-tenants); 25 Edw. III (1352) St. V, c. 11 (tenants *in capite*).
[2] Cap. II (S.C. 297).
[3] 28 Edw. I (Statute of Wards and Reliefs).
[4] Cap. 6 (S.C. 297).
[5] By the 12 Car. II c. 24.
[6] 52 Hen. III (Marlborough, 1267), c. 17.
[7] Perhaps the 'merchet,' or marriage fine of the villein's daughter, may be regarded as a 'value of marriage.'

be very sure that the socager and the villein would not have submitted without a severe struggle to any legal rule which attempted to deprive them of the land which their forefathers had ploughed from time immemorial. The very wording of the custumal of 1299, before alluded to,[1] suggests that the socage heir was with difficulty brought to recognize the fitness of a 'relief'; and that, in his case, it was a question of the rules to be followed, rather than any question of the right of inheritance generally. There can be little doubt, that the general English rule survives in the gavelkind principle of equal division among males in the nearest degree; and Glanville seems to regard it as in force for socage in his day.[2] On the other hand, no such antiquity consecrated the claim of the heirs of military tenants; and reason weighed somewhat heavily against the transmission to heirs of military fiefs. Nevertheless, it is clear that, at least by the time of the Great Charter, inheritance of such estates is fully recognized as normal. What is more, the rule of primogeniture among males, not unreasonable for military tenure, early succeeded in establishing itself also for socage tenants, in lieu of the old rule of equal division among males. Inheritance in villeinage remained, and remains, a matter of local custom. But the rule that the grant of land 'without words of inheritance' confers only a life estate, a rule which still prevails, is a significant reminder of the original characteristics of tenure.

Inheritance

Escheat is rather an inevitable consequence, than an incident, of the principle of tenure. When the interest, or 'estate' granted, or supposed to have been granted, to the vassal came to an end, the land would naturally return to the lord. If the estate was for life, it came to an end on the death of the man or men for whose lives it had been granted. These, of course, need not have been the tenant or tenants themselves; the estate *pur autre vie* was quite common in this period. Where the estate was inheritable by the tenant's heirs, it came to an end when these failed. In either case, the lord resumed the land; it was said to 'escheat,' or fall back, to him. Before estates of inheritance became common, and especially among the great tenants *in capite* of the Crown, escheats were a

Escheat

[1] *Ante*, p. 34.
[2] Lib. VII, cap. 3.

valuable source of revenue; and the Crown employed regular officials and held periodical enquiries, or 'inquests,' to discover and enforce them. In later days, the term 'escheat' was employed strictly to designate the falling in of estates through actual failure of heirs, or through the fictitious failure caused by the doctrine of corruption of blood by attaint of felony. The land which went back to the lord at the end of a life estate was said to 'revert'; and the lord's interest during the running of that estate was called a 'reversion.' But there is no difference, in principle, between the two cases; the difference of terms was brought about by certain arbitrary changes in the law of alienation.

This brings us, in conclusion, to a question of first-rate importance, to which this period gives no certain answer. Might a tenant alienate his holding? At the present day, such a question would appear to be absurd; and the man who ventured to suggest a negative would lie under a heavy *onus* of proof. In the period with which we are dealing, the presumption was all the other way. The peasant held his land as a member of a group; perhaps, as has been hinted, it was not a definite area of land at all, but a 'shifting severalty,' *i.e.* a share which changed from year to year, or from 'course' to 'course' of husbandry. His co-farmers would, naturally, object to the introduction of a stranger, at any rate without the full agreement of the group. This is the *retrait communal.* Also his heirs, who looked forward to succeeding to the ancestral claims, would object to alienation. This is the *retrait lignager:* probably it affected the socager as well as the villein. Finally, and especially in the knightly tenures, the lord might strongly object to a change of vassals; there is even some presumption, and, what is more, evidence, that the tenant might object to have a new lord thrust upon him — to be 'attorned,' or handed over, to a strange lord. This is the *retrait féodal.*

Alienation

Evidently these considerations puzzled the authorities a good deal; and their attitude was hesitating.

In spite of some doubts, the practice of **subinfeudation** rapidly made its way. By this process the tenant did not, in theory, impose upon his lord a new vassal, or deprive his heir of a fief. He merely, as a modern lawyer would say, 'sub-let' the land, and drew the rents instead of cultivating

Subinfeudation

the soil, or collecting the peasant's dues, on his own account. The very structure of feudalism must have rendered this process familiar; and even the King seems to have regarded it as a matter of course.[1] Nevertheless, it was, in fact, open to objections, from the point of view of the original lord. It is one thing to have a tenant who holds land 'in demesne'; he is there, his doings and happenings are known, the 'incidents' of his tenancy can be promptly claimed. With a tenant who holds 'in service,' it is otherwise. True the land is there; and the beasts of the actual occupant can be distrained for withholding of service. But if it comes to escheat or forfeiture, the under-tenant may say that his estate was lawfully created, and that, so long as he renders the services reserved on the creation of *his* tenancy, he cannot be disturbed. Now these services may be considerably less than the services reserved on the original grant — a fact which will also be productive of loss to the overlord in enforcing his claims of 'wardship' and 'marriage.' Most especially will this be the case if the sub-grant has been for an estate of inheritance; for the process may go on indefinitely, and the original grantor may find himself further and further divorced from the soil. Nevertheless, in spite of some evidence of protest,[2] the right of 'subinfeudation' appears to have been generally admitted during this period. Bracton, in a well-known passage,[3] strongly denied that it was wrongful.

Substitution

The total alienation of the tenant was regarded with more disfavour. This was a complete rupture of the feudal tie, and, in effect, deprived both lord and heir of valuable rights. It was, probably, to this kind of alienation that Glanville alluded, in the passage in which he lays down somewhat severe restrictions on its exercise.[4] He distinguishes between the *hereditas*, or inherited estate of the tenant, and his *questum* or newly acquired estate. In respect of the latter, the tenant has a fairly free hand; in respect of the former, his rights are much more limited. He can alienate a 'reasonable' part of it for proper purposes, such as the endowment of a son or

[1] This appears to be a fair inference from the Inquest of Knights Fees in 1166 (*Red Book of the Exechequer*). But it is also implied in Domesday Book.

[2] Great Charter of 1217, cap. 39 (S.C. 346). Possibly, however, the clause refers to substitution.

[3] Lib. II, cap. XIX (1, 2).

[4] Lib. VII, caps. 1, 2.

daughter, the rewarding of faithful service, or even the satisfaction of the claims of religion or charity. But, in the latter case, the alienation must be made when the tenant is in full health; Glanville has a strong suspicion of death-bed gifts. Of course, the devise of lands, as we understand it, was not recognized in this period; probably because the new doctrines about 'livery of seisin' made it impossible to set up a title dependent on an oral or merely written gift. But even the formal conveyance to take effect on death was regarded with suspicion, and required confirmation by the heir.[1]

[1] Glanville, Lib. VII, 1. 'In extremis tamen.' The language suggests that the rule may possibly be altered in the near future ('hactenus').

CHAPTER IV

IMPROVED LEGAL PROCEDURE

THE second great triumph, not unworthy to rank beside the creation of a land law, which the royal officials achieved during this period, was the establishment of a new set of royal tribunals, with a definite legal procedure.

In order to understand the greatness of this achievement, we must once more put from us modern ideas, and remember that the assumption, now everywhere prevailing, that the administration of justice is the exclusive function of the Crown or State, is the result of a long period of bitter struggle, nowhere better illustrated than in English legal history. In so far as there was any regular 'administration of justice' at all in England in the latter half of the eleventh century, it took place in the local moots of the Hundred and the Shire, possibly, in trifling matters, in the hall of the thegn. So far from desiring to abolish the jurisdiction of the local moots, the kings, at first at any rate, were constantly insisting that they should be held as of old.[1] In the Laws of Cnut, it is formally laid down that no one is to bother the King with his complaints, so long as he can get justice in the Hundred.[2] Even before the Conquest, the land was covered with thegns, *judices regis* as they are called in the *Leges Henrici;*[3] and the latter title suggests that they exercised a certain amount of local jurisdiction.

Local Moots

Church Courts

After the Conquest, as has been said, the Church courts rapidly developed a large business, both 'criminal' and 'civil'; they dealt with such offences as, not being recognized as wrongs by the lay tribunals, were yet, in the view of the Church, sins against the laws of God. Examples are, perjury, fornication, usury, defamation, neglect to pay tithes

[1] *E.g.* S.C. 84 (William I), 104 (Henry I).

[2] Cnut, II, 17 (Liebermann, 320). For an earlier enunciation of the same principle, see Edgar, III, 2 (Liebermann, 200).

[3] Art. 29 (Liebermann, 563).

and other dues of the Church; the Church courts dealt also with all questions (save one)[1] of legitimacy or divorce. Then too, there were the feudal courts, which, feeble as they were beside some of their great models on the Continent, yet flourished in large numbers during the whole of this period. Finally, the charters granted to merchant gilds and burgesses expressly or by implication recognized the existence of market and other courts, in which the Law Merchant and not the Common Law was administered.[2] Even the King's own judges had eventually to admit that to every market a court of piepowders (*pieds poudrés*) was appendant as of common right. It was only in the face of keen rivalry that the royal jurisdiction won its way; and its ultimate triumph, complete and unquestioned, over its many rivals, is the result of its inherent superiority, and a striking proof of the ability of the men who organized it. Again we need not suppose their motives to have been very lofty. Legal business has, from the beginning of time, been profitable — to those who have conducted it; because it is concerned with things that touch men's passions very deeply, and because men are willing to pay, and pay highly, for wisdom and skill in the conduct of it. The real merits of the Norman lawyers were, not altruism, but ability, energy, and enthusiasm for their work.

Feudal Courts

Courts Merchant

One of the first definite steps taken was to develop that branch of the royal claims which, as has been said,[3] was the beginning of criminal law in the modern sense. By the famous **Assise of Clarendon,**[4] issued in 1166, there was substituted for the ancient and somewhat casual 'hue and cry,' a regular, formal 'presentation,' or indictment, before the King's justices and sheriffs, by twelve sworn men from the Hundred and four from the township, of robbers, murderers, thieves, and their accomplices. Apparently, a very full shire-moot was to be assembled for the purpose, and a sort of preliminary enquiry held by the sheriff, who was to remand under

Criminal Procedure

[1] The exception was the well-known 'plea of special bastardy,' which involved the question of post-legitimated children. The King's Courts could not trust the Church to accept the famous clause of the Statute of Merton (cap. 9).

[2] The records already edited by Professor Gross (S.S. Vol. 23) 1238 (Torksey Piepowders. App. I), show that such courts were in working order as early as the first half of the thirteenth century.

[3] *Ante*, p. 10.

[4] Given in full in Stubbs, S.C., at p. 140.

custody or bail all against whom there seemed to be a *primâ facie* case, to await the arrival of the justices. The accused were then to be given a rough sort of trial. If they had been hitherto of good repute, they were allowed to clear themselves by the ordeal of water; if they were of bad fame, or if they failed at the ordeal, they were, apparently, mutilated and turned adrift, their chattels being forfeited to the Crown. Ten years later, after the Inquest of 1170[1] had revealed the iniquities of the sheriffs, the process was made more definite and severe by the **Assise of Northampton** in 1176.[2] To the list of offences indictable under the Assise, were added treason, arson, and false coining. Even if the accused satisfied the ordeal, he was, nevertheless, to give pledges for his future good behaviour; if his character was bad, he was even to abjure the realm, though he might take his goods with him.[3] If he failed at the ordeal, or was not entitled to it, he was to lose both hand and foot, be banished the realm, and, of course, forfeit his goods. As will shortly appear[4] the disuse of the ordeal introduced the modern method of trial by jury for criminal cases, and thus completed the scheme of criminal procedure in outline. But the Assises of 1166 and 1176 definitely marked off the 'felony' or public offence entailing forfeiture of goods and banishment, not only from the mere private wrong, but also from those minor misbehaviours, or misdemeanours, which were punished in the local moots.[5] These appear to have remained in their old vague position until the later development of the local Justices of the Peace, when they became subject to true criminal prosecution. By the end of the twelfth century, conviction of felony worked a forfeiture, not only of chattels but of the offender's land. But, though King John had claimed otherwise,[6] the forfeiture of land did not, save in the case of treason, go to the Crown, but, as an 'escheat,' to the tenant's immediate lord; subject to the royal right of 'year, day, and waste.'[7]

[1] S.C. 147. (Note the reference in art. 5 to the Assise of Clarendon.)

[2] S.C. 150.

[3] Art. 1. There is a puzzle here. If the accused was of bad fame, he ought not to have been allowed to go to the ordeal at all. (See Assise of Clarendon, art. 12.)

[4] *Post*, pp. 51, 52.

[5] Assise of Clarendon, art. 5 (S.C. 144).

[6] Magna Carta, cap. 32 (S.C. 300).

[7] *I.e.* the right of the Crown to wreak its vengeance on the offender by plundering his land for a year. The right was usually bought off by the lord who claimed the escheat.

In the matter of private disputes, the royal officials achieved their revolution, partly by putting still further limits to extra-judicial procedure, partly by tempting the litigants, with offers of superior remedies, to resort to the royal jurisdiction.

Civil Procedure

The efforts of the later English kings appear to have been successful in restricting the feud to cases of personal violence, including theft. In such cases, not unnaturally, the lust of vengeance was keenest; and, under the name of an **appeal,** the blood feud, reduced to order and system, and limited to the parties immediately interested, remained, at least until Bracton's day, the ordinary remedy.[1] The introduction of true criminal procedure, just described, set up a very powerful rival of the private 'appeal'; for, as will be remembered, the 'felonies' of the Assises of Clarendon and Northampton comprised just those very offences of violence which were the ordinary subject of appeals. And, inasmuch as the consequences of a successful appeal were much the same as those of a criminal prosecution, viz. death or mutilation of the offender, and forfeiture of his land and goods, it was obvious that appeals and indictments tended to become alternative methods of procedure for the same offences. In fact, the well-known expression 'appeal of felony' is almost proof conclusive of the common ground; though whether the term 'felony' itself originated with the royal officials or in popular usage, seems to be an insoluble problem.

Appeals

The chapters in Bracton's book, just alluded to, show pretty clearly the steps taken by the royal judges to discredit appeals and substitute for them the newer process of indictment. Here again, the motive is obvious. No doubt it was a good thing to put down what was, in fact, private war; it was still better, from the point of view of the royal judge, to secure the offender's goods for the Crown. And so the man who was 'appealed,' or challenged, was encouraged to apply to the royal judges on every kind of side issue. He might plead every sort of objection, or *exceptio*, that he could think of, *e.g.* that the 'hue and cry' had not been properly conducted, that the 'words of appeal,' or formal accusation, had not been pronounced, or

Restrictions on Appeals

[1] Lib. III, cap. 19–34. The appeals mentioned by Bracton are those of homicide, mayhem, false imprisonment, robbery, arson, rape, and larceny.

were wrong in some petty detail, that the accuser, or 'appellor,' did not show his wounds to the coroner, that the demand was a stale one, or, generally, that it had been put forward 'of hatred and malice' (*de odio et atiâ*). Thereupon the royal judges would hold, by a process to be later alluded to, a sort of preliminary enquiry into the truth of the 'exception' or excuse; and if the accused, or 'appellee,' was successful in this enquiry, the appeal would be sternly put down by the King's officers. A somewhat obscure passage in the Great Charter of 1215[1] is now generally construed as a promise by the King that an appellee shall in the future be entitled, gratuitously and as a matter of right, to an inquest *de odio et atiâ*. If this view be correct, and the clause was observed, it is tolerably clear that, by the beginning of the thirteenth century, an appellee who wished to avoid battle could do so. Another significant passage in Bracton[2] suggests, that if the King's itinerant justices came into the county after the commission of the alleged offence and before the raising of the appeal, the right of private vengeance was suspended until the alleged offender had stood his trial at the King's suit.[3] If this was so, we can well understand that the 'appeal,' though in theory not abolished until 1819,[4] was practically becoming obsolete at the end of the thirteenth century.

Alternative Remedies

The great alternatives offered to the litigant for the older remedies of the popular tribunals were the writ of summons and trial by jury.

Writ of Summons

The **writ**, or **breve**, as its names imply, is a short written document; but, pre-eminently and almost universally, a short written command of the King. In the great majority of early cases, it was addressed to a royal official, and was merely, as we should say, an administrative order. At first, it was used for all kinds of purposes, not specially connected with litigation; the King summoned his army and his Great Council by writ, bade his officials levy taxes by writ, and so on. But, very soon after the Conquest, we begin to see writs issued from the royal Chancery for the purpose of influencing legal

[1] Cap. 36 (S.C. 301).

[2] Lib. III, cap. 24, 2 (fo. 145).

[3] On the other hand, it is clear from later law that acquittal at the King's suit was no bar to an appeal.

[4] After its well-known dramatic revival in *Rex v. Thornton*. The abolishing statute is 59 Geo. III, c. 46.

proceedings; and, what is even more suggestive, we find that these writs are 'purchased' (probably at substantial fees) by litigants themselves. What were the attractions?

In the first place, they applied to the accused person a stronger pressure than any that could be brought to bear without them.

Compulsion

The summons by the party aggrieved was probably a very formal and complicated affair, delivered by word of mouth in the presence of witnesses;[1] and any flaw in it probably justified the accused in treating the proceedings with contempt. Even if it were correctly delivered, with proper words and at a proper time and place, it might prove inefficacious; and the recent restrictions on the right of **distress,** previously alluded to, rendered it dangerous for the accuser to take the law into his own hands.[2] But the **writ of summons,** addressed to the sheriff, bade that official relieve the accuser (or 'plaintiff' as we may now call him) of the fruitless task of trying to get the defendant before the court; and directed *him* (the sheriff) to summon the defendant 'by good summoners.' Now it is one thing to disobey the summons of a private person; and quite another to disobey the summons of the King. And though, in later times, the curious hesitation of a primitive tribunal to proceed in the absence of a defendant still allowed much scope for evasion, it is quite clear that the royal official had means of compelling attendance which were not exerciseable directly by the private litigant.

But a second and even greater service was performed by the new writ-procedure. Hitherto, the definition of offences had

Definition

been left to the 'doomsmen' of the court, in whose memory was supposed to lie a store of immemorial wisdom. There were no written records; nothing to which the aggrieved party could turn, to see whether the court would give him a remedy. Now, he knew that if he could get his complaint described in a royal message, he could hardly be met by the defence that such complaint 'disclosed no cause of action.' Doubtless there would remain scope for discussion, as to whether

[1] The causes of the formal and sacro-sanct character of early legal procedure are: (1) The necessity for relying on the memory before the introduction of writing; (2) the ignorance of primitive litigants, who cannot be trusted to distinguish between spirit and letter.

[2] These restrictions culminated in the reign of Henry II, in the action of 'replevin.' (Glanville, XII, 12, 15.) The date is significant.

the plaintiff could bring the defendant within the terms of the writ. But it was a great step gained to have it declared, or at least implied, that, if the facts were as alleged, the plaintiff had a good ground of complaint; and this result was achieved when it was clear that any one could have, as of course, a writ of Debt, or Trespass, or the like.

That this point had been reached before the end of the twelfth century, is clear from Glanville's famous treatise. It is obvious that this book is speaking throughout of well-established procedure, open to any litigant on payment of the proper fees. It is even possible to classify its examples. They are either writs 'original,' *i.e.* writs destined to commence legal proceedings,[1] or 'judicial,' such as are merely incidental to the carrying on of proceedings already begun.[2] The latter are, it may be said, 'mere machinery.' The former, when, in course of time, they were collected into a Register, of which more or less correct copies were in circulation, really became a dictionary of the Common Law. Even the so-called 'prerogative' writs, which were only issued by special leave of the court, shared this character;[3] because, if satisfied that a case has arisen to which they are applicable, the Court would certainly allow them to issue. The invention of writs was really the making of the English Common Law; and the credit of this momentous achievement, which took place chiefly between 1150 and 1250, must be shared between the officials of the royal Chancery, who framed new forms, and the royal judges, who either allowed or quashed them. Before the end of the thirteenth century, the stream of new writs began to run dry. As we shall see, an attempt was made to revive it in a famous statute of 1285;[4] but the effort was not wholly successful. Other methods of declaring new law took the place of the Register of Writs.

The Register of Writs

The need of a new method of trial was, at the beginning of the twelfth century, quite as urgent as a new method of summons. Roughly speaking, the old English courts knew of three methods; and all three were, obviously, unworthy of a

Old Methods of Trial

[1] *E.g.* the 'Writ of Right' (Lib. I, 6).

[2] *E.g.* the 'Writ of View' (Lib. II, 3). In later days, these were issued by the court having charge of the case, not by the Chancery.

[3] The distinction appears in the Provisions of Oxford (Chancellor's Oath, S.C. 389).

[4] Statute of Westminster the Second (13 Edw. I, c. 24).

civilized system of justice. The accused against whom no suspicion rested, was entitled to **wage his law**, *i.e.* to get a proper number of his friends (the number varying with his social rank) to swear in a prescribed form, and 'with united hand and mouth,' that he was innocent. This process, which probably dates back to the days when the kindred of the accused were prepared to fight the 'suit' or supporters of the accuser, was rapidly becoming a farce, as the reality of its meaning became lost. In the next period, if a defendant could prove that he was entitled to resort to it, his opponent usually gave up the case as hopeless. There was, however, no direct attempt to abolish it in this period, save in the case of a man indicted, under the Assises of Clarendon and Northampton, at the King's suit. Such a person could not wage his law.[1]

Neither, in any case, could the man against whom lay a presumption of guilt, *e.g.* the man who was taken red-handed, or on whom the stolen property was found, wage his law. If such a man were not prepared to fight his accuser, his only alternative was a resort to the **ordeal**, *i.e.* to invoke a miracle; and, inasmuch as the belief in miracles to order was dying out, even in the twelfth century, it gradually became clear that, in the absence of collusion, a resort to the ordeal practically meant certain condemnation. Moreover, the ordeal system could not be worked without the active aid of the Church; and the Church definitely abolished the judicial ordeal at the Lateran Council of 1216.

There remained then, apart from some special cases, such as trial by charters and trial by official witnesses,[2] only the ancient resort of trial by **battle**, the last formal survival of the blood feud; and this, as we have seen in the case of the 'appeals,' the royal judges were striving, might and main, to put down. It is true that, in their famous procedure of the Writ of Right, they virtually legalized it under the name of the duel, or judicial combat;[3] but, as we shall see, before very long, they found a

[1] The curious expression 'wager of law' seems to be due to the fact that the accused gave pledges (*vadia*) to appear with his 'oath-helpers' on a given day.

[2] *E.g.* where the accused relied upon direct proof of title by royal gift, or where he had bought the disputed article in open market under the provisions of William's Law (Liebermann, 487).

[3] It appears to be orthodox to deny the connection between the feud and the judicial combat. But may not the latter have been simply a later and more humane stage of the former? The fact that the Conqueror seems to have had some difficulty in persuading his subjects to accept it (Will. I, 1; art. 6) seems merely to point to the fact that the English clung to the rougher joys of a less formal scramble.

substitute for it, though the Writ of Right itself was not formally abolished till the year 1833. This substitute was the still more famous **trial by jury**.

The Jury

A jury is, as the word implies, a body of sworn men. But not all bodies of sworn men are juries, in the technical sense of the word. The oath-helpers of the 'wager of law,' of which we have just spoken, were, obviously, sworn men; but they were not a trial jury, because they simply testified to the truth of the accused's denial. Neither are witnesses, in the modern sense, though they, too, are sworn, a trial jury; and for a similar reason. The doomsmen of the popular moots may, very possibly, have taken some oath; but they were a tribunal, not a method of trial. To find the origin of trial by jury, we must turn, not to ancient popular custom, but to royal privilege.

In the later Roman Empire, the Imperial Treasury had often found itself at a loss in dealing with fiscal questions in the provinces. It was not unnatural that the imperial claims should often be met, especially in districts remote from centres of administration, with professions of ignorance very hard to disprove. Was a particular farm, or was it not, part of the property of a deceased person who had bequeathed all his belongings to Caesar? To solve this and similar problems, the imperial officials used to seize upon a certain number of the most responsible persons in the neighbourhood, and compel them to find an answer. The privilege, under the name of 'inquest,' passed to the Frankish emperors, Charles the Great and his successors, from them to the Norman dukes who conquered an outlying province of the Frank Empire, from the Norman dukes to the English kings. It was at first intensely unpopular; and not unnaturally, for it was used mainly as an engine to extort information which, it was easily foreseen, would lead to taxation. The 'inquests' which resulted in the compilation of Domesday Book made a vivid and unfavourable impression on the country. A similar effect was produced by the inquests of 1166 and 1170, before alluded to.[1] Even to this day, the word 'inquisitorial' bears the burden of historical unpopularity.

A new turn was given to the royal privilege when the royal officials began to use it for the decision of private disputes, and

[1] *Ante*, pp. 40, 41.

especially for disputes about land. By the common law of feudalism, such disputes were settled in the court of the lord of both disputants. Properly speaking, the verdict or judgment should have been found by the *pares curtis*, or other vassals of the lord, and pronounced by the lord's mouth. This plan was adopted in more than one of the big lawsuits of the early twelfth century; and, in the famous clause of the Great Charter, so long and so profoundly misunderstood, it was again asserted as a fundamental principle of justice.[1]

The Jury in Law Suits

But in fact we find, from the earliest years of the twelfth century, that the King was using another method to decide disputes between his tenants *in capite*. In the year 1101, Rollo of Avranches and the Abbot of Abingdon were disputing the title to three virgates of land in Oxfordshire. The King, instead of summoning his Great Council, sent a writ to Hugh of Buckland (? sheriff of Berks) and the sheriff of Oxford, bidding the men of the two counties, 'on the part of the King,' say the truth as to the title to the three virgates.[2] In the year 1122, a dispute between the monks of St. Stephen of 'Brideton' and the tenants of the royal manor of Bridport was, on the King's command, referred to a sworn jury of sixteen men of the neighbourhood, who found that the land in dispute belonged to the manor of Brideton, granted to the monks by William the Conqueror.[3]

Reforms of Henry II

The judicial activity of the reign of Henry II comprised a vast development of the jury trial. At some unknown date, the King, while admitting the principle of feudal jurisdiction in land suits, added, as a new rule of administration, that no suit touching a freehold should be commenced, even in a feudal court, without the royal writ.[4] There was, probably, some colour for this startling innovation in the historic oath of Sarum, by which the Conqueror had striven to make himself, not merely overlord, but direct lord, of all land-holders in the kingdom. Obviously, it gave the royal officials notice of all land suits, and thus provided them

[1] Cap. 39 (S.C. 301). The judgment by peers survives in the trial of a peer in the House of Lords.

[2] Bigelow, *Placita, Anglo-Normannica,* p. 74.

[3] *Ibid.*, p. 120.

[4] Glanville, Lib. II, cap. 15. There was an exception for a purely clerical dispute about a frankalmoign estate.

with abundant opportunities of further interference, which they were not slow to use.

One of the most famous and sweeping of these interferences was that known as the **Grand Assise**. The defendant against

Grand Assise

whom a Writ of Right had been issued, might, if he pleased, instead of running the risks of battle, apply to the King for a counter-writ which bade the sheriff summon sixteen knights of the county wherein the disputed land lay, to recognize, upon their oaths, which of the parties had the greater right.[1] Thereupon, the proceedings towards battle in the lord's court were peremptorily stopped by the sheriff; and the dispute remitted to the jury of sixteen.[2]

Another innovation of the same reign was equally drastic. The proceedings on the Writ of Right were apt to prove dilatory,

Petty Assises

by reason of the number of 'essoins,' or excuses allowed to the defendant, as well as by 'vouchers to warranty.' It would have been unsportsmanlike to expect a man to fight while he was in poor health, or to deprive him of his land because, being absent on the King's business, he failed to respond to the challenge. Again, it had been recognized in England, from very early times, that one of the best ways of defending a challenged title, either to goods or land, was to call in the help of the person from whom the defendant had received them. This person might either have expressly guaranteed the defendant's title; or he might have been held by the law to have done so. In either case, he was bound to intervene and take up the burden of the defence; unless he himself, in turn, 'vouched to warranty' *his* vendor, and so on.

But all this caused delay; and, in the meantime, who was to hold the land? This question the royal justices took upon themselves to settle; presumably on the ground that the King must know to whom to look for military service and taxes. Accordingly, a brief inquest on some simple question of fact was held by sworn men; and, according to the result, interim possession was awarded. Generally speaking, the principle adopted was that of the *status quo*. By the **Assise of Mort d'Ancestor**,[3] the heir of the person who had actually been in

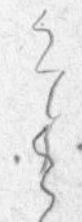

[1] Glanville, Lib. II, cap. 11. Four knights were chosen directly by the sheriff; and these elected the other twelve.

[2] *Ibid.*, cap. 8.

[3] *Ibid.*, Lib. XIII, capp. 2–18.

possession at his death was given possession. By the **Assise of Novel Disseisin,**[1] the man who had but just ejected his peaceful opponent was compelled to hand back the land. By the **Assise d'Arrein Presentment,**[2] the patron who had presented the last incumbent was given power to fill the existing vacancy. All was 'without prejudice' (as a modern lawyer would say) to the ultimate decision of the 'right' or title; but, in fact, the delay and expense of trying the 'right' or ultimate title, were so great, that an award on a possessory assise frequently settled the dispute for ever. This fact, naturally, tended to increase the popularity of the possessory assises, and, through them, to draw a sharp line between 'right' and mere possession, or, as it was called, 'seisin.' This again, led judges and lawyers to insist on the importance of possession, or seisin, as evidence and presumption of title, and thus to give to the seisin of land that unique importance in English land law which it has ever since held.

Writs of Entry

The next stage in the story is the development of remedies for the protection of seisin or possession, independently of a Writ of Right. It soon became clear, that the real essence of a 'novel disseisin' was the disturbance of good order which had been caused by the unsuccessful party. Let the idea be extended a little further; and we get an independent action based on disturbance of seisin as a wrong *per se*. Thus appear the **writs of entry,** which, at first only available between the ejector and the ejected, were gradually extended in favour of persons deriving title through each of them.[3] The man who 'had no entry' to the land in dispute, save by a disseisin, was bidden to give up the land at once, or appear in the King's court to show the reason why. If he appeared, the simple question of disseisin, or disturbance of the King's peace, was submitted to a jury; and, according as the jury found, so the seisin—in theory only pending the decision of the 'right,' in substance for ever—was awarded. No wonder the feudal lords, who saw themselves deprived of their jurisdiction by this novel procedure, protested vigorously, and, in form at least,

[1] Glanville, Lib. XIII, capp. 32–39.

[2] *Ibid.* capp. 18–21.

[3] This is the meaning of the mysterious *per*, *post*, and *cui*, so often associated with the Writs of Entry. The details are too long to give. All limits were removed by the Statute of Marlborough in 1267 (cap. 29). The Writ of Entry thus became a simple means of recovering seisin.

procured the abolition of the obnoxious 'Præcipe' by the Great Charter.[1] But the tide was running against them. Under cover of the glaring fiction that the 'lord of that fee had renounced his court,' the King's judges granted, almost as of course, on the issue even of a Writ of Right, a supplementary writ (the *tolt*) to remove the case from the lord's court to the shire court, and another (the *pone*) to remove it from the shire court to the King's court.[2] In their despair, the feudal lords seem to have grasped at royal privileges, and, at any rate during the troubled years of Henry III, to have attempted to attract litigants to their own courts by the offer of jury trial. But this was too much to be borne; and the claim was repudiated, after the royalist victories, by the Statute of Marlborough.[3]

The Criminal Jury

We have seen that the jury of accusation, as distinct from the jury of trial, was introduced into the new criminal procedure by the Assise of Clarendon.[4] But it is equally clear from that document, that the trial jury formed no part of its original plan. With the abolition of ordeals, however, the machinery of the Assise threatened to break down. Public opinion, even in the thirteenth century, would hardly permit of a man of good character being condemned off-hand, even on the accusation of a jury. Apparently, the judges who found themselves called upon for a practical solution of the difficulty got into the habit of asking the accused whether he would submit to a trial by the 'country,' *i.e.* by a second jury, chosen from the neighbours present. The purely voluntary character of the submission is shown by the (to us) amazing fact that, until the year 1772,[5] a prisoner who refused to plead before such a tribunal could not be tried at all; he could merely be subjected to the *peine forte et dure* — *i.e.* to judicial torture, to compel him to plead.[6] Apparently, the pressure literally applied to the accused to 'put himself upon his country' was successful in establishing the **petty jury**, or jury of trial in criminal

[1] Cap. 34.

[2] This process had begun in Glanville's day (Lib. I, capp. 4–6). The later forms are given in Blackstone's *Commentaries*, Vol. III, Appx. I.

[3] 52 Hen. III (1267) c. 22.

[4] *Ante*, p. 40–1.

[5] 12 Geo. III, c. 20.

[6] This barbaric means of introducing an amendment of legal procedure was actually authorized by the Statute of Westminster the First (3 Edw. (1275) c. 12). That it should have been necessary to resort to it, is a vivid illustration of the difficulty of openly making changes in primitive law.

cases, as an ordinary institution, soon after the close of the thirteenth century. At any rate, a statute of the year 1352[1] makes a clear distinction between the jury of indictment ('grand jury') and the 'jury of deliverance,' by enacting that no member of the former should be put upon the latter, if the accused objected. We may, therefore, not unfairly assume, though the story is very dark,[2] that, by the middle of the fourteenth century, the outlines of English criminal procedure, as we know it now, had been definitely drawn.[3]

Finally, in their determination to win all litigation for the King's courts, the royal justices, at the very end of this period, invented or adopted a new writ, destined to be of enormous importance in all branches of our law.

Trespass

This was the **Writ of Trespass**, which makes its appearance in the middle of the thirteenth century, just at the outbreak of the Barons' War. Doubtless, in those troubled times, offences of violence were unusually frequent; whilst the old methods of redress only tended to aggravate the disorder. The notion of the 'peace,' or suspension of hostilities, was very familiar in theory; whatever its rarity in practice. And, of all 'peaces,' the peace of the King was the most powerful and best protected. If the royal officials could once establish the rule, that any interference with possession, however slight, was a breach of the King's peace, and subjected the offender to be summoned before the King's justices, the ultimate triumph of the royal courts was secure. With a little ingenious straining, almost any offence known in a simple state of society could be treated as a breach of the peace. The notion of the sanctity of possession had, as has been seen, been growing by means of the protection afforded to 'seisin' by the 'petty (or 'possessory') assises' and the Writs of Entry. But the notion of seisin was becoming technical. It was, for special reasons, gradually being restricted to the possession of land (as distinct from chattels), and of land by a freeholder, or a man who claimed as

[1] Printed as 25 Edw. III, st. V, c. 3.

[2] It may be studied in the work of the late Professor Thayer, *Evidence at the Common Law*, cap. II.

[3] It seems also, though the story is not very clear, that the decision of those 'exceptions,' which, as we have seen (*ante*, pp. 42, 43), were allowed by the royal judges to evade an appeal of felony, was also referred to a jury of recognitors. If this were so, the step by which the issue of guilt or innocence was referred to a similar body would not be long or distant.

such. Moreover, the notion of 'disseisin' was held to imply a deliberate attempt to assert a right of possession. Something simpler was wanted — some process which should make the mere casual raid or blow punishable by sharp and speedy process in the royal courts.

This is exactly what the Writ of Trepass did, as the following form will show.

> "If A gives pledges to prosecute his complaint, then put B by gage and pledge that he (B) be before our Justices at Westminster (on such a day) prepared to show why with force and arms he assaulted the said A at N (or broke the close of A at N, or took and carried away the sheep of A) and other enormities to him did, to the grave damage of the said A, *and against our peace*."[1]

In somewhat later days, there appears to have been a second form, in which the sheriff was bid to hear the plaint; and the allegations of 'force and arms' and 'against our peace' were omitted. But it may be doubted whether the 'viscontiel' Writ of Trespass was known in the period under review.[2] At any rate, the great merit of the Writ of Trespass was, that it offered to the injured party a tempting alternative of the somewhat unsatisfactory remedies previously open to him. Instead of bringing a dangerous 'appeal,' in which his opponent might complete his triumph by doing the complainant to death, instead of resorting to a probably unavailing summons before the Hundred moot, the complainant could bring his adversary before the royal justices and get him fined and outlawed, while, out of the offender's goods, compensation would be awarded to the complainant in proportion to the extent of his loss. Almost from the first, it would seem, the very simple question involved in an action of Trespass ('Did or did not the defendant offer violence to the plaintiff?') was referred to that new 'inquest' tribunal which, as we have seen, was becoming the favourite method of settling all short questions of fact. At any rate, we know that, when Edward I, in 1284, was forcing English

[1] Fitzherbert, *Natura Brevium*, I, 86. Of course Fitzherbert lived long after the thirteenth century; but the form may be traced back to 1254 (*Abbreviatio Placitorum*, 141, &c.).

[2] This doubt is suggested by the curious name which, in later days, distinguished the royal from the local Writ of Trespass. The former was said to be 'returnable.' But are not all writs of summons 'returnable'?

legal procedure on the conquered Welsh, he spoke of trial by the *patria* (the technical name for a jury) as the almost inevitable method of deciding a plea of Trespass;[1] and he announced his intention of standing no nonsense about refusal of consent.[2] The new Writ of Trespass would, therefore, present the double merit of a speedy decision and a new remedy. It is true that the complainant ran some risk. If his complaint turned out to be unfounded, he was *in misericordiâ regis* — *i.e.* liable to fine and imprisonment. But this was, after all, a smaller risk than the risk of an 'appeal.'

By these and other means, of which no account can here be attempted, the royal officials of the twelfth and thirteenth centuries had accomplished the chief part of that heavy task which lay before the State, if it was to justify its existence by establishing order and justice in the land. They had not only provided a machinery which would, in the not very distant future, draw well-nigh all causes to the King's courts, and thus prepare the way for one uniform system of law; they had, in the process, almost of necessity brought into existence a whole set of tribunals to deal with such causes. The steps by which the old irregular progresses of the King and his officers throughout the land had developed into an elaborate system of circuit courts for the trial of assises and gaol-deliveries and offences against the peace, are matters of Constitutional Law, and cannot here be traced; so with the process by which the old *Curia Regis*, sitting occasionally to settle disputes between tenants in *capite*, had produced the regular tribunals of the Upper Bench, Common Bench, and Exchequer of Pleas. These weighty matters are for separate study.[3] Here it has been attempted only to show, how the royal justices, faced with the duty of strengthening the authority and revenue of their master, had, by silent innovation and subtle ingenuity, gone far to bring about the day when that master should be 'over all causes and in all matters within his dominions supreme.' This was a great ideal; for it meant, ultimately, one people under one law.

[1] Statutum Walliae, cap. 11. [2] *Ibid.*

[3] They may be studied briefly in the late Professor Maitland's posthumously published *Constitutional History*, and in Book I, chapter VII, of the great *History* of Pollock and Maitland; at more length in volume I of Holdsworth's *History of English Law.*

CHAPTER V

THE LAW OF CHATTELS

IT is not due to carelessness that, in the arrangement of the chapters dealing with this period, the subject of legal procedure is placed between what a modern lawyer would regard as two equally important branches of substantive law. This is a work on history; and such a work should follow historical lines, which in the present connexion appear to fall in the direction indicated. The feudal scheme of land law was deliberately built up with a view of administering the newly won country of England. The new procedure, which the last chapter has attempted to describe, was very largely produced by the desire to strengthen the feudal scheme of land law. The common law of chattels, that is to say, the law ultimately adopted by the King's courts for the regulation of disputes about the ownership and possession of goods, was, to a substantial extent, a by-product of that new procedure which had been mainly introduced to perfect the feudal scheme of land law.

The Writ of Right and the Writ of Debt

We have seen[1] that the foundation stone of the new royal procedure for the decision of land suits was the Writ of Right. Doubtless, as has also appeared, this primordial but rather costly and dilatory remedy had, in practice, been largely superseded by newer and more speedy remedies, which, originally intended to decide only 'interlocutory' questions, had come to be regarded as disposing of final questions. Nevertheless, it remained an assumption, all through the Middle Ages, that the claimant of land who was really in earnest, could insist on the original remedy of a Writ of Right.[2]

[1] *Ante*, p. 49.

[2] Even the theoretical right to trial by battle was not abolished till 1819 (59 Geo. III, c. 46, s. 2 — the statute which also abolished appeals). The Writs of Right themselves (for there were several varieties) were not formally abolished till 1833 (3 and 4 Will. IV, c. 27, s. 36).

Now in that treatise attributed to Glanville, which tells us most of what we know about the procedure of the royal courts in the twelfth century, there is another writ, the **Writ of Debt**, which strikingly resembles it, and, indeed, appears to overlap it in certain cases. Let us put the two writs side by side.

Right	Debt
'*The King to the Sheriff.* Bid A that to justly and without delay render to B one hide of land in such a vill, of which the said B complains that the said A unjustly deforceth him. And unless he does it, summon him,' &c. (Glanv. lib. I, cap. 5).	'*The King to the Sheriff.* Bid N that he justly and without delay render to R 100 marks which he owes him, as he (R) saith, and of which he (R) complains that he (N) unjustly deforceth him. And, unless he does it, summon him,' &c. (Glanv. lib. X, cap. 2).

This resemblance, already, as we have said, striking enough, becomes all the more striking when we observe that there was actually a form of the Writ of Debt applicable to the recovery of land. This form[1] supposes that the land was given in pledge by the plaintiff to the defendant, for a term of years which has expired, and that the defendant refuses to give back the land. This is a most interesting writ from other points of view also. Something will have to be said of it when we speak of terms of years, and also when we speak of mortgages. At present we confine ourselves to asking why, contrary to all experience of early legal systems, there should apparently be a double remedy for the same grievance?

But, if we look a little more closely, we shall probably soon discover that the grievance is not exactly the same in the two cases. In the case of the Writ of Right, as in the case of the popular 'appeal of larceny,' there is an underlying assumption, that the thing sought to be recovered has been taken from the claimant by force or fraud. Therefore, if all other methods fail, the dispute must be decided by battle. In the case of the Writ of Debt, it is not so; though it is possible that, incidentally, a question involving an appeal to arms may arise in the course of an action of Debt — as, for example, if the defendant from whom a chattel is claimed sets up a hostile title, and 'vouches to warranty' a third party who takes up the challenge.[2] In the ordinary way, the Writ of Debt assumes

Not Based on Violence

[1] Glanville, lib. X, cap. 9.

[2] *Ibid.*, cap. 17.

that the thing sought to be recovered has been voluntarily handed over (or 'bailed') to the defendant by the plaintiff, for a specific purpose, such as hiring, pledge, or loan, which has now expired. According to the ideas of the day, refusal to return a thing thus 'bailed' was no very serious offence; probably, in spite of King Alfred's injunctions, the plaintiff in such a case was looked upon as rather a fool for letting his land or chattels go out of his hands. So the stern remedy of battle was not part of the proceedings. The defendant (even, apparently, if the plaintiff has a tally or other record of the transaction) was allowed to clear himself by the process of 'waging his law.'

Now, at this point, the student of English legal history ought to begin to feel a serious difficulty. He has been taught to believe, on the great authority of Bracton,[1] that there never was, in English law, an action to recover a specific chattel, a 'real' action to recover a movable; and he knows that, until a very recent day, the defendant in an action of Detinue (which was only a special form of Debt) could always evade delivery of the subject matter by paying its value. And yet it looks, if Glanville speaks the truth, as though the earliest and, for some time, the only chattel action known to the King's courts, was of the most thoroughly 'real' type.

A 'Real Action'

The difficulty is great; but a fairly plausible solution may be offered.

It seems quite clear, that the original notion of the Writ of Debt was as 'real' as anything could possibly be. Even when the subject of the action was a sum of money, as in the first example given by Glanville,[2] the mind of the framer of the writ is evidently bent on getting back the specific coins lent. There is no question of a 'debt' in the wide modern sense, which includes any liability to pay money. The defendant is to restore the very coins lent.

'Fungibility' of Money

But, even in the twelfth century, though, doubtless, the quality of coins was very far from uniform, a plaintiff would have been unwise if he refused to accept 100 marks from a defendant, on the ground that they were

[1] Lib. III, cap. 3 (4). [2] Lib. X, cap. 2.

not his identical coins. Naturally, the defendant had not borrowed the money for the purpose of looking at it; he had borrowed it to trade with, or to pay his rent, or for some other purpose which involved parting with it. What is technically called the 'fungibility' of money, is its chief value as an article of commerce; and this fact could not long remain unrecognized, even by such a conservative class as legal officials. Accordingly, it soon became clear, that an action of Debt based on a loan of money was merely an action to recover money of a certain value. But the originally 'real' character, even of a money claim, survived, to the latest days of its history, in the rule that a Writ of Debt could only be issued for a specific sum — the 'very debt itself' was to be recovered. The action could not be employed to recover 'unliquidated damages'; because there was no jury to assess them. If the defendant was so unlucky as to fail in his wager of law, he was liable for the whole of the plaintiff's claim.[1]

The change was by no means complete when the thing sought to be recovered was, not money, but 'non-fungible' chattels.

Other Chattels

The difference is marked by the appearance, just at the end of this period, of the distinction between 'Debt' and 'Detinue.' If the plaintiff is suing for a sum of current money, he alleges that the defendant 'debet' — *i.e.* ought to pay it; and the Court, if the defence fails, will issue a judicial writ (*Fi. Fa.*) to the sheriff, bidding him 'cause the sum to be made' from the defendant's goods. But if the plaintiff is seeking the recovery, say, of a horse or a plough, he must say that the defendant 'detains' it (*detinet*); and then he may be met by the simple denial, strictly in accordance with ancient tradition[2] — *non detinet.* But that simple denial opened up all sorts of questions, on some of which the law of the thirteenth century was very vague. It may be quite true that the defendant no longer 'detinet'; because he has sold the article and pocketed the money. And yet, surely, he ought not to get off. On the other hand, the horse may have died or been killed without his (the defendant's) fault; and then the case would be different.

[1] Professor Maitland has pointed out that this result was actually embalmed in a verse of medieval doggerel (*The Court Baron*, S.S. vol. 4, p. 17).

[2] This was the 'twertutnay' or direct denial (word for word) which the primitive moot expected from an accused.

Accordingly, as Bracton informs us,[1] it was the business of every plaintiff who sought to recover a chattel by action, to put a price upon it; and then, even if the defendant no longer held the chattel, he might be made liable for the value. And thus the Court, unwilling to allow the plaintiff to be tricked at the last moment by the defendant destroying the chattel or allowing it to escape, seems to have got into the habit of giving judgment for the return of the article *or its value,* an alternative not unnaturally interpreted by defendants in their own favour.

Alternative Remedy

A much more interesting explanation of this apparently stupid anomaly is so often given, that a word must be said about it. It is alleged that the maxim or rule enunciated by Bracton is founded on a fundamental principle of Teutonic law, usually expressed in the adage '*Hand muss Hand wahren,*' or, in French form, '*meuble n'a suyte.*' With great respect, the adage alluded to seems, in practice at any rate, to have led to a result exactly the opposite of the rule under consideration. Surely we see the primitive Teutonic mind at work, if anywhere in legal procedure, in that ancient 'appeal of larceny' which the King's courts are, in this period, trying to put down. But it is just in the appeal of larceny that the successful appellor gets back his very goods. The possessor may clear himself by 'vouching to warranty,' or by showing that he bought the goods before formal witnesses; but he has to give them up all the same, if the plaintiff can prove his allegations. If the appellee is worsted in battle, he loses, not merely the article in dispute, but his other chattels as well. In the picturesque language of an ancient Assise Roll, 'he (the appellor) gets his (the appellee's) chattels, for beheading him.'[2] It is suggested that this primitive right could not be enforced if the claimant had voluntarily parted with the possession of the chattel sought to be recovered.[3] It may be so; though the reasoning is not obvious. It looks much more as though, when money became common, and most things had acquired a 'market value,' and when the new jury tribunal was

Another Explanation

[1] Lib. III, cap. 3 (4) 'alioquin non valebit rei mobilis vindicatio, pretio non apposito.' As Bracton goes on to point out, the necessity for valuation is still greater where the object 'in pondere, numero, mensura, consistit.'

[2] *Assise Rolls of Northumberland* (Surtees Society), p. 70.

[3] See the question elaborately discussed by P. & M. (Vol. II, pp. 155–183).

there to assess 'unliquidated damages,'[1] it was found convenient to substitute a money judgment for a decree of specific restoration. But it was a singular and obvious gap in the legal procedure of the Middle Ages; and it worked a good deal of injustice.

Law of Succession

So far we have learned, incidentally, that, according to English law in the thirteenth century, chattels might be stolen, aliened (finally or temporarily), and recovered by legal process. But it is also clear, though the rules themselves are far from certain, that chattels may be disposed of by will, and that, if they are not so disposed of, they can be claimed under rules of intestate succession.

Intestacy

The latter is obviously the older method; and it is somewhat surprising to discover how long its first principles remained unsettled. The Laws of Cnut give the undisposed of possessions (*æhte*) of a deceased person to his wife and children; subject only to the just claims of his lord.[2] The coronation charter of Henry I allots them to his wife, children, or relatives, and his liege men; to be divided for the good of his (the deceased's) soul.[3] The Custumal known as the *Leges Willelmi* says that the goods of a deceased intestate are to be divided equally among his children.[4] Glanville gives them to his lord.[5] The Great Charter supports the claims of the Church to undertake the distribution;[6] and Bracton follows the Charter.[7]

The Reasonable Parts

Thus the victory appeared to rest with the Church; but it is clear from Bracton's pages, that the Church was not allowed to carry off all the goods of a deceased intestate. From whatever source derived, whether from Roman Law or Teutonic custom, there was an ancient division which, differing in detail from place to place, is everywhere recognizable in principle. The deceased's widow (unless sufficiently provided for by dower) gets one third of the goods; one half if

[1] In this connection, the new Writ of Trespass (*de bonis asportatis*) previously alluded to, was important; but it did not apply to chattels voluntarily bailed to the defendant.

[2] Cnut, II, 70.

[3] S.C. 101.

[4] Liebermann, 514.

[5] Lib. VII, cap. 16. (Possibly this passage refers only to the case of the bastard, which Glanville has just been discussing. But the forty manorial courts which claimed probate jurisdiction so late as the year 1831 (*Report on Ecclesiastical Courts*, Appx. D, p. 509) suggest a formerly widespread claim.)

[6] Cap. 27 (S.C. 300).

[7] Lib. II, cap. 26 (2).

there are no children. The children get a third, or, if there is no widow, a half. The remaining third (or half) is the 'deads' part'; and, if not disposed of by the deceased's will, goes to the Church, or, possibly, if the deceased man was a serf, to his lord.[1]

This brings us to an important question. Is the will (of chattels) a primitive English institution? The passage above quoted from the Laws of Cnut refers to a man who dies '*cwydeleas*'; it suggests, therefore, that a man might if he liked, make a will. But it seems to be the better opinion that, before the twelfth century, the only form of testamentary disposition in England (except in the case of privileged persons) was the 'post-obit gift,' *i.e.* the actual delivery of goods to a trustee or executor, who undertook to distribute them after the owner's death in accordance with the latter's wishes.

The Testament

Now the Church disliked this way of doing business; because it left little scope for that practice of making death bed gifts which, during the whole of the Middle Ages, brought so much wealth to ecclesiastical coffers. And so we find, everywhere throughout Western Europe,[2] as one of the most striking results of the establishment of separate ecclesiastical courts, the introduction of the genuine will of chattels, *i.e.* the purely 'ambulatory' disposal, usually by mere word of mouth, of the 'dead's part,' to take effect on his decease. Such wills, being revocable and secret, were usually made *in articulo mortis*, and were really part of the dying confession. Naturally, the execution of these fell into the hands of the Church, which, also, usually turned out to be chief legatee. Naturally, also, the Church insisted strenuously upon the duty of making a will, and almost stigmatized as doomed to perdition the unlucky man who omitted this duty—at least if he had fair warning of his impending death. Naturally, in the last place, the Church contended strongly, that such a lapse from duty should not deprive her of property which should have been left for pious uses; and, as has been seen, she seems to have made good her claim by the end of the period under review.

Influence of the Church

Thus the Church in England acquired that unrivalled position in the matter of wills of chattels which remained almost

[1] See Bracton, lib. II, cap. 26 (2), ff. 60 b–61 a.

[2] See Caillemer, *The Executor in England and on the Continent* (Select Essays in Anglo-American Legal History, III, 746–769).

unbroken for six centuries. If the deceased's legatees set up a will, they must prove its existence in the court of the 'Ordinary' of the diocese; otherwise the Church's claim to the 'dead's part' prevailed. Thus the 'probate' of the will. All questions of interpretation were naturally referred also to the same tribunal. If intestacy were admitted, the Church appointed an 'administrator'; and it was long before the next-of-kin could make him answerable for the 'dead's part.' Until the 'letters of administration' were formally granted, the goods were the property of the 'Ordinary.' No doubt there were, in privileged places, *e.g.* chartered towns, special customs which ousted the control of the Church courts.[1] But, speaking generally, the Church had, by the end of the thirteenth century, established a monopoly of testamentary jurisdiction in all matters not affecting land. The efforts of the royal courts seem to have been confined to a vigorous defence of all land jurisdiction against the Church, and to the enforcement, in favour of the creditors of the deceased, of the payment of the latter's debts. This last point is so important, that a few words must be said about it.

Testamentary Jurisdiction

Once more, the student familiar only with modern ideas finds himself in a maze when he attempts to understand the attitude of primitive society towards the liabilities of a deceased person. To him it appears inevitable, that the claims of a dead man's creditors should be confined to his 'estate,' *i.e.* the proprety which the dead man leaves behind him. Every student of English law is also familiar with the fact that, until less than a century ago, it was with difficulty, and only in exceptional cases, that the deceased's land could be made available to satisfy his creditors. It may, therefore, come upon him as a shock to find, that there are, in English law of the twelfth century, unmistakable traces of personal and unlimited liability on the part of the **heir** to satisfy his ancestor's debts, irrespective of 'assets.' Glanville,[2] for example, distinctly says that, if the goods of the deceased are insufficient to pay his debts, the heir 'is held bound to make up the deficiency out of his own estate, if he is of age.' As late as the year 1275, the Statute of Westminster the First[3]

The Deceased's Debts

[1] See Gross, *Mediæval Intestacy* (Select Essays in Anglo-American Legal History, III, 723–736). [2] Lib. VII, cap. 8. [3] 3 Edw. I, c. 19.

re-affirmed this rule; so far as Crown debts were concerned.

The explanation seems to lie in the fact that, in early times, the liabilities of a deceased person are not 'debts' in the modern sense of the term, but, rather, sacred family responsibilities connected with religion and the blood feud, which are indelible, and fall alike on all members of the kin. It was only the recent and extraordinary change in the law which, as we have seen, substituted primogeniture for equal division among males, that, in England, made the liability of the single heir look so grotesque. And so we are not surprised to find that a great change took place also in the law of liability for the dead man's debts.

Primitive Notions

The change is marked by the introduction of a new figure into the scene. In the middle of the twelfth century, the heir is contemplated as the person who will succeed, not only to the deceased's land, but to his chattels, at any rate for purposes of distribution. 'If,' says the Assise of Northampton,[1] 'a free tenant dies, his heir shall continue in the seisin [2] which his father had on the day when he (the father) was alive and dead, as regards his fief; and he (the heir) *shall have the chattels that he may make the division of the deceased.*'

The Executor

But it was natural that the new practice of will-making introduced by the Church should work a change in this rule; and, accordingly, we find that, by the early years of the thirteenth century, the person entrusted with the distribution of the chattels of the deceased is not his heir, but a new person called an 'executor,' *i.e.* a person specially appointed by the deceased to execute, or carry into effect, his will.[3] This person may be, as is sometimes suggested, a survival of the old *Treuhander* or *Salmann,* to whom was entrusted, by post-obit gift, the fulfilment of the deceased's wishes in primitive times.[4] But he is sufficiently accounted for by the desire of the Church courts, jealously excluded from all control over the deceased's land, but vested, as we have seen, with administration of his chattels, to have a separate 'personal representative,' who should

[1] Art. 4 (S.C. 151).
[2] This is the famous doctrine: '*Le mort saisit le vif.*'
[3] 'The rest (of the deceased's chattels) shall be left to his executors for the performance of his will' (Magna Carta of 1215, cap. 26, S.C. 300).
[4] *Ante*, p. 61.

derive his authority entirely from them, and undertake to carry out the administration under their supervision, and according to their rules. In the case of intestacy, it was still more important for the Church courts to appoint an 'administrator,' who would look sharply after the substantial claims of the Church in respect of the undisposed of 'dead's part.'

Release of the Heir

But it was equally natural that the heir, thus deprived of what was gradually growing, as commerce and industry developed, to be a more and more important part of his ancestor's estate, should decline responsibility for his ancestor's liabilities; the more so as these also gradually ceased to wear a religious and personal character, and became mere commercial debts. The liability of the deceased's chattels themselves to be employed for payment of his debts is clear; even in the passage of Glanville which has been quoted to show the ultimate liability of the heir at that date.[1] By the time of Bracton,[2] we find that the heir's liability is limited to the value of the deceased's property inherited by him. The great Statute of Westminster the Second, in 1285, informs us, incidentally, that the executors of a deceased person are bound to pay his debts,[3] and imposes a similar liability on the 'Ordinary' in the case of intestacy. The same statute[4] gives to executors a Writ of Account against the debtors of the deceased; and thus relieves them from the necessity of resorting to the Church courts for less efficient remedies. For the King's courts did not allow the Church courts to entertain actions of Debt, even *fide interpositâ*.[5]

In some such way as this appear to have arisen those two fundamental rules of the Common Law which were, until recently, and, to a considerable extent, are still, such striking features of the English Law of Succession. Land[6] goes to the heir; because the executor was appointed by a will, and the King's courts would recognize no will of lands. And it went, until

[1] Perhaps, however, at that date only when the testator had so expressly directed (Lib. VII, cap. 8).

[2] Lib. II, cap. 26 (2). 'But the heir of the deceased will be bound to pay the debts of the deceased . . . so far as the inheritance goes, and no farther' (fo. 61a).

[3] 13 Edw. I, st. I, c. 19.

[4] Cap. 23.

[5] Glanville, lib. X, cap. 12.

[6] It must, of course, be remembered that, for this purpose, 'land' does not include terms of years ('leaseholds').

lately, to the heir free of all the liabilities of the deceased; except such as could be enforced, under the law of warranty, against the land itself ('specialities in which the heir is bound'). If the Church claimed the chattels, let her pay the debts. This medieval quarrel is largely responsible for one of the most characteristic and important rules of English property law, viz. the distinction between 'real' and 'personal' property.

At first sight it looks as though the period before us did nothing to develop that branch of the law which, to every modern lawyer, is of supreme importance, viz. the **Law of Contract**. For the modern lawyer inevitably thinks of a contract as an accepted offer, or agreement; and Glanville lays it down emphatically, in spite of the somewhat ambiguous wording of the Constitutions of Clarendon[1] (with which he must have been familiar), that the King's court will not concern itself with 'private agreements.'[2] Bracton, who wrote at the very end of our period, was, as a scholar and a student of Roman Law, perfectly well aware of the hideous gap left in the structure of the common law by the absence of a general theory of contract; and made a half-hearted attempt to fill it with bricks and mortar from the Institutes.[3] But, in the opinion of eminent critics, his treatment of this topic is purely academic, and bears little relation to the facts of his day.[4]

Contract

Looking, however, again at Glanville, we seem to discover that, under the disguise of '*diracionatio*' or '*probatio*,'[5] contracts (for Glanville expressly uses the term)[6] are making their way into the action of **Debt**. And this ought not to surprise us; for, as we have seen,[7] an action of Debt was originally an action to recover a chattel; and, as we also know, both from general sources and Old English law in particular,[8] the delivery or pledge of a chattel was one of the earliest known means of securing the performance of an undertaking. How does this apparently irrelevant treatment lead to anything like a recognition of a Law of Contract? Apparently, in this way.

Debt and Contract

The man who brings an action of Debt must show some ground for his assertion that the defendant ought to render to him the

[1] Cap. XV (S.C. 140).
[2] Lib. X, cap. 18.
[3] Lib. III, cap. 2 (ff. 99–101).
[4] *Bracton and Azo* (S.S. Vol. 8). See Introd. pp. xix, xx.
[5] Lib. X, cap. 12.
[6] *Ibid.*, cap. 18.
[7] *Ante*, p. 57.
[8] *Ante*, p. 13.

sum of money or other thing that he is claiming.[1] He must show that he gave the article as a pledge, and that he has redeemed it, or is prepared to redeem it.[2] He must allege that the defendant gave himself as security for A's debt, and that A is in default;[3] or that he (the plaintiff) hired to the defendant the article claimed;[4] or sold to him the chattel, the price of which he is seeking to recover.[5] Only in one case does Glanville, in his famous Book on Debts, recognize anything that we should call a 'purely executory contract.' This is when the plaintiff produces in court a charter bearing the defendant's seal. Then the defendant 'will be held to warrant without contradiction all that is contained in that charter.'[6] But as to the kind of claim a charter may be brought to enforce, Glanville says nothing; and it is quite possible that, at first, it was only in support of a common claim for money lent, as we should say, 'on a bond,' that such a proof could be adduced. The real difficulty for the modern reader of Glanville's book is, that his author does not clearly distinguish between the nature of a transaction and the proof of it. If we take his words literally, he seems to demand that, for every action of Debt, there must either be (*a*) pledge, (*b*) surety, (*c*) *causa* — *i.e.* some well-recognized and familiar transaction, such as sale, hiring, gratuitous loan of a chattel, and the like. Illogical as this classification may sound, it is not at all unlike the kind of classification which one meets with everywhere in early law. Once more we must remember, that the sharp distinction of ideas with which we are familiar is a very modern thing.

But if this view of Glanville's meaning is correct, we have the beginnings of a Law of Contract. It is only necessary to increase the list of *causae*,[7] and we shall increase the list of contracts. It is true, that a Law of Contract based on *causae* will always be an arbitrary and inelastic law; but it is a kind of law with which

[1] It is true that the first example of the Writ of Debt given by Glanville (lib. X, cap. 2) contains nothing but a bare demand of money. But this seems to be a mere skeleton form. The statement in cap. 12 is explicit.

[2] Capp. 7, 9. [3] Cap. 4. [4] Cap. 18. [5] Cap. 14. [6] Cap. 12.

[7] A very promising opening appears in the action of Debt on a sale (Glanville, lib. X, cap. 14). In all probability, this action was at first given only when the article or the price had already been handed over, and it would have been iniquitous to allow the other party to refuse to fulfil his share of the bargain. But, when Glanville wrote, the sale was 'perfected' as soon as the price was fixed — a rule which will account for the 'passing of the property' without delivery. Bracton protested against this conclusion (lib. II, cap. 17 (1)), but in vain.

some great nations are satisfied at the present day. It is, in fact, one of the unique peculiarities of English law that, having started on this unpromising road of *causae*, it should very soon have abandoned it for the broad highway of 'innominate' contracts. But that is a story which belongs to the next period.

Finally, we may note that, to the very close of this period, there is nothing that would satisfy the modern definition of a

Torts

Tort, as a purely civil wrong, not being a breach of contract, and remediable only in damages. The private citizen could (under difficulties) bring his 'appeal of felony,' sue out his Writ of Right, Assise of Novel Disseisin, or Writ of Entry, or even his Writ of Trespass. But even this last remedy, though it is now classed as an action of Tort, is anomalous in that connection. It aimed originally, and, to a certain extent, aims still, at punishment, rather than compensation — at fine and imprisonment, rather than 'damages' in the modern sense. It was not long before English Law took the one step needed to produce the modern scheme of legal remedies. And when it did, it used the Writ of Trespass as the starting point. For, as our masters have told us, "the King's courts were approaching the field of tort through the field of crime." [1]

[1] P. & M. II, 530. The writer's reasons for thinking that this is a truer view of the situation than that of Sir Henry Maine, will be found at p. 13, *ante*.

PERIOD III

EDWARD I TO THE COMMONWEALTH

1272–1660

AUTHORITIES

Statutes of the Realm (including *Acts and Ordinances of the Interregnum*), ed. Firth and Rait (Stationery Office, 1911, 3 vols.).

Registrum Brevium, ed. Fitzherbert.

Year Books.
(New edition proceeding in S.S. publications.)

Littleton. *Tenures.*

Fortescue. *De Laudibus Legum Angliæ.*

Fitzherbert. (Novel) *Natura Brevium.*

Coke. *Institutes.*
I. Commentary on Littleton.
II. Commentary on certain statutes.
III. High Treason.
IV. Jurisdiction.
Compleate Copyholder.
Book of Entries.

Reports by various reporters (quoted in footnotes).

West. *Symbolæographia.*

TEXT-BOOKS

Ames, J. B. *Origin of Uses and Trusts* (Select Essays in Anglo-American Legal History, II, 737–752).
History of Parol Contracts Prior to, and of, Assumpsit (Select Essays in Anglo-American Legal History, III, 259–319).
The History of Trover (Select Essays in Anglo-American Legal History, III, 417–445.)

Caillemer, R. *The Executor in England* (Select Essays in Anglo-American Legal History, III, 746–769).

Campbell. *Lives of the Chancellors* (not entirely trustworthy in detail).

Gross, C. *The Mediæval Law of Intestacy* (Select Essays in Anglo-American Legal History, III, 723–745).

Holdsworth, W. S. *A History of English Law*, Book II, Part I, chapters III–end, and Part II (Methuen, 1909).

Holmes. *The Common Law* (Macmillan, 1882).

Maitland, F. W. *Canon Law in England* (Methuen).
English Law and the Renaissance (Select Essays in Anglo-American Legal History, I, 168–207).
The History of the Register of Original Writs (Select Essays in Anglo-American Legal History, II, 549–596).

Scrutton. *Land in Fetters* (1886), *Commons and Common Fields* (1887).

Sedgwick, A. G., and Wait, F. S. *The History of the Action of Ejectment* (Select Essays in Anglo-American Legal History, III, 611–645).

Stephen. *History of the Criminal Law of England*, chapters IV–X (Macmillan, 1883, 3 vols.).

CHAPTER VI

THE TRIUMPH OF THE KING'S COURTS

THE long period which we must now attempt to survey is, at first sight, lacking in unity. Politically and constitutionally, it begins with a strong but progressive monarchy, followed by a period of internal disturbance, verging on anarchy, itself succeeded by a strong and brilliant, but stern and somewhat unsympathetic autocracy, finally, by a political convulsion which shakes the State to its foundations. And yet, disjointed as the period is to the student of public or constitutional law, to the student of private law it is marked by a singular and steady unity, which makes it one period for his purpose. The outstanding feature is the slow but relentless crushing out, by the King's courts, of those many rivals which, as we saw, divided with them the administration of justice at the close of the preceding period. The preceding chapters have attempted to show how the way was prepared for this achievement; it will now be well to say a few words as to the steps by which it was accomplished.

The Feudal Courts

We have seen[1] how skilfully the royal officials of the Norman and Angevin reigns, especially the reign of Henry II, had undermined, whilst professing to respect, the fundamental feudal principle, that questions of land tenure are for the decision of the lord of the disputants, of whom they hold their lands. In some countries, this principle went far beyond the bare claim to decide land suits; it involved claims to High, Middle, and Low Justice of all kinds. Thanks to the circumstances of the Norman Conquest, and to the virility and political genius of the Norman and Angevin kings, such claims were never successfully established in England, save in the rare cases of the Palatinate earldoms; the many judicial franchises claimed by the Church and the lay barons in the thirteenth century were

[1] *Ante*, pp. 48–51.

rather appropriations of the old local moots than assertions of independent feudal right. These were carefully regulated by the Statute of Gloucester, passed in the year 1278,[1] after the compilation of the Hundred Rolls, with a view to the holding of the great 'Quo Warranto' enquiry; and though it was certainly deemed necessary, so late as the years 1391 and 1392, to enact that 'from henceforth none of the King's subjects be forced, compelled, nor in any way constrained, to come or appear before the Council of any Lord or Lady, there to answer concerning his freehold,'[2] yet it may fairly be surmised, that this necessity was due rather to the general disturbance of that period, than to any serious revival of feudal jurisdiction.

But the final blow which destroyed the feudal courts did not fall until the fifteenth century. Even the statutes of 1391 and 1392 speak only of freeholders; from which it may be inferred, that there was as yet no suggestion of interfering with a lord's feudal jurisdiction over his serfs, at any rate in questions relating to their tenements. But we remember that it was just precisely in the reign of Richard II that the Peasants' War, following upon the changes wrought by the visitations of the Great Plague, virtually destroyed serfdom as a personal status. It is not, therefore, surprising to find that, half a century later, the villein tenants, or **copyholders** as they were by that time called,[3] had succeeded in obtaining the protection of the King's courts for their holdings. In language of extreme caution, which marks the novelty of the proposition, Littleton admits[4] that, though a tenant in villenage holds, in theory, at the will of his lord, yet eminent authorities have stated from the Bench that, if such a tenant, duly rendering his services, should be ejected by his lord, 'he shall have an action of trespass against him.' For some little time longer, the King's courts hesitated to interfere when the dispute was merely between rival claimants of the tenement, in which case the lord would,

Copyholds

[1] 6 Edw. I.

[2] 15 Ric. II, c. 12; confirmed in the following year (16 Ric. II, c. 2).

[3] Because the particulars of their holdings were entered on the rolls or records of the manor, and copies of such entries were (and are) in practice used as title-deeds. The practice of keeping such rolls became universal after the Inquest which resulted in the compilation of the Hundred Rolls.

[4] *Tenures*, s. 77. Littleton's famous treatise was written in the last quarter of the fifteenth century. (Dr. Holdsworth informs one that the passage alluded to was not incorporated into it till 1530.)

presumably, be impartial. But, ultimately, by the indirect method of a 'Mandamus,' or order to the lord to carry out the view taken of such a dispute by the King's court, the royal judges assumed control in such matters also; and, by the end of this period, the law of copyholds had become part of the common law, in the sense that it was recognized and enforced by the King's courts, though an indelible mark of its origin still survives, in the rule that each holding is governed by the local custom of the manor, in all those points not deemed to be 'unreasonable.' The change is marked in legal literature by the appearance of Coke's little treatise entitled *The Compleate Copyholder*, written about 1630. The change virtually put an end to feudal jurisdiction in England.

The Popular Courts

The triumph of the royal jurisdiction over the old **popular courts** was equally complete. We have seen[1] that, according to Fitzherbert, the new action of Trespass, which was to work such a revolution in legal procedure, could be heard before the sheriff in the County Court as well as before the King's justices. After all, the sheriff was a royal officer; and, in a way, the County Court was a royal court.[2] Moreover, a chapter of the famous Statute of Gloucester, of 1278,[3] expressly affirms the jurisdiction of the sheriff in pleas of Trespass, and enacts that such pleas shall not come before the royal justices, unless the plaintiff will swear that he has lost goods to the value of forty shillings — a large sum in 1278. But, somehow, this clause was interpreted in a way exactly opposite to its apparent intention; and it became a maxim that no claim could be heard in the County Court, if it were for more than forty shillings. As the value of money steadily sank, this maxim steadily reduced the scope of the County Court jurisdiction; and, though that court lingered until the eighteenth century, its vitality was gone. The still more humble Hundred Court, having largely fallen into private hands, went the way of the feudal jurisdictions; and, though it, like the County Court, lingered on until the establishment of the new statutory 'County Courts' in the year 1848, it was rather as a 'franchise' or form of feudal prop-

[1] *Ante*, p. 53.

[2] Not only did the early kings, as has been said, encourage the holding of the Shire and Hundred courts; they described them in official documents as 'our courts' (see, for example, the Writ of Tolt, in Blackstone, *Comm.*, III, Appx. I).

[3] 6 Edw. I, c. 8 (1).

erty, than as part of the system of administering justice. In the form of property, it can be, and is, claimed at the present day.

Church Courts

The activity of the **Church courts** was great until the Reformation; and, before that momentous change, the King's courts found in them formidable rivals. At the very beginning of the period, the so-called statute of *Circumspecte Agatis*,[1] makes handsome admissions as to the competence of ecclesiastical tribunals; though it incidentally affirms the hotly contested claim of the royal judges to issue Writs of Prohibition when the Church courts are exceeding their jurisdiction. The famous Statute of Heresies, in 1414,[2] virtually gave the ecclesiastical judge the power of life and death, as well as forfeiture, over laymen. Even the Reformation, though it affirmed the sovereign judicial supremacy of the Crown, and virtually destroyed the legislative independence of the Church, did not, at first, seriously curtail the jurisdiction of the Church courts. It was not until the greatly abused privilege of 'benefit of clergy' was taken in hand by Parliament, that a serious breach was made in ecclesiastical jurisdiction; for the failure of the royal judges to maintain the compromise laid down by the Constitutions of Clarendon on the subject of 'criminous clerks,'[3] is the one striking defeat in their history. But a statute of 1531[4] deprived all but genuine clerics of the privilege of exemption from criminal liability, in serious charges, and, five years later,[5] the deprivation was extended to genuine clerics. A statute of Elizabeth[6] effected a sweeping reform in this direction; and thus the most scandalous of all ecclesiastical privileges tended to disappear. The greatest changes were, however, brought about by the Civil War. For, though the statute of the Long Parliament, which abolished episcopacy and ecclesiastical jurisdiction in 'root and branch,' was formally repealed at the Restoration,[7] much of the work formerly done by the Church courts had, during the Commonwealth, been performed by the secular courts; and the successors of these, though they paid lip-service to the restored

[1] Now generally attributed to the year 1285, and printed as 13 Edw. I, st. III.

[2] Hen. V, c. 7.

[3] Cap. III (S.C. 138). The failure was, doubtless, due to the horror excited by the murder of Becket.

[4] 23 Hen. VIII, c. 1. [5] 28 Hen. VIII, c. 1. [6] 18 Eliz. (1576) c. 7.

[7] 13 Car. II (1661) st. I, cc. 2, 12. (But the latter statute contains significant restrictions.)

Church, were resolutely bent on retaining their newly-acquired jurisdiction. The wonder really is, not that the Church courts should have lost, during the Interregnum, practically all their jurisdiction in such matters as defamation, fraud, and perjury, but that they should have succeeded in recovering jurisdiction in matrimonial and testamentary matters.

The Courts Merchant

Over the last of their serious rivals, the **mercantile courts** of the borough and the gild, the royal jurisdiction won no complete triumph in this period. The medieval line of distinction between the merchant and the ordinary citizen was breaking down; though the restriction of the new bankruptcy jurisdiction, set up by Henry VIII and developed by Elizabeth and James I,[1] to the merchant or trading class, served to perpetuate it. The publication of Malynes' *Lex Mercatoria* in the early seventeenth century, by revealing, to a profession always eager to extend the sphere of its operations, a new and profitable territory, must have done a good deal to prepare the way for the change which took place in the next period, under the auspices of Lord Mansfield. The break-down of the old exclusive trading privileges, which followed on the expansion of world-commerce after the great discoveries of the fifteenth and sixteenth centuries, must have also laid open the secret monopolies of the mercantile courts. But we should do wrongly to suppose that, by the time of the Restoration, the King's courts were thoroughly familiar with mercantile transactions.

Sources

Not unnaturally, we find it easier to describe the sources of this unified Common Law than it was to range the scattered materials for the previous period. For now the canons of legal authority were becoming firmly settled; and judges and pleaders no longer considered themselves justified in clutching at any text which would serve their purpose. In other words, the meaning of the term 'source,' always ambiguous in legal literature, undergoes a change in this period. We must not think now of 'authorities' as being the origin of legal rules, but merely as the indisputable evidence of their existence. For the King's courts have by now adopted the celebrated theory

[1] 34 and 35 Hen. VIII (1542) c. 4; 13 Eliz. (1570) c. 7; 1 Jac. (1603) c. 15; 21 Jac. (1623) c. 10. The first of these statutes is not in terms confined to traders; but the last three are. Their whole machinery was worked through the royal judges. It must have done much to familiarize them with mercantile law.

of the immemorial antiquity of the Common Law; and are loth to admit that it can be changed or created by human agency, even by Parliamentary statutes. But they will admit that there are certain records or monuments whose testimony is unimpeachable. Where these are silent, it is the duty of the judges themselves to apply existing principles to the new facts. The famous theory was, perhaps, on the whole, the wisest that could have been adopted. If it led to a somewhat oppressive conservatism, it served as a strong barrier against arbitrary despotism.

Foremost among the sources of this period, are the Acts of Parliament, which, from the establishment of the great scheme of Edward I in 1295, increase in volume and number. Some, however, of the most important statutes in the Book, such as those of Westminster (I and II),[1] Gloucester,[2] and Winchester,[3] come before the definite and final Parliamentary scheme of 1295; and, at least until the end of the reign of Edward II, there was a good deal of difficulty in distinguishing technically between a true Act of Parliament, an Ordinance of the Council,[4] a Writ of general import issued by the King,[5] and even a privately compiled report which had commended itself to people in authority.[6] Perhaps this is the reason why, on the introduction of printing, the compilers of the first printed editions of the Statute Book began their collections with the accession of Edward III;[7] later editions produced the older and omitted documents, under the title of *Antiqua Statuta*.[8] There is not even agreement as to the authoritative form of such documents. Perhaps the orthodox view is, that everything which appears on the Chancery Statute Rolls (which run from 1278 to 1469) is authoritative; and nothing else for that period.[9] But, from the year 1290, it was the practice also to record statutes on the Rolls of Parliament,

Statutes of the Realm

[1] 3 Edw. I (1275); 13 Edw. I (1285) st. I.

[2] 6 Edw. I (1278).

[3] 13 Edw. I (1285) st. II.

[4] *E.g.* the 'Statute of Merchants,' or 'Acton Burnel' (1283).

[5] *E.g.* '*Circumspecte Agatis*,' attributed to 1285.

[6] *E.g.* '*Modus Levandi Fines*' (printed as 18 Edw. I (1290) st. IV).

[7] Afterwards called the *Nova Statuta*.

[8] The first attempt (by Pynson) was incomplete. It was supplemented by Berthelet in his *Secunda Pars Veterum Statutorum*.

[9] From 1407 onwards, the Acts seem to have been engrossed separately and retained in the custody of the Clerk of the Parliaments. Certified transcripts are, however, sent to the Record Office.

which contain matter of all kinds; and it has been judicially assumed that the Rolls of Parliament are also authoritative.[1] At first the statutes were recorded indifferently in French and Latin; from the accession of Henry VII, they appear to have been passed and recorded in English.

Of hardly less importance than the Statute Book, as an authority for the law of this period, is the so-called **Registrum Brevium**, the collection of the writs used for beginning or carrying on legal proceedings. Of the origin of this collection, something has previously been said;[2] but its origin is far easier to understand than its character. The perverse thing about it (to modern ideas) is, that there was no official or absolutely conclusive edition or text of the Register; no standard to which copies could be referred if their accuracy was questioned. It is easy to understand that such a compilation would require, as we should say, re-editing from time to time; as additions and corrections were rendered necessary by legislation and judicial decision. But that is not the point. The point is that, even though what purported to be an authoritative copy of the Register was sent to Ireland in 1227,[3] on the introduction of English Law into the Pale, yet, in truth, no official edition ever existed. Many copies were in the hands of the Chancery officials; but there is no reason to suppose that they were identical — the probability is all the other way. Many copies found their way into private hands; they would be precious possessions for pleaders and litigants. But whether a form of writ found in any copy of the Register was authentic, would depend upon the view taken by the clerk to whom application was made for its issue, and, ultimately, on the attitude of the Court which tried the action.

The Register of Writs

As is well known, an important statute, dating from the very commencement of this period, professed to lay it down that new writs were to be framed whenever occasion for them arose.[4] It is easy to exaggerate both the importance and the failure of this celebrated *Consimilis Casus* clause. A study of the statute, which is evidently concerned with minor

Consimilis Casus

[1] *Earl of Macclesfield's Case* (1725) 16 St. Tr. pp. 1388–1390.

[2] *Ante*, pp. 45–6.

[3] On this and all other points connected with the early history of the Register, students should consult the brilliant series of articles by the late Professor Maitland, published in the *Harvard Law Review* for 1889, and reprinted in the Select Essays in Anglo-American Legal History (II, 549–596).

[4] Statute of Westminster the Second (13 Edw. I (1285) c. 24).

technical objections rather than with defects of principle, may well cause us to doubt whether the Parliament of 1285 intended to place in the hands of the Chancery clerks[1] what appears, at first sight, to be practically an unlimited power to make new law. On the other hand, the great and undeniable development of the Action of Case, which followed swiftly upon the passing of the statute, seems to suggest that, though the inventive vigour and bold spirit of innovation which had characterized the judges of Bracton's day, had been replaced by the more timid and conservative attitude of their successors in the fourteenth century, yet that the Register of Writs remained a flexible and expanding document until the commencement of the sixteenth century. By that time, the invention of printing had come to revolutionize the world; and editions of the Register promptly appeared in the new stereotyped form. Then the days of expansion were really over. Rastell's edition of 1531 was made by Fitzherbert the basis of his celebrated commentary;[2] but Theloall's edition of 1579 seems ultimately to have been accepted as the quasi-official version.

The Year Books

Hardly less anomalous than the Register of Writs, and still more mysterious, are the celebrated **Year Books**, which profess to be reports of cases decided in the King's courts between the middle of the thirteenth and the middle of the sixteenth centuries. They are entirely anonymous, and, as their popular title implies, are grouped under the regnal years of the various kings with whose reigns they deal. It was, apparently, these two facts which, supported by certain misunderstood words of Plowden, Coke, and Sir Francis Bacon, begot the extraordinary legend that the Year Books are official compilations, drawn up by the prothonotaries or other officials of the various courts, appointed and paid for the purpose. That such a belief should be held by intelligent men who had actually

[1] This statutory provision produced a yet further classification of Writs Original into (*a*) *De Cursu*, or writs of course in the strictest sense, issued by the Cursitors on payment of the ordinary fee, and (*b*) *Magistralia*, *i.e.* those issued by the Clerk or Masters in Chancery under the Statute of 1285.

[2] *New Natura Brevium*. Many editions, of which the most convenient for students is that which appeared in English in the eighteenth century, with notes attributed to Sir Matthew Hale and Sir Wadham Windham. The word "New" in Fitzherbert's title is due to the fact that, as he himself says in his brief Preface, a previous commentary (generally described as the *Old Natura Brevium*) had appeared, and had been vulgarized by being translated into English. In the early sixteenth century, it was still heretical to write in English.

made acquaintance with the Year Books, seems well-nigh impossible; nothing more unlike an official publication can well be imagined. And yet, that it was the accepted view of the eighteenth century, seems proved by the well-known passage in Blackstone's *Commentaries*,[1] in which that great writer states it without a shadow of suspicion or comment. Perhaps the true explanation is, that the Year Books had ceased to be read in their original form by the end of the seventeenth century; having been superseded by the **Abridgements** of Fitzherbert, Brooke, Rolle, Hale, and other eminent and industrious analyists.

For this fact, if it be a fact, there was every excuse. If the editions of the Register are confusing, the older printed editions of the Year Books[2] are a weltering mass of inaccuracies and contradictions, through which none but a specially trained expert can make his way. It is one of the many reasons for which the student of English legal history laments the untimely death of Professor Maitland, that it cut him off from the completion of the task which, at the instance of the Selden Society, he had undertaken, of editing an intelligible and trustworthy edition of the Year Books. That great scholar was, however, happily permitted to live until he had given to the world three instalments of his projected enterprise;[3] and in the first of these, in the early pages of a masterly Introduction, the editor disposes for ever of the ancient legend, and convinces us that in the Year Books we have, not a dry official publication (for why, indeed, duplicate that magnificent series of records which was every year accumulating in the royal archives?), but a series of informal notes, very human, very gossipy, probably not free from gross inaccuracy, but, on the whole, extraordinarily vivid and realistic, compiled by the students and apprentices of the law, who haunted the King's courts, and jotted down things worthy of remembrance by themselves and those who should come after them. Slowly these note-books were accumulated by the practitioners of the law;[4] and, by the end of the period, were regarded with almost

[1] I, 72.

[2] The best known is that printed in 1679. But there are fragmentary printed editions scattered all over the latter half of the sixteenth century.

[3] These are vols. 17, 19, and 20 in the S.S. series. Two other volumes (22, 24), partly by other hands, have since appeared.

[4] The most famous of the later collectors was the great Serjeant Maynard. The story told by Roger North of his passionate fondness for the Year Books is well known, and is reprinted on the title-pages of the Selden Society's volumes.

superstitious reverence. Whether they can safely be treated as trustworthy, is a problem which each student must solve for himself.

A few other accounts of the decisions of the King's courts in the earlier part of this period are available. The new **Court of Chancery** which acquired an independent existence as a judicial tribunal in the fourteenth century, and took up the task of expanding the common law[1] when the Register of Writs was inclined to drop it, was not likely to be deficient in the matter of records; and some of these have been published by the Selden Society.[2] The Court of Star Chamber had a great and permanent influence in the development of the Common Law; and, fortunately, some accounts of its proceedings have been preserved and published.[3] For the later part of the period, we have the works of the 'nominate' reporters — Dyer, Leonard, Plowden, Coke, Croke, and others. Some of these are of high merit; almost all of them are infinitely easier for a student to understand than the grotesque language of the Year Books. The **Books of Entries**, or forms of pleading, which appeared soon after the introduction of printing, are really in the nature of reports; for the precedents which they give us are, obviously, those, and only those, which have stood the fire of judicial criticism.[4]

Other Reports

Finally, a word must be said about the text-books of this period; for, whatever may have been their reception by their contemporaries, some of them, at least, were accepted as gospel by the succeeding generation. Passing by the epitomes of Bracton's great work, known under the titles of *Fleta* and *Britton*, and the picturesque but untrustworthy *Mirror of Justices*, attributed to Andrew Horn, Town Clerk of London in the late thirteenth century,[5] we must mention the names of

Text-Books

[1] To the practitioner, Equity, the rules of the Court of Chancery, is contrasted with the Common Law, or doctrines developed by the older royal tribunals. But, in the historical sense, Equity is part of the Common Law, the law administered by the King's courts, and common to all the land.

[2] *Select Cases in Chancery*, edited by W. P. Baildon (S.S. vol. 10). There is an older volume in the Record Series (*Calendar of the Proceedings in Chancery*, edited by J. Bayley, 3 vols. 1827–1832).

[3] *Select Pleas of the Court of Star Chamber*, edited by I. S. Leadam (S.S. vols. 16, 25); *Les Reportes del Cases in Camera Stellata* (Hawarde MS.) edited by W. P. Baildon (1894, priv. print.).

[4] Early compilers are Smythe (1546), Rastell (1564), Coke (1614).

[5] Edited by Whittaker and Maitland (S.S. vol. 7).

Littleton, Fortescue, Fitzherbert, and Coke. The first was

Littleton

the author of the treatise to which Coke has given immortality, viz. **The New Tenures,** probably composed in Norman French about the year 1475, but speedily translated into English, and printed in both languages.[1] As with Fitzherbert's **Natura Brevium,** it had been preceded by an anonymous treatise on Tenures, which still survives, and, to distinguish it from its famous successor, is known as *The Old Tenures.* Littleton's treatise is written in the form of letters to the author's son, supposed to be a student at Cambridge; and, if, as family correspondence, it appears to be a trifle heavy, we may console ourselves with the reflection that, as legal literature, it is unusually clear and brief. Separated from Coke's ponderous commentary, it is a mere pamphlet; but a pamphlet of which every word has been weighed with scrupulous accuracy.

Fortescue

Fortescue, whose work *De Laudibus Legum Angliae,*[4] may be mentioned, was a contemporary of Littleton; a Lancastrian, while Littleton was a Yorkist. Fortescue was, however, a politician rather than a lawyer; and his treatise is

Fitzherbert

useful rather for its general observations than as a precise statement of legal rules. Fitzherbert, whose *New Natura Brevium* has already been mentioned, lived half a century after Littleton, was, like him, a Justice of the Common Pleas, and was the author also of an *Abridgement* of the Year Books, as well as of treatises on *The Diversity of Courts* and *The Justice of the Peace.* To him is also attributed, though he modestly laid no claim to it, a deeply interesting *Treatise on Husbandry,* in which we see the beginnings of the great dispute between the old-fashioned open field (or 'champaign') farming, and the new 'several' or enclosed system.

Coke

Coke's weighty volumes are known to most students of law. His chief work was his **Institutes of the Laws of England,** in four parts; the first consisting of the famous commentary on Littleton's treatise, the second of an *Exposition of Many Ancient and Other Statutes,* the third of a treatise on *Pleas of the Crown,* and the fourth of the *Jurisdiction of Courts.* The first two parts were published in Coke's lifetime (about

[1] Printed copies appear dated from 1516. Editions supposed to reach back to 1418, but undated, are extant.

[2] Ed. Lord Clermont.

1628); the last two, somewhat disfigured by the heat of the political combat into which Coke was drawn, after his death (about 1644). Beyond the Institutes, Coke wrote another book, previously referred to, of first-class importance, viz. *The Compleate Copyholder*, first published in 1630. The list of his works includes also the *Little Treatise on Bail and Mainprize* (1635).

Finally, reference should be made to William West's valuable *Symbolaeographia*, or collection of forms used by notaries and scriveners at the end of the sixteenth century, published by Tothill in 1590. These have, of course, no official value; but they throw great light on the conveyancing practice of the day. It is interesting to note that, although attorneys were apparently excluded from conveyancing (at least in London) till the seventeenth century, the author of this collection was himself an attorney.

CHAPTER VII

NEW INTERESTS IN LAND

THE broad outlines of English real property law had been drawn in the scheme of tenures described in a previous chapter;[1] and they remained substantially unaltered, in theory at least, for a period of four hundred years. Even the Act of Abolition of Military Tenures,[2] with which the next period opens, though it removed a part of the ancient fabric and some picturesque details of the remainder, left the building perfectly recognizable. It may be claimed, indeed, that even the sweeping legislation of the nineteenth century has not affected the ground-plan of the edifice; though it has revolutionized the internal arrangements. At this stage, therefore, we have but to fill in the chief details added to the original scheme by the later medieval judges and conveyancers.

The original idea of the scheme of tenures was, as we have seen, based upon the seisin or possession of land by the tenant.

Future Interests

This seisin might be for life only ('freehold'), or for an hereditary interest ('fee'); but, in either case, the tenant was seised 'in his demesne,' *i.e.* as actual occupant or 'terre-tenant,' responsible to the State for military service and other dues, and, therefore, entitled to claim the protection of the royal tribunals.

But it will be remembered, that the principle of tenure is essentially relative. If it implies possession in the tenant, it

Reversions

also implies lordship, with its attendant rights to fealty, service, and other profits, in the lord. So long also as the tenant's interest was limited by existing lives, the lord had a substantial prospect of resuming possession of the land after its expiry; and, even after hereditary estates had come to be recognized, in days when the extinction of whole

[1] *Ante*, pp. 27–31.
[2] 12 Car. II (1660) c. 24. The credit of the measure belongs, of course, to the Long Parliament, whose Act the Restoration Parliament adopted.

families by war was no uncommon event, there was the ultimate prospect of an 'escheat' on failure of the tenant's heirs, or corruption of his blood by attaint.

It is quite impossible to imagine that, in the later years of the preceding period, this valuable interest of the lord was not recognized as a legal institution. We are, in fact, expressly told by the famous Statute *De Donis*,[1] that, in 1285, the royal Chancery was familiar with a writ framed for the purpose of protecting a much more shadowy interest, viz. the right of the lord to recover the land after the expiry of an hereditary estate limited to the issue of the tenant — of which more presently. We may, therefore, fairly assume that, under the names of 'lordship,' 'seignory,' 'reversion,' and other equivalents, the interest of the lord, and particularly his right that the land should 'revert' to him after the expiry of the tenant's interest, was fully recognized by law, even before the commencement of the period now under discussion. Moreover, it was not in the least necessary that any express claim to the right should have been made when the tenure was created. A **reversion** has always been 'an estate which arises by operation of law.' Any express reservation was merely redundant, and, before modern legislation, purely inoperative.

Remainders

A different idea began to develop when the creator of a tenancy was allowed to name a succession of tenants, instead of creating an hereditary estate — to say that after A was dead the land should go to B, and so on. Here would arise a difficulty which, to a primitive tribunal, is always formidable, but, to tribunals which were beginning to attach a special value to seisin or possession, was peculiarly formidable, viz. the difficulty of recognizing a claim not evidenced by possession. During A's lifetime, what was the position of B? He was merely a person who might, if he chanced to survive A, put in a claim to the land. But such a claim must, in the days when most tenures were created by word of mouth, have appeared to be very shadowy, very likely to lead to quarrels between the claimant and the lord who desired to resume possession after the first tenant's death. In any case, it was not an estate, but a 'mere right.' Nevertheless, there is some reason to believe

[1] 13 Edw. I, c. 1 (4). It seems to have been a Writ of Entry. Professor Maitland has traced it back to the year 1219 (*Bracton's Note Book*, Vol. II, 54).

that even a **remainder** after an estate of inheritance was beginning to be recognized by the authorities before the death of Henry III; though we must remember that Bracton, from whom we learn most about it,[1] is always inclined to anticipate the slow development of practice. At least we can say that, at the very beginning of our present period, the technical distinction between a 'reversion' and a 'remainder' appears to be familiar to the framers of a first-class statute.[2]

But, when the notion of the future estate is once admitted, there is no reason why it should stop at the simple limitations of the early remainders. The real difficulty had been, to persuade the courts that an interest in land could be conferred otherwise than by way of corporal investiture or delivery — a mode of creation obviously inapplicable to a future interest. That difficulty once overcome, it was certain that, in course of time, conveyancers would claim to be able to dispose of future interests in favour of persons unknown or unascertained at the date of the conveyance. If, on the expiry of the preceding estate, such persons were not in a position to claim seisin of the land, of course their rights would vanish. The land would either go to the claimant next in succession, or revert to the lord; for the seisin could not be allowed to fall into abeyance. For a similar reason, the donor could not, in naming the order of succession, interpolate the slightest interval between the expiry of one interest and the succession of the next. For that also would have been a deliberate provision for **abeyance of seisin.**

Contingent Remainders

Abeyance of Seisin

Apparently, this further development was struggling to obtain recognition in the middle of the fourteenth century; for we find it elaborately discussed at that time by the new Court of Chancery, or at any rate by the Chancellor.[3] The earliest form in which it was attempted to create **contingent remainders** seems to have been that of a limitation to the heirs of a living person. Now a living person cannot, of course, have an heir (*nemo est haeres viventis*); whence

Contingent Remainders

[1] Lib. II, cap. 6 (1). Bracton describes such a remainder as an estate on condition. Later on (lib. II, cap. 31 (3), he announces his intention of setting out the special writ which will enable the remainder-man to get the land when his turn comes. Bracton does not, however, fulfil his promise.

[2] 3 Edw. I (1275) c. 40 ('lands or tenements . . . which ought to descend, revert, remain, or escheat').

[3] Y.B. 38 Edw. III, Mich. (1364) fo. 26.

it follows that, unless the person in question dies before the right of the remainderman to claim possession arises, the latter's right, for the reason given above, is gone. But, in 1364, the Chancellor said that such a limitation would be void from the beginning; and though, more than half a century later,[1] it seems to have passed as good, the later case was one of a devise under local custom, and so does not count for very much. Littleton, who was as inclined to be conservative, as Bracton had been to take the enterprising line, says boldly, that 'every remainder which beginneth by deed, it behoveth that the remainder be in him to whom the remainder is entailed by force of the same deed, before the livery of seisin is made to him which shall have the freehold';[2] which, obviously, could not be the case if the remainderman were then unascertained. By Coke's time, however, the law had completely changed;[3] and, subject to certain rules about remote or improbable contingencies, the lawfulness of contingent remainders was then fully admitted. One of the earliest and best cases is that of *Colthirst v. Bejushin,* in 1550.[4] By that time, also, the distinction between a remainder and a conditional estate had become clearly marked by the adoption of the rule, that no condition could be made enforceable by a third party; a rule which was probably dictated by fear of 'maintenance,' or stirring up of lawsuits, but which was connected also with another event, of which a brief account must now be given.

Entails

We have seen,[5] that Bracton was familiar, in theory at least, with the estate of inheritance confined to the actual issue of the original tenant, and that he assumed that it was even possible to limit a remainder after it. Such an estate seems generally to have been given as a *maritagium,* or endowment on the marriage of one of the donor's children. It was naturally assumed by the donor that, on the failure of the donee's issue, the land would revert to the family stock; but, apparently led away by the idea of 'conditional gifts,' the King's courts had come to hold, in the early thirteenth century, that a gift 'to A and the heirs of his body' was a gift which, on the birth of issue to A, became an absolute gift of an estate of full inheritance in A, to do what he liked with.

[1] Y.B. 9 Hen. VI, Trin. (1431) pl. 19.
[2] S. 721.
[3] Co. Litt. 378a.
[4] Plowd. 21.
[5] *Ante,* p. 85.

Naturally, such doctrine was extremely unpalatable to the great landowners, who had created appanages out of their family estates, and who saw these appanages now finally split away from the main stock. Signs of their wrath appear during the previous period;[1] but their great triumph was not achieved until 1285, when the first chapter of the Statute of Westminster the Second,[2] the famous chapter *De Donis Conditionalibus*, enacted that, on failure of the donee's issue, the land should revert to the donor or his heirs; notwithstanding any intervening alienation. The statute, however, went far beyond the demand of the donors; and, perhaps unconsciously, in its anxiety to justify its policy, proceeded to protect, not only the donors and their heirs, but the issue of the donee himself, from unauthorized alienation, and to provide a special remedy (the Writ of Formedon in the Descender) for this object. Thus the statute created a new kind of inheritable estate, differing from the older 'fee simple,' not only in the fact that it could only be inherited by the direct lineal issue of the original donee, but in the fact that no alienation, however solemn,[3] by the holder for the time being, could avail against the rights of the 'issue in tail.' Such an interest, though an estate of inheritance, was manifestly inferior, from the point of view of the holder, to the wider 'fee simple'; it went back on history, and deprived the holder of that right of free alienation which, as we have seen,[4] he had gradually won against his lord and his heirs. His fee was *talliatum*, or cut down, into a 'fee tail.' It is true that, by somewhat later doctrine, he could, even by a common foeffment, put the issue in tail to some inconvenience, by depriving them of their right of entry on his death, and compelling them to resort to their statutory right of action (*formedon*).[5]

De Donis

But this was probably not until after, with the connivance of the courts, and by clever use of the doctrine of warranty, the tenant in tail had achieved the far completer triumph

[1] Provisions of Oxford of 1258, art. 27 (S.C. 386).

[2] 13 Edw. I, c. 1.

[3] The statute (s. 4) expressly provides that a Fine (of which something later) shall be ineffectual to alienate the new estate.

[4] *Ante*, pp. 37–39.

[5] Litt. s. 597. To the layman, the inconvenience might appear to be slight. In fact, it caused the heir in tail considerable expense and delay. He could not use the simple process of 'Ejectment,' to be hereafter explained.

of defeating entirely the claims of lord and issue alike, by the process afterwards known as a **Common Recovery.** The date usually quoted for this complete defeat of the statute De Donis is 1473, the date of the celebrated decision in *Taltarum's Case;* [1] but the device can easily be traced back for nearly a century,[2] and is even suggested by a case of the year 1340.[3] Thus it would appear, that the inalienable inheritance, the ideal of every feudal aristocracy, was in fact realized in England for little longer than half a century. Its abolition is the classical justification of the somewhat clumsy reforming agency known as the 'legal fiction.' Of the nature of Fines and Recoveries, somewhat will be said in the next chapter.

Common Recovery

A third, and, for the future, highly important interest, must next be noticed. The term of years was already familiar to Glanville, who gives[4] a form of writ to recover land which has been pledged to the defendant '*ad terminum qui praeteriit*'; and this will suggest to us, that the early holders for terms of years were creditors who, unable by reason of the laws against usury, to charge interest openly, had bargained to be allowed to hold their debtor's land until, out of the rents and profits, they had repaid themselves with interest.[5]

Terms of Years

Such a transaction is treated by Glanville as a mere 'contract' or 'cause.' It did not give the creditor seisin of the land which had been 'bailed' or pledged to him; in all probability he was merely entitled to secure himself by acting as the lord's bailiff or manager of the land, in which capacity rents in money and kind would come into his hands. It is conceivable, also, that, even in those early days, a lord who was starting off on a Crusade might think it safer and more convenient to give his steward a promise of a fixed term of office, in return for a promise of a *ferm*, or fixed annual rent, instead of an account of the actual receipts and outgoings.

But, by the time of Bracton, it becomes obvious that the

[1] Y.B. 12 Edw. IV. fo. 19, pl. 25.

[2] 9 Ric. II (1385) c. 3. As the statute alludes to 'tenant in tail after possibility,' it can hardly have overlooked the case of the ordinary tenant in tail.

[3] Y.B. (Record Series) 14 Edw. III, 104.

[4] Lib X, cap. 9.

[5] This was *vif gage*, a more merciful form than the *mort gage*, in which the rents did not go to reduce the capital debt.

creation of **terms of years** is proceeding apace, and with objects other than providing security for debts. Bracton[1] treats the 'donee for term of years' as acquiring property; not, he is careful to explain, a free tenement, but still, something a good deal more than a mere pledge. He cannot deny that the termor has possession; and thereupon arises a question, which evidently causes Bracton much perplexity. What about the lessor's seisin? If you deprive the lessor of his seisin, he will not be able to protect his interests, should these be assailed by a stranger, by using the possessory assises, or even the Writs of Entry. This is a heavy penalty; so Bracton cannot bring himself to impose it. On the other hand, if the lessor has seisin, what about the termor? Obviously, there cannot be two independent seisins of the same land. So, probably as the result of Bracton's reasoning, the historic question was settled; and it was decided that the interest of the termor was a chattel interest, which could be bequeathed by will even though it was an interest in land, could be seized by a judgment creditor as part of the debtor's goods, and could be created and transferred by mere word of mouth or writing, without livery of seisin.

Bracton's View

But the view that the termor had not a free tenement left him somewhat naked against attack. If, as became common in the later thirteenth century, his term had been created by a sealed covenant, he could protect himself by the appropriate Writ of Covenant against his lord. But, in the first place, such an action, even if successful, would only entitle the termor to damages,[2] not to delivery of the land itself. In the second, if the disturbance of the termor had been by a stranger, he (the termor) could sue neither the stranger, for the stranger was no party to the covenant, nor the lessor, for the latter had not interfered; while, in Bracton's day, a lease for years implied no warranty of title.[3] Apparently, Bracton considered that the termor was amply protected

Seisin and Possession

[1] Lib. I, cap. 9.

[2] At least, this was so in later days. But see Statute of Gloucester (6 Edw. I (1278)) c. 11 ('recovery by Writ of Covenant'). And note the explicit statement attributed to Belknap, C.J., by Bellewe, in his *Les Ans du Roy Richard Le Second* at p. 159, under the year 1382. The 'covenant real,' as a common law remedy, probably died out with the improvement in the remedy by Ejectment, to be afterwards explained (*Post*, pp. 175–177).

[3] Lib. II, cap. 9, *ad fin.*

by a special Writ of *Quare Ejecit infra Terminum;*[1] but, for some unknown reason, the later law refused to allow this action to be brought against any but the lessor and the latter's feoffees. Ultimately, the termor found salvation in the Writ of **ejectio firmae**, a variety of that Writ of Trespass, which, as we have seen,[2] was so striking a feature of the last quarter of the thirteenth century, and which protected, not merely seisin, but any physical possession. It is true that, until the middle of the fifteenth century, only damages could be recovered by the Writ of Ejectment; but, as we shall later see, a momentous step was then taken, which made the term of years the best protected of all interests in land. Meanwhile, the Statute of Gloucester[3] had enabled the termor to defeat the lessor who was endeavouring to get rid of him by suffering a 'Common Recovery,' by showing the real facts;[4] and this statute, which seems to have applied only to London, was made general in 1529.[5] Before this latter date, however, the termor had definitely established his footing in the scheme of tenure; for Littleton[6] treats him as a tenant, and even compels him, though with evident hesitation, to do fealty to his lessor;[7] while, shortly after, the Covenants Act of 1540,[8] by making conditions and covenants in leases enforceable against purchasers of the reversion, must have added greatly to the stability and value of terms of years. But the curious history of the term of years remains, to the present day, vividly impressed upon its present position; it stands midway between real and personal property — neither wholly real, nor wholly chattel, but a 'chattel real.'

Waste

The gradual definition of the various estates in land which, as we have seen, took place in the thirteenth century, was, without doubt, responsible also for the appearance of the law of **waste.** A man who has but a temporary interest in a piece of land cannot be allowed to treat it as if he were absolute owner. His natural tendency is to make

[1] Lib. IV, cap. 36. The form of the writ is given. Bracton, forgetful of his former distinction, here makes the termor recover his 'seisin.'

[2] *Ante*, pp. 52–54.

[3] 6 Edw. I (1278) c. 11.

[4] The fiction appears to have been, that the title of the collusive plaintiff was deemed to have accrued before the date of the termor's lease. Thus, if the collusive plaintiff had recovered judgment against the true lessor, he could have ejected the lessee, and handed the land back to the lessor.

[5] 21 Hen. VIII, c. 36.

[6] Ss. 58–60.

[7] S. 132.

[8] 32 Hen. VIII, c. 34.

the most of his brief opportunities, regardless of the interests of his successors. But, equally naturally, these latter will seek to be protected against unfair treatment.

As a matter of fact, the appearance of an express Law of Waste begins, not with ordinary tenants, but with **guardians.**

Guardians As we have seen,[1] the custody of the infant heir of a deceased tenant in chivalry belonged, on feudal principles, to his lord, and was accompanied by custody of the ward's inheritance. This position was frequently abused by guardians, who treated their positions simply as opportunities for plunder; and particularly in the numerous guardianships which fell to the Crown as supreme lord of every fief, and direct lord of the *tenants in capite*. Accordingly, the Great Charter of John contains strict promise of amendment in this respect; the guardian is to take from the land nothing more than the customary issues, and he is to maintain the buildings and other plenishings of the estate in good condition.[2] The Charter of 1215 apparently applied only to **guardians in chivalry**; but the prohibition against waste was extended by the Statute of Marlborough[3] to **guardians in socage**. The same statute[4] also enacted that '**termors**, during their terms, shall not make waste, sale, nor exile, of houses, woods, or men'; and the Statute of Gloucester,[5] enumerating the persons against whom a Writ of Waste will lie, includes also **tenants for life**, whether by act of the parties or by operation of law.[6] The Writ of Waste entitled the successful plaintiff to forfeiture of the place wasted and three-fold damages; but, though a solemn decision of the King in Parliament in *Gawin Butler's Case*[7] laid it down, that the heir of the reversioner or remainderman in whose lifetime the waste had been committed should be entitled to the Writ of Waste, yet there remained other technicalities which made the Writ of Waste a somewhat imperfect remedy, and its place was largely taken by the new action of Trespass on the Case, to be hereafter described.[8] According to later law, the tenant for years (though not the tenant for life) is responsible, not merely

[1] *Ante*, pp. 34–35.

[2] Magna Carta, capp. 4, 5 (S.C. 297). The prohibition was re-enacted by the Statute of Westminster the First (3 Edw. I (1275) c. 21).

[3] 52 Hen. III (1267) c. 17.

[4] Cap. 23.

[5] 6 Edw. 1 (1278) c. 5.

[6] *E.g.* a dowress, or a tenant 'by the *curtesy*.'

[7] Printed among the statutes as 20 Edw. I (1291) st. II.

[8] *Post*, pp. 136–144.

for 'active' or 'positive' waste, but for mere failure to keep the premises in repair; the thirteenth century statutes, however, afford no authority for such a proposition. The Statute of Marlborough also clearly recognizes[1] the right of the creator of the estate to release his tenant from liability for 'waste'; and the 'tenant for life without impeachment of waste' became a very common figure in the books of later days. So full an advantage, indeed, did such persons take of the liberty thus accorded to them, that, early in the succeeding period,[2] they had to be curbed by the introduction of the doctrine of **equitable waste,** *i.e.* waste so outrageous, that even a tenant 'without impeachment' would be restrained by a Court of Equity from committing it.

Incorporeal Heredita-ments

At the very beginning of our present period, the King's courts were faced with the peculiarly difficult task of applying the new and highly popular possessory remedies to a class of interests ill fitted to receive them. These were the 'incorporeal hereditaments' of later times, *i.e.* those limited and strictly defined rights over land which do not include possession of the soil, but merely the power to do certain definite acts which the possessor of the soil would otherwise be entitled to resent, or to restrain the possessor of the soil from doing something which he would otherwise, as a matter of common right, be entitled to do. Such limited rights are especially suitable for philosophic analysis; and the terms '*jura in re aliena,*' 'servitudes,' 'fractional rights,' applied to them by jurists, are useful as impressing upon students their peculiar characteristics. Historically, however, they appear to have arisen in an entirely haphazard way; partly by the gradual conversion of official functions into property rights ('franchises'), partly by the change in the conditions of agriculture which was slowly transmuting communal usages into individual privileges, partly by economic restrictions, such as the Usury Laws, which compelled people to resort to indirect methods, like rent-charges, to disguise the fact that they were lending money at interest.

It might appear natural to a modern lawyer to treat such rights as *choses in action*, *i.e.* as personal claims by one individual

[1] 52 Hen. III (1267) c. 23 (2).
[2] *Vane v. Lord Barnard* (1716) 2 Vern. 738.

against another. But, to the men of the twelfth and thirteenth centuries, such a course would have seemed fraught with danger. Whilst the personal remedies of that day, at any rate in the King's courts, were few and imperfect, the remedies based on 'real' or proprietary claims were rapidly becoming scientific and effectual; and the royal judges did not shrink from the task of including incorporeal hereditaments in their scope. Already in Glanville's day, the Writ of Right, the great proprietary action, had been adapted to the case of servitudes by the modification known as the Writ of *Quod Permittat.*[1] The owner of woods and pastures is ordered to permit the plaintiff to have the easements therein which he claims that he ought to have; and the King's officer, the sheriff, would even be ordered to take upon himself the task of measuring the meadows of a township, to see whether any of the commoners were putting in an undue number of beasts, and thus 'overloading the pasture.'[2] But, apparently, in all these cases, the strict question of title had to be tried before any redress could be actually given; and, as we have seen,[3] such a trial might involve long delay.

Not Choses in Action

It will not, however, have escaped the reader's memory, that the more speedy remedy of the 'petty' or 'possessory' assises had been applied, so far back as the reign of Henry II, to one very important kind of interest which we now class as an 'incorporeal hereditament.' This was the **advowson**, or right of presentation to an ecclesiastical benefice, with regard to which a speedy remedy was given by the Assise *d'arrein presentment.*[4] It is true that an advowson was, by the lawyers of the medieval period, regarded almost as much as a 'corporeal' as an 'incorporeal' hereditament. It could be made the subject of tenure;[5] though it could not be transferred by corporeal investiture or livery of seisin.[6] Still, it obviously differed from the ordinary estate of which the owner was 'seised in demesne as of his fee' (or 'freehold'); and the existence of the Assise *d'arrein presentment* must have rendered a speedy remedy for disturbance of incorporeal interests desirable. Unfortunately,

Advowsons

[1] Glanville, lib. XII, cap. 15. [2] *Ibid.*, cap. 14. [3] *Ante*, pp. 49–50.

[4] Glanville, lib. XIII, capp. 18, 19. It was also protected by the powerful remedy of the *Quare impedit.*

[5] Co. Litt. 85a; *Hartopp's and Cock's Case* (1627) Hutt. 88.

[6] Co. Litt. 332a, 335b.

both the Writs of Entry and the Writ of Trespass were obviously inapplicable to interests which did not confer seisin or possession; and, though the highly popular Assise of Novel Disseisin had been applied, as early as Glanville's time,[1] to protect pasturage rights, the difficulty of extending it to other incorporeal hereditaments seemed to be insuperable. In the year 1285, however, the Statute of Westminster the Second, by a chapter which incidentally reveals the existence of many of our most familiar modern 'easements and profits,'[2] extends the remedy to 'estovers' and other profits of woods, toll, tronage, passage, pontage, offices, and commons of all kinds. The position of rents charge was altogether anomalous. Though they could not, unlike rents service, be distrained for (unless an express power of distress had been granted), they could virtually be treated as land for purposes of litigation. If the person seised of the land *(terre-tenant)* refused to pay the rent, he could be regarded as disseising the rent-charger of the land itself; if a stranger procured payment of the rent instead of the lawful claimant, he could be similarly treated.[3] So closely was the rent, even the rent charge, identified with the land, that, in later days, when the Assise of Novel Disseisin had dropped out of use, it could be gravely argued that there was no personal remedy for the recovery of a rent charge.[4]

For the various 'easements and profits' not protected by the Assise of Novel Disseisin, a speedy remedy was soon found in the Action of Case, the development of which must, in its proper place, be traced with some care.[5] Here it is sufficient to say, that the method of the Action of Case was to take some ancient remedy, the value of which was impaired by technical restrictions, and cut away those restrictions, by making the remedy universally applicable under the guise of analogy, or 'like case.' In the matter of incorporeal hereditaments, the ancient Assise of Nuisance, given by Glanville,[6] at first only available for freeholders, was, by means of the Action of Case, rendered generally available to recover damages for actual interference with the enjoyment of such rights. And, so popular did the Action of Case become, that the older remedy of the

[1] Lib. XIII, cap. 37. [2] 13 Edw. I (1285) c. 25. [3] Litt. ss. 233–40.
[4] *Thomas v. Sylvester* (1873) L. R. 8 Q. B. 368.
[5] *Post*, pp. 136–144. [6] Lib. XIII, capp. 35–38.

Assise, even where it was available, soon tended to disappear. Nevertheless, it is possible that, in the original distinction of remedies, we have the key to the apparently anomalous difference between those rights, the mere technical disturbance of which is a 'cause of action,' and those other rights which are only infringed when actual damage occurs.[1]

Finally, in the period now under review, we note the appearance of an entirely novel and modern conception of interests in land, the introduction of which threatened to shake to its foundations the whole fabric of feudal land law. That this fabric succeeded ultimately, in spite of almost overwhelming difficulties, in incorporating into itself the new and revolutionary features of the 'use,' without depriving those features of their essential value, is a striking tribute both to the tenacity and to the adaptability of the medieval system of tenure.

Uses of Land

The **use of lands** was, originally, a device for enjoying the benefits of landownership without incurring any of its legal responsibilities. As we have seen, one of the fundamental principles of tenure is, that the position (the *status* or 'estate') of the tenant is burdened with various services and 'incidents of tenure.'[2] Regarded as a means of achieving certain political objects, these liabilities were essential. Regarded as a condition of the enjoyment of the profits of the land, they were mere encumbrances, to be got rid of if possible. Moreover, they were liabilities which, in many cases, could not actually be performed by certain classes of persons. Thus, an infant, a woman, or a religious house, could not in person perform military service; though, doubtless, in such cases, a substitute could be sent. On the other hand, a certain class of person was only too liable to commit treason or felony, and thus incur a forfeiture of his estate, or to run into debt, and have his land seized by his creditors under the new remedy of Elegit provided by the Statute of Westminster the Second.[3] Finally, the desire to extend to land that power of testamentary disposition which, as we have seen,[4] had been acquired for

[1] The reader familiar with modern English law will not need to be reminded of the famous decision in *Colls v. Home and Colonial Stores* [1904] A.C. 179. It turned entirely on the distinction referred to in the text.

[2] *Ante*, chap. III. [3] 13 Edw. I (1285) c. 18. [4] *Ante*, p. 61.

chattels in the twelfth and thirteenth centuries, grew stronger with each generation.

Feoffee and Cestui que Use

The method of the 'use,' as distinguished from its objects, was, to vest the **seisin** of the land in some person who would, for all public and legal purposes, be the tenant of the land, but to bind him by a solemn promise or oath, to permit another person to enjoy the benefit (**Use**) of the land, after satisfaction of the claims of the State and the lord. So far as these authorities were concerned, the only person was he who was vested with the seisin, the 'feoffee to uses,' as he came to be called. Upon his death, felony, infancy, marriage, and the like, the usual incidents of tenure arose; against him were made the claims for all services, though, it is hardly necessary to say, the right of distress gave the lord a still more powerful remedy against the land itself. As for the beneficiary, the *cestui que use*, he was out of the picture, so far as the State and the lord were concerned.

Origin of Uses

The popularity of the famous device of the use of lands into England is said to be largely due to the mendicant friars of the then new Orders of St. Dominic and St. Francis, who, arriving in this country in the first half of the thirteenth century, found themselves hampered by their own vows of poverty, no less than by the growing feeling against 'Mortmain,'[1] in acquiring the provision of land absolutely necessary for their rapidly developing work. Churches, schools, and hospitals were their material stock-in-trade; and these required sites, even if the brethren themselves were prepared to lodge in poverty and obscurity. But the device soon found imitators with inferior motives. A statute of 1376[2] is aimed at persons who, having inherited tenements and borrowed chattels, give such tenements and chattels to their friends, 'by collusion to have the profits thereof at their will,' and then, fleeing to sanctuary, waste these profits 'with an high countenance,' in defiance of their long-suffering creditors. Other statutes allude to the practice of covering defective titles by transferring them to powerful men against whom the lawful claimants can make no way,[3] to the evasion of the Mortmain rule and the rule against alien incumbents, by the same de-

[1] *Ante*, p. 31.

[2] 50 & 51 Edw. III, c. 6.

[3] 1 Ric. II (1377) c. 9.

vice,[1] and to the practice of alienating lands on a similar understanding, in order to be able to commit waste with impunity.[2]

Protection of the Use

But here it will not unnaturally be asked, with what assurance could the adopters of this device expect, from those to whom they had confided such enormous power, any better faith than they themselves had shown? What was there to prevent a feoffee to uses denying the claim of his *cestui que use* to the profits of the land? According to law, he (the feoffee to uses) was the tenant, the owner of the estate. What was to prevent him taking the profits for his own use, instead of leaving them for the use of another?

The Court of Chancery

Probably, in the early days of the use of lands, nothing at all; save the popularity of the friars, and the general scandal which a breach of ecclesiastical confidence would have occasioned. The Church courts, which would, doubtless, have been only too eager to interfere for the protection of the *cestui que use,* had been excluded in advance from enforcing promises, even when a breach of them amounted to a *laesio fidei;* they were still more strictly prohibited by the royal judges from holding plea of lands. But, in the latter half of the fourteenth century, a powerful champion of the *cestui que use* arose in the Court of Chancery; and, from the end of the fifteenth century[3] (probably long before) we find the Court issuing its powerful Writ of **subpœna** against the man who, having received land to hold for the use of another, refuses to allow that other to enjoy it. After this, it is merely a question of time when the 'equitable ownership' of land shall assume the character of a definite and recognized system alongside of the older system of legal estates. The details of the story are too long to be told here. Suffice it to say that, by gradually assimilating the interest of the *cestui que use* to that of the legal tenant, by imposing, not merely on the original feoffee to uses, but on all persons who acquired his estate in circumstances which rendered them morally bound to respect the claims of the *cestui que use,* the liability to do so,[4] above all,

[1] 7 Ric. II (1383) c. 12; 15 Ric. II (1391) c. 5. (The latter statute put an end to this particular evasion of the Mortmain rule.)

[2] 11 Hen. VI (1433) c. 5.

[3] See the precedents in *Select Cases in Chancery,* ed. Baildon (S.S. vol. 10).

[4] See this process worked out in detail in Maitland's *Equity,* pp. 117–121; also in the author's *Modern Land Law,* at pp. 141, 142, where the decisions are referred to. They range from 1485 to 1589.

by raising implied or constructive uses from circumstances which, in the opinion of the Court, rendered the legal owner bound in conscience to act as a trustee for the *cestui que use*, the Court of Chancery, powerfully aided by Parliament,[1] had, even before the passing of the statute of 1535, in effect created a dual system of land-ownership in England. Unlike the older system or estates, which was based on the conspicuous fact of seisin of possession of the land, the new system was based on conscience, *i.e.* on the moral duty of the person seised (the feoffee to uses) to allow the beneficial owner, or *cestui que use*, to enjoy the profits of the land. This moral duty was not recognized by the older royal tribunals, the Benches and the Exchequer,[2] which, indeed, with their jury-process, were ill-fitted for the decision of moral questions.[3] But the new Court of Chancery, with its ecclesiastical Chancellor, well versed in the mysteries of theological casuistry, and unhampered by the presence of a secular jury, set itself with eagerness to defend the *cestui que use* against the tenant of the legal estate. Only where such tenant had acquired his estate as a *bonâ fide* purchaser, without knowledge of the trust affecting it, was the Chancery powerless to protect the equitable ownership; for in that case there was no 'equity' that could be set up against the legal tenant. In all other cases, the equitable interest dogged the heels of the legal tenant like an inevitable shadow; a shadow which, from the standpoint of pecuniary value, was worth more than the substance of the legal estate. Even Littleton, though he represents the strictest orthodoxy of the older feudal law, was obviously familiar with the use of lands; for he admits[4] that the *cestui que use* is put on assises and inquests under the Jury Act of 1414,[5] and his will shows that he had lands of his own in 'use.'

But the peaceful development of the use of lands was threat-

[1] See 11 Hen. VI (1433) c. 5 (*cestui que use* liable for waste); 4 Hen. VII (1488) c. 17 (heir of *c.q.u.* to be in ward and pay relief, and to have action against guardian); 19 Hen. VII (1503) c. 15 (use of land liable to be taken in execution on judgment, &c.; heriots, reliefs, &c. to apply).

[2] It is, of course, well known that, in later times, the Court of Exchequer exercised equitable jurisdiction. But it was evidently borrowed from Chancery.

[3] Fitzherbert (*Natura Brevium*, 117 A) does indeed state that the *cestui que use* may have a Writ of Account against the feoffee. But he gives no form; and the statement is of doubtful authority. Anyhow, the Writ of Account was never a great success.

[4] Ss. 462–464.

[5] 2 Hen. V, st. II, c. 3.

ened with violent interruption in the first half of the sixteenth century. The King's advisers had in immediate view the dissolution of the monasteries, and the confiscation of their lands. It was known that a vast quantity of these lands were held for the monasteries under the convenient protection of uses, presumably created before the mortmain statute of 1391.[1] The royal advisers were determined that these lands should not escape forfeiture under the disguise of mere equitable interests; such a result would merely have benefited the feoffees to uses, whereas the King's advisers destined the lands for quite other persons. Accordingly, the famous Statute of Uses, passed at the close of the year 1535,[2] in effect enacts (for the language is unspeakably involved and obscure) that, whenever A is or shall hereafter be 'seised' to the use of B, of any interest in land, B shall be deemed to have a corresponding legal estate; A disappearing altogether from the scene.[3] One of the popular titles given to the statute, viz. 'An Act for the Transmutation of Uses into Possession,' perhaps hits, as clearly as any brief formula, the intention of the measure; for, though it was afterwards held,[4] that mere trespassory possession was a question of fact which could not be disguised, even by the words of a statute, yet all that the recognition of the legal seisin could do for the *cestui que use* would be done.

The Statute of Uses

The fate of the Statute of Uses is one of the most curious in legal history. Its secret and unavowed purpose, of securing the estates of the monasteries for the Crown, it accomplished. Its ostensible purpose, fortified by a wealth of hypocritical justification,[5] it entirely failed to achieve. Not only were devises of lands, after a brief interval, put on a legal footing;[6] but, as is well known, uses of lands, as distinguished from legal estates, soon re-appeared in full vigour. Whilst, in unforeseen directions, the statute worked havoc in the medieval system of conveyancing; and gradually modernized it out of existence. At this point we are concerned to notice only the failure of its avowed object. This failure took

Effects of the Statute

[1] 15 Ric. II, c. 5.
[2] 27 Hen. VIII, c. 10.
[3] This seems to be a fair summary of the long first section.
[4] *Lutwich v. Milton* (1620) Cro. Jac. 604 ('not to have *trespass* without entry and actual possession').
[5] See the long list of supposed grievances quoted in the preamble.
[6] 32 Hen. VIII (1540) c. 1.

the form of a discovery that three important classes of uses of land did not fall within the operation of the statute.

Uses not within the Statute

In all probability, the framers of the Act had never contemplated the inclusion within it of 'active trusts'—*i.e.* arrangements under which the feoffee to uses did not merely lend his name as a cover for the *cestui que use*, but genuinely conducted himself as manager and administrator of the estate, handing over the net profits to the *cestui que use*. At any rate, such **active trusts** were soon treated as being outside the statute;[1] although, owing to the important fact that no technical words were ever essential to the creation of a use, it was sometimes difficult to discover whether an 'active' or a 'passive' use or trust was intended.

Another loophole was discovered in the employment of the word 'seised' by the framers of the statute. For, as we have seen,[2] the word 'seised,' and its analogues, had long been reserved for the free tenement; the owner of a term of years was not seised. Consequently, an assignment of a **term of years** to A to the use of B was not 'executed' by the statute, so as to make B legal owner; though a feoffment to A and his heirs to the use of B for the same number of years, would have that effect.[3]

Finally, by what can only be regarded as sheer quibbling, it was resolved, in a famous decision of the Court of Wards,[4] that if the donor of lands has placed an **use upon an use** (*e.g.* has enfeoffed A, to the use of B, to the use of, or in trust for, C), the second use is not 'executed' by the statute; for that 'an use cannot be engendered of an use.' It was not long before the ingenuity of conveyancers saw in this decision a simple means of evading the statute in any case; and so we get the common formula of a conveyance 'into and to the use of A,' in trust for B, which, as was said in a well-known case,[5] merely added three (? five) words to the conveyance, and, at the same time, entirely excluded the operation of the statute.

Thus, after a temporary check, the development of the doctrine of uses resumed its full course. The Court of Chancery, aided from time to time by Parliament, imposed upon the interest of the *cestui que use* the incidents of the legal estate,

[1] *Nevil v. Saunders* (1686) 1 Vern. 415.
[2] *Ante*, pp. 52, 53, 89.
[3] This is expressly enacted by the statute (s. 1).
[4] *Tyrrel's Case* (1557) Dyer, 155.
[5] *Hopkins v. Hopkins* (1738) 1 Atk., at p. 591.

and vested him with its powers; while, on the other hand, it relieved the estate of the trustee from the legal liabilities which, owing to the default or incapacity of the trustee, threatened to endanger the beneficial interest, though not, of course, from the ordinary incidents of tenure. Thus, by a series of steps, the course of which will be traced in the history of the next period, the 'use, trust, or confidence of lands,' which the good friars of the thirteenth century adopted to enable themselves to reconcile the enjoyment of property with their vows of perpetual poverty, has developed into a new form of ownership which, to all but trained eyes, completely resembles the older feudal form of tenure.

Later History of Trusts

CHAPTER VIII

RIGHTS AND METHODS OF ALIENATION

IT has been shewn, in a previous chapter,[1] how that right of alienating property in land which, to a modern student, seems an inevitable feature of every civilized system of law, but which primitive society long declines to recognize, had won substantial victories during the preceding period. Just at the close of the thirteenth century, was passed a famous statute which is the charter of free alienation in England. This, the so-called *Quia Emptores*, from its opening words, appears as the Statute of Westminster the Third;[2] and from its wording we may gather that it was something in the nature of a diplomatic move in the struggle between the conservative forces which opposed free alienation and the progressive forces which favoured it. Apparently, the great feudal landowners had complained that their tenants had 'subinfeudated' their lands in such a way that the benefits of the overlordship were lost, and had prayed relief. The King, assuming sympathy, had, with the advice of his Parliament, and 'at the instance of the great men, of the realm,' enacted that such subinfeudation should no longer be lawful; but, at the same time, that 'it shall be lawful to every free man to sell at his own pleasure his lands and tenements, or part thereof; so nevertheless that the feoffee shall hold the same lands or tenements of the same chief lord of the fee, and by the same services and customs as his feoffor held them before.' Thus the famous rule, which has ever since governed English conveyancing, was laid down: a fee simple may be transferred, it cannot be created, by a subject. The statute is expressly limited[3] to estates in fee simple. It was not intended to affect the entails just made inalienable by *De Donis;*[4] nor to prevent

Quia Emptores

[1] *Ante*, pp. 36–38.
[2] 18 Edw I (1290) st. I.
[3] Cap. 3.
[4] *Ante*, pp. 86–88.

the creation of such limited fees or of life estates. Moreover, according to a well-known rule of Constitutional Law, it does not bind the Crown, which can accordingly, and does, create fee simple estates at the present day. But, so far as the right of alienation by tenants *in capite* of the Crown was concerned, that was tacitly granted by a statute of the year 1327,[1] which substituted a reasonable fine for the previous forfeiture incurred by such alienation.[2]

Thus, by the end of the thirteenth century, slightly later for immediate tenants of the Crown, the right of alienation of land had been established as a general principle, at least for free tenants. How far the claims of servile tenants to similar privileges had progressed at that date, it is difficult to say. When copyholds come within the jurisdiction of the King's courts, we find the practice of alienation by surrender of the tenant's interest to his lord and the admittance of his alienee in his place, so firmly established, that the King's courts treat it as part of the general law of copyholds.[3] The form of the process suggests a compromise between seignorial and tenant rights. No doubt appears to have ever been raised as to the alienability of terms of years, in spite of the fact that contractual rights were, in general, long inalienable. But there were certain rules about the enforcement of conditions of forfeiture which, until the passing of the statute of 1540,[4] must have rendered the alienation of reversions somewhat difficult; and, though vested remainders probably fell within the provisions of *Quia Emptores*, it was long before the possibility of alienating contingent estates, by ordinary conveyance *inter vivos*, was openly admitted.[5] As has been before stated,[6] the statutory prohibition against alienating entailed estates, was evaded by the use of fictions, probably before the end of the fourteenth century.

Copyholds

[1] 1 Edw. III, st. II, c. 12.

[2] It would seem, from the wording of the *Prærogativâ Regis* (17 Edw. II, st. II, c. 7) that, even before 1327, the tenant *in capite* was allowed to alienate a portion of his fee; in other words, the matter was governed by cap. 32 of the charter of 1225 (9 Hen. III).

[3] Coke, *Compleate Copyholder*, s. xxxvi.

[4] 32 Hen. VIII, c. 34.

[5] Statutory recognition was not accorded until 1845 (8 & 9 Vic. c. 106, s. 6). As a matter of fact, the rule had long been relaxed for wills; and this fact was formally recognized by the Wills Act of 1837 (7 Will. IV & 1 Vic. c. 26, s. 3).

[6] *Ante*, pp. 37, 38.

The next great step in the progress of free alienation was the result of the introduction of uses of land, described in the last preceding chapter. Though the older King's courts, the Benches and the Exchequer, adhered sternly to the rule, that the legal estate in lands was not devisable, the Court of Chancery freely recognized the right of the *cestui que use* to dispose of his equitable interest by will—provided, of course, that such interest was capable of continuing after his death. Accordingly, it was every-day practice in the fifteenth and early sixteenth centuries, for a landowner, who felt his end approaching, to enfeoff a trustworthy person or persons 'to the uses of his will'; and those uses would, after his death, be enforced against his feoffees by the Court of Chancery.[1] It was, probably, in this way that 'future uses,' *i.e.* uses not to take effect, or possibly not even to be declared, until the happening of some future and uncertain event, acquired their first recognition. By this means, undoubtedly, our law gained acquaintance with those 'executory devises' which still, on some points, defy the rules of ordinary conveyancing. For, inasmuch as the will of uses could by no means affect the seisin of the land, which still remained peacefully vested in the feoffee to uses, the Court of Chancery saw no harm in allowing free disposition of the use itself. It is worthy of notice, too, that the practice of surrendering to the uses of the tenant's will, obviously framed on the analogy of the Chancery model, had acquired a footing in copyholds by the beginning of the seventeenth century.

Wills of Uses

The Statute of Uses avowedly aimed at putting an end to devises of land, by converting uses into legal estates.[2] But such a result was so repugnant to a generation which had become familiar with testamentary dispositions of land through the medium of uses, that public opinion compelled the passing, in the year 1540,[3] of a statute which openly sanctioned the devise of legal interests; excepting only, for the benefit of reversioners, one third of knight-service estates. So wide, indeed, was the wording of the statute of 1540, that it was found necessary to correct it, two years later, by an explana-

First Statute of Wills

[1] A statutory recognition of this practice may be found in 1488 (4 Hen. VII, c. 4).

[2] 27 Hen. VIII (1535) c. 10 ('Where(as) by the common laws of this realm, lands, tenements, and hereditaments be not devisable by testament').

[3] 32 Hen. VIII, c. 1.

tory statute,[1] which restricted the operation of devises to fee simple estates. The restriction was, probably, intended to exclude only estates tail; but it had the effect of shutting out estates *pur autre vie*, which remained, accordingly, undevisable until the passing of the Statute of Frauds,[2] in the next period. On the other hand, the explanatory statute of 1542[3] withdrew at least some of the restrictions which had been placed by the principal statute on devises of estates held *in capite* of the Crown,[4] and expressly allowed undivided shares of devisable estates to be devised.[5] This last provision completed the policy of allowing all co-owners to demand a 'partition,' or breaking up into severalty of their lands, which had been begun by the

Partition

Partition Act of 1539,[6] and must be regarded as the climax of the movement in favour of free alienation brought about by the Reformation statutes.

On the other hand, Parliament, in this period, clung firmly to the rule against alienation in mortmain, which, as we have

Mortmain

seen,[7] had begun to establish itself in the preceding period, and even extended its scope. A statute of the year 1279,[8] devoted entirely to the subject, laid it down that the immediate lord should, in the event of a breach of the rule, be entitled to enter the land and claim it as forfeited at any time within a year after the breach; if he failed to do so his right passed for six months to his next overlord, and so, ultimately, to the Crown. The Statute of Westminster the Second introduced two new writs specially concerned with enforcing the rule.[9] *Quia Emptores* is careful to explain[10] that the recognition of the free right of alienation does not extend to gifts in mortmain. The Crown was not bound by the statute of 1279. But the King promised, in the year 1299,[11] that no license to acquire lands in mortmain should be granted until an enquiry had been held as to its effect upon the interests of 'mesne' or intervening lords; and this promise was renewed in 1306.[12]

[1] 34 & 35 Hen. VIII (1542) c. 5. [2] 29 Car. II (1677) c. 3, s. 12.
[3] 34 & 35 Hen. VIII (1542) c. 5. [4] *Ibid.*, ss. 5–8. [5] *Ibid.*, s. 4.
[6] 31 Hen. VIII, c. 1. (Co-heirs were entitled to partition by the older law.)
[7] *Ante*, p. 31. [8] Printed as 7 Edw. I, st. II.
[9] 13 Edw. I, c. 41. (The writs are: *Contra Formam Collationis* and *Cessavit in Biennium*.)
[10] 18 Edw. I (1290) c. 3.
[11] 27 Edw. I, st. II. (This is the writ of *Ad Quod Damnum*.)
[12] 34 Edw. I, st. III.

A statute of 1344[1] shows some weakness; but the statute of 1391[2] is memorable, not merely as being the Mortmain Code of three centuries, but as extending the rule of mortmain to all bodies, religious and secular alike, having perpetual succession. For this extension marks the definite recognition by English Law of the corporation, or, as it is sometimes called, the 'fictitious person' — the legal personality which is not restricted to the limits of individual life. The gradual evolution of this institution is one of the most fascinating chapters in legal history; but space forbids any attempt to describe it here.[3] The Reformation statutes still further strengthened the policy of mortmain by declaring void (though not a cause of forfeiture) all gifts of lands to parish churches, chapels, or religious gilds,[4] and by defining the scope of lawful charitable gifts.[5]

Passing now from the right of alienation to the forms by which that right was exercised, we find it everywhere assumed, in the earlier years of this period, that an alienation of land, whether by way of 'subinfeudation' or 'substitution,' will be effected by a 'feoffment with livery of seisin,' *i.e.* by a physical transfer of possession. Analytically, this process is two-fold. The present possessor vacates possession, indicating to the intending acquirer that he (the purchaser) may now take peaceful possession of the land so left vacant. Thereupon, the purchaser enters and takes possession of the land. Usually, however, the process is effected by a single ceremony which disguises the dual character of the transaction ('livery in deed'). It is possible, however, that a considerable interval may elapse between the retirement of the transferor and the entry of the transferee. In that case, until the latter event has taken place, the delivery of possession is imperfect ('livery in law'). In any case, it is essential to the transaction that the possession shall be vacant when the transferee enters; otherwise his act is a disseisin, it may be a forcible disseisin, which will subject him to criminal punishment.[6] That is why entry must take place in the lifetime of the feoffor;[7] before

Feoffments

[1] 18 Edw. III, st. III, c. 3.
[2] 15 Ric. II, c. 5.
[3] The reader should refer to the account given in P. & M. (Vol. II, pp. 486–511.)
[4] 23 Hen. VIII (1531) c. 10. There was an exception for interests not exceeding twenty years (s. 3).
[5] 43 Eliz. (1601) c. 4, s. 1.
[6] Statutes of Forcible Entry (5 Ric. II (1381) st. I, c. 8; 8 Hen. VI (1429) c. 9).
[7] Co. Litt. 48 b.

the latter's seisin descends to his heir in pursuance of the rule: *le mort saisit le vif.* During the whole of the period under review, no written evidence of the feoffment was required; though, for convenience of record, 'charters of feoffment' became common before the end of the fifteenth century. But the form of such documents tells its own tale. It is recitative only, not operative — 'I have given and granted,' not, 'I give and grant.'

Around this primitive type of conveyance an almost superstitious atmosphere of reverence had accumulated before the close of our period; and, in addition to what a modern lawyer would esteem the proper and normal effect of a conveyance, viz., the transfer of undisputed rights, the feoffment was marked by at least three qualities which, to a modern lawyer, seem grotesque.

Beneficial Operation

The first of these is what may be called (though the expression is not orthodox) its 'beneficial operation.' Provided only that the entry of the feoffor to make livery be lawful, the feoffment 'cleareth all disseisins, abatements, intrusions, and other wrongfull or defeasible estates';[1] in other words, it starts the feoffee again with a clear title, unhampered by any previous defects caused by unlawful claims. That was one reason why the 'right of entry' was so jealously guarded; and why, therefore, a 'discontinuance' by a tenant in tail, which, though it did not deprive the heir in tail of his estate, robbed the latter of his 'right of entry,' and so rendered it impossible for him to alienate until he had recovered the land by action, was so serious a step.[2] The doctrine of beneficial operation was justified by the subordinate and very difficult principle of 'remitter,' *i.e.* the rule whereby a man who has two titles, one older and better, the other younger and more disputable, if he comes to the land by the latter, will be deemed by the law to be 'in' by force of the former.[3] In the days of disturbed titles, it was of great importance, and is so treated, both by Littleton and Coke.[4]

The second peculiar quality of a feoffment is officially described[5] as its 'tortious operation.' For, a livery in deed being an

[1] Co. Litt. 9a. An 'abatement' is the entry of a stranger between the death of an ancestor and the entry of the heir; an 'intrusion' a similar entry between the death of a tenant for life and the entry of the remainderman (Co. Litt. 277a).

[2] See *ante*, p. 87.

[3] Litt. s. 659.

[4] Co. Litt. 347 b–364 b.

[5] *E.g.* in the Real Property Act, 1845, s. 4.

undeniable fact, it at least transferred seisin to the feoffee — not necessarily a rightful seisin, but, if the feoffor professed to transfer more than he himself had, a wrongful or 'tortious' seisin. And, inasmuch as there could only be one seisin of the land, it followed that this tortious feoffment might work disastrous results to lawful interests. Thus, for example, if made a lessee for years, it deprived the lessor of the seisin which, as we have seen,[1] remained in him, notwithstanding the grant of the term. If made by a tenant for life, it 'devested' the remainders or reversion on his estate. In both cases, the estates of the remainderman or reversioner were reduced to mere rights of entry, which, if exercised at all, must have been exercised promptly, or the 'disseisor' would have acquired a seisin protected by the possessory assises, and the claims of the injured party would then have been reduced to mere rights of action, which were liable to perish by lapse of time, and which could not be alienated.[2] If the wrongful possessor succeeded in holding possession until the death of the rightful claimant of the seisin (the 'disseisee'), the latter's heir was likewise restricted to a mere right of action; the 'descent cast tolled the entry.'[3] Naturally, such a grievous wrong was not committed with impunity; a tortious feoffment by a feoffor who had no fee worked a forfeiture of his estate, and entitled the next vested remainderman or reversioner to enter and claim the land at once.[4] But this very righteous rule itself ultimately became an engine of fraud; for, by means of it, tenant for life in possession could, by collusion with the next vested remainderman, cause a forfeiture of his (the tenant for life's) estate, and thus destroy the intervening contingent remainders. It was this device which led to the institution of 'trustees to preserve contingent remainders' — necessary parties to every family settlement, until the Real Property Act, 1845, abolished altogether the tortious operation of a feoffment.[5]

Tortious Operation

Thirdly, a feoffment might involve a warranty by the feoffor

[1] *Ante*, p. 89.

[2] If the disseisor could hold possession for three years, even though his entry had been forcible, he could not be turned out by the summary remedy given by the 8 Hen. VI (1429) c. 9 (see s. 7). Of this more in a later chapter.

[3] Litt. s. 386. The Note of Hargraves and Butler appended to this section in their edition of Coke's Commentary on Littleton gives an excellent summary of the effects of disseisin.

[4] Co. Litt. p. 251.

[5] 8 & 9 Vic. c. 106, s. 4.

of the feoffee's title — *i.e.* a liability, in the event of the feoffee losing the lands by a claim inconsistent with the title of the feoffor, to make up to him the loss out of his (the feoffor's) other lands. This liability is, historically, of such importance, that a few words must be devoted to it.

Warranty

The feudal warranty is, doubtless, derived from the ancient duty of the feudal lord to protect his liege man 'with fire and sword against all deadly.' It was of the essence of the feudal bond, that the vassal should be under his lord's protection. But, with the gradual transmutation of the feudal tie into a mere symbol of property, we notice a desire on the part of the State to restrict the operation and frequency of a liability so dangerous to social order. For, even when the ancient military protection had degenerated into the mere liability to replace the lost estate, the fact that a vassal was known to be 'warranted' by a powerful lord, might well prejudice the just claims of humble claimants of his land.

Accordingly, we are not surprised to find, that one of the earliest statutes of the period under review proceeds to discuss the question of the liability of feoffors to warranty. In the so-called Statute of Bigamy, passed in the year 1276,[1] it is laid down that, where the technical words '*dedi et concessi*' have been used, and a tenure created between the feoffee and the feoffor, then the latter and his heirs are bound to warranty; even though no homage is rendered, nor any express warranty given. But where the feoffment is by way of 'substitution,' *i.e.* where the feoffee is to hold, not of the feoffor, but of the chief lord or some other person, then, although the feoffor will be bound to warranty during his own life, 'by force of his own gift,' yet his heirs will not be bound, without express words.

Now it will be remembered that, fourteen years after the passing of the Statute of Bigamy, the statute *Quia Emptores* [2] put an end to the practice of subinfeudation in fee simple; thus bringing the most important class of conveyances within the restricting clause of the older statute. In other words, after 1290, the ordinary feoffment in fee simple would not impose any warranty upon the feoffor's heirs, because it created no

[1] 4 Edw. I, st. III, c. 6. (The statute takes its name from its 5th chapter, which deals with a certain theological prejudice against second marriages.)

[2] 18 Edw. I (1290) c. 1. (See *ante*, p. 102.)

tenure between him and the feoffee; it would merely, as a modern lawyer would say, impose a personal liability on the feoffor himself. Of course, if the feoffment were accompanied by a charter containing an express clause of warranty, the case might be otherwise.

But now the question has to be asked: How was a warranty in fact enforced? And to this question only a general answer can be given; for the subject bristles with difficulties and obscurities.

Let us take, in the first place, what may be called the 'active' enforcement of a warranty; *i.e.* the feoffee, being threatened with a hostile claim to the land by a third party 'vouches to warranty' the feoffor ('warrantor') or his heir. The latter is then summoned by Writ of Warranty, to appear in the proceedings which have been commenced against the feoffee, and make good his warranty. Four courses are open to the warrantor. He can either deny the warranty; in which case he subjects himself to a kind of interlocutory lawsuit, possibly ending in a duel, with the feoffee.[1] Or he may take up the feoffee's defence, and carry on the original action brought by the hostile claimant; thus either securing the land to the feoffee, or, if the action goes against him, replacing the lost estate. Or, thirdly, he may admit his liability at once, in which case the original plaintiff gets judgment against the feoffee, and the latter judgment against the feoffor for an equivalent estate. Or, finally, the feoffor may himself 'vouch to warranty' *his* feoffor; in which case the proceedings turn against the latter. Naturally, the original plaintiff would find this dilatory procedure very annoying; and the possibility of numerous warranties was, in fact, one of the great reasons for the unpopularity of the old real actions, though the plaintiff was, by the Statute of Westminster the First, to a certain extent relieved against abuse of the process.[2] Subject, however, to this statutory restriction, the practice of 'vouching to warranty,' already well known in Glanville's

Vouching to Warranty

[1] If the feoffee was sued by Writ of Right, he could vouch the feoffor; and the main action was then suspended until the side issue between him and the feoffor was settled. If the feoffee had been turned out by a possessory assise, in which a warranty could not have been pleaded, he could have a separate Writ of *Warrantia Cartae* against the feoffor.

[2] 3 Edw. I (1275) c. 40. It will be observed, that the relief given by the statute only applied to 'Writs of Possession,' not to the Writ of Right. It was slightly extended, however, by the 20 Edw. I (1292) st. I, the so-called Statute of Vouchers.

time,[1] seems to have lasted until the practical disappearance of real actions; and, as we shall shortly see, it formed an essential part of the fiction of the Common Recovery.[2] Further than this, the strict doctrine was, that the liability to satisfy the warranty was not merely personal, but extended to all the lands belonging to the warrantor at the date when the warranty was entered into, even after they had passed into the hands of innocent purchasers for value. So that, not merely the original warrantor and his heirs, but all purchasers from him, could be 'vouched to warranty.'

In early times, when ancestral liabilities were regarded as indelible, and the possibility that an heir might be called upon to undertake inherited responsibilities irrespective of inherited assets, was treated as natural, this extreme operation of the doctrine of warranty might be tolerated. But, with the change in the law of inheritance which, as we have seen,[3] took place in the twelfth and thirteenth centuries, and especially after the separation between the heir and the executor, we notice a distinct modification of the liability on warranty. Briefly put, the change was from active to passive liability. The heir of the feoffor was no longer liable to replace the estate conveyed by his ancestor; but he was 'barred,' or, as a modern lawyer would say, 'estopped,'[4] at any rate in certain cases, from claiming, through his ancestor, the estate which that ancestor had conveyed 'with warranty.' In all probability, this liability had a good deal to do with breaking down the ancient *retrait lignager*, *i.e.* the right of the heir to set aside his ancestor's alienation;[5] probably, also, it was the origin of the rule that, even after the introduction of the executor, the heir was liable (at least to the extent of assets) for specialty debts in which he was expressly bound. But, at the very beginning of our period, we find the doctrine of 'bar' further cut down by a famous distinction. If the right to the estate claimed descended to the heir from the same ancestor, and by the same course, as the liability to warranty, then the liability was a bar to the claim to the estate, assets or no assets;

Estoppel

[1] See lib. III of Glanville's work. [2] *Post*, pp. 113, 114. [3] *Ante*, pp. 64–65.

[4] The technical difference between a bar by warranty and an estoppel is pointed out by Coke (Co. Litt. 365b).

[5] *Ante*, p. 36.

for this is 'lineal warranty.' If, on the other hand, the liability to warranty came to the heir from an ancestor different from him from whom he inherited the estate, then the heir will only be bound to the extent of the assets he had received from the ancestor who imposed on him the liability to warrant; for this is 'collateral warranty.' Thus, if A, tenant in fee simple, enfeoffs B with warranty and dies, A's heir is bound by the warranty, and cannot claim the estate against B; even though he has received no assets from A. But if A is merely tenant by the curtesy of his (A's) wife's estate, and enfeoffs B with warranty, then, though A's heir probably inherits the estate and the warranty, he will not be barred from claiming the estate, unless, and to the extent to which, he has inherited land from A. For the warranty descended on him from his father; while the estate came to him from his mother. This is the very case put by the Statute of Gloucester;[1] but it seems to have been quickly generalized into a principle. And thus we get the famous rule: 'lineal warranty without assets is a bar; collateral warranty without assets is no bar.' The passing of the Statute *De Donis*[2] caused some little difficulty; for the statute made no express provision against lineal warranty. But by the time of Littleton,[3] it was admitted that even lineal warranty did not bind the heir in tail, except to the extent of assets received from the warrantor.[4] A warranty by a tenant for life or years did not usually bind the heirs of the feoffor, because such warranty 'commenced by disseisin';[5] for a tenant for life or years could not convey a lawful fee. It might, however, conceivably have that effect; until such warranties were wholly abolished by statute, in the next period.[6]

Common Recoveries

The subject of warranties brings us naturally, though with some possible violation of strict chronological order, to the form of conveyance known as a Common Recovery. This was, in its origin, a genuine 'real' action, *i.e.* an action to recover seisin; but, in its application as a form of conveyance, was a collusive proceeding between the parties,

[1] 6 Edw. I (1278) c. 3.
[2] 13 Edw. I (1285) c. 1.
[3] S. 708.
[4] Litt. ss. 711–712.
[5] *Ibid.*, s. 698. Where such warranty did not 'commence by disseisin,' *e.g.* in the cases of tenant by the curtesy or in dower, who were lawfully seized, the effect of the warranty was, as has been said, nullified by statute (6 Edw. I (1278) c. 3 (curtesy); II Hen. VII (1494) c. 20 (dower)).
[6] 4 & 5 Anne (1705) c. 3, s. 16.

entered into for the purpose of barring the lawful claims of strangers. We have seen already[1] that use was made of it to defeat the rights of lessees for years; and from the statute which gave protection to the lessee, we infer that the collusive recovery had been used also to defeat the claims of dowresses, tenants by the curtesy, reversioners, and heirs. In other words, any person being actually seised of land could, by 'making default' in any 'real' action brought against him by a collusive plaintiff, practically defeat all claims which had arisen since the date at which the collusive plaintiff's fictitious title was supposed to have accrued.

The Statute of Westminster the Second appeared,[2] by allowing any person injured by a collusive action of this kind, to 'falsify' or show the fraudulent character of the proceedings, to have put an end to the practice. But, as was natural, the statute did not expressly safeguard the rights of contingent remaindermen and donees of powers; for such interests were not, at the time of its passing, yet invented. It is, however, a little surprising, that it did not expressly safeguard from destruction by such means the interest of the issue and remainderman in and after the new estate tail introduced by the statute itself. This omission led directly to the most famous application of the fictitious real action as a 'common assurance.'

As Bar of Entail

For, although it would have been too bold for the courts to have allowed the tenant in tail to 'bar' or destroy the rights of the issue in tail and remaindermen or reversioner, by the simple process of making default in a collusive action brought against him by a stranger who claimed to be seised in fee simple, by a title older than the date of the creation of the fee tail, yet, under the disguise of a recompense in warranty, this was just what the courts, probably before the end of the fourteenth century,[3] permitted him to do. The tenant in tail did not himself defend the action; before it commenced, he created a '*tenant to the praecipe,*' *i.e.* a defendant to the action, by transferring the seisin with warranty to a collusive nominee. Upon being sued, the nominal defendant 'vouched to warranty' the tenant in tail, who himself vouched to warranty another

[1] *Ante*, p. 90. [2] 13 Edw. I (1285) cc. 3, 4.
[3] The reasons which have led Sir Howard Elphinstone to this conclusion will be found in his article in L.Q.R. VI, 280.

collusive person, and he again, it may be, others; until at last some 'man of straw,' usually a petty court official, was vouched, and the process of vouching ceased. But then the collusive plaintiff 'craved leave to imparl,' or talk matters over, with the 'common vouchee'; and, on leave being granted by the court, the two withdraw for the imaginary conference. In due course, the collusive plaintiff re-appeared; but the common vouchee made default. Whereupon the judgment of the court was given in favour of the collusive plaintiff against the common vouchee, who was condemned, in pursuance of his imaginary warranty, to recompense the issue in tail and the other parties under the settlement, with lands of equivalent value. Needless to say, the latter part of the judgment was purely illusory; but the earlier gave to the collusive plaintiff a title to the land, guaranteed by the judgment of the court. If the plaintiff were intending to purchase the land, he thus acquired an exceptionally good title; if he were merely acting to oblige the tenant in tail, he re-conveyed to the latter, as soon as possible, an estate in fee simple, clear of the claims of the issue in tail and remaindermen.

Other Purposes

Revived for the purpose of barring entails, the Common Recovery was also applied to defeat other interests not expressly protected by statute, *e.g.* contingent remainders and executory interests, and powers appendant or in gross.[1] This effect seems to have been produced, at least in the case of a tenant for life, by the doctrine that the suffering of a Common Recovery worked a forfeiture, in the same manner as a feoffment in fee.[2] The process was also frequently used to bar claims to dower; but only with the consent of the dowress, whose rights had been, as we have seen, expressly protected by statute.[3] Statutory restrictions prevented its operation against Crown reversions;[4] and threw some doubt upon its efficacy when employed by a tenant for life.[5] A statute of the year 1540 also expressly made it void, at least so far as a bar of the entail was concerned, in the hands

[1] *Plunket v. Holmes* (1661) 1 Lev. 11; *King v. Melling* (1673) 2 Lev. 58.

[2] *Sir W. Pelham's Case* (1590) 1 Rep. 8.

[3] *Ante*, p. 113; *Eare v. Snow* (1578) Plowd., at p. 515.

[4] 34 & 35 Hen. VIII (1542) c. 20. In such cases the Common Recovery did not even bar the heirs in tail (ss. 2, 3).

[5] 14 Eliz. (1572) c. 8.

of a 'tenant after possibility,' *i.e.* a tenant in tail under a limitation which cannot continue after his death.[1]

Fines

The **Fine** is a still older form of fictitious lawsuit employed as a 'common assurance'; and may, conceivably, be traced back in origin to the 'shire witness' of pre-Conquest times. As a process in the royal courts, it is certainly as old as the twelfth century; and records of Fines in the Court of Our Lord the King are extant from the year 1179. In the year 1195, an important official regulation with regard to their formalities was issued; and from that day until their abolition by statute in 1833, the records of Fines are complete.

Unlike the Common Recovery, the Fine was, in form, a personal action; though it 'savoured of the realty.' It was usually commenced by a Writ of Covenant (*Quod ei teneat conventionem*) founded on a real or imaginary contract under seal to do the act which was the object of the intended conveyance. In later days, the intending alienor actually covenanted to levy a Fine to the specified uses. The intending alienee, or 'conusee' (as he was later known) was the plaintiff in the fictitious action, which, instead of being carried through all its stages (as was the Common Recovery), was speedily compromised, with the permission of the Court, on the terms arranged between the parties (the 'concord'), which were then embodied in the judgment of the Court, and entered on the record.[2] Thus the alienee secured, not merely unimpeachable evidence of his title, but judicial authority for its validity. The form which the proceedings assumed at the end of the thirteenth century is described, probably with accuracy, in a document known as *Modus Levandi Fines*, which is printed among the Statutes of the Realm.[3]

Advantages of a Fine

The Fine was a much more flexible instrument than the Common Recovery. The latter, being a 'real' action, could only be employed by, or with the concurrence of, the person actually seised of the land; because he alone could defend the action. Consequently, it was unsuitable for the trans-

[1] 32 Hen. VIII, c. 31. The familiar example is, when land has been given to 'A and the heirs of his body by his wife B.' B dies leaving no issue, or only issue who die in A's lifetime without issue. A is then said to be 'tenant in tail after possibility of issue extinct;' because no issue of A and B can now possibly exist.

[2] These terms frequently included a 'warranty' of title by the conusor; which seems inconsistent with the fiction that the concord is the judgment of the Court.

[3] As 18 Edw. I (1290).

fer or release of 'mere rights,' such as reversions, rights of dower, claims of easements, and the like. Moreover, in practice, it was only used to pass an estate in fee simple; because it was difficult, in a judgment in a real action, to make any more elaborate limitations. The Fine suffered from no such restrictions; and, as a fact, was as often used to effect an elaborate settlement (*sur don, grant, et render*) as to convey an absolute, or at any rate a simple interest[1] (*come ceo qu'il a de son don*) or release a right (*droit tantum*).[2] Moreover, the process gave an opportunity for the 'separate examination' of a married woman; and was thus specially suited for binding her interests.[3]

Safeguards

Not unnaturally, these fictitious conveyances, and especially the Fine, were open to abuses. There was not so much danger in the case of the Common Recovery; on account of the rule which made the person actually seised of the land a necessary party. But, as we have seen,[4] even in the case of a Common Recovery, it was necessary to provide, in certain events, for the 'falsification' by a party interested. The danger with Fines was much greater; for what was to prevent any pair of enterprising strangers arranging that one should convey to the other by Fine an interest in the land of a third party? The Court would pass the transaction as of course, on payment of the fees; and the number and value of these rendered every official of the Court anxious to facilitate the levying of Fines. Then the conusee would appear to have an indefeasible title by record to an estate to which he had not, in truth, the remotest claim.

So obvious was this danger, that certain pleas appear to have early been allowed when a title depending on a Fine was set up in a law court. Thus the party sought to be ousted could plead that the conusor of the Fine *nil habuit in tenementis*, when he levied it;[5] or that he (the defendant), and his ancestors, *semper fuerunt seisiti* of the land, from a date prior to the levy of the Fine. Again, it was expressly provided by statute, that Fines levied by certain persons, such as husbands

[1] *Hunt v. Bourne* (1703) 1 Salk., at p. 340.

[2] See the differences explained by Blackstone, *Comm.* II, pp. 352–3, and forms in Appendix IV. There was a fourth form (*sur concessit*) which did not acknowledge the justice of the fictitious claim, but, for the sake of peace, conveyed the estate.

[3] Statute of Gloucester (6 Edw. I (1278) c. 3).

[4] *Ante*, p. 90.

[5] This plea was expressly preserved by the statute of 1487 (4 Hen. VII, c. 24).

holding their wives' lands by 'curtesy,'[1] and tenants in tail,[2] should not be effective to bar the rights of other persons. Moreover, it seems to have been a rule of the Common Law (probably dating back to the old 'court days' of the popular moots), that the so-called 'preclusive' effect of a Fine should not begin till a year and a day after the levy;[3] and, even then, could be staved off by regular protest or 'continual claim.'[4] But the best protection was, probably, afforded by the practice of 'proclamations.'

Proclamations

This practice seems to have begun with the statute of 1299 (*De Finibus Levatis*),[5] which must not be confused with the *Modus Levandi Fines*, before alluded to. By the statute of 1299, the plea of *semper fuerunt seisiti* was abolished, or at least restricted; but it was enacted that Notes and (? of) Fines levied in the King's Court, should be read openly and solemnly, two days in the weeks, at the discretion of the Justices; all pleas ceasing for the purpose. Apparently, these proclamations only bound 'parties and privies,' *i.e.* persons related in blood to the persons levying the Fine.[6] But a later statute of 1483[7] (repealed but substantially re-enacted by another of 1487),[8] increased the number of the proclamations,[9] and provided that any one, privy or stranger, who did not, by action or lawful entry, dispute the Fine within the next five years, or, in the case of infancy, coverture, or other disability, within five years after the cesser of the disability, should be for ever bound, or 'concluded' by the Fine. But the greatest increase in the popularity of Fines occurred, when a statute of 1540,[10] reversing the policy of *De Donis*,[11] enacted that a Fine levied by a tenant in tail, with proclamations under the statute

[1] 6 Edw. I (1278) c. 3; 32 Hen. VIII (1540) c. 28, s. 6.

[2] 13 Edw. I (1285) c. 1 (De Donis).

[3] *Modus Levandi Fines* (18 Edw. I, 1290) *ad fin.*

[4] The actual necessity for repeated claim seems to have been abolished by statute in 1360 (34 Edw. III, c. 16).

[5] 27 Edw. I, c. 1.

[6] This view seems inconsistent with the express language of *Modus Levandi Fines;* but it is difficult to explain otherwise the necessity for the statutes of 1483 and 1488.

[7] 1 Ric. III, c. 7.

[8] 4 Hen. VII, c. 24.

[9] The Act of Richard had provided for proclamations at Quarter Sessions as well as in the Common Pleas. But this provision was not adopted by the statute of 1487. The details of these proclamations were subsequently modified by statute (23 Eliz. (1581) c. 3, s. 7; 31 Eliz. (1589) c. 2).

[10] 32 Hen. VIII, c. 36.

[11] 13 Edw. I, c. 1, *ad fin.*

of 1487, should bind the issue in tail. Thus a Fine became an alternative means of barring an entail; and it had this advantage over a Common Recovery, that it could be levied by a tenant in tail in remainder, because a Fine, not being a 'real' action, did not require the concurrence of the person seised of the land. On the other hand, it did not bar the estates in remainder after the estate tail; for the words of the statute of 1540 only extended to persons claiming 'by force of any such entail.' Lastly, it may be remarked, that it was found necessary to enact expressly that neither a Common Recovery nor a Fine should enable a widow to convert her dower estate into a fee simple.[1]

The tenacity with which the Common Law clung to the principle that only by transfer of seisin could an estate, or corporeal hereditament, in land be alienated, is shown by the fact that even a Common Recovery and a Fine required, to complete their effect, a Writ of Seisin, directed to the sheriff, bidding him put the recoveree or conusee into actual possession of the land.[2] But, as we have seen,[3] the Common Law had, from the very beginning of our period, recognized certain interests, such as reversions, remainders, and 'hereditaments purely incorporeal,' which did not admit of seisin; and, though these could, no doubt, often be created or transferred by Fine, still it would have been oppressive to have compelled a resort to that costly process for every simple case.

Grant

Accordingly, we find it well established by the time of Littleton, that any interest in land which does not confer seisin may be created and transferred by simple deed, or writing under seal,[4] apparently without any notarial or other public sanction. Thus, true reversions, remainders, rents, advowsons, easements, and profits[5] 'lay in grant'—*i.e.* could be created or transferred by deed. There was some doubt as to the so-called reversion on a term of years. For, it will be remembered,[6] no term of years confers seisin; and, therefore, the reversioner remains seised of the land. Yet, in fact, the

[1] 11 Hen. VII (1495) c. 20; 32 Hen. VIII (1540) c. 36, s. 2.

[2] After the passing of the Statute of Uses, this writ became unnecessary, if the vendor were seised at the time when the proceedings commenced, and the Recovery were suffered or the Fine levied, to uses. But Cruise (II, 134) seems to deny this as to Recoveries.

[3] *Ante*, pp. 83–86; 92–95.

[4] Litt. s. 1; Co. Litt. 9a.

[5] Litt. ss. 627–628.

[6] *Ante*, p. 89.

termor is probably in possession; and, therefore, feoffment, which implies vacant possession, is hardly appropriate. In the end, it seems to have been settled, that either feoffment (with the tenant's consent), or Fine (where the process of the Court had to be invoked to compel the tenant to attorn), was appropriate; while merely the services of the tenant, as distinct from the lordship, could be transferred by deed of grant.[1] It must be remembered, that for the creation and transfer of terms of years themselves, no deed, or even writing, was required before 1677;[2] whilst, on the assumption by the Common Law Courts, towards the end of the fifteenth century, of jurisdiction in copyholds, the King's judges found the system of conveying these interests by surrender and admittance duly recorded on the manorial rolls, fully established. This process, being thoroughly in accordance with feudal principles, they did not seek to change; on the contrary, they enforced it by Writs of Mandamus directed to manorial lords.

Surrender and Admittance

But the passing of the Statute of Uses[3] rapidly disintegrated the strict feudal theory of transfer. It will be remembered, that the ostensible object of this statute was to get rid of the alleged evils attendant upon the practice of creating 'uses,' or beneficial interests in land. Inasmuch as these interests did not confer seisin, and were recognized only by the Court of Chancery, there seem to have been no rules of form as to their creation and transfer. Originally, they were created by way of supplement to feoffments; and it might have been in the highest degree inconvenient to record their nature in writing. Secrecy was of the essence of the transaction. Later on, the feoffment was seen to be unnecessary; if the donor 'covenanted to stand seised to the use of' the donee, that was quite sufficient for the Court of Chancery, which could as well make the donor and his heir, as any third party, a trustee. In this last case, no doubt, the uses were expressed in the deed; but the Court of Chancery would equally hold that if A had 'bargained and sold,' or agreed to sell, land to B, and B had paid the purchase money to A, A was seised 'to the use of' B. And, in such a case, there need have been no writing at all before 1535.

[1] Bracton, fo. 82; Co. Litt. 48b, 49a.
[2] 29 Car. II, c. 3 (Statute of Frauds), ss. 1–3.
[3] 27 Hen. VIII (1535) c. 10, ss. 1–3.

But it was not only in matters of evidence that the Court of Chancery was, according to Common Law principles, deplorably lax. That Court would enforce all kinds of 'future' or 'executory' uses, quite inconsistent with Common Law theories about remainders. Thus, a man might be seised of land to the use of A's unborn children, without any prior use. Such a 'springing' use would have been impossible as a Common Law estate; for it made no provision for the seisin before the birth of the children. Again, a man might be seised of land to the use of B and his heirs, with a provision that if B died childless the use should 'shift' away to C and his heirs. Such an interest as C's would have been impossible at Common Law; being, in effect, either a right to take advantage of a condition imposed by a stranger, or a remainder after a fee simple.

Springing and Shifting Uses

The passing of the Statute of Uses had a revolutionary effect on this system; for it converted all these hitherto 'equitable' interests into legal limitations. We have seen[1] how this result was evaded, by the collusion of the Courts, in the case of trusts. The legislature itself attempted to avert the unforeseen and undesired consequences in the matter of alienation.

Apparently it was determined to tolerate the 'covenant to stand seised.' For, by some process of reasoning, it had been held by the Courts, that such an instrument was only applicable to settlements intended to 'build up a family,' and only valid when based on 'natural love and affection.' Moreover, by its very nature it involved a deed. And so, seemingly to this day, a legal estate can be created by means of a **covenant to stand seised** through the medium of a use; provided only that it is part of a marriage or family settlement. But it was impossible to allow a sale of land to be effected by mere word of mouth through a '**bargain and sale**'; and so the Statute of Inrolments[2] was hastily passed to prohibit such a catastrophe.

Covenant to Stand Seised

The Statute of Inrolments provided that no 'estate of inheritance or freehold should be made or take effect in any persons, or any use thereof be made, by reason only of any bargain and sale thereof, except the same bargain and sale were made by writing indented sealed and enrolled'

Statute of Inrolments

[1] *Ante*, pp. 100–101. [2] 27 Hen. VIII (1536) c. 16.

(in one of the King's Courts at Westminster, or with the *Custos Rotulorum* of the county in which the lands lay), within six months after the date of the indenture.

Whatever the obscurities of style of this famous enactment, it was, obviously, intended to prevent, not merely oral, but secret dealings in land. Apparently, it was really operative for about seventy years; for we can trace a recognition of it in statute,[1] text-book,[2] and decision,[3] down to about 1615. But then a daring evasion by a leading conveyancer, known as the **Lease and Release,** received judicial sanction; and commenced a successful career of more than 200 years. The Lease and Release, attributed to Serjeant Moore, was based on the fact that the Statute of Inrolments did not apply to terms of years.[4] Probably the permission was intentional; for, as we have seen,[5] neither the making nor the transfer of leases for years was attended by any formality at the common law. But certainly the framers of the Act did not foresee the extent of the loop-hole. For, by making an oral bargain and sale for one year, at a money price,[6] the intending vendor could raise a use for a year in favour of the purchaser; and this use would be 'executed' by the Statute of Uses, and become a legal estate. Then, by a well-established common law practice, a simple deed of Release would enable the vendor to transfer his reversion to the bargainee, without the latter even taking possession.[7] Thus, by this dual process, when once formally recognized by the Courts,[8] it was possible at last for a conveyance of a freehold to be made, not, it is true, without a deed, but without transfer of seisin. Thus the country lost the chance of establishing, not indeed a Register of Titles, but a Register of Sales, which might have done much to obviate the uncertainty of later titles.

[1] 5 Eliz. (1562) c. 26, extending the principal Act to the palatine counties of Chester, Lancaster, and Durham.

[2] Co. Litt. 35b. (pub. 1628).

[3] *Hynde's Case* (1591) 4 Rep. 70b; *Edward Seymor's Case* (1613) 10 Rep. 95b.

[4] This fact had been pointed out in *Heyward's Case* (1595) at fo. 36a.

[5] *Ante*, p. 118.

[6] Perhaps at first the price was actually paid; but in 1677 it was decided (*Barker v. Keat*, 2 Mod. 249) that nominal consideration was sufficient.

[7] Apparently, Serjeant Moore, like every other inventor, had predecessors; for a common law process of Lease and Release was known. But it had this disadvantage, that the lessee was obliged to take possession, in order to convert his *interesse termini* into an estate. For the reversioner could not convey to the owner of a mere *interesse termini* by way of Release (Litt. s. 459).

[8] The leading case is *Lutwich v. Mitton* (1620) Cro. Jac. 604.

Incidentally, also, the simple theory of feudal seisin became greatly complicated by the grafting upon it of the new statutory seisin of the Statute of Uses. For, though the Courts would not admit that a mere legal seisin, unaccompanied by possession, would entitle the person seised to the protection of the Writ of Trespass,[1] they were obliged to hold him seised for other purposes, *e.g.* to make him a stock of descent, or to entitle him to use the possessory assises and Writs of Entry. The use of the words 'bargain and sale,' as applied to the creation of a term of years, had previously been sanctioned by judicial decision;[2] and, a few years later, judicial dictum laid it down, that the use of 'words of inheritance' was necessary to pass a fee by bargain and sale, as well as by feoffment.[3] Thus assimilated to an ordinary conveyance, the Lease and Release became practically the normal method of transfer of lands until the passing of the Real Property Act, 1845,[4] in the next period. In addition to the merit of secrecy, it had the further merits of avoiding the necessity for attornment of the tenant on a transfer of a reversion,[5] and of being free from the peculiar consequences attending the use of a feoffment. For all conveyances by deed were 'innocent' conveyances, *i.e.* they passed nothing but what the conveying party had; while a feoffment, as we have seen,[6] might, until 1845, have a 'tortious operation.'

Thus the period we are studying is remarkable for achieving, not merely the right of free alienation of land, but also the right of alienation by secret conveyance. The latter achievement we may sometimes regret; but it was, probably, necessary for the complete emancipation of land from its ancient tribal and feudal bonds.

[1] 'Not to have trespass without entry and actual possession' (*Lutwich v. Mitton, ubi sup.*).

[2] *Heyward's Case* (1595) 2 Rep. 35a.

[3] *Corbet's Case* (1599) 1 Rep., at 87b.

[4] 8 & 9 Vic. c. 106. (A statute of the year 1840 had allowed a deed of Release, expressed to be made under it, to take the place of the former 'Lease and Release.')

[5] *Heyward's Case* (1595) 2 Rep., 34b.

[6] *Ante*, p. 108.

CHAPTER IX

THE LAW OF PERSONAL PROPERTY

A SHORT chapter will suffice to deal with the law of personal property in this period; not, as has been suggested, because personal property was of small value in the eyes of the law, but for other and more interesting reasons. No doubt it is true, that the King's Courts had for their original and primary purpose the protection and adjustment of seisin and property in land. But, long before our period ends, they had developed a very elaborate procedure for the protection of that movable wealth which was increasing so rapidly in England with the discoveries of the fifteenth and sixteenth centuries, and the growth of international commerce. Only, so far as chattels corporeal, or 'goods' were concerned, they did not build up this law as a code relating to proprietary interests. They approached it through the Law of Tort, by means of the new writs of Trespass and Trover, and the modification of the old writ of Detinue. It will be convenient, therefore, to postpone our examination of it till we come to the discussion of the Law of Tort, in the following chapter. Here we need deal only with chattels incorporeal, or, as they are more commonly called, 'choses in action,' which, though they were at first regarded by the Courts with some suspicion, became active towards the end of our period, and, in modern times are, of course, of vast importance.

Mortgages

First in point of time and interest comes the mortgage debt, *i.e.* the claim for the return of money lent on the security of some tangible object. Such claims are among the earliest fruits of a commercial civilization, and are nearly always effected in the same way, viz. by the deposit or pledge of the security with the creditor, to be redeemed or returned on the payment of the debt. We have seen[1] that,

[1] *Ante*, p. 56.

even in Glanville's time, this process was applied indiscriminately to land and chattels corporeal; and, with regard to the latter, there is really very little more to say, for the contract of pledge of chattels, though in recent times regulated by the Pawnbrokers' Acts, is still, substantially, what it was in Glanville's day.

But the pledge or 'gage' of land, though it remained, as a debt, the personal property of the creditor, yet, owing to its connection with the 'realty,' was, almost inevitably, drawn by the powerful influence of feudalism within the orbit of land law. For though, as has been said,[1] Glanville did not treat the pledgee of land as an owner or tenant, yet, in fact, the pledgee was probably put in possession of the land, in order that he might take the profits, either as interest (*mortgage*) or in reduction of the debt (*vifgage*). Without some such protection, he would have had little by way of security;[2] and so it could hardly be denied that he had an interest, of some sort, in the land. Glanville[3] called this interest 'seisin'; and though, as we have seen,[4] seisin came ultimately to be regarded as an improper description of the possession of the termor, yet the increased protection given in the thirteenth century to the lessee for years must have tended to strengthen the position of the mortgagee of land, so long as mortgages were effected by mere pledge, or delivery of possession.

Apparently, however, this way of effecting a mortgage came to be regarded by conveyancers as dangerous. The growing importance of seisin, the special remedies open to the person seised, induced them to demand that their clients, the mortgagees, should obtain a freehold in the land. Possibly, also, as has been suggested by learned writers,[5] there was a technical difficulty in the practice which arose later, of making the pledge forfeitable if the debt was not paid by a certain day. This was, in itself, a natural arrangement; though the Court of Chancery did its best to nullify it by establishing and developing its famous maxim: 'Once a mortgage, always a mortgage.' But the Common Law Courts did not like the idea of a term of years enlarging automatically into a freehold; for one thing,

[1] *Ante*, p. 88.

[2] Glanville expressly says that the King's Courts would not, in his day, interfere; unless the land was actually in the 'seisin' of the creditor (Lib. X, cap. VIII, *ad fin.*).

[3] *Ibid.* [4] *Ante*, p. 89. [5] P. & M. II, 122.

the process was an evasion of the rule that a freehold could only be transferred by feoffment with livery of seisin. So, by Littleton's day,[1] it appears to have become the practice for mortgages of land to be effected by way of feoffments on condition. The mortgagor (borrower) enfeoffed the lender (mortgagee) in simple, but attached a condition that, upon repayment of the money, the mortgagor might re-enter the land, and avoid the estate of the mortgagee. Of course this arrangement threw upon the mortgagor the whole risk of omitting to make the payment on the prescribed day; and it was the severity with which the Common Law Courts enforced the condition, that led to the high-handed interference of the Court of Chancery in mortgage transactions. The Chancery, as is well known, insisted in regarding the mortgage simply as a security for the payment of the money, and would allow the borrower to recover his land by payment of the principal and interest at any time, making the creditor account rigidly for any profits derived from his occupation, if he had been in possession of the land. But the formal recognition of the lawfulness of taking moderate interest in mortgage transactions, which occurred in 1545,[2] seems to have speedily substituted for the old mortgage, under which the creditor took possession of the land at once, something like the modern arrangement, in which the debtor covenants to pay a fixed interest, and, so long as he does so regularly, the creditor does not take possession. The substitution for the old Feoffment of the new conveyance by Lease and Release[3] would, obviously, facilitate such a change, by rendering actual transfer of seisin unnecessary. Nevertheless, in spite of the efforts of Chancery, the freehold mortgage retained serious defects till quite recent times; one of the most serious being that, whereas the debt itself was personalty, and went to the mortgagee's executor on his death, the estate in the land was realty, and went to his heir.[4] Accordingly, we are not surprised to find it stated by a learned conveyancer of later days, that, at the end of the sixteenth century, there was a revival of the

[1] Ss. 332–344. Apparently the *vifgage* was still known in Littleton's day (s. 327), but rather as a supplement to the right of distress than as a substantive transaction.
[2] 37 Hen. VIII, c. 9, s. 4; 13 Eliz. (1570) c. 8. (The maximum rate was 10 *per cent.*)
[3] *Ante*, pp. 121–122.
[4] There were other drawbacks, *e.g.* the claim of the mortgagee's widow to dower.

practice of effecting mortgages by creating terms of years.[1] But these were effected by deed, not by delivery of the land in pledge, as in the days of Glanville.

Statutes

It must not be supposed, however, that the formal mortgage was the only 'real' security known to the English creditor in the later Middle Ages. The famous statute of Acton Burnel[2] enabled a merchant to enter into a sealed recognizance, or acknowledgment of debt, before the mayor of a chartered borough; and empowered the creditor, on default, to seize the body of the debtor. If, after three months further delay, the debt were still unpaid, the lands and goods of the debtor were delivered by the sheriff to the creditor 'by a reasonable extent' (*i.e.* estimate); the creditor being entitled to hold them until his debt was satisfied out of the profits, and having his possession of the land protected by the then highly popular Assise of Novel Disseisin.[3] The great Statute of the Staple, in 1353,[4] extended a similar protection to recognizances entered into before the mayors of staple towns; and, so popular did the new form of security become, that, under cover of fictions, it was resorted to by persons who were neither merchants nor staplers. Accordingly, in the year 1531,[5] the 'recognizance in the nature of a statute staple' was formally sanctioned by the legislature; and the 'statute' appears in Elizabethan literature, among such other treasures as bonds, mortgages, and bills, as part of the normal equipment of the grasping money-lender. The Acts of Parliament authorizing statutes merchant and staple were not repealed till 1863;[6] but the 'statutes' themselves had then long been obsolete. Nevertheless, they are interesting as the nearest approach to a 'hypothec,' or real charge, of land, which English Law has known.

Of still greater historical and practical importance are bills of exchange, cases about which do not begin to come into the

[1] Barton, *Modern Precedents*, V, 133. There was certainly the form of absolute conveyance (bargain and sale) accompanied by deed of defeasance (West, *Symbolæographia*, s. 269).

[2] 11 Edw. I (1283), amended by the Statute of Merchants (13 Edw. I (1285) c. 1). In the latter year, a similar remedy (but restricted to half the debtor's land), was given to judgment creditors by the Statute of Westminister II (13 Edw. I, st. 1 (1285) c. 18).

[3] This was anomalous; for the Assise was, properly, a freeholder's remedy.

[4] 27 Edw. III, st. II, c. 9.

[5] 23 Hen. VIII, c. 6.

[6] Statute Law Revision Act of that year.

King's Courts till towards the end of our present period,[1] though they were probably familiar, long ere that date, to the courts administering the Law Merchant. The subject has never been satisfactorily investigated, so far as England is concerned; but it is clear that such documents were known on the Continent from a very early date,[2] and it is unlikely that they remained long unknown in this country after the beginning of the thirteenth century. Probably they were first introduced to overcome the risk and expense of the actual transport of coins. European roads were very unsafe in the Middle Ages; and a merchant of Paris, who owed a debt to a London merchant, would hesitate long before trusting the money to the perils of the journey between Paris and London. If, as was not unlikely, a second London merchant owed him (the Paris merchant) a similar or larger sum, he would save much risk and expense by simply directing the second London merchant to pay over the sum to the first; and the letter, or 'bill,' containing this request would, naturally, be sent to the first London merchant for presentation to the second. If the latter did not admit that he was indebted to the writer or drawer of the letter or bill, he refused to accept, or 'dishonoured,' the request; but, at any rate, the dishonoured missive served as an acknowledgment by the merchant at Paris of his indebtedness.

Bills of Exchange

Probably, also, letters or bills of exchange were used at an early date to get over the difficulties of foreign exchange. In the days when the coinage of Western Europe was in a thoroughly unsatisfactory condition, the terms of exchange were a matter of the highest importance for international trade. Accordingly, we find Edward III, in his Statute of Money,[3] providing that Tables of Exchange shall be set up at Dover and other places approved by the Council, and exchanges there effected by Wardens under the inspection of Royal Comptrollers. In all probability, this statute contemplated the actual exchange of coins at a physical table; but this clumsy method must, one

[1] The earliest reported is said to be *Martin v. Bure*, in 1602 (Cro. Jac. 6). The Court seems to be perfectly familiar with the document.

[2] See the author's *Early History of Negotiable Instruments* (Select Essays in Anglo-American Legal History, III, 51–71).

[3] 9 Edw. III, st. II (1335) c. 7. The enactment was repealed in 1344, on the issue of the new gold coinage (18 Edw. III, st. II, c. 6).

would think, have soon given way before a documentary system of notes based on a schedule, or 'table,' of rates of exchange. It is also probable, that the protectionist policy of the later fourteenth century, which aimed at preventing the export of English coin,[1] did a good deal to encourage the use of negotiable paper. At any rate, we get a definite mention of 'letters of exchange' in a statute of 1379.[2] In the year 1390, Richard II's Parliament enacted that every foreign merchant who sent English money abroad should give a bond to the Chancellor to buy within three months staple English goods of the same value, which must, presumably, have been paid for in English coin.[3] What more likely than that this rule should induce merchants to conduct their transactions by means of letters of credit, easily transportable?[4] The elaborate Money Statute of 1477[5] expressly provides that the foreign merchant, before his departure, shall prove his compliance with the policy of Richard's statute, by a 'writing' to the merchants to whom he sold his goods, or by other sufficient proof. An Act of 1487,[6] aimed at eradicating a species of 'new Chevisaunce' called 'dry exchange,' speaks of 'buying any obligation or bill'; and Malynes, who wrote in 1622,[7] expressly says, referring to this statute, that this process of 'dry exchange' was carried on by means of bills of exchange. It is obvious that such documents were familiar to Malynes, who, in his *Lex Mercatoria,* incorporated a treatise on them by John Marius, a notary public.

Patents

A more notorious, and equally valuable, form of personal property appeared also as a lawful institution at the end of the period we are now discussing; but it had an earlier, and somewhat stormy career, as a chartered libertine. The powers claimed for the prerogative in the Middle Ages in the matter of the regulation of trade and commerce were extensive and vague; and, with the expansion of trade which took place in the early sixteenth century, it was not unnatural that the Crown, always suspicious of international

[1] *E.g.* 27 Edw. III, st. II (1353) c. 14.

[2] 3 Ric. II, c. 3 (2).

[3] 14 Ric. II, c. 2. A note (or 'estreat') of these bonds had to be sent to the Exchequer every fifteen days (11 Hen. IV (1409) c. 8).

[4] The statute of 1353 provides that the searchers at the ports shall give the foreign merchant a 'writing' showing the amount of foreign money brought into the realm by him.

[5] 17 Edw. IV, c. 1.

[6] 3 Hen. VII, c. 6.

[7] *Lex Mercatoria,* Part III, ch. 1 (p. 261).

dealings which it did not itself supervise, should attempt to regulate foreign trade by granting the monopoly of dealing with various countries to different companies of merchants. So long as any respectable English merchant who wished to join the company could do so, there was nothing opposed to the spirit of the age in such an arrangement. But when it came to granting **monopolies** of articles like soap, playing cards, silver lace, and so forth, not to adventurous companies, but to Court favourites, who simply made use of their privileges to sweat the public, popular feeling began to rise. As is well known, the question of the legality of Letters Patent conferring such monopolies slumbered uneasily, or awoke but fitfully, during the reign of Elizabeth; but with the advent of her successor, it arose to vigorous life. At length, by the Statute of Monopolies of 1623,[1] it was enacted that all monopolies, however granted, should be absolutely void; with the exception of Letters Patent and grants of privileges for terms not exceeding fourteen years, for the working or making of new manufactures within the realm, in favour of the true and first inventors thereof. This exception is still the basis of our Patent Law; though, as we shall see, in considering the next period, the simple provision of 1623 has expanded into a great Patent Code.

Copyright

The last form of personal property to which reference need be made under this period is **copyright**. No formal recognition of an author's right to secure the profits of his publications appears to have been accorded. But it seems to have been the practice to regard a license to publish as conferring something in the nature of exclusive rights; and there are traces of such rights having been made the subject of Letters Patent.[2] As is well known, it was the policy of the State, from the time of the introduction of printing, to keep a tight hand on the operations of the press. Again, the action of the State must not be hastily condemned. The appearance of the printing-press speedily revolutionized politics, and at first rendered the task of government enormously difficult. It was against the abuses of the licensing system, especially in the later days of the Star Chamber, more than against the system itself, that popular feeling rose. Still, the appearance of Milton's

[1] 21 Jac. I, c. 3.

[2] Licensing Act of 1662 (13 Car. II, c. 33, s. 6).

splendid *Areopagitica: or Speech for the Liberty of Unlicensed Printing,* in the year 1644, showed which way the tide was turning; and, as we shall see, in discussing the next period, the licensing system did not, in England, survive the seventeenth century. Unfortunately, when it fell, it left the hapless author unprotected; and it was not until 1709[1] that the first statutory recognition of copyright was granted.

Wills and Intestacies

It now remains only to point out, that succession to personal property after the death of its owner received some further treatment in this period on the lines described in an earlier chapter. The Statute of Westminster the Second,[2] as we have seen, clearly recognizes the responsibility of the executor for the deceased's debts, to the amount of his personalty, and extends it to the 'Ordinary' of the Church on intestacy. It likewise gives the executor a remedy by Writ of Account against the deceased's debtors. A statute of 1330 set aside the maxim: *actio poenalis moritur cum personâ,* to the extent of allowing executors to sue for trespasses *de bonis asportatis* committed against their testator during his lifetime;[3] and another, of 1352,[4] puts the executor's executor in the same position, both as regards rights and liabilities, as the original executor. This last Act, also, tells us incidentally, that statutes merchant and recognizances were enforceable by executors. Seven years later, the 'Ordinary' is compelled to appoint, as 'administrator' of the intestate's goods, 'the next and most lawful friends of the deceased,'[5] who are to have the rights and liabilities of executors in respect of the estate. The fees demanded by the ecclesiastical courts for probates and grants of administration were severely regulated by statute at the Reformation;[6] but, as we have said, the jurisdiction in testamentary matters was not taken away from them, and even survived the Civil War and the Commonwealth. Nevertheless, the latter period was disastrous to it; for, during the Interregnum, the King's courts began to entertain suits for the payment of legacies;[7] and the King's courts rarely gave up any jurisdiction which they had once acquired. The most startling development of the law of succession to personalty in this period is, however,

[1] 8 Anne, c. 19.
[2] 13 Edw. I (1285) cc. 19, 23.
[3] 4 Edw. III, c. 7.
[4] 25 Edw. III, st. V, c. 5.
[5] *I.e.* his nearest relatives.
[6] 21 Hen. VIII (1529) c. 5.
[7] *Nicholson v. Sharman* (1661) 1 Sid., at p. 46.

the claim of the executor to keep for his own benefit any property not disposed of by the will; unless the testator had, directly or by implication, excluded him. How this remarkable doctrine came to be accepted, it is not easy to discover.[1] It is true, that the executor had always distributed the 'dead's part,' and that the rule of 'legitim'[2] seems to have largely disappeared in the sixteenth and seventeenth centuries, leaving scope for the familiar residuary bequest. But the rules of intestate succession were settled by the Statutes of Distribution in 1670 and 1685;[3] and yet the rule in favour of executors, despite judicial criticism,[4] lingered until 1830, when it was partially, but not entirely, altered by the Executors Act.[5] Even now it prevails against the claim of the Crown;[6] and this is the more remarkable, that the Crown has long claimed, as *bona vacantia*, personal property in the hands of a trustee, where the trusts have failed and there are no representatives of the settlor. In the case of land, the theory of tenure gave the beneficial interest, in similar circumstances, to the trustee;[7] but even this rule has lately been altered by statute.[8]

[1] See on this point the essay of Caillemer, previously referred to (Select Essays in Anglo-American Legal History, III, 746–769).

[2] *Ante*, pp. 60, 61. [3] 22 & 23 Car. II, c. 10; 1 Jac. II, c. 17, ss. 6, 7.

[4] *A. G. v. Hooker* (1725) 2 P. Wms. 338 (King, C.).

[5] 11 Geo. IV & 1 Will. IV, c. 40.

[6] *Re Bacon's Will* (1881) 31 Ch. D. 460.

[7] *Burgess v. Wheate* (1759) 1 Ed. 177.

[8] Intestates Estates Act, 1884, s. 4.

CHAPTER X

CONTRACT AND TORT

IT has previously been pointed out in this book, in more than one passage, that one of the most striking lessons to be learned from a study of legal history is, that ideas which to us now seem absolutely distinct, and even opposed, are found originally to have been blended in a common stock, from which they have subsequently split off by a process of specialization. No better example of this truth could be found than in the history of Contract and Tort. To us, these two institutions seem wholly distinct; separate books are written about them, and Acts of Parliament treat them as mutually exclusive. We regard an action of Contract as an action to prevent or compensate for a breach of a promise; an action of Tort as an action to punish or compensate for a wrong, such as assault or defamation, which has not any necessary connection with a promise. An ordinary defence to an action of Contract is, in effect: 'I did not promise.' What should we think if a defendant in an action for libel defended himself on the ground that he had not promised not to libel the plaintiff? It is true that, occasionally, a case arises which causes some difficulty;[1] and it would hardly be possible to throw a more effective apple of discord into a company of lawyers, than by starting a discussion on the question whether Detinue was an action of Contract or of Tort. But we are apt to regard these difficulties as inseparable from any legal classification; whereas a little knowledge of history would enable us to trace them to their true source. As a matter of historical fact, the simple contract and the ordinary tort spring from the same stock; and the wonder would be if they did not, in some points, betray signs of their common origin.

[1] *E.g. Bryant v. Herbert* (1878) 3 C.P.D. 389; *Du Pasquier v. Cadbury* [1903] 1 K.B. 104.

We have seen that, in the previous period, the only remedy of a general nature for anything like what we understand by a contract, was the Action of Debt.[1] This action was, at first, in truth an action to recover a specific object; usually a moveable, because actions to recover land were conducted by other and more elaborate machinery. By Bracton's time, as we have seen, it had specialized into two forms, the Writ of Debt, strictly, in which a fixed sum of money was sought to be recovered, and the Writ of Detinue, in which a specific chattel was the object pursued.

Debt

In the period we are now discussing, the Writ of Debt speedily lost its original character as an action to recover money lent or bailed, and was applicable to any case in which the plaintiff sought to recover a fixed sum of money, due to him on grounds which the law considered to be adequate. Thus, for example, if a tenant failed to pay his rent (though he had not expressly covenanted to do so),[2] if a sheriff,[3] or the Warden of the Fleet,[4] allowed a debtor to escape, if a sum was found due from a debtor on account stated,[5] all these were liable to an Action of Debt. In some cases, *e.g.* the case of rent, there had, no doubt, been something very like a contract; where the Action of Debt was brought on a bond, we should consider it strictly contractual. Still, the old rule of Glanville, that in an Action for Debt the King's Courts would not enforce a mere 'private agreement,' held good throughout the whole history of the Action of Debt; and so that action can only be held to have contributed in a very minor degree to the development of the Law of Contract. Moreover, it rapidly became unpopular in this period, owing to the fact that unless the plaintiff could show exceptionally good proof of his claim, *e.g.* a sealed charter, the defendant could get off by 'waging his law.' It was, therefore, in spite of the provisions of the Statute of Westminster the Second,[6] very unsuitable for use against executors; and in fact, it could not be brought against them in cases in which their testator, had he lived, would have been entitled to 'wage his law.'

[1] *Ante* pp. 56–58.

[2] 8 Anne (1709) c. 14, s. 4. (This statute merely extended the liability to tenant for life. The tenant for years was liable at common law.)

[3] Statute of Westminster II (13 Edw. I, st. I (1285) c. 11).

[4] 1 Ric. II (1377) c. 12. (The sheriff or warden was liable for the sum owed by the debtor.)

[5] 5 Hen. IV (1403) c. 8.

[6] *Ante*, p. 64.

The Action of Detinue, as we have said,[1] lay where a specific chattel belonging to the plaintiff was in the hands of the defendant, who refused to give it up. But it behoved the plaintiff to be cautious in stating in what manner he alleged the chattel to have come into the defendant's hands. He had to be careful to avoid 'words of felony,' *i.e.* anything that might sound like a charge of theft or robbery; for, if he did not, he laid himself open to being met by the argument that his proper procedure was an 'appeal of larceny,' upon which he was obliged to offer battle. So it appears to have been the practice in the early Writs of Detinue for the plaintiff to allege (what was, no doubt, in many cases, the strict truth), that he had himself 'bailed' or delivered the chattel to the defendant in the first instance. Thus the form of action known as 'Detinue *sur bailment*' became the orthodox form; and thus Detinue appeared to be an action founded on contract.[2] For a voluntary delivery or bailment of a chattel, accepted by the defendant, is something very like an agreement, from which a promise to return the chattel can well be implied. Nevertheless, the promise is only implied; and it is very doubtful whether, to the mind of Glanville or Bracton, Detinue was really regarded as a contractual action. In the middle of the fourteenth century,[3] the plaintiff was allowed to substitute for the allegation of bailment the wider allegation that the goods 'came to the hands' (*devenerunt ad manus*) of the defendant, without saying how; and thus the Action of Detinue lost whatever contractual character it may once have had. How it acquired its tortious character, we shall see later on. At any rate, there was no possibility of a general theory of contract developing out of the Action of Detinue.

Detinue

A third possible source of contract at the beginning of the period was the Action of Covenant, about which, unfortunately, we know very little. We have seen[4] that Glanville treats a deed or charter as one of the *causae* or grounds of Debt; and it is very significant that Debt and

Covenant

[1] *Ante*, p. 57.

[2] This is the view taken by the late Professor Ames, whose brilliant studies of the history of Contract and Tort are reprinted in Select Essays in Anglo-American Legal History Vol. III, pp. 259–319, 417–445. But the difficulties of trying to build a theory of contract on bailment are well illustrated by the famous case of *Coggs v. Bernard* (1703) 2 Ld. Raym. 909.

[3] *Wagworth v. Halyday*, Y.B. 29 Edw. III (1355), fo. 38b.

[4] *Ante*, p. 66.

not Covenant remained the proper form of action on a common money bond until quite late in this period.[1] This curious fact may be accounted for by assuming (as we are warranted in doing) that in early times the sealed bond was looked upon rather as the symbol than as the ground of the debtor's liability; in other words, that the debtor was regarded as the object pledged, or bound,[2] the document being given as a security for his return to captivity if he failed to pay the debt. Nevertheless, the language of Glanville, that, if the defendant acknowledges the genuineness of the charter, he is bound to warrant its terms, and to observe the compact expressed in it, points to the fact that, even in the twelfth century, the sealed charter was assuming a wider form than the mere acknowledgment of a debt. Indeed, we know independently that at least two very important transactions, viz. a lease for years and an agreement to levy a Fine, were being made by deed before the end of the thirteenth century. But both these were rather in the nature of 'covenants real' than personal contracts; and the remedy for breach of them seems to have been more in the nature of specific performance than a money compensation.[3]

Nevertheless, it is clear that, before the end of the fourteenth century, the Writ of Covenant enabled an action to be brought for 'unliquidated damages' on breach of any of the terms of a sealed instrument. And this rule has prevailed to the present day; giving us our 'specialty' or 'formal' contract, which includes any lawful promise made under seal.

By far the greater number of contracts entered into in ordinary life are, however, not embodied in sealed documents.

Simple Contracts

They are either contained in ordinary correspondence or mere written memoranda, or they are made solely by word of mouth or conduct. These are all now, by English Law, termed 'simple' or 'parol' contracts; and our problem is, to discover how they obtained a foothold in the common law, despite the attitude of the King's Courts so clearly stated by Glanville. To do this, we must turn aside entirely from the realm of Debt and Covenant, and enter what seems, at first sight, a very unlikely quarter.

[1] Thus in 1584 (*Anon.* 3 Leon. 119) it was doubted if covenant lay on a specialty promise to pay a fixed sum.

[2] The word points to the original physical bondage of the debtor. Early legal history is full of such cases.

[3] 6 Ed. I (1278) c. 11 (1), 'recover by Writ of Covenant.'

Apparently, the inventiveness of the Chancellor and judges in the matter of making new writs had come to an end in the latter half of the thirteenth century. At any rate, there were complaints in Parliament of suitors being turned away empty-handed because there was no writ to suit their cases. Accordingly, the great Statute of Westminster the Second [1] sought to provide a remedy by enacting, that 'whensoever from henceforth it shall fortune in the Chancery, that in one case a writ is found, and in like case falling under like law, and requiring like remedy, is found none, the Clerks of the Chancery shall agree in making a writ' (and, if they don't there is to be an appeal to Parliament).

Case

This enactment, though it appears only at the end of a chapter on special cases, seems to have been taken as a general authority for the expansion of legal remedies; and under it were formed many new writs on the analogy of the older writs found in the Register. These new writs were all grouped together under the name of '**Case**'; apparently from the words used in the Statute of Westminster the Second — *in consimili casu.* Another feature common to them all was, that each was framed on the model of a specific older writ; enlarging its scope by omitting one or more of the technical requirements of the older document.

Trespass on the Case

One of the first, if not the very first model made use of for this purpose was the famous Writ of Trespass, which, as we have seen,[2] had been introduced into the Register at the end of the preceding period, and which speedily became very popular. The gist of the Writ of Trespass was an allegation that the defendant had, 'with force and arms,' (*vi et armis*) and 'against the peace of our Lord the King' (*contra pacem domini regis*) interfered with the plaintiff's possession of his body, land, or goods. No doubt at first the 'force and arms' were taken seriously; but the writ speedily came to cover every interference with possession, however trifling and accidental. Nevertheless, the Courts held fast to the technical point, that, to amount to a trespass, there must have been interference with the plaintiff's possession by some voluntary act of the defendant, his servants, or his cattle.

It speedily came to be perceived, however, that there were many circumstances in which the plaintiff had suffered serious

[1] 13 Edw. I, st. I (1275) c. 24 (2).

[2] *Ante*, pp. 52–54.

loss by the defendant's action, though the latter had not, technically, been guilty of trespass. Thus, in the middle of the fourteenth century, a Humber ferryman so overloaded his boat, that the plaintiff's horse, which was on board, was drowned.[1] There was no trespass; because the plaintiff had voluntarily parted with the possession of his horse when he put him on the defendant's boat. Similarly, when a smith lamed a horse entrusted to him to be shod,[2] or a leech so negligently did his cure, that the horse died,[3] or a surgeon mismanaged the plaintiff's hand which he undertook to cure.[4] In all these cases, though there was no trespass, there was actual **malfeasance** or wrongdoing in respect of a physical object by the defendant, from which the plaintiff suffered loss; and so the analogous action of 'Case,' or 'Trespass on the Case,' [5] was allowed. For some time, the action was restricted to cases in which the defendant pursued a 'common calling' — *i.e.* that of a smith, or ferryman, or surgeon, in which he was bound to attend all comers. But, by the middle of the fifteenth century, for the general 'holding out' implied in the **assumption** of a common calling, the alternative of a 'special assumption,' or undertaking, might be pleaded. One or the other was necessary.[6] And so we find the allegations: *assumpsit super se, emprist sur lui, manucepit,* and other forms, appearing in the Writs of Case. Now these allegations do not, perhaps, necessarily imply promises; but they are very near it. Perhaps if we say that a man 'takes upon himself' to do a thing, we do not necessarily allege that he promises to do it. But what if we say 'he undertakes' to do it? The difference is not great. Still, in Trespass on the Case, the stress was laid on the physical damage, rather than on the breach of undertaking.

Half a century after the full recognition of the Trespass class of cases, we find another model followed, viz. the Writ of Deceit. The old Writ of Deceit was very technical; it could, practically, only be used where the defendant had been guilty of trickery in legal proceedings in the

Deceit on the Case

[1] Y.B. 22 Ass. (1348) 94, pl. 41.
[2] Y.B. 46 Edw. III (1372) fo. 19, pl. 19.
[3] Y.B. 43 Edw. III (1369) fo. 33, pl.38.
[4] Y.B. 48 Edw. III (1374) fo. 6, pl. 11.
[5] The proper title is: 'Action on the Case in the Nature of Trespass.' But the form in the text is the more usual.
[6] Y.B. 19 Hen. VI (1441) fo. 49, pl. 5, *per* Paston, J.

King's Courts.[1] But, before the end of the first half of the fifteenth century, we get two cases, at least, in which the plaintiff was allowed to recover, because, although there had been no physical damage to the plaintiff or his goods, he had suffered loss by the deliberate fraud of the defendant in breaking his undertaking. In *Somerton's Case*, three times reported,[2] and so, presumably, regarded as of great interest, the defendant had been employed by the plaintiff to buy a manor, and had persuaded some one else to buy it over the plaintiff's head. In a slightly later case,[3] the defendant had agreed to sell the plaintiff a manor, and subsequently enfeoffed a third person. In each case the plaintiff suffered damage, though not of a physical kind. The second case is called a 'Bill of Deceit'; but, as it was brought in the King's Bench, this probably only meant that the fiction of the marshal's custody was employed.[4] Any way, these two cases bring us a step nearer to a law of contract. We may call them the Deceit or **misfeasance** cases.

Lastly, we come to the **non-feasance** group. Here the sole ground of alleged liability is the failure to fulfil a promise; and, when this group is established, we have clearly a law of simple contract. Unfortunately, at this stage, another and more obscure question arises.

Non-feasance

So early as the year 1424, we find a case which looks very much like one of mere non-feasance. It was an action against a mill-maker for failing to build a mill according to his promise.[5] The action seems to have been allowed, with some hesitation. Professor Ames strongly urges that this and a slightly later case to the same effect [6] were premature freaks, due to the idiosyncrasy of a particular judge, and that it is not till the very end of the sixteenth century, that we get a definite legal recognition of the truth that a man may be just as much harmed by his neighbour's mere non-fulfilment of his promise, as by his active fraud or deceit.[7] But by this time it had been perceived, that to allow an action to be brought for the non-fulfilment of any promise would be to open the door too wide; and accordingly we

[1] Fitzherbert, *Natura Brevium*, 95 E.
[2] Y.B. 11 Hen. VI (1433) fo. 18, pl. 10; fo. 24, pl. 1; fo. 55, pl. 26.
[3] Y.B. 20 Hen. VI (1442) fo. 34, pl. 4. [4] *Post*, p. 171.
[5] Y.B. 3 Hen. VI (1424) fo. 36, pl. 33.
[6] Y.B. 14 Hen. VI (1435) fo. 18, pl. 58.
[7] Select Essays in Anglo-American Legal History, III, 270.

find, that only those promises were actionable which had been given in return for some recompense received by the promisor, or some detriment suffered by the promisee.

This is the famous doctrine of '**consideration**,' without which no simple contract is valid. How it exactly arose, we do not know. The writer suggests that it is a compound doctrine, of which the positive side (recompense or benefit to the promisor) is a reflection from the original character of the older action of Debt, while the negative side (detriment to the promisee) is merely a slight ante-dating of the damage which was necessary to support an action of 'Case.' The action of Debt, as we have seen, was, originally, an action to recover something of the plaintiff's which had been bailed to the defendant (*quid pro quo*). Strictly speaking, the damage to the plaintiff should have been that which he suffered by breach of the defendant's promise; but it is not difficult to see how this requirement could be changed into damage suffered in exchange for the promise. Whatever be the explanation, the doctrine itself was clearly known by the beginning of the sixteenth century; for it was made the basis of an elaborate discussion in the *Dialogues between a Doctor of Divinity and a Student of the Laws of England,* published in 1523, and attributed to St. Germain. The parties are debating the respective merits of the Canon and English Laws; and they come into sharp conflict over the theory of the simple contract. The Doctor wishes to make the enforceability of a contract depend on the occasion on which it was made, and the intention of the promisor.[1] This is the old doctrine of *causae,* with a new touch of casuistry added. The Student maintains the doctrine of English Law; though, oddly enough, he does not, in that place, employ the word 'consideration.' *Ex nudo pacto non oritur actio,* he alleges, with a triumphant quotation from the Institutes; but then he goes on to explain, that a 'nude contract' is one made without any 'recompence' appointed for it — an explanation which would have sounded strange to a Roman lawyer. It is the Doctor who uses the word 'consideration' in the chapter; and, with him, it obviously means merely 'motive' or 'object,' in which sense it is also adopted by the Student in another passage,[2] when he says that the 'consideration' of the Statute of Fines

Consideration

[1] *Dialogues,* II, cap. 25.

[2] *Dialogues,* I, cap. 26.

was to ensure the certainty of titles. But the word had become appropriate to the new doctrine by the middle of the sixteenth century, and appears in the Reports shortly afterwards.[1] By that time, it was admitted that the consideration to support a simple promise might itself be a promise;[2] and so the purely executory contract became a recognized institution. After that, it was not difficult to clear away the surviving vestiges of its origin, and allow it to appear as a substantive and distinct institution. In 1520,[3] the Court had allowed **Assumpsit** to be brought against executors, in spite of the fact that it was then, in form, clearly an action of Tort; but this decision had been scoffed at by Fitzherbert.[4] In 1557,[5] however, and again in 1611,[6] the Court allowed Assumpsit against executors, and thus removed a substantial grievance; for, as has been pointed out, Debt could not be maintained against them where the deceased could have 'waged his law.' Finally, it was resolved, in *Slade's Case*,[7] that 'every contract executory imports in itself an assumpsit'; and thus the necessity of suing in Debt,[8] which let in the 'wager of law,' was abolished, practically in all cases. This case gave rise to the well-known sub-division of contractual actions into *indebitatus assumpsit* (where the defendant was really liable apart from express promise, *e.g.* for rent), and *special assumpsit*, where the promise was the true cause of action. Thus freed entirely from its early restrictions, the Action of Assumpsit took its place in the legal armoury as the typical action of contract; though, as we have seen, it was, historically, an action founded on a tort. Thus it became possible, also, to classify personal actions into actions of Contract and actions of Tort.

It must not be supposed, however, that the Action of Case had exhausted its possibilities when it had given birth to Assumpsit; for, though, for a long time, the action founded on Deceit

[1] *Jocelyn v. Skelton* (1558) Benloe, 57; *Gill v. Harewood* (1587) 1 Leon. 61.

[2] *Peske v. Redman* (1555) Dyer, 113. The point was discussed in *Wichals v. Johns* (1599) Cro. Eliz. 703.

[3] *Cleymond v. Vincent*, Y.B. 12 Hen. VIII, fo. 11, pl. 3.

[4] Y.B. 27 Hen. VIII (1535) fo. 23, pl. 21.

[5] *Norwood v. Read*, Plowd. 180.

[6] *Pinchon's Case*, 9 Rep. 86b.

[7] (1603) 4 Rep. 92b.

[8] This necessity was not merely due to the absence of an express promise, but also to the old theory that a man who had a 'higher' remedy, might not resort to a lower.

lingered on only as a special and peculiar remedy for breach of warranty,[1] we soon find a new and highly popular form of Case in the variety known as **trover.**

As we have seen, the Action of Detinue had its drawbacks; for, though it was no longer restricted to the case of the bailee, it was obviously unsuitable when the defendant, though willing to give up the chattel, had wilfully or carelessly damaged it, or where he had parted with the possession of it. True, Trespass might have come in here, if the original taking had been unlawful; but, if the plaintiff had, in fact, parted voluntarily, or, perhaps, unconsciously, with his chattel, Trespass, which implies at least some degree of violence, was unsuitable. Moreover, Trespass itself was risky; for the unsuccessful party was, at least in theory, liable to pay a fine to the King. Again, Detinue suffered from the drawback of being open to the antiquated 'wager of law.'

Trover

Accordingly, we are not surprised to find that, before the end of the fifteenth century,[2] the Court considered that the Action of Case might well be held to cover a bailee who had wilfully misused the chattel bailed to him; and that, a few years later,[3] the new action was stretched to cover a case in which he had sold it. The former case was very like Trespass; the latter, luckily for the defendant, just escaped being larceny. By Coke's time,[4] the pleaders had agreed upon a form which alleged that the plaintiff 'casually lost the chattel from his hands and possession, and afterwards . . . it came to the hands and possession of the defendant by finding (*trover*), who nevertheless put and converted it to his own use.' This form anticipated and guarded against two objections by the defendant, viz. (i) 'I did not *take* it' (Trespass), and (ii) 'I have not *got* it' (Detinue). But, later on, these fine distinctions were ignored; and, in 1627, Trover was allowed as a substitute for Trespass,[5] where the defendant took the chattel in the presence of the plaintiff, and, in 1674, for Detinue,[6] where there was a mere demand and refusal. Before this time, moreover, Detinue had been held to cover cases in

[1] *Stuart v. Wilkins* (1778) 1 Doug. 18.
[2] Y.B. 18 Edw. IV (1479) fo. 23, pl. 5.
[3] (1510) Keil. 160, pl. 2.
[4] *Entries*, 37d, 40c, 41d, &c.
[5] *Kynaston v. Moore*, Cro. Car. 89.
[6] *Sykes v. Walls*, 3 Keb. 382 (3).

which there had been no bailment. This was regarded as a novelty in 1455;[1] but by 1510 Detinue *sur trover* had taken its place as common form alongside Detinue *sur bailment*.[2] Thus the three forms of action largely overlapped, as alternative actions of Tort; though there were still cases which could only be brought under one of them. Their later history may be quickly disposed of. In 1833,[3] the abolition of 'wager of law' caused a revival of Detinue, which was fostered by a judicious alternation of the rules of pleading in the action. In 1852, the Common Law Procedure Act[4] rendered allegations of bailment and finding unnecessary, whilst they had long been 'untraversable — *i.e.* undeniable; and thus the essence of the action of Trover, viz. the conversion to the use of the defendant, became more clear, and the name **conversion** is now more common than Trover, whilst the action, in spite of some difficulties, tends more and more to be regarded as one of Tort. Of course, the necessity for choosing a special form of action has long since disappeared.

Independently of the desire to protect chattels, many new forms of Tort made their appearance during this period, and have survived to the present day. Various causes are to be assigned for their introduction, among which the most prominent are: (i) the necessity for abolishing some of the technical restrictions of the older writs; (ii) the absorption of other jurisdictions by the King's Courts; and (iii) the passing of legislation intended to meet the exigencies of special occasions. Of these in their order.

Malicious Prosecution

The new forms of Tort which came into existence as varieties of the action of Case, because the older writs dealing with similar offences were unavailable, were, notably, Malicious Prosecution and Nuisance. Malicious Prosecution was an adaptation of the old Writ of Conspiracy, which was itself based on a statute and ordinance of the years 1300 and 1305 respectively.[5] These enactments, however, only applied to cases where 'two, three, or more persons of malice and covin do conspire and devise to indict any person falsely, and afterwards he who is so indicted is acquitted.' The old writ was, consequently, confined to such cases; and subsequent judicial rulings

[1] Y.B. 33 Hen. VI, fo. 26, pl. 12.
[2] *Liber Intrationum* (ed. 1546) fo. lxxxiv (B).
[3] Civil Procedure Act, 1833, s. 13.
[4] S. 49.
[5] 28 Edw. I, st. III, c. 10; 33 Edw. I, st. II.

seem to have restricted it still further, to cases of false indictments for treason or felony, whereby the accused's life was endangered.[1] Obviously, there were many other cases in which oppression could be used, not merely by a group of persons acting together, but even by a single unscrupulous person, through the medium of baseless prosecutions. And so, after the Church Courts had tried to acquire jurisdiction in such cases through proceedings for defamation,[2] we find in the King's Courts, by the end of the fifteenth century,[3] an action of Case in the Nature of Conspiracy, which applied against single individuals and on false indictments for mere misdemeanours. This new form of action gradually acquired the name of Malicious Prosecution,[4] and was further extended to cover the malicious procuring of search warrants against the plaintiff.[5] It should be observed, however, that, unlike strict Conspiracy, the gist of the action of Malicious Prosecution is damage to the plaintiff, not the mere conspiring of the defendants; though, if a false and malicious prosecution is brought, damage to the party prosecuted will be presumed. Apparently, though the closely related Writ of Champerty (against persons buying shares in lawsuits with a view of aiding in carrying them on) retained the form given to it by statute,[6] the Action of Maintenance (against persons taking part in lawsuits in which they had no interest) was also a typical example of Case; being an enlargement of the narrower statutory remedy against royal officials.[7]

Nuisance

Equally clear is the widely popular Action of Nuisance, devised to protect immovable rights of all kinds from physical disturbance. There was an old Assise of Nuisance; but this, as a real action, could only be used by and against freeholders, while the action of Case framed upon the analogy of it was open to all persons having an interest in posses-

[1] *Skinner v. Gunton* (1669) 1 Wms. Saund. 228.

[2] 1 Edw. III (1327) c. 11.

[3] Y.B. 11 Hen. VII (1496) fo. 25 pl. 7.

[4] The transition appears clearly in the leading case of *Savile v. Roberts* (1698) 1 Salk. 13.

[5] *Windham v. Clere* (1589) Cro. Eliz. 130.

[6] 33 Edw. I (1305) st. III, cap. 2. Champerty had been made a criminal offence by 3 Edw. I (1275), c. 25; 13 Edw. I, st. I (1285) c. 49; 28 Edw. I, st. III (1300) c. 11.

[7] 33 Edw. I (1305), cc. 28, 33. (The latter statute also made Maintenance a criminal offence.) The form of the writ is not, apparently, given in Fitzherbert's *Natura Brevium*.

sion, against all persons causing a physical injury to their land. A curious and not altogether commendable survival of the right of self-help marks the transition. Under the old Assise of Nuisance, and the still older Writ of *Quod Permittat,* the successful plaintiff was entitled to have the nuisance 'abated,' or taken away by the sheriff and the power of the county.[1] The judgment in the action of Case in the Nature of Nuisance was merely for damages; but the complainant was, apparently, permitted to abate the nuisance himself, and the right survives to the present day, though the exercise of it has been largely superseded by the issue of mandatory injunctions.[2]

The second group of new torts produced in this period was that which sprang from the absorption by the King's Courts of other jurisdictions. Of this group by far the best example is Defamation.

Defamation

As is well known, Defamation is of two kinds, viz. libel (where the defamatory publication is printed or written, or is contained in pictures or other permanent record), and slander, where the defamation is by spoken words only. There are many legal differences between the two. For instance, libel may be punished both criminally and civilly; and, even in the civil action, no special damage need be alleged, while, in the criminal proceedings, it need not always be proved that the defamatory matter was published to a third person. On the other hand, slander, except in certain cases, is not actionable unless special damage is shown; and it is never punishable criminally. Moreover, the period for bringing an action of Slander, where the words are 'actionable *per se,*' is limited to two years after the commission of the offence; while libel and ordinary slander can be pursued, even civilly, at any time within six years after the commission of the offence, or, in the case of slander, after the occurrence of the damage.

It is natural to surmise, that such differences of character proceed from differences of historical origin; and we find, as a fact, that slander and libel, as legal offences, have had different sources.

It seems clear that cases of oral slander were, in early times,

[1] Blackstone, *Comm.* III, 222. The forms of the Assise and the *Quod Permittat* are given in Fitzherbert, *op. cit.*, 183, K; 124 H. See remarks of Cresswell, J., in *Battishill v. Reed* (1856) 18 C.B., at p. 715.

[2] *Lane v. Capsey* [1891] 3 Ch. 411.

matter for the local moots. In the records of feudal courts recently published by the Selden Society,[1] we find precedents and forms in slander going back to the thirteenth century; and it can hardly be doubted that this branch of feudal jurisdiction resulted from the absorption of the popular authority of the leet court of the Hundred. In the cases given in the publications referred to, the charges of slander are frequently supplementary to charges of trespass and other offences against good order;[2] but there seems little reason to doubt that slander alone, at any rate if damage followed, was a generally recognized cause of action,[3] though, probably, in such matters, each court had its own rules.

Slander

With the decay of the feudal courts, previously referred to,[4] the jurisdiction in slander appears to have passed, not at first to the King's Courts, but to the Courts of the Church. A clause of the statute of 1315,[5] commonly known as *Articuli Cleri*, fully recognizes the authority of the bishop in defamation; and we find the King's Bench, in the year 1498,[6] declaring that actions for slander are matter for the spiritual tribunals. It is not until after the crucial years of the Reformation, viz. in the year 1536,[7] that we find an action of **slander** reported in the King's Courts;[8] and, as is well known, the jurisdiction of the ecclesiastical tribunals in defamation lingered on, though with diminished vigour, until 1855.[9] From the middle of the sixteenth century, however, it is clear that the action of Case for spoken words becomes increasingly frequent in the King's Courts; and, in the year 1647, a special text-book on the subject was published by John March, the reporter, and attained considerable favour. Before the end of our present period, the action of Slander had virtually assumed its modern form. In this example, as elsewhere, it may well be, that the action of Case was framed on an older model; and we think, naturally,

[1] *Select Pleas in Manorial . . . Courts* (Maitland) S.S. Vol. 2; *The Court Baron* (Maitland and Baildon), S.S. Vol. 4. The former volume is a record of actual cases; the latter a collection of court forms.

[2] *Court Baron*, 28, 30, &c. (The language is picturesque.)

[3] *Ibid.*, 40, 48; Manorial Courts, 19, 36, 82, &c.

[4] *Ante*, pp. 71–73.

[5] 9 Edw. II, st. I, c. 4.

[6] Y.B. 12 Hen. VII, fo. 22, pl. 2.

[7] *Anon.* Dyer, 19a.

[8] There was, however, a disposition earlier to check excess of ecclesiastical jurisdiction, *e.g.* where the Church courts entertained actions for defamation against preferrers of indictments (1 Edw. III (1327) c. 11).

[9] Ecclesiastical Courts Acts (18 &19 Vic. c. 41).

in this connection, of the statutory offence of *Scandalum Magnatum*, which appears in the Statute Book on several occasions, from 1275 to 1558.[1] But, if we look at these statutes, we shall find that they are of a purely criminal character; and it is not easy to see how any writ of Case could be framed upon them.

Very different was the history of libel. Probably, in the days before the invention of printing, there were not many opportunities of committing this offence; though there seems little reason to doubt that the ecclesiastical courts, even then, entertained suits for written defamation. But the appearance of the printing press, as has been pointed out in another connection, brought the subject into prominence; and the Court of **Star Chamber**, though it declined to trouble itself about slander,[2] soon became an active centre of criminal prosecutions for libel. Apparently, however, the jurisdiction of the Star Chamber did not exclude the more open jurisdiction of the King's Bench; for, in the well-known *Case of Scandalous Libels*,[3] which came before the former tribunal in the year 1605, it was resolved, that 'a libeller shall be punished either by indictment at the common law, or by bill, if he deny it, or *ore tenus* on his confession, in the Star Chamber.' The strongly criminal character of the proceedings in libel at that time is also emphasized by the ruling, that the truth of the libel is no justification for its issue; while a slightly later case in the Star Chamber[4] added the well-known distinction between criminal and civil libel, viz. that the former may be committed without publication to a third party.

Libel

It appears, however, that the Star Chamber itself, at any rate in its later years, adopted the practice of awarding damages to the party injured by a libel, as well as punishment for the criminal offence;[5] and this practice naturally led to the growth of the idea that **libel** might be treated also as a civil offence. References to a possible action of Case for libel appear in the

[1] 3 Edw. 1 (1275) c. 34; 2 Ric. II, st. I (1378) c. 5; 12 Ric. II (1388) c. 11; 1 & 2 Ph. & M. (1554) c. 3; 1 Eliz. (1558) c. 6.

[2] *Select Cases . . . in the Star Chamber* (SS. vol. 16) 28–45.

[3] 5 Rep. 124b.

[4] *Edwardes v. Wootton* (1607) reported in Hawarde's *Cases in the Star Chamber*, ed. by Baildon, and privately printed, 343–344.

[5] *Edwardes v. Wootton, ubi sup.;* and *Lake's Case* (1619), reported in *Calendar of State Papers* (Dom.) III, 19, 21.

Reports from the beginning of the seventeenth century;[1] and, on the abolition of the Court of Star Chamber by the Long Parliament in 1641, civil actions for libel begin, though far more slowly than might have been expected, to be reported.[2] A marked survival of the criminal origin of libel is to be found in the rule that, to succeed, even in a civil action, no actual damage need be proved; though the action is, historically, one of Case.

Statutory Torts

Finally, more than one new tort was created by express statute during the period at present under review. Of these, some were of little permanent importance; such as the offences created by the statute of 1400,[3] which gave a defendant wrongfully sued in the Admiralty Court an action against his adversary, and another of the year 1531,[4] which gave a similar remedy to a person aggrieved by the irregularity of an ecclesiastical official. But the offences created by the series of Labour statutes and ordinances[5] which followed on the occurrence of the Black Death and the Peasants' Revolt, have left a permanent mark on our law. It was part of the policy of that code to compel all persons under a certain rank to serve any one who was willing to employ them, at the statutory rate of wages; and severe penalties were imposed upon a servant who refused to serve or departed from his service. Naturally, the Courts regarded any attempt to seduce a servant from his employment as violating the spirit of the Acts; and, accordingly, the action of Case for the **seduction** or **harbouring** of a servant made its way into the books. The form of the writ is given by Fitzherbert,[6] who expressly bases it on the statute of 1349, and says that it lies against both enticer and servant. By a well-meaning, but rather clumsy analogy, this action was, later on, extended to cover the case of debauching a woman; but the many anomalies of that form of action show how ill-fitted is the machinery to achieve its object. The Statutes of Labourers, and their amendment in the reign of Elizabeth, ultimately gave birth to another important branch of the Law of Tort, viz. the actions for **procur-**

[1] *Barrow v. Lewellin* (1616) Hob. 62; *Lake v. Hatton* (1618) *ibid.*, 252; *Hicks' Case* (1619) *ibid.*, 215.

[2] One of the earliest is *Lake v. King* (1668) 1 Wms. Saund. 131, b, on Parliamentary privilege.

[3] 2 Hen. IV, c. 11.

[4] 23 Hen. VIII, c. 9, s. 3.

[5] 23 Edw. III (1349); 25 Edw. III, st. II (1351); 34 Edw. III (1360) cc. 9–11.

[6] *Natura Brevium*, 167–168.

ing **breach of contract**, and **civil conspiracy**. But this development belongs to a later period. It is not difficult to see how a social upheaval such as that of the late fourteenth century, which virtually abolished serfdom and profoundly affected the policy of the State, would naturally be reflected in a legal system which was, above all things, a mirror of the ideas of the ruling classes.

CHAPTER XI

CRIMINAL LAW AND PROCEDURE

THERE is not much to be said about the substantive Law of Crime in this period. The Law of Treason was codified in the year 1352 by the great Statute of Treasons,[1] which is still the foundation of the law on the subject; for, though a good many new treasons were introduced in the reign of Henry VIII, they were, together with most of the new felonies created by the Reformation statutes, swept away on the accession of his son.[2] The progress of the nation in wealth and refinement, however, naturally brought with it an increase in the number of crimes, as the old definition of offences became inadequate.

New Crimes

Among the new crimes may be mentioned that of maiming by cutting out the eyes or tongue, made a felony by a statute of 1403,[3] the unauthorized multiplication of gold and silver, by the same statute,[4] the recognition of embezzlement and obtaining goods by false pretences as but variations of the ancient crime of theft,[5] unnatural offences,[6] forgery,[7] and bigamy (in the modern sense).[8] Witchcraft with evil intent was made felony by statute in 1541;[9] and this statutory recognition of one of the very oldest of social offences looks somewhat reactionary. It may well be, however, that a regular prosecution before the King's judges rescued many a wretched outcast from the terrors of Lynch law.

The really important changes in criminal justice during this

[1] 25 Edw. III, st. V, c. 2.

[2] 1 Edw. VI (1547) c. 12, s. 2. (It must be admitted, however, that even this statute, in its later sections, introduced or continued one or two newfangled treasons, and was followed by the 23 Eliz. (1581) c. 1.)

[3] 5 Hen. IV, cc. 4, 5.

[4] *Ibid.*

[5] 21 Hen. VIII (1529) c. 7; 33 Hen. VIII (1541) c. 1. But obtaining goods by false pretences was not made felony; and embezzlement was not felonious unless it amounted to forty shillings.

[6] 25 Hen. VIII (1533) c. 3.

[7] 5 Eliz. (1562) c. 14, s. 8 (felony on second offence; but no corruption of blood).

[8] 1 Jac. I (1604) c. 11.

[9] 33 Hen. VIII, c. 8; succeeded by 5 Eliz. (1562) c. 16; 1 Jac. I (1603) c. 12.

period are, however, not the new crimes introduced by statute, but the alterations in classification and procedure brought about by the growth in importance of the jurisdiction of the Justices of the Peace, and the virtual abolitions of 'appeals' and clerical privileges.

Justices of the Peace

All students of English Constitutional History will be aware, that, after a tentative introduction as 'Conservators' at the end of the thirteenth century, the **Justices of the Peace** were definitely accepted and organized as part of the normal scheme of government in the fourteenth. The great statute of 1360[1] recognizes that dual character of the Justices' office with which we are now familiar—the magisterial and the judicial. The Justices are to have power to 'restrain' offenders, rioters, and other barrators; they are to make enquiries and arrest and imprison all suspicious persons; these, and the numerous duties imposed upon them by the Statutes of Labourers, previously alluded to, belong to them as magistrates or keepers of the peace. But, in their judicial capacity, they may 'hear and determine at the King's suit all manner of felonies and trespasses done in the same county.' A slightly earlier statute[2] had already established the General or **Quarter Sessions** of the Justices as a regular institution. A statute of 1483[3] conferred upon the Justices the important power of granting bail; and, though this power was somewhat restricted by a later statute,[4] yet the last Act, and its amendment[5] in the following year, by directing the Justices to examine the accused and transmit the information of his accusers to the next gaol-delivery, really regularized and strengthened the magisterial side of the Justices' powers. Two books dealing with the jurisdiction of the Justices of the Peace were published in this period, and point to a growth of interest in the subject. These are *L'Office et Aucthorite de Justices de Peace*, a posthumous work attributed to Sir Anthony Fitzherbert, and published with 'enlargements' by Crompton in 1583,[6] and *Eirenarcha, or the Office of the Justices of the Peace*, by William Lambard, published in 1619; and they are of great value for a study of criminal procedure during this period.

[1] 34 Edw. III, c. 1. [2] 25 Edw. III, st. II (1351) c. 7. [3] 1 Ric. III, c. 3.
[4] 1 & 2 Ph. & M. (1554) c. 13. [5] 2 & 3 Ph. & M. (1555) c. 10.
[6] There is said to be an earlier edition extant; but the author has not seen a copy of it.

Felonies and Trespasses

The first thing that we note from them is, that an important distinction is growing up between those crimes which are punishable with death, forfeiture of goods and lands, and corruption of blood, and a newer class of offences, mostly statutory, for which are prescribed merely fine and imprisonment. It is possible, by a reference to the valuable collection of indictments given as a supplement to Fitzherbert's book, to form a tolerably accurate idea of how this classification stood when his work was published, *i.e.* it must be remembered, not in the author's lifetime, but in 1583.[1] According to these forms, the classification of crimes in the last quarter of the sixteenth century would be somewhat as follows: —

Treasons and Felonies

Offence	Form
High Treason Rebellion Counterfeiting Letters Patent False Coining	'proditorie'
Clipping of gold coin	'felonice et proditorie'
Murder Homicide Arson Burglary Larceny above 12 pence Purse-cutting Rape Unnatural Crime Conniving at escape of felon Witchcraft resulting in death Maiming	'felonice'
Suicide	

Trespasses ('Misdemeanors')

- Breach of safe conduct
- Extortion
- Forcible entry
- Riot
- Assaults of various kinds
- Brawling in certain places
- Unlawful hunting
- Not following hue and cry
- Barratry (*i.e.* stirring up of strife)
- Nuisance
- Forgery (? 1st offence)
- Religious offences
- Scandalum Magnatum
- Shooting in prohibited places
- Stealing heiresses
- Perjury
- Rescue
- Maintenance
- Embracery
- Offences against Statute of Liveries
- Conspiracy

It will be seen at once, by a glance at the above lists, that there had been very little disposition to extend the class of capital offences, or felonies, since the days of the Assise of Northampton;[2] only three or four really new felonies had been added, for the statutory felony of cutting out eyes or tongue, for which the form of indictment is given, is really only a statutory definition of the old offence of 'mayhem,' (which was certainly

[1] This is quite clear from the dates used in the forms, *e.g.* 'anno regni Reg. Eliz. XV,' in the indictment for forcible entry (fo. 183b).

[2] *Ante*, p. 41.

felonious, because an 'appeal' lay for it), while suicide is, of course, only a variety of homicide. The minor offences, usually described in the statutes of the period as 'trespasses,' but just beginning to be known also as 'misdemeanors,'[1] were nearly all statutory; though, again, failure to follow the 'hue and cry' is a very ancient offence, which was merely defined and strengthened by statute.

Indictments

But another point should not escape attention. All the offences above enumerated were **indictable,** *i.e.* could only be prosecuted by accusation of the grand jury and conviction by the petty jury. During this period, the widest interpretation was evidently put upon the section of the statute of 1360,[2] which empowered the Justices of the Peace to hear and determine felonies; and, if we may judge by the attitude of Fitzherbert's editor, there was no limit to the exercise of this jurisdiction. Apparently the most serious felonies, even High Treason itself,[3] could be tried at Quarter Sessions, no less than before the itinerant Justices of the Benches. It must not be supposed, however, that the authority of the Justice of the Peace was confined to his work in sessions. At the close of the second Book of Lambard's *Eirenarcha* will be found a formidable list of things 'which one Justice of the Peace may doe out of the Sessions'; and from this we learn that, not merely what we should consider strictly magisterial acts, such as taking sureties for good behaviour, arresting and committing to prison, and searching for stolen goods, but acts of at least a quasi-judicial character, could be performed by the Justice in the privacy of his own hall. Thus, he could decide controversies between masters and servants,[4] hear and determine offences against the Ordinance relating to Tile-Making,[5] punish offences against the Assize of Fuel,[6] hear disputes under the Statute of Watermen,[7] examine for breaches of the statute against illegal shooting,[8] and try and punish hedge-breakers and robbers of orchards and

[1] There is a title of 'Misdemeanors' in the index to Fitzherbert's book, or, rather the edition of Crompton. But the reference to the text cannot be traced.

[2] 34 Edw. III, c. 1 (7).

[3] Lambard, Bk. II. cap. 7 (p. 226) seems to be a little doubtful on this point.

[4] Lambard, 190. (The authority was the Statute of Labourers.)

[5] *Ibid.*, 193–194. (The Ordinance is 17 Edw. IV. (1477) c. 4).

[6] *Ibid.*, 196–197 (7 Edw. VI (1553) c. 7).

[7] *Ibid.*, 203 (2 & 3 Ph. & M. (1555) c. 16).

[8] *Ibid.*, 296 (33 Hen. VIII. (1541) c. 6).

gardens.[1] Other powers were expressly conferred on two or more Justices, to be exercised out of sessions; notably under the Riot Act of 1411,[2] and the Elizabethan Poor Law.[3] It will be noted, that all these powers are statutory; because the Justices themselves are statutory officials, having no traditional or 'common law' powers. But it is hardly going too far to suggest that, in many cases, these statutory offences were really mere recognitions of ancient communal misdoings, which, in the earliest times, would have been the subject of fine or other punishment in the Hundred Court, and, somewhat later, in the Leet sessions of the High Constable. Just in the same way as the new Justices had succeeded to the position of the sheriff as apprehender and custodian of persons charged with serious offences, so they had succeeded to the jurisdiction of the decaying popular moots in the punishment of petty offences.

General and Special Sessions

Before leaving them, a passing reference must be made to a question which has later become of importance. Was the modern distinction between Quarter (or General) and **Petty Sessions** recognized in the period under review?

It is easy to make a mistake on this point. The modern lawyer thinks of Quarter Sessions as a Court by which more serious offences are tried, and as a court of appeal from Petty Sessions, which decides, in a 'summary' manner (*i.e.* without a jury) on accusations of petty offences. But we have seen that, in the sixteenth century, petty offences were, to a large extent, tried and disposed of 'out of sessions'; and this practice continued, to the great discredit of 'Justices' justice,' until the passing of Sir John Jervis' Acts, in the nineteenth century. So there appears to be no room for any sessions but Quarter or General Sessions.

Nevertheless, it is quite clear that Lambard, at least, if not Fitzherbert, was familiar with 'special' as distinct from 'general' sessions. He tells us,[4] that they are holden 'at other times, when it shall please the Justices themselves, . . . to appoint them,' and, usually, only for special business, such as the delivery of gaols in populous towns. It appears to have been a moot point between Fitzherbert and Lambard whether at 'special'

[1] Lambard, 303 (43 Eliz. (1601) c. 7).
[2] 13 Hen. IV, c. 7.
[3] 39 Eliz. (1597) c. 3, s. 3.
[4] Book IV, cap. 20.

session the Justices were at liberty to 'give in charge' all the statutes alluded to in their Commission; and the matter was complicated, for a particular reason. Just after Fitzherbert's death in 1538, a statute had been passed [1] for the institution of what were known as 'six weeks' sessions,' being, in fact, very much like the modern Petty Sessions, for the trial of minor offences in limited divisions of the county. But this statute, having been found oppressive, had been repealed in 1545; [2] and the business of 'the six weeks' sessions' had, thereupon, reverted to the Justices out of sessions. It was possible, therefore, to argue, that 'special sessions' were an attempt to revive an abolished institution, and therefore invalid.

Borough Justices

Finally, on the subject of Justices, it may be remarked, that, speaking generally, the Commission of the Peace, of which a specimen appears in Fitzherbert,[3] is a commission for the county; but that Commissions of the Peace for boroughs were, evidently, not unknown in the sixteenth century.[4] During the Commonwealth period, indeed, some of the boroughs developed an elected magistracy; but this practice, except as regards the Mayor (who was not, necessarily, a Justice of the Peace) was put down with a strong hand after the Restoration. Save for these exceptions, however, it has been statute law since 1535,[5] that the appointment of Justices of the Peace, even in counties palatine, is an exclusive right of the royal prerogative.

Next in importance, in changing the character of criminal procedure in this period, to the appearance of the peace jurisdiction, was the practical disappearance of the ancient procedure by way of appeal of felony. The nature of this procedure has been discussed at an earlier stage; and we have seen how, by means of the new jury-system, the King's judges had succeeded in restricting the use of it.[6]

Appeals

Nevertheless, it is clear that, at the commencement of our present period, the **appeal of felony** was regarded, if not with favour, at least with toleration, by the State. For the Statute of Gloucester [7] abolished the necessity for 'fresh suit' in conducting an appeal; and enacted

[1] 33 Hen. VIII (1541) c. 10.
[2] 37 Hen. VIII, c. 7.
[3] *Op. cit.* ff. 1, 2.
[4] *Ibid.* fo. 77a.
[5] 27 Hen. VIII, c. 24, s. 2.
[6] *Ante*, pp. 51, 52.
[7] 6 Edw. I (1278) c. 9.

that an appeal brought within a year and a day of the commission of the alleged offence should not abate for delay. But the tide quickly turned. The Statute of Westminster II[1] provides for the punishment of persons bringing unsuccessful appeals. The Statute of Appeals of 1300[2] allows any person appealed by an 'approver' (*i.e.* an accomplice turning King's evidence) to put himself upon his country, *i.e.* claim to be tried by a jury. A statute of 1399[3] forbade the hearing of appeals in Parliament — a rule which practically put a stop to appeals of treason. But the two steps which did most towards abolishing appeals were taken in the years 1486 and 1529 respectively, and were both of an indirect nature.

Nothing is more characteristic of the sacredness with which the ancient right of revenge was regarded, even so late as the fourteenth century, than the rule which grew up as the result of the clause of the Statute of Gloucester, above alluded to. We have seen[4] that, when indictments were first introduced by the Assises of the twelfth century, there was considerable doubt as to the respective priorities of the Crown and the persons entitled to prosecute an offence by way of appeal. The Statute of Gloucester, which, as just stated, gave the appellor a year and a day from the commission of the offence in which to bring his appeal, seems to have been taken as creating a 'close time' in the appellor's favour. During that time, accordingly, the public prosecution was suspended; with, probably, the result that, in many cases, the offender made good his escape entirely. This rule was, however, abolished by statute in 1486, so far as appeals of murder were concerned.[5]

Again, one of the drawbacks to a prosecution by indictment, from the injured person's point of view, was that, a convicted felon's chattels being forfeited to the Crown, no restitution of stolen property could be claimed by the prosecutor. Naturally in such circumstances, a prosecutor who was a powerful man of his hands preferred an appeal of larceny. But, in the year 1529,[6] it was enacted that whenever a person was convicted of felonious robbery or larceny, 'by reason of evidence given by the party so robbed, or owner,' the latter should be entitled to

[1] 13 Edw. I, st. I (1285) c. 12.
[2] 28 Edw. I.
[3] 1 Hen. IV, c. 14 (4).
[4] *Ante*, pp. 42, 43.
[5] 3 Hen. VII (1486) c. 1 (14).
[6] 21 Hen. VIII, c. 11.

a **writ of restitution** of his goods, 'in like manner as though any such felon or felons were attained at the suit of the party in appeal'; thus removing one of the chief inducements to bring an appeal of robbery or larceny. This provision had a substantial effect on the civil as well as the criminal law; for it overrode the rule that purchase in market overt by a *bonâ fide* purchaser conferred a valid title, and the exception prevails to the present day. It is not to be supposed, that even these changes in the law caused the immediate and total disappearance of the appeal of felony; and it is quite worthy of notice that the Appendix to Fitzherbert's work on the Justice of the Peace, published in 1583, contains a full set of forms of 'appeals,' and there are several references to 'appeals' in Dyer's reports. On the other hand, it is equally fair to point out, that the later Lambard, who wrote at the beginning of the seventeenth century, though he closely follows Fitzherbert's order, does not think it necessary to give forms of appeals. He gives, however, the form of the Writ of Restitution.[1] As is well known, the appeal of murder was revived, with dramatic effect, in *Thornton's Case,* in 1819; but the total abolition of appeals immediately followed.[2]

Finally, criminal procedure was rendered greatly more effective in this period by the severe restrictions placed upon the absurd privileges known as '**benefit of clergy**' and '**sanctuary**.' As we have said,[3] the former arose out of the struggle between State and Church in the twelfth century, on the subject of 'criminous clerks'—*i.e.* jurisdiction to try clerks accused of crime. The compromise arrived at in the Constitutions of Clarendon[4] was not kept, mainly owing to the indignation felt for the murder of Becket; and it was well understood, that the handing back of the accused to the clerical tribunal on the plea of privilege, was a mere formality precedent to his liberation. Moreover, in the twelfth century, the line between cleric and lay was very vaguely drawn, owing to the existence of a number of 'minor orders'; while the rough and ready test adopted by the royal judges enabled practically any man who could get up the small quantity of Latin necessary to enable him to repeat a well-known verse of

Benefit of Clergy

[1] *Processes, ad fin.*
[2] 59 Geo. III, c. 46, s. 1.
[3] *Ante*, p. 74.
[4] Cap. III S.C. 138.

Scripture, to escape a conviction by 'pleading his clergy.'[1] The only merit of the privilege was, that it served as a mitigation of a rather savage criminal law. But, even in this respect, it was defective; for no woman could be a cleric, and, therefore, no woman could plead benefit of clergy.

The privilege was one of the first attacked by the Reformation statutes. In 1531,[2] all persons below the rank of subdeacon were excluded from the benefit of it in the case of the more serious felonies; and even those who were admitted to it were to be kept in prison by the Ordinary, or made to find sureties for good behaviour. The exclusion was extended to persons in higher or genuine holy orders in 1536.[3] Forty years later, a still more stringent statute was passed.[4] Where the privilege was allowed, the layman pleading it was to be branded in the hand; and, instead of being delivered over to the Ordinary, to undergo imaginary purgation, he was to be at the disposal of the Justices, who might either set him free at once, or imprison him for any period not exceeding a year, while no one was to be allowed to plead his clergy a second time. But the most effective reduction of the privilege resulted from the practice, which began in the sixteenth century, of enacting that certain offences should be 'without benefit of clergy'; and, as new crimes were thus created, and older ones passed through the sieve of legislation,[5] the privilege became of less and less value. In 1706, the farce of applying the reading test was abolished;[6] but in 1827 the privilege itself was entirely swept away.[7]

Sanctuary

The privilege of sanctuary was, originally, a notable achievement in the crusade waged by the Church in the Dark Ages against violence and disorder. Whilst unable, as has been before pointed out,[8] wholly to repress the waging of the blood-feud, the Church did succeed in establishing the doctrine, that the feud should be suspended during certain seasons and in certain places. The former restriction is the origin of the legal holidays (*i.e.* 'holy days') and vacations, when no legal process was possible. The latter gave rise to the privilege

[1] The mechanical way in which the privilege was exercised may be guessed at by the fact, that the copy of the Gospels kept in Court for the purpose of administering the test was officially known as 'The Clergy.' (Somers Tracts, VI, 235.)

[2] 23 Hen. VIII, c. 1. [3] 28 Hen. VIII, c. 1. [4] 18 Eliz. (1576) c. 7.

[5] *E.g.* 1 Edw. VI (1547) c. 12, s. 10; 5 and 6 Edw. VI (1552) c. 10; 8 Eliz. (1565) c. 4; 18 Eliz. (1576) c. 7, s. 1; 39 Eliz. (1597) c. 9.

[6] 5 Anne, c. 6, s. 4. [7] 7 & 8 Geo. IV, c. 28, s. 6. [8] *Ante*, p. 8.

of **sanctuary**, which we are now discussing. If the accused could succeed in reaching some place which was sheltered by the protection of the Church, before the avenger of blood caught him, he could, practically, evade the challenge to battle; for the thunders of the Church would have blasted the daring 'appellor' who had ventured to drag the fugitive from the sacred precincts. But the privilege was confined, strictly, to the locality; and worked a suspension, only, not an extinction of the feud.

The situation was, however, at that, intolerable to both parties. The fugitive was, virtually, condemned to perpetual imprisonment;[1] for, the moment he left the place of sanctuary, he could be attacked. The accuser was, virtually, condemned to perpetual watching outside the sacred spot; unless he was prepared to allow his adversary to escape. No doubt, advantage was often taken of the delay to arrange some kind of a compromise between the parties, *i.e.* generally, the payment of the blood-fine or 'wergild.' But, as has been explained in an earlier chapter,[2] there seems to have been no power, at any rate in the earliest days, to compel the acceptance of 'wer' or 'wite.'

Apparently, however, a way had been found out of the difficulty, before the close of the Middle Ages, in the practice of 'abjuring the realm,' which we find fully recognized in the Assises of Clarendon and Northampton.[3] The accused, in the presence of the coroner, took the oath of abjuration, became, in fact, an outlaw, and was then given a safe-conduct, under shelter of which he was passed from constable to constable to the sea, where he took ship for a foreign clime, and was seen no more in his native land.

Perhaps the most remarkable fact in the history of 'sanctuary' is that, as the evidence abundantly shows, it was incorporated, apparently without question, into that new royal criminal procedure by indictment which, as we have seen,[4] was introduced in the twelfth century. It was quite natural, according to our ideas, that the wild justice of revenge should be curbed by some such restriction as that afforded by the privilege of sanctuary; but it is somewhat startling to find what we should consider

[1] The inconveniences attendant on this state of affairs are detailed, with more directness than elegance, in the *Articuli Cleri* of 1315.

[2] *Ante*, pp. 8, 9.

[3] Clarendon, cap. 14; Northampton, cap. 1 (S.C. 145, 151).

[4] *Ante*, pp. 40, 41.

to be the passionless justice of the State subjected to a similar control. Perhaps the impartiality of the State was not so complete as in modern times; perhaps the idea (which we have traced in other quarters),[1] that the King ought not to have any unfair advantage over the private prosecutor, was responsible for the incorporation of the privilege into true criminal law. At any rate, the adoption is beyond question; for we find the *Articuli Cleri* of 1315,[2] not merely providing remedies for some of the minor defects of the situation, but exempting clerics altogether from the necessity of abjuring the realm after taking sanctuary.[3]

It was not, apparently, until the sixteenth century, that the mischief of the privilege began to be realized; and, even then, the first thought of the reformers seems to have been in a direction which to us appears quaint enough. The advisers of Henry VIII seem to have regretted the loss to the kingdom, by the process of abjuration, of so many active spirits, who, though not exactly modelled after a Sunday school pattern, had in them, doubtless, the making of 'expert mariners,' and 'very able and apt men for the wars.'[4] Accordingly, the person who has fled to sanctuary, was not, after taking the oath of abjuration, to avoid the realm, but to remain a perpetual prisoner under the control of the authorities of his chosen sanctuary, whence he could, doubtless, be released by the royal officers anxious to secure recruits for army and navy. He was not, however, allowed to disport himself in his former lawless manner; for the commission of felony after abjuration was to involve loss of the privilege of sanctuary.

But, a few years later, probably under the double influence of the decay of appeals and the feeling against Church privileges, we find a stringent statute[5] on the subject, which, whilst not reversing entirely the policy of 1530, in effect renders it of less importance. A large number of sanctuaries are abolished; and, in fact, only parish, cathedral, and collegiate churches, together with eight other specially favoured places, are to retain what was, doubtless, a very lucrative privilege. Moreover, persons committing murder, rape, burglary, highway robbery, house-

[1] *Ante*, p. 155. [2] 9 Edw. II, st. I, cc. 12, 15.

[3] This provision (c. 15) clearly demonstrates that the compromise of the Constitutions of Clarendon, on the subject of criminous clerks, had broken down. Clerical immunity from lay jurisdiction is openly admitted by the statute.

[4] 22 Hen. VIII (1530) c. 14. [5] 32 Hen. VIII (1540) c. 12.

breaking, or arson, are excluded entirely from privilege of sanctuary; and the number of fugitives which may be sheltered in any one sanctuary is restricted to twenty. All this legislation was repealed by a statute of James I, passed in the year 1604,[1] which is noteworthy as an early example of what would now be called a 'Statute Law Revision Act.' But, whatever may have been the object of this apparently retrograde step, it was of no great importance; for, in a statute of the year 1623,[2] the privilege of sanctuary was entirely abolished.

[1] 1 Jac. I, c. 26, s. 34.

[2] 21 Jac. I, c. 28, s. 7.

CHAPTER XII

CIVIL PROCEDURE IN THE LATER MIDDLE AGES

THE gradual severance of criminal from civil proceedings which, as has been explained in the preceding chapter, resulted from the introduction of indictments and the gradual abolition of 'appeals,' paved the way for the development, on scientific lines, of purely civil procedure, *i.e.* of procedure in actions between citizen and citizen for the vindication of private rights. For, whilst the direct connection between true criminal procedure and the ancient right of vengeance lingered long in the public mind, and produced that intense conservatism which retained, in criminal procedure, the archaic oral pleadings and the minute correctness of detail which characterized the appeal of battle; in the less heated atmosphere of civil procedure, convenience and legal science were allowed freer play. Thus it seems quite clear, though the exact dates elude us, that, by the beginning of the sixteenth century, the ancient oral pleadings in open court, uttered by the 'serjeant' or 'countor' of the parties, had given way to the more convenient written pleadings which, after being exchanged between the parties, were enrolled on the records of the tribunal. At any rate, it seems impossible to believe that the elaborate and lengthy pleadings set forth in the *Liber Intrationum* of 1510, and the other early 'Books of Entries,'[1] were really intended to be delivered by word of mouth;[2] though the perpetual recurrence of the phrase 'comes and says' reminds us of the earlier practice. These books show us also, that the sequence of steps so familiar to the later pleaders was already established in the sixteenth century. After the *narratio* or 'declaration' of the plaintiff,

Written Pleadings

[1] The most famous of these in the period now under discussion are those of Rastell (1564), Coke (1614), and Brownlow (1652).

[2] On the other hand, the statute of 1362 (36 Edw. III, st. I, c. 15) which required pleadings to be in the English tongue, appears to assume that they were delivered orally in Court by the 'serjeants and other pleaders.'

comes the 'bar' or 'plea' of the defendant, followed by the *replicatio* or 'reply' of the plaintiff, and this again, if necessary, by the rejoinder of the defendant; till, at last, the parties attain their desired end, viz. the joinder of issue on some definite question which can be submitted to the jury. But this process was rendered even more artificial and complicated than it need otherwise have been, by a curious reaction which seems to have taken place quite early in this period, and which led to the development of the highly technical process known as 'giving colour.'

We have seen [1] that, as a result of a series of procedural reforms extending over part of the twelfth and the whole of the thirteenth centuries, the jury had gradually ousted the older methods of trial as the ordinary procedure in civil as well as criminal cases. Though the details of this important development, especially in the later stages, are still among the unsolved mysteries of English legal history,[2] we may take it as settled that, at any rate by the middle of the fourteenth century, the ordinary civil action at common law was tried by a jury of twelve men.

Colour

But, apparently, the defects of the jury system had already made themselves felt; and from the beginning of the fifteenth century, and especially in those very proceedings, *e.g.* assises, entries, and trespasses, to which the jury-system had from the first been essential, we notice a curious plan adopted for the purpose of mitigating its defects. Thus, in a case of the year 1400,[3] the parson of Saltash brought a Writ of Trespass for goods taken in Saltash. Now there can be little doubt that the defendant had taken the goods; and, therefore, that if he had contented himself with a simple denial, or, in the words of later days, 'pleaded the general issue' of 'not guilty,' the jury would infallibly have found against him. But the defendant believed himself able to justify his proceedings as servant to the Dean of Windsor, who was 'parson' or rector of Saltash; and so he alleged a taking in that capacity and an attempted seizure by the plaintiff. Thus he raised a question of law, the decision of which was for the Court, not for the jury; and though, in that

[1] *Ante*, pp. 46–52.
[2] The most notable contribution to the subject is Thayer's *Treatise on Evidence at the Common Law* (London and Boston, 1898).
[3] Y.B. 2 Hen. IV, fo. 5, pl. 16.

particular case, the point of law went against the defendant, the propriety of the fictitious story was not questioned. The illustration given in *Doctor and Student* [1] is an Assise of Novel Disseisin brought against an occupant of land by a stranger of whose title the defendant knows nothing. If the defendant were to plead simply 'no wrong nor disseisin,' *i.e.* the general issue, he might find himself defeated by a hostile verdict on some technical disseisin committed by a predecessor in title. Even if he were to put his own title in evidence, that would not help him; for that would be a plea 'amounting to the general issue,' and, therefore, going to the jury as a whole. But, by giving the plaintiff a 'show,' or 'colour,' *i.e.* by imagining a fictitious title for the plaintiff, specious, but inferior to his own,[2] and asking the judgment of the Court upon it, he avoided the general issue. Naturally, the plaintiff, unwilling to have an inferior title thus 'surmised' or put upon him, replied with his real title; and thus the question came before the Court as one of law. In the report of the leading case on the subject of 'colour,' viz. *Doctor Leyfield's Case,* decided in 1611,[3] it is said by Coke, that every 'colour' ought to have four qualities, viz.: —

1. It ought to be a doubt to lay people (or, as it is sometimes put, to 'the lay gents');
2. It ought to have continuance, *i.e.* it must feign a state of things existing at the date of the cause of action;
3. It ought to be such as, if it were of effect (*i.e.* true) it would maintain the action;
4. It should be given by him who is in by the first conveyance, *i.e.* has apparently the older title; because he is the true defendant, the presumption being in his favour.

It must, of course, be remembered that, during the latter part of the period now under discussion, there was growing up,

Equity Procedure

alongside this common law, technical, 'litigatory' procedure, another system of civil procedure of a wholly different character. This was the procedure of the

[1] *Dialogue*, II, chap. 53.

[2] The example in *Doctor and Student* is that the plantiff claims 'by colour of a *deed* of feoffment,' which, without livery, would not have passed seisin. This appears to have become common form; for in 1606 an ignorant pleader actually applied it to goods, with disastrous results, for goods did pass by deed without livery (*Radford v. Harbyn*, Cro. Jac. 122).

[3] 10 Rep. 88.

Court of Chancery, which, at least from the end of the fourteenth century,[1] had become a tribunal of resort for suitors whose cases were not covered by the common law Register of Writs. Chancery procedure differed in almost every conceivable respect from the procedure of the Common Law courts. In the first place, it did not treat the parties as equal rivals, coming for a decision of strict right; but as petitioner and respondent in a matter of grace. Accordingly, the proceedings in a Chancery suit did not begin with the issue of a Writ Original, in a stereotyped form, but with an informal petition, or Bill, in which the complainant set forth his grievance in artless language. Then, if the petition disclosed a *primâ facie* case for the interference of Equity, the Chancellor issued a judicial Writ of Subpœna[2] against the respondent, or defendant, bidding him, under pain of £100, appear and answer on oath the petitioner's complaint. No doubt, at first, as in the Common Law courts, the pleadings in Chancery were oral; but, by the beginning of the seventeenth century at the latest, it is clear that a regular succession of written pleadings — bill, answer or plea, and replication or reply — had been established.[3] Only, it must be remembered again, these pleadings were not, like those of the Common Law courts, technical and often imaginary arguments drawn out to an issue; but merely statements of facts. Even the 'demurrer,'[4] which at Common Law was a highly technical step, raising a

[1] The earliest Chancery reports that are conveniently accessible are those printed in the Record Commission's *Calendars of Proceedings in Chancery* (1827), and in the Selden Society's *Select Cases in Chancery* (Vol. 10), together with occasional examples in Bellewe's *Les Ans du Roy Richard Le Second*. These cases show that the Equity jurisdiction of the Court was well established in the latter half of the fourteenth century.

[2] The Subpœna *ad respondendum*, which must be carefully distinguished from the Subpœna *ad testificandum* (to compel the attendance of a witness), is attributed to the invention of John Waltham, Master of the Rolls, 1381–1386. It is said, but with doubtful truth, by the Serjeant in his comment on *Doctor and Student* (Appendix, Part II), to be the process alluded to in a statute of 1393 (17 Ric. II, c. 6). It is, however, certainly pointed at by the 15 Hen. VI (1436) c. 4; and the increasing power of the Chancery jurisdiction at the commencement of the sixteenth century is obvious from the Appendix to *Doctor and Student*. The Serjeant maliciously points out, that the Writ of Subpœna will not be found in Fitzherbert (*Natura Brevium*), obviously the classical treatise on writs of that peroid, *i.e.* about 1520.

[3] See Bacon's celebrated *Ordinances*, published in his *Law Tracts* (ed. 1737). Bacon became Lord Chancellor in 1618.

[4] A demurrer was a plea by which the person demurring admitted the facts stated by his opponent, but denied that they warranted the legal conclusion drawn from them. It was a highly dangerous step; for, if the demurrer was overruled, the other party got judgment at once, on the admitted facts.

technical question of law, was, in Chancery, merely a suggestion that the plaintiff was already provided with a legal remedy, and had no need, therefore, to resort to the aid of Equity.

Again, the Court of Chancery was by no means content to play the part of indifferent umpire in a judicial duel; its business was to examine the defendant and purge his conscience of its burden of guilt. Its proceedings were 'inquisitorial,' in the strict sense. They involved the administering of a searching examination to the respondent; and, though the course of this examination was, doubtless, suggested by the plaintiff, it was, in theory, administered by the Court.[1] Thirdly, there was no jury, for whose sake the pleadings had to be worked up to a definite issue of 'aye' or 'no'; it was for the Court to pronounce a decree on consideration of the whole facts. Therefore, though Equity pleadings in later times often assumed portentous length, they were free from the technical rules of Common Law pleading. Finally, in its decree, the Court of Chancery proceeded *in personam*, by imprisoning the defendant until he obeyed the order of the Court, or even, if necessary, issuing a 'commission of rebellion' against him; whereas the Common Law judgment either directly bound the property *in rem*, or was restricted to the award of damages, to be 'made' by sale of the defendant's chattels or body (*Ca. Sa.*), or, at the option of the plaintiff, by seizure of half his lands, under the new remedy of Elegit introduced by the Statute of Westminster the Second.[2] It will, of course, not be forgotten, that, towards the end of the period under discussion, the superiority of the Equity jurisdiction in cases of conflict between it and the Common Law courts was vindicated in the well-known dispute between Chief Justice Coke and Lord Chancellor Ellesmere, in which, Coke having procured the indictment at the Middlesex Sessions of two defendants in Common Law actions who had applied to Chancery for injunctions to stop the plaintiff's proceeding, the Grand

[1] The defendant is not to be examined upon interrogatories, except "it be in very special cases, by express order of the Court" (Bacon, *Ordinances*, No. 70).

[2] 13 Edw. I, (1285) st. I. c. 18. Of course, by means of arrest on mesne process, the Common Law courts had also considerable powers against the person of the defendant. But that is a different matter, to be explained later. No doubt, on the other hand, Chancery had invented the process of sequestration, by which property in dispute could be seized into the hands of officials appointed by the Court, to put pressure on a contumacious defendant. But Lord Chancellor Hatton's attempt to make a Chancery decree bind the legal estate directly, like a Fine, was not successful.

Jury ignored the indictment, and, the matter having been taken up by the Law Officers, the King decided (though in somewhat ambiguous terms) in favour of the Chancellor.[1]

It is hardly possible to leave this part of the subject, without pointing out, that the procedure of the Court of Chancery resembled that of the Court of Star Chamber, almost as completely as it differed from that of the Common Law courts. So striking, indeed, is the resemblance, that the Star Chamber is sometimes called a 'court of criminal equity'; and suggestions of a common origin are frequently met with. The latter raise a constitutional, rather than a legal question; but the resemblance between Chancery and Star Chamber in the matter of procedure is indisputable. Like the Chancery, the Star Chamber began with a Bill, followed by arrest and examination of the defendant. As became the criminal character of the proceedings, the examination was more stringent than in Chancery; sometimes, it is to be feared, leading to actual torture. But the principle was the same. So too, the fact that the accuser and the accused were not on equal terms. The accuser was merely the informant, on whose evidence the Court might, if it thought fit, act, but who was not brought face to face with the accused. There was no jury, as there was none in Chancery, to decide between the parties. Finally, the decree of the Court of Star Chamber, like that of the Chancery, was against the person of the defendant; though, doubtless, a heavy fine might also be levied from his goods. So striking are the resemblances and differences between the procedures of the three jurisdictions that it may be of interest to set them out in tabular form. (See page 167.) From this it will be seen, that the procedure of the Court of Chancery agrees with that of the Court of Star Chamber in no less than seven points, and differs from it only in two; while, conversely, it differs from the Common Law courts in seven points, and agrees only in two.

Chancery and Star Chamber

Finally, on this point, it is not unworthy of mention, that when, in accordance with somewhat later practice, it became common to appoint a Lord Keeper, or Commissioners for executing the office of the Great Seal, instead of a Chancellor, the commissions of these officials, until the abolition of the Court of Star Chamber, specially empowered them to hear causes in that tribunal.

[1] Bacon alludes to the royal decree (26 July, 1616) in his *Ordinances* (No. 33).

[THE PERIOD IS SUPPOSED TO BE ABOUT THE YEAR 1500]

COMMON LAW COURTS	STAR CHAMBER	CHANCERY
1. Right.	Grace.	Grace.
2. Writ (*i.e.* special form of action).	Bill (no form of action).	Bill (no form of action).
3. Pleadings (? oral) to issue.	Written pleadings (no issue).	Written pleadings (no issue).
4. No examination of parties.	Defendant on oath.	Defendant on oath.
5. Precedents.	Discretion.	Discretion.
6. Jury.	No jury.	No jury.
7. *In rem.*	*In personam.*	*In personam.*
8. Open accusation.	Accuser unknown.	Open accusation.
9. Reasons given for judgment.	No reasons given.	Reasons given.

With regard to the topics specially dealt with by the Court of Chancery at the beginning of the sixteenth century, a very useful summary will be found in a criticism of the work known as *Doctor and Student*, previously alluded to. This is supposed to be a commentary, by a 'Serjeant of the laws of England,' on certain subjects dealt with in the two Dialogues which compose the main treatise; and though, being obviously written from the point of view of a common lawyer, it must be regarded with some suspicion, its temperate and reasonable tone, together with the verifiable truth of many of its allegations, forbid us to treat it as a mere party squib. In Part II. of his criticism, the Serjeant enumerates the following cases in which it is admitted that a Subpœna will lie, viz.: —

1. Discovery of documents;
2. Perfecting of imperfect conveyances for valuable consideration (where there was an express promise, the Action of Case lay at the common law);
3. Recovery of rents reserved in conveyances of the whole estate of the grantor;[1]
4. Defence against unconscionable claims, *e.g.* when the plaintiff has been sued at common law on a bond

[1] These were void at Common Law, because, as the grantor had no reversion after the execution of the conveyance, he could not 'reserve' anything to himself. Of course by using the proper forms he could have given himself a rent charge, for which an assise would have lain.

which he has really discharged. (This was, probably, an early case of the 'common injunction');

5. Performance of 'uses.'[1]

This list agrees fairly well with the doggerel summary attributed to Sir Thomas More —

> 'Three things are to be judged in Court of Conscience,
> Covin (fraud), accident, and breach of confidence.'

But it is noteworthy that, as the Serjeant has no difficulty in showing,[2] there were many other hard cases for which no remedy lay, either in the Common Law courts or in Chancery; as, for example, that of the man in respect of whose land a Fine with proclamations had been levied by another who knew perfectly well of his opponent's title, and yet took no steps to make him aware of the proceedings, or, a still more glaring case, when a man had bought goods on credit and died, and the creditor could not bring Debt against the debtor's executors, because the debtor would have been entitled to 'wage his law.' Thus it is clear that there was ample scope, despite the efforts of the Chancellors, for the enterprising law reformer, in the first half of the sixteenth century.

Apart from these general features, the period is marked by three events of first-class importance in the history of civil procedure, viz: (i) The establishment of a common jurisdiction in the three Common Law courts at Westminster by means of legal fictions; (ii) the introduction of arrest on mesne process as an ordinary step in civil proceedings; and (iii) the perfection of the Action of Ejectment as a general process for trying title to land. A few words must be said about each of these events; but the first two are so closely interwoven, as reciprocal cause and effect, that it will be necessary to treat of them together.

It will be known to all students of Constitutional History, that, of the three 'Courts of Common Law at Westminster,' which, for nearly six centuries, administered the Common Law in the name of the King, only one was, in origin, a court of general jurisdiction for civil causes. This was the Court of Common Bench, attributed to the action of Henry II, who, according to Benedict of Peterborough, selected, in the year

[1] Chaps. II–VI.

[2] Chaps. VII and VIII.

1178, five persons from his household, and directed that they 'should not depart from the King's Court, but there remain to hear all the complaints of the kingdom, and do right'; cases of peculiar difficulty being reserved for the hearing of the King himself, with the advice of his wise men.[1] Thus arose the Court held before 'Our Justices at Westminster,' the 'certain place' chosen in obedience to article XVII of the Great Charter. In theory, the King's or Upper Bench, the *Curia ad placita coram Rege tenenda*, only exercised the reserved jurisdiction described above, for cases of peculiar difficulty,[2] and dealt with matters in which the Crown was peculiarly interested, *e.g.* the 'prerogative' writs of Certiorari, Prohibition, and the like, and the prosecution of criminal offences. So too, the Exchequer of Pleas, which, as we have seen,[3] dates from 1268, at first dealt only with matters really arising in the course of the collection of and accounting for, the revenue, as described in the *Dialogue of the Exchequer*.[4]

Process in the Common Bench

The Common Bench, or Common Pleas, then, was the normal and proper court for the commencement of ordinary civil process; and, in the absence of special circumstances, the forms of writ assume that the defendant will be ordered to appear 'before Our Justices at Westminster.' It was not, however, very easy to compel the defendant to obey a writ of summons; for, as we have previously seen, early tribunals find themselves in the greatest possible difficulty in the face of a contumacious defendant. Apparently, during the earlier part of our period, in an ordinary civil action in the Common Bench, after the service of the summons by the sheriff's officers, and the failure of the defendant to appear, the sheriff could then 'attach' the defendant, *i.e.* order him to find sureties ('gages and pledges') to appear; and, if he refused, or broke his pledges, could then by various degrees of seizure, distrain him by all his lands and chattels to appear.[4] But if these steps proved unavailing, there was, apparently, no power to proceed

[1] S.C. 131.

[2] This was, probably, the origin of the jurisdiction in appeals from the Common Pleas, which was exercised by the Court of King's Bench until the re-organization of the Exchequer Chamber in 1830 (11 Geo. IV and 1 Will. IV, c. 70).

[3] *Ante*, p. 24.

[4] S.C. 168–248.

[4] These various forms are given in the *Registrum Brevium (Judicialium)* of 1687, at p. 1. In their somewhat later shape they may be seen in Blackstone *Comm.* Vol. III, Appx. III.

in the defendant's absence; and the only thing to be done was to go through the cumbrous and dilatory process of 'outlawing' the defendant, after which, if he appeared in public, he could be arrested by the Writ of *Capias utlagatum*. But the process of outlawry was laborious and costly, involving no less than five 'exactions' at successive monthly County Courts, interspersed with proclamations, before the issue of the *Capias utlagatum*.

The Capias

It was, in all probability, this helplessness of the Common Pleas in the face of a contumacious defendant, that gave the rival Courts of the King's Bench and Exchequer their opportunity of stealing some of the business normally belonging to the first-named tribunal. For these latter courts, being specially concerned with enforcing the King's claims, were armed with the powerful weapon of a *Capias ad respondendum*, *i.e.* a writ directed to the sheriff, bidding him arrest the defendant at once to answer the plea of our Lord the King. For it was not to be tolerated, that a person accused, for example, of force and arms against the King's peace, should be allowed to defy the tribunal before which he was called to account.

Ac Etiam

The King's Bench, therefore, if the plaintiff wished to enforce a debt, offered him a cunning device. He issued a writ based on a wholly fictitious trespass alleged to have been committed by the defendant. This trespass, had it, in fact, taken place, would have given the King's Bench genuine jurisdiction; for all Trespass, as has been said, involves, technically, a breach of the King's peace, and subjects the offender to fine and imprisonment. But, as it had not, in the case supposed, really taken place, and, moreover, was not the object of the action, the plaintiff was allowed to add ('*ac etiam*') to his claim in Trespass, a claim in Debt for his real demand; and, thus, as the action was nominally Trespass, the plaintiff could secure the defendant's arrest by a *Capias ad respondendum*. When the proceedings came before the court, the allegation of a trespass was quietly dropped, and the case proceeded as though the action had originally been in Debt. Thus the plaintiff obtained the benefit of the superior process, while the Court of King's Bench secured the profitable jurisdiction in Debt. But a simpler expedient was soon devised.

The right of the King's Bench to proceed in Debt on a Writ of Trespass was based on the old established doctrine, that that Court could take summary proceedings to regulate the affairs of all prisoners in the custody of the King's officers. Having been arrested for Trespass, the defendant was, *de facto*, in the custody of the sheriff, and, therefore, came within this principle.

Bill of Middlesex

But it was easier still, and less costly, to avoid the necessity for the actual issue of a Writ of Trespass, and simply to *assume* that the defendant was already in the custody of a royal officer. This, of course, could only be done with the connivance of the Court; but, this connivance being secured, the plaintiff then simply presented a petition or Bill, called an 'English Bill' from the fact that it was in English (whereas a writ was in Latin), and, more usually, a 'Bill of Middlesex,' from the fact that the King's Bench usually sat in Middlesex. This Bill stated,[1] that the defendant was in the custody of the Marshal of the King's Bench on a plea of Trespass within the verge,[2] and that the King was petitioned to make him pay a debt due to the plaintiff. Thereupon a precept was issued to the sheriff of Middlesex, bidding him produce the defendant to answer to the plea of Trespass 'and also' (*ac etiam*) to the plea of debt; and, in the highly probable event of his not being found within the county of Middlesex, a further writ, known as the *Latitat*, was issued to the sheriff of the county where he was really believed to be, or where, in the picturesque language of the writ, 'it is sufficiently attested that the aforesaid R. lurks (*latitat*) and runs about.' Thus the defendant would be arrested; and the proceedings would continue in the King's Bench.

The Quominus

The Exchequer acquired jurisdiction in ordinary cases by an equally ingenious device. The normal process in the Exchequer was by 'suggestion,' or 'information,' *i.e.* giving notice to the royal officials of a possible claim on behalf of the royal revenue. This process was apt to be abused; and, as will be seen later,[3] special precautions were afterwards taken to prevent it being adopted as a means of oppression. A particular variety of suggestion, however, known

[1] The form is given in Blackstone *Comm.* Vol. III, Appx. III.
[2] *I.e.* assault within the verge of the Court, a peculiarly heinous offence.
[3] *Post*, pp. 335, 336.

as the Writ of Quominus,[1] seems to have been used for no more harmful purpose than the acquiring of jurisdiction by the Court of Exchequer in ordinary civil cases. The fiction was, that the plaintiff owed money to the King, and the defendant to the plaintiff; so that the delay of the defendant to pay the plaintiff caused the latter to be in default to the King—'whereby (the plaintiff) is the less (*quominus*) able to satisfy Us the debts which he owes Us in Our said Exchequer.' Here, too, as a claim of the King was involved, arrest by the sheriff followed as a matter of course; and then the proceedings continued in the Exchequer.

'Ac Etiam' Again

It is not to be supposed, that the Court of Common Bench would peaceably stand by, and allow its monopoly to be infringed in this glaring manner, without making an effort to retaliate. Accordingly, that Court seems to have claimed original jurisdiction in Trespass from a very early date,[2] and, also by means of an '*ac etiam*' clause, to have allowed suitors to add to a plea of Trespass a claim of debt or any other civil claim,[3] with the consequent advantage of being able to secure the arrest of the defendant on mesne process. No doubt at first the plaintiff also went through the form of issuing the ordinary process of 'attachment' and 'distringas' also; but, as Blackstone informs us,[4] these steps were ultimately dropped, and the issue of the writ of summons (or 'original') was followed immediately by that of a *Capias ad respondendum*. It should be observed, also, that, by direct legislation, the power of arrest on mesne process had been extended, in 1352, to the actions of Debt, Detinue, and Replevin,[5] and, in 1503, to the comprehensive action of Case,[6] which, as we have seen,[7] by that

[1] The form is given in Blackstone *Comm.* Vol. III, Appx. III. It seems to have been founded on the practice described in Sect. XV of Part II of the *Dialogue of Exchequer* (S.C. 237).

[2] By Fitzherbert's time Trespass lay indifferently in the King's Bench and the Common Pleas (*Natura Brevium*, 86 I); and see the statement of Hale, C. J., in his posthumous *Discourse Concerning the Courts of King's Bench and Common Pleas*, reprinted in Hargrave's *Law Tracts*, Vol. I, p. 367.

[3] Blackstone, *Comm.* Vol. III, 281. (Blackstone does not quote any authority; but his statement is borne out by the wording of the statute of 1661, to be described in next period.)

[4] *Ibid.*

[5] 25 Edw. III, c. 17. Blackstone *Comm.* III, 281, says that it was also extended to the action of Account, by the Statutes of Marlbridge and Westminster the Second. But the passages quoted do not bear out his contention.

[6] 19 Hen. VII, c. 9.

[7] *Ante*, pp. 136–148.

time included the action on the simple contract, as well as many actions of Tort, and which certainly lay in the Common Bench. Thus, not only did the three Common Law courts practically acquire an identical jurisdiction in civil cases,[1] but, incidentally, the power of arrest on mesne process became firmly fixed as a normal step in civil procedure. It was mitigated only by the clause in a statute of 1444,[2] which enacted that the sheriff and other officers should let out of prison on 'reasonable' bail, all manner of persons being in their custody by force of any writ, bill, or warrant in any action personal. And even this mitigation was soon severely restricted by evasions, which ultimately established, that not merely 'common' or reasonable, but

Special Bail

'special' bail might be demanded as of right for the defendant's appearance in actions of Debt, Detinue, Trespass to goods, or Case (other than slander), if the debt or damages claimed exceeded twenty pounds, and that it might be insisted on by the Court, at its discretion or on a specific application, in other cases such as Covenant, Battery, Conspiracy, and False imprisonment.[3] Apparently Slander (not being 'slander of title,' which was not defamation at all, but an ordinary action of Case) was the one instance in which 'special bail' could not be exacted.[4]

The third great change in the civil procedure of this period is the invention and gradual development of the action of Ejectment.

As was previously pointed out, in dealing with the early history of terms of years,[5] the Writ of Ejectio Firmae was, originally,

Ejectio Firmae

a mere variety of the great Writ of Trespass, and, therefore, sounded in damages only, not in specific recovery. As such, however, it remained, substantially, the only

[1] It is clearly assumed by the statute of 1585 (27 Eliz. c. 9, s. 2) which made appeals from the King's Bench lie to the Court of Exchequer Chamber, that actions of Debt, Detinue, Account, and Case, as well as Ejectment and Trespass, even when between private persons, are within the jurisdiction of the 'King's Bench.' (It is odd that, even in Elizabeth's reign, the term 'King's Bench' is retained.)

[2] 23 Hen. VI, c. 9 (5).

[3] *Rules and Orders for the Common Pleas*, made in Michaelmas Term, 1654 (Cooke, *Rules, Orders, and Notices*, Sect. XII). Apparently this Rule was originally made in 1582 (24 Eliz.). There was an exception when the defendant was sued as heir or personal representative.

[4] This was, probably, because of its recent adoption from the ecclesiastical courts (see *ante*, pp. 145, 146).

[5] *Ante*, p. 90.

remedy open to the lessee for years,[1] against a mere stranger, until the middle of the fifteenth century; and, so long as its original limitations remained, the lessee for years could hardly be said to have an estate in the land. But, about the middle of the fifteenth century,[2] the Courts began to toy with the notion that not merely damages, but the term itself (*i.e.* possession of the land) could be recovered by the Writ of Ejectio Firmae. In an important case, which came before both the Benches in 1467,[3] for Debt on a lease made by a man and his wife, Catesby and Fairfax, two eminent counsel who soon afterwards became judges, argued without protest from the assumption that, in an action of Ejectment, the plaintiffs could have recovered their term. By the year 1481, the doctrine had become, apparently, unquestionable; for in that year we find it uttered by no less a person than the Chief Justice of the King's Bench.[4] The first actual decision, however, is said to have been in the year 1499, when judgment was given in Ejectment, not only for damages, but for the recovery of the house and appurtenances.[5] Fitzherbert, who wrote in the first half of the sixteenth century, states the new rule without hesitation;[6] and by the second half of the sixteenth century it was in full working order.[7] Thus the lessee for years acquired full status as a tenant, and was able to recover his term, both as against a stranger, as well as against the lessor and the latter's feoffees.[8]

But the action of Ejectment would not have fulfilled its

[1] He had, of course, the remedy of Covenant and Quare Ejecit; and by those could recover his term. But the Quare Ejecit only lay against the lessor and the lessor's feoffee (Y.B. 19 Hen. VI (1440) fo. 56, pl. 19); and the Covenant only against the lessor and his heirs, and when the lease was under seal.

[2] The doubt is mooted by Choke (afterwards a judge) in 1454 (Y.B. 33 Hen. VI, p. 42, pl. 19).

[3] Y.B. 7 Edw. IV, fo. 6, pl. 16.

[4] Y.B. 21 Edw. IV, fo. 11, pl. 2.

[5] The case is not reported; but a full copy of the pleadings, with a reference to the record, is given in Rastell's *Entries*, at ff. 252–253. A suggestion has been made, by Finlason, the editor of Reeve's *History* (III, p. 31 n.), that the *dicta* in the older cases mentioned above have been misunderstood; and that the remedy of recovery or the term is much older than 1499. But the case of 1499 was evidently regarded as a leading authority; and, if Bellewe may be trusted (p. 169), Sir Robert Belknap, Chief Justice of the Common Pleas, in 1382, expressly stated it, as a matter of general knowledge, and with the approval of the whole Court, that nothing but damages could be recovered by a Writ of Ejectio Firmae.

[6] *Natura Brevium*, 220 H (referring to the case of 1499).

[7] See, for examples, the cases reported by Dyer.

[8] It will be remembered that in the year 1529 the lessee had been given complete statutory protection against fictitious recoveries suffered by his lessor (21 Hen. VIII, c. 15).

destiny, had it remained merely a remedy for lessees for years. The important thing about it is, that it became, as we have said, a general action to try title to land, not only for termors, but also for freeholders. We have now to see how this result came about.

In theory, of course, the freeholder was amply protected by the numerous 'real' remedies at his disposal. Owing to the care with which the Assises and the Writs of Entry [1] had been worked out, provision had been made for every possible case. But, apparently, early in the fifteenth century, these 'real' remedies had become unpopular. Probably this result was due to their great technicality, and the consequent danger of choosing the wrong procedure. According to Sir Matthew Hale,[2] they were largely superseded in the later fifteenth century by proceedings under the Statutes of Forcible Entry.[3] These statutes were, primarily, of a criminal character; but the elaborate Act of 1429 provided [4] that the Justices should not merely punish the offender, but should restore possession to the party grieved. Inasmuch as this Act applied not merely to persons making forcible entry, but to persons (wrongfully) entering without force and afterwards holding possession by force, and inasmuch, moreover, as it provided that if the ejected party chose to bring an Assise or Trespass, he might recover treble damages against the offender, it will be seen that a fairly complete remedy, of a summary nature, was offered by the statutes to the ejected freeholder;[5] though it should be observed that, in the case of peaceable entry forcibly held, the remedy on the statutes was barred after three years.[6]

Decay of the Real Actions

Statutes of Forcible Entry

Possibly it was the last-named fact that rendered proceedings under the Statutes of Forcible Entry ultimately unpopular, as the 'real' actions had also become. At any rate it is clear that, just as proceedings under the statutes were the favourite remedy for the recovery of land in the

The Fictitious Ejectment

[1] *Ante*, pp. 49–51. [2] *History of the Common Law* (ed. 1794), p. 301.

[3] 5 Ric. II, st. I (1381) c. 8; 15 Ric. II (1391) c. 2; 8 Hen. VI (1429) c. 9.

[4] 8 Hen. VI, c. 9, s. 3 (2).

[5] 8 Hen. VI, c. 9, s. 7; confirmed by 31 Eliz. (1589), c. 11.

[6] The benefit of the statutes was extended to lessees for years, copyholders, guardians in chivalry, and tenants by Elegit, Statute Merchant, and Statute Staple, by the 21 Jac. I (1623) c. 15. The decision in *Taltarum's Case* was given on an entry against the statute of Richard II.

sixteenth century, so the action of Ejectment was the favourite remedy in the seventeenth. The machinery which adapted it to the requirements of the freeholder was ingenious. At first, the intending plaintiff made an actual entry on the land, to avoid the risk of being proceeded against on a charge of Maintenance, to which he would have been liable if he had attempted to aliene whilst actually out of possession.[1] His entry was only momentary; but, during its continuance, he handed a lease of the premises to a person who had agreed to act as nominal plaintiff in the action. The latter made entry upon the premises under the lease, and thereby acquired an estate for years in the land. He was then ejected, or 'ousted,' either by the genuine defendant, or by a friendly person who had agreed to act as such. In the former event, the nominal plaintiff immediately commenced an action of Ejectment against the true defendant, founded on the actual ouster. In the latter, he commenced it against the fictitious defendant, or 'casual ejector.' In either event, the validity of the lease to the nominal plaintiff necessarily came in issue; and as this could not be lawful unless the claim of the lessor (the real plaintiff) were valid, a judgment for the plaintiff implied that the Court was in his favour. Only, it will be observed, that such judgment merely affirmed the claimant's right *to grant the lease;* and therefore, in theory, his title could still be disputed on any ground that did not involve this right. Thus, it might be argued, in a later proceeding, that the true plaintiff had only an estate for life. But, in effect, the judgment in Ejectment was treated as conclusive of title; because the plaintiff in that action took care to set up his full claim.[2] The difficulty that, when the nominal defendant was only a 'casual ejector,' the whole proceedings might be conducted without the knowledge of the true defendant, was got over by a Rule of Court,[3] to the effect that no judgment should be given against

[1] 32 Hen. VII (1540) c. 9, s. 2. This provision was not formally repealed until 1897 (Land Transfer Act, 1897, s. 11). There had been several earlier statutes to a similar effect.

[2] And Chancery would, probably, have granted an injunction against repeated attempts to try the same title.

[3] Messrs. Sedgwick and Wait, to whose admirable Essay on Ejectment (Select Essays in Anglo-American Legal History, III, pp. 611–645) all students of English legal history are deeply indebted, say, that this Rule was made in 1662, and refer to Cooke's well-known *Rules and Orders*. But the writer cannot find the Rule there. It is clear, however, that such a Rule was observed in practice before the close of the period.

a casual ejector; unless due notice of the action had been given to the actual tenant in possession of the land, to enable him to offer a genuine defence, if he wished to do so.

Improvement by Rolle

In the event of the tenant in possession wishing to defend the action, he was admitted as of course to do so, upon indemnifying the 'casual ejector' for his costs; and, at first, he was then able to raise any objection to the form, though, probably, not to the genuineness, of the fictitious plaintiff's story. Quite at the end of our present period, however, a great saving of time and expense was effected by a practice, said to have been introduced by Chief Justice Rolle, of compelling the genuine defendant, as a condition of being allowed to defend, to 'confess lease, entry, and ouster.' [1] These three proceedings thereupon became really unnecessary, and were, in fact, omitted; being merely recited in the plaintiff's statement of his case, or 'Declaration.' Thus, in theory, every action of Ejectment was between fictitious or, at least, nominal parties; the proper title being '*Doe on the demise of X* (the true plaintiff) *against Roe*' (the casual ejector) or, more shortly, '*Doe v. Roe*'; though, for the sake of reference, the name of the real defendant was often substituted in the report for that of the casual ejector.

Clumsy as it seems to modern eyes, this curious procedure appears to have been the universal method of trying title to land from the close of the present period, until the great reforms of 1833 and subsequent years; in other words, for a period of nearly two centuries. Not only did it take complete possession of the Courts in England; but, as we are informed,[2] the name, at least, of the action of Ejectment passed, with other institutions of more value, to the English colonies in America, where, however, the necessities of practical life, combined with the stern Puritan dislike of fictions, soon caused great modification in the forms used.

It is hardly possible to leave the period which ended at the Restoration of Charles II, without saying a few words about

[1] The early stages of this practice may be traced in a Note in Style's Reports (p. 368) under the year 1652. The difference between the Upper (or King's) Bench and the Common Pleas should be noted. Manifestly, the action could be brought in either Court. By the end of the seventeenth century, the admission of the true defendant by the 'consent rule' had, apparently, become universal (*The Practick Part of the Law*, 3d ed. 1702, p. 156).

[2] By Messrs. Sedgwick and Wait, in the Essay before alluded to (Select Essays in Anglo-American Legal History, III, pp. 611–645).

one of the most remarkable documents in English legal history which dates from the close of that period.

Scheme of the Little Parliament

The 'Little' or 'Barebones' Parliament, summoned by Oliver Cromwell to meet at Westminster on 4th July, 1653, after the dissolution of the remains of the Long Parliament, may have been an unpractical body, so far as the task of administration in troublous times was concerned. But it seems quite possible that the wealth of contumely and scorn which has been poured upon it was, originally, due quite as much to the fierce anger of vested interests against outspoken criticism, as to any real vagueness or want of practical wisdom in the plans of the House itself. At any rate, the scheme of reform prepared by the Committee 'to consider of the Inconvenience, Delay, Charge, and Irregularity in the Proceedings of the Law,' and ordered to be printed on 12th July, 1653,[1] reads like a revelation of the future; and if it be really true that it was prepared in the course of a week, even with the assistance of eminent lawyers outside the House, it is a striking testimony to the capacity, or at least to the intelligence, of those members of the House who adopted it. For, of the long series of changes which it recommends, more than two thirds have since become law, practically in the shape forecast by the Committee; and, if it appears somewhat out of place to give a brief account of this scheme at the end of a chapter on Civil Procedure, it will probably be admitted, that no more fitting place for it could be found than between the close of the period of which it was, in a sense, the final act, and the commencement of that in which, after long delay, so many of its proposals were at last adopted.

After a brief preamble, in which the Committee proposes to abrogate fines on the commencement of civil proceedings, the

Marriage Law

scheme proceeds to a draft of a measure of marriage law reform, which recommends the establishment of a system of registries in which notices of intended marriages shall be given, as essential preliminaries of valid celebration. Then follows a proposal for universal civil marriage, not before the registrar, but before a Justice of the Peace. Not only marriages, but births and deaths, are to be entered in the local register. No person under twenty-one is to marry without the

[1] It will be found in full in the *Somers Tracts*, Vol. VI, pp. 177–245.

consent of parents or guardian; and the age of consent is fixed at seventeen for men and fifteen for women.

The Marriage Bill, the proposals of which, as will have been noticed, have only b en partially realized, is succeeded by the draft of an Act for the suppression of extrajudicial oath, and, immediately afterwards, by another of an Act for cutting off entails and providing for 'acknowledgments' in conveyances by married women. This draft, which most strikingly resembles the measure actually passed into law with the same object nearly two centuries later,[1] was framed, of course, with the object of abolishing the costly and cumbrous conveyances known as Fines and Recoveries.[2] It concludes with certain useful provisions on the subject of the liability of lands for payment of their deceased owner's debts, which had, likewise, to wait nearly two centuries for their realization.

Fines and Recoveries

This remarkable draft is succeeded by a short Bill for ascertaining 'arbitrary' fines on copyholds, which, unfortunately, has never been passed, a second for abolishing certain technical details in the law of tenure which made it difficult to transfer reversions,[3] and a third, excluding members of Parliament from acting as counsel on private lawsuits during the session, and regulating pleaders' fees. Then follows a wide scheme for the establishment of Small Debts courts throughout the country, under lay Commissioners appointed jointly by the Grand Jury and Justices of the Peace in each county; a scheme which was carried out piecemeal by the erection, usually by private Acts of Parliament, of local Courts of Requests during the eighteenth and early nineteenth centuries, and, more effectively, by the later County Courts Acts.

Small Debts Courts

After this come short Bills for making void voluntary conveyances as against creditors, for recovery of debts owing by corporations, and for enabling debts, or 'choses-in-action' to be assigned; interspersed with more distinctly Puritanic proposals for prohibiting traffic in offices, duels, bribery, drunkenness, swearing, and Sabbath-breaking. Many, though not all, of these proposals have since been carried into effect.

The draft code, for such in effect it is, concludes with a thorough

[1] 3 & 4 Will. IV (1833) c. 74.

[2] *Ante*, pp. 112–119.

[3] Some of these recommendations were carried into effect in the eighteenth century by the Act for the Amendment of the Law (4 & 5 Anne (1705) c. 16, s. 9), and the Landlord and Tenant Act, 1730.

Procedural Reforms

Register of Titles

Probate

overhauling of the machinery of legal procedure, judicial and extra-judicial, treated under five heads. Under the first, which deals with conveyancing, the Committee proposes to set up a universal Register of Titles, in which every incumbrance affecting land, and every conveyance dealing with it, is to be entered. As is well known, the latter of these objects was partially achieved in the early eighteenth century, by the establishment of county registers in Yorkshire and Middlesex;[1] while general registers of judgments, executions, and other incumbrances were set up under various statutes ranging from the Revolution to the end of the nineteenth century. Under the second head, the whole scheme of the probate of wills and administration of estates is to be removed from the jurisdiction of the ecclesiastical courts, and transferred to county officials, acting under the control of the county jurisdictions proposed to be set up for the conduct of higher civil litigation.

Chancery and Common Law Procedure

Under the third, a drastic reform of Chancery procedure, and under the fourth, of that of the Common Law courts, is proposed; and, though these are, in many respects, too technical for discussion here, it may be stated broadly that, while some of their more moderate suggestions were, almost immediately, brought into operation by Regulations issued by the Keepers of the Great Seal and the common Law Judges,[2] the whole course of procedural reform during the last two centuries has been in the direction indicated by their proposals. These proposals are by no means confined to procedure in the strict sense; but comprise suggestions for the abolition of survivorship in joint-tenancy (especially among partners), the recognition of the right to bar dower, the power of excluding the principle of merger, by which a smaller and a larger immediately succeeding interest cannot be separately held by the same person in the same land, the abolition of 'col-

[1] 2 & 3 Anne (1703) c. 4 (Yorkshire); 7 Anne (1708) c. 20 (Middlesex).

[2] A great reforming Order for the Common Bench was issued directly after the fall of the Little Parliament. It is given in Cooke's *Rules &c. in the Common Pleas* (not paged). The Chancery reforms were longer in arriving; but a comprehensive set of Orders was issued by Lord Clarendon (Chancellor) and Sir Harbottle Grimston (Master of the Rolls) shortly after the Restoration. These were published separately by Pawlet in 1669; and are included in the general collection of *Rules and Orders in the High Court of Chancery*, issued by Worrall in 1739.

lateral warranties,'[1] the admission of the half-blood heirs to inheritance, and the modification of the rule of primogeniture.

In no direction, however, is the foresight of the Law Committee of the Little Parliament more strikingly vindicated, than in its proposals for the reform of criminal procedure. It proposed to substitute for the barbaric *peine forte et dure*[2] a simple admission of guilt,[3] to allow prisoners to be defended by counsel (at least when counsel appeared against them), and to have their witnesses examined on oath, to abolish all penalties when death occurred by misadventure,[4] to modify the feudal doctrine of corruption of blood by attaint of felony, to set convicted thieves to work with the object of compensating the persons from whom they have stolen, to do away with the capital punishment of burning,[5] to make compensation to poor prosecutors for loss of time and trouble, and, in the case of a few most serious crimes, to reward persons coming forward to prosecute; finally, to make provision for the spiritual needs of prisoners in gaol.[6] Incidentally, it disposed, in a sentence of four lines, of a question which, even to the present day, is in a state of disgraceful uncertainty, viz. the question whether a person who has suffered loss by the felonious conduct of another, may bring a civil action for redress before criminal proceedings have been taken. Historically, as we have seen,[7] there was much justification for the doubt; practically, the question could be settled satisfactorily at any time by a single section of an Act of Parliament. And we have waited, in vain, two centuries and a half for its enactment!

Criminal Procedure

[1] *Ante*, p. 112. [2] *Ante*, p. 51.

[3] The modern practice, as will appear, is to substitute a plea of 'not guilty,' which requires a trial.

[4] One of the most curious survivals in English law was that of the 'deodand,' or article which caused death by misadventure. Thus, if a man was killed by a falling beam, it was the duty of the coroner's jury to find the value of the beam, in order that the Crown might claim it as a forfeiture. In spite of the recommendation of the Little Parliament, deodands were not formally abolished until 1846 (9 & 10 Vict. c. 62).

[5] This, practically, was confined to women convicted of treason, high or petty.

[6] It must not be supposed, however, that the Committee showed itself to be entirely free from the superstitions of its age or the special defects of Puritanism. The punishment of death is freely distributed; and mutilation of the face and head is prescribed for perjury. But the sense of mercy, as well as of justice, shows itself in the proposal to abolish the death penalty for horse-stealing and pocket-picking, and in the provision that no accused person shall be called upon to pay any fee until conviction, and no acquitted person at all.

[7] *Ante*, pp. 155, 156.

All the procedural reforms projected by the Committee were accompanied by a rigid tariff of fees, issued with the object of reducing the cost of legal proceedings; and it may be that the hostility aroused by its Report, and the oblivion into which it soon fell, were due, more than to any other cause, to the official hostility aroused by this feature. Whatever the cause or causes, the fact remains that, after a few spasmodic efforts at reform in the reigns of William and his immediate successor, of which some account will be given in their proper order, Parliament settled down, so far as legal questions were concerned, to the almost unbroken slumber of the eighteenth century, and the first quarter of the nineteenth. Then indeed, as we shall see, law reform came like a river; and has never since ceased to flow. As has been previously said, the almost complete failure of the scheme of the Little Parliament is generally attributed to its unpractical character. But it is difficult to suppose that suggestions which have, almost unconsciously, been adopted by the most enlightened reformers of modern times, could ever have been really unpractical. It is far more likely, that the profound hostility produced by the more extreme manifestations of the Puritan movement re-acted against the proposals of the wiser and better members of the party, and condemned them to two centuries of ostracism.

Failure of the Report

PERIOD IV

THE RESTORATION TO THE PRESENT DAY

1661–1911

AUTHORITIES

Statutes of the Realm.

Statutory Rules and Orders (prior to 1890 revised, afterwards in full).

Reports of judicial decisions (see *post*, pp. 190–195).

Rules and Orders of the Supreme Court (annually published with full notes).

Books of Entries (see p. 197).

TEXT-BOOKS

Blackstone. *Commentaries on the Laws of England* (Clarendon Press, 1765). [This work has been re-edited from time to time; and its best known form is that now appearing under the name of the late Judge Stephen (Butterworth, 15th edition, 1908).]

Bowen, Lord. *Progress . . . in the Victorian Period* (Select Essays in Anglo-American Legal History, I, 516–557).

Dicey, A. V. *Law and Public Opinion in England* (Macmillan, 1905).

Scrutton, T. E. *History of the Law Merchant* (Select Essays in Anglo-American Legal History, III, 7–15).

Stephen. *History of the Criminal Lawl of England*, chapters XI–end (Macmillan, 1883, 3 vols.).

Underhill, A. *Changes in the Law of Real Property* (Select Essays in Anglo-American Legal History, III, 673–719).

Veeder, Van V. *A Century of English Judicature* (Select Essays in Anglo-American Legal History, I, 730–836). *The English Reports*, 1537–1865 (Select Essays in Anglo-American Legal History, II, 123–168).

Wilson, Sir R. K. *History of Modern English Law* (Rivingtons, 1875).

CHAPTER XIII

MODERN AUTHORITIES AND THE LEGAL PROFESSION

THE process of specialization tends, almost inevitably, to narrow the sources from which the rules of any science are drawn; and English law is no exception from this rule. We have seen that, in its earlier stages, judges and lawyers borrowed freely from all sorts of authorities which appeared to have any bearing on the subject under discussion. Ancient customs, maxims of the wise, royal decrees, official regulations, text-books, even foreign systems such as those of the *Corpus Juris Civilis* and the *Corpus Juris Canonici*, were called in aid; no less than Acts of Parliament and formal judicial decisions.

So long as such practices prevailed, the liberty of choice open to a tribunal, and the doubt prevailing as to the comparative weight of these rival authorities, must have left much to the discretion or idiosyncrasy of the Court in each case.

Parliamentary Sovereignty

But one of the great changes which took place in the last century of the period last considered was the rapid sweeping away of all rival authorities, and the ultimate concentration of the power of the State in the King in Parliament. In the earlier stages of the struggle, indeed, it seemed as though the Crown would emerge sole victor; but the effect of the Civil War was to bring about a compromise, in which sovereign authority ultimately vested, not in the Crown alone, nor in the Houses alone, but in the Crown and Parliament acting together. And, though subsequent developments have shown that, when the sovereign is a composite body, there may, and, indeed, generally will, be a struggle for supremacy within that body itself, yet, for legal purposes, the verdict of the Civil War, which decided the sovereignty to be in the Crown and Parliament, is still undisturbed. At the present day, the only ultimate source of law is the King in Parliament; though, by force of a tradition which is older than

Parliament itself, the Crown, within certain well-defined limits, and the Courts, within limits less well defined, still exercise their ancient prerogative of declaring, formulating, and, we might almost say, making, new law. No one doubts, however, that the action of the Crown and of the Courts in this respect is liable to be overruled by the action of Parliament; and, in fact, not a few modern statutes have been passed expressly for the purpose of altering the law as laid down by judicial decisions.

Obviously, therefore, the chief authority for the law of the period we are now approaching is the Statute Book; and a glance at the shelves of any law library will show how enormously this source of authority has increased in bulk in recent years. Roughly speaking, the whole of the public statutes passed in the period which lasted from the birth of Parliament, in the late thirteenth century, down to the restoration of Charles II (a period of about 400 years) occupy less than three quarto volumes in the common edition of the Statutes at Large. The statutes from 1660 to 1868 (a period of about half that length) occupy rather more than forty-three volumes of the same edition. Of this vast bulk, as well as of the numerous Acts of Parliament passed since 1868, every word which has not been expressly or by implication repealed by a later statute, is binding law of the highest authority. Whatever doubts may have existed in the mind or language of Coke and his contemporaries, with regard to the limits of Parliamentary authority, disappeared in the Civil War; and Blackstone, no worshipper of representative institutions, in his immortal work,[1] fully, though not without reluctance, accepts the doctrine that, however apparently absurd and unjust an Act of Parliament, yet if the words are clear, 'there is no court that has power to defeat the intent of the legislature.'

Acts of Parliament

Happily for the student of existing law (though the historian is less relieved by the practice), Parliament freely, and, of recent years systematically, by means of Statute Law Revision Acts, has repealed much of its former enactments; and a convenient edition of *The Statutes Revised*, issued by the Statute Law Revision Committee, enables the practitioner to distinguish readily between dead and living statutes. Be it observed, also, that though the *ipsissima verba* of an unrepealed statute

[1] *Comm.*, Vol. I, p. 91.

are binding, even on the Crown if the Crown be expressly named therein, it is not permissible for legal purposes, to go behind a statute to the discussions in Parliament which preceded its passing.[1] This tempting addition to the possibilities of forensic argument has always been sternly repressed by the Courts, which have also laid it down, that the side notes usually appearing in the authoritative or King's Printer's editions of the statutes, are of no authority, even for the interpretation of a statute.[2] On the other hand, the preamble, and the title, are now parts of a statute;[3] and are, indeed, often valuable guides to the policy of the enactment.

Orders in Council

Midway between purely Parliamentary and purely judicial legislation, come the various Orders in Council, Proclamations, and other formal legislative and administrative enactments issued by the executive authority in the State. These are capable of simple and instructive classification. In the first place, they are either (*a*) prerogative or (*b*) issued under Parliamentary authority. The former, now rare in number, were at one time, as every student of English Constitutional History knows, the source of much debate and feeling. They played no inconsiderable part in the differences of opinion which led to the Civil War; they were conspicuous in the Revolution of 1688. The net result of those two important events is: (1) That any purely prerogative Order or Proclamation inconsistent with or derogating from the express terms of an Act of Parliament, is wholly void; but, (2) that, subject to this rule, the Crown's ancient rights, in so far as they have actually been exercised with fairly definite continuity, still remain. In fact, a certain number of Prerogative Orders are from time to time published.[4] But, even where the rights still exist, as, for example, in the case of the government of the navy, the army, and the 'Crown Colonies,' and the summoning and dissolution of Parliament,

Prerogative

[1] For a recent statement of this rule, see *R. v. West Riding C.C.* [1906] 2 K.B. at p. 716. Of course the rule does not prevent consideration of the circumstances which led to the passing of a statute.

[2] This at any rate was the older view. But it appears that the recent (but not uniform) practice of printing the marginal notes on the Parliament Roll, has given rise to some doubts (*Sutton v. Sutton* (1882) 22 Ch. D., at p. 513).

[3] *Income Tax Commrs. v. Pemsel* [1891] A.C., at p. 543 (preamble); *Fielding v. Morley (Corpn.)* [1899] 1 Ch., at pp. 3, 4 (title).

[4] They now appear as an Appendix to the *Statutory Rules and Orders*. This has been the practice since 1893.

they are often now exercised under express Parliamentary authority — a fact which much diminishes their 'prerogative' character. It is, also, highly improbable, that any exercise of this prerogative authority in new directions would now be tolerated by Parliament; even though that exercise did not conflict with the express provisions of an Act of Parliament.

Parliamentary

The second, and far larger group, of Executive 'Orders' which, in their operation, resemble Acts of Parliament, are those which are made under the express authority of Parliament. Owing partly to the necessity for leaving the application of discretionary legislation to the Executive, but still more to the impossibility of discussing details in an overworked Parliament, it has become increasingly common for Parliament to delegate, either to the Crown (*i.e.* the Executive as a whole) or even to the Minister at the head of the department charged with carrying out the Act, the power of making Rules or Orders under it. These Rules and Orders are, in effect, so long as they keep within the authority prescribed by their respective Acts, themselves Parliamentary statutes, and are enforced by the Courts as such. It is, of course, in theory, possible to raise against any of them the plea of *ultra vires;* but they are usually drawn with sufficient skill to render such an attack hopeless. They are now published periodically by royal authority;[1] and their bulk bids fair soon to rival that of the Statute Book. Like the statutes, they are also periodically revised by authority. The difference between Orders made by the Crown in Council and those made by a single Minister, is more apparent than real. For, in the former case, as in the latter, the form and contents are virtually settled by the departments concerned; the approval by the Privy Council is a pure formality.

Rules and Orders of Court

Technically on the same legal footing as the modern Statutory Orders in Council, but in fact, and historically, inclining somewhat heavily towards judicial legislation, are the various Rules and Orders affecting the practice of the Courts, which have from time to time been published. These go back for a long period in English legal history; and it is impossible, without further research into the archives of the fourteenth century, to state definitely when they began. Among

[1] Pursuant to the Rules Publication Act, 1893, s. 3.

the oldest are the General Orders (as distinct from decrees affecting only particular cases) made by the Chancellors for the regulation of Chancery procedure; and it may have been that, until this example of prerogative legislation had been set by the holders of the Great Seal, the judges of the Common Law courts did not venture to exercise similar powers. At any rate, while the known Chancery Orders go back to 1388,[1] the oldest Common Law Rules (viz. those of the Common Pleas)[2] date only from 1457; but the oldest of these latter refers clearly to still older Rules, which seem to have disappeared. The oldest published Rules of the King's Bench appear to be of 1604;[3] but it is more than probable that these are not in fact the first made. The oldest Exchequer (Plea) Rules known to the writer date from 1571; but these were issued by the Lord Privy Seal, not by the Barons.[4] Other Exchequer Orders, undated, were published in 1698.[5]

As has been suggested, these Rules and Orders appear to have been for long issued by the Chancellor and Justices on their own responsibility, as controllers of the business of their courts; and, so long as they stood in that position, they belonged entirely to the judicial branch of legal authority. But, as with the Crown, so with the judges. Parliament began to look with more and more jealousy on any rival in the business of legislation; and, as it was clearly advisable not to withdraw in fact from the judges the very necessary function of issuing Rules of Practice, Parliament, in the first half of the nineteenth century, began definitely, as in the case of the Crown, to authorize the judges to exercise it. A beginning was made with the Civil Procedure Act, 1833,[6] which authorized any eight of the Common Law judges (including the three Chiefs) to make Rules for the reform of pleading; and the step, having

[1] These are collected in *Orders of the High Court of Chancery*, by G. W. Sanders (Chief Secretary at the Rolls), and published in 1845 (Maxwell).

[2] *The Rules and Orders of the Common Pleas*, from 1457–1743, were published anonymously in the latter year (Lintot); but an earlier collection, from 1457 to 1741, was annexed to Sir George Cooke's *Reports and Cases of Practice in the Court of Common Pleas*, published in 1742.

[3] Published by the anonymous compilers of the Rules of the Common Pleas, and bound up with them in the edition of 1747.

[4] These Orders were confirmed by statute in 1604 (1 Jac. I, c. 26).

[5] These Orders are bound up with the *Ordines Cancellariae* of 1698. They deal chiefly with Equity business.

[6] 3 & 4 Will. IV, c. 42, s. 3.

been found beneficial, was repeated, with wider reach, in the year 1850.[1] These two statutes, which were temporary in their effect, were incorporated, with many additional powers, into the Common Law Procedure Acts of 1852 and 1854.[2] Meanwhile, in the year 1850, a similar provision, with a limited scope, had been introduced into the Chancery Amendment Act of that year;[3] empowering the Chancellor, with the concurrence of the Master of the Rolls and one of the Vice-Chancellors, to make General Rules and Orders for carrying out the objects of the Act. In the Chancery Amendment Act of 1858, this power was extended to cover virtually the whole procedure of the Court;[4] the Rule-making body being enlarged to include the newly created Lords Justices of Appeal in Chancery. Under this power, the great Consolidated Orders of 1860 were issued; and thus the way made easier for the reform undertaken by the Judicature Act of 1873. An account of this measure must be reserved for a future chapter;[5] here it is sufficient to say, that it contains provision[6] for a judicial Council consisting of the judges of all the tribunals incorporated into the new Supreme Court of Judicature, with powers to issue Rules and Orders regulating the practice of all branches of the Court. This power has been fully and constantly exercised ever since the Judicature Acts came into force in 1875; and now the *Rules and Orders of the Supreme Court*, annually republished with copious notes and comments, are as necessary for the practitioner as the Statutes of the Realm or the Law Reports.

Judicial Decisions

Mention of the Law Reports brings us naturally to the last of the great sources of legal authority at the present day. We have seen[7] that the doctrine of judicial precedent had been fully established in the preceding period, through the agency of the Year Books, those anonymous compilations in which the decisions, and even the *dicta*, of the Courts

[1] 13 & 14 Vict. c. 16.
[2] Act of 1852, ss. 223–225; Act of 1854, ss. 97–98.
[3] 13 & 14 Vict. c. 35, ss. 30–32.
[4] 21 & 22 Vict. c. 27, ss. 11–12.
[5] *Post*, pp. 364–371.
[6] 36 & 37 Vict. c. 66, ss. 68–74, repealed before coming into operation by s. 33, and replaced by ss. 17–21 of the Judicature Act, 1875, itself subsequently amended by s. 17 of the Appellate Jurisdiction Act, 1876, and by s. 19 of the Judicature Act, 1881. The present authority is the Judicature (Rule Committee) Act, 1909, by virtue of which statute the Rule Committee now includes (in addition to eight judges) two members of the General Council of the Bar, one member of the Council of the Law Society, and one other solicitor.
[7] *Ante*, pp. 78, 79.

were stored up, by unknown hands, for reference and quotation in the argument of cases. We have seen also, how these anonymous reports gave way, in the middle of the sixteenth century, to the nominate works of Dyer, Leonard, Plowden, Coke, Croke, and others.[1] Nor can there be any serious doubt that, with due allowance for the somewhat lax canons of criticism which prevailed until a recent date, it was fully admitted before the end of the last period, that a decision of a Court of co-ordinate or higher jurisdiction was binding on its successors and inferiors. Probably, too, the three superior Courts of Common Law, though technically independent of one another, respected one another's decisions; while, if there was no interchange of authority between the Common Law and the Equity tribunals, this was because, in theory at least, there could be no common ground between them.

The 'Authorized Reports'

The flow of nominate reports continued with unabated vigour after the Restoration; the only official restriction on the output of rival volumes being that imposed by the Licensing Act of 1662. With this statute, which plays an important part with the history of copyright, we shall have to deal in a later chapter.[2] Here it is sufficient to say that, by its provisions, all law books required the license of the Lord Chancellor or one of the Chiefs of the superior Courts of Common Law; and whoever is familiar with the Reports of the later seventeenth century in the original editions will recognize the solemn *Imprimatur* prefixed so conspicuously to them, and will note also, that the prudent reporter did not confine himself to the express directions of the Act, but took care to get the signatures of as many as possible of the judges of the tribunals whose decisions he reported.

It is a curious testimony to the conservatism of the legal profession, that, long after the refusal of Parliament, in 1695, to renew the Licensing Act, it continued to be the practice of the reporters to obtain judicial authority for their efforts. The volumes of Vernin, Levinz, and Lutwyche, all published after 1695, are still adorned by the judicial license; and, long after the formal license had disappeared, the race of 'authorised

[1] The older tradition of anonymity lingered in the publications known familiarly as *Reports in Chancery*, *Cases in Chancery*, and *Equity Cases Abridged*. But these were, in some cases at least, mere abstracts of nominate reports.

[2] *Post*, pp. 277, 278.

reporters' continued to flourish. It must not be supposed, however, that the judicial license or authority afforded any official guarantee of the accuracy of the reports which it adorned. Save for a very small exception, hereafter to be noticed, there never has been in England any official publication (in the strict sense) of law reports. But it was well understood that the 'authorised reporters' enjoyed in a special way the favour of the courts to which they were attached; and it is obvious to every lawyer that judge and reporter, if harmonious, could be useful to one another in many ways which would tend to improve the quality of the reporter's work.[1]

It was not until the beginning of the nineteenth century that there was any apparent break in this individualist system.

Anonymous Series

But from the year 1823 onwards, and at frequent intervals, there appeared, usually as a publisher's enterprise, a series of anonymous, or, at least, quasi-anonymous reports, the chief *raisons d'être* of which seem to have been the length and prolixity of the 'authorised' reports, and the delay which occurred in their appearance. The first of these series was the *Law Journal Reports*, which, with a literary supplement entitled *The Law Advertiser* (afterwards known as *The Law Journal*), made its appearance in 1823, and continues to flourish to the present day.[2] It was followed by the *Jurist*, which, starting as half magazine, half gazette, in 1837, became, from 1841 till its decease in 1866,[3] purely a reporter. Almost contemporaneously with the *Jurist*, viz. in 1837, appeared *The Justice of the Peace*, a combination of magazine and reporter which, as its name implies, deals exclusively with magisterial business. The decisions reported by it are, however, not, as might be rashly supposed, those of the Justices of the Peace, which are, of course, of no judicial authority, but of the superior Courts reviewing magisterial decisions, or deciding on matters of special interest to Justices.

[1] Useful information regarding the various nominate reporters will be found in Wallace's *The Reporters Arranged and Characterized* (4th edn. Boston, U.S.A., 1882). A summary of dates and chronological lists under the various Courts will be found in a handy form in Sweet & Maxwell's *Lawyers' Reference Book* (1907), and Stevens & Haynes' *Alphabetical Catalogue of the Reports of Cases* (1875). These little works contain also lists of abbreviated citations, regnal years, &c., which will be found indispensable to the student of legal history. Soule's *Lawyer's Reference Manual* (Boston, U.S.A., 1883) is a larger work with similar objects, which includes the American reporters.

[2] A 'New Series' began in 1832.

[3] A 'New Series' began in 1855.

Then came the *Law Times* in 1845, at first with reports and general matter mixed, but, since the commencement of its 'New Series' in 1859, in separate volumes. It still flourishes. The *Weekly Reporter*, first published in 1852, with a view of giving brief and speedy notes of current decisions, was incorporated in 1857 into the newly-founded and still flourishing *Solicitors' Journal and Reporter*. Finally, in 1884, commenced the excellent series of *Times Law Reports*, which, published weekly during the sittings of the Courts, give a rapid and yet careful account of current legal business, and, also in 1884, the solitary example of official law reporting known to English legal history, viz. the *Reports of Patent Cases*, issued as a supplement to *The Journal of the Board of Trade*. But the greatest event in the modern history of English law-reporting has, undoubtedly, been the foundation, in the year 1864, of the series known as *The Law Reports*.

It appears from the interesting account of this movement, written by Mr. Daniel,[1] one of its most active promoters, that the multiplicity, inconsistency, want of authenticity, delay, and expense of the many competing reports published in the middle of the nineteenth century, had for some time given rise to a feeling in favour of reform. The difficulties in the way were obvious. Not merely did the wholesome independence of the English Bar react strongly against any proposals for an official system; but the subject bristled with vested interests (always tenderly regarded by lawyers), of reporters, publishers, and printers. Nevertheless, so great were the practical inconveniences of the unregulated condition of affairs, that a memorial was numerously signed by members of the Equity Bar, less numerously (but sufficiently) by their brethren of the Common Law, suggesting the summoning of a general meeting of the Bar to consider the whole subject. This memorial was presented, in November, 1863, to Sir Roundell Palmer (afterwards Lord Selborne), who was then, as Attorney-General, at the head of the legal profession; and he, after some little hesitation, acquiesced in its prayer. The meeting was duly held on 2d December, 1863; and a Committee appointed to draw up a definite scheme. The scheme was produced at a meeting held on 1st July, 1864, and then dis-

The 'Law Reports'

[1] *The History and Origin of the Law Reports* (Clowes, 1884).

cussed. Objections of detail were taken; but it was obvious that the sense of the majority was strongly in favour of a reform on the lines broadly indicated by the report of the Committee. On only two points does there appear to have been any serious division of opinion among the supporters of the proposal. One of these was whether the new reports were to be official in the strict sense, or at least in the sense that no others could be quoted in Court. The affirmative of this proposition, though supported by eminent names, was ultimately rejected without a division at the adjourned meeting, held on 28th July, 1864, at which the reform proposals were finally carried.[1] A similar fate befell a proposal to maintain the old individual responsibility of the reporters by rejecting the proposals of the Committee in favour of editorial supervision.[2] These points of principle having been cleared up, objections resolved themselves into matters of financial detail; and the latter were finally overcome by generous offers on the part of three of the Inns of Court and the Council of the Law Society (then known as the 'Incorporated Law Society') to guarantee the expenses of the first year's publication. Vested interests were conciliated, where possible, by the offer of posts on the reporting staff of the newly created Council of Law Reporting, and by liberal offers of remuneration to publishers and booksellers.

The new series, which, as every lawyer knows, comprises reports of moderate length of cases decided in all the various branches of the Supreme Court, as well as in the House of Lords, the Judicial Committee of the Privy Council, the Court of Criminal Appeal, and the old Court of Crown Cases Reserved, commenced its career in November 1865, and has, in the general opinion, been an unqualified success, both literary and financial. An indication of its achievements in the latter direction may be gathered from the fact that whereas, in the estimate of Mr. Daniel, a complete set of the reports current in 1863 could not be obtained for a less annual expense than £45, the annual subscription to the complete series of Law Reports is now only £4, which includes, not merely the Reports proper, but such useful appendages as *The Weekly Notes*, *The Quarterly Current Index of Cases*, and *The Consolidated and Decennial Digests* which are from time to time published by the Council. The

[1] Daniel, *op. cit.*, p. 225. [2] *Ibid.*, pp. 224–245.

Council itself consists of two representatives of each of the four Inns of Court, the General Council of the Bar, and the Law Society, and of three *ex-officio* members, viz. the Attorney-General, the Solicitor-General, and the President of the Law Society for the time being. It is, therefore, thoroughly representative of both branches of the legal profession; whilst at the same time, through the Law Officers, just sufficiently in touch with the State to enable it to be assured of adequate consideration for its views, should occasion arise for it to express an opinion on official matters. Despite their success, however, the *Law Reports* are still faced by wholesome competition. Not only do the *Law Journal Reports* continue to appear in volumes which for trustworthiness and convenience are hardly, if at all, inferior to the *Law Reports;* but, as we have seen, several other series, not professing to give such complete reports as the two series named, continue to attract sufficient public support.

Other Sources of Law

It is, perhaps, not strictly true to say, that the sources of authority previously described in this chapter are the only possible authorities for the guidance of English Courts at the present day. For the ecclesiastical courts, though, as we have seen,[1] shorn of much of their dignity and profit by the Reformation and the Civil War, were not finally deprived even of their temporal jurisdiction in matters matrimonial and testamentary until 1857; while they exercise, of course, some jurisdiction in purely ecclesiastical matters to the present day. Again, the Court of Admiralty was not merged into the Supreme Court until 1875; and, when it was so merged, it took over with it, like the ecclesiastical courts of Probate and Divorce, its existing law, subject, of course, to statutory and judicial modifications. In theory, therefore, both the Canon and the Roman Civil Law may be quoted as authorities in the English Courts; when these are exercising what was formerly ecclesiastical or Admiralty jurisdiction. But the legal positions of the two are not precisely the same. So

Roman Law

far as Roman Law is concerned, it stands where it did, as the admitted basis of testamentary jurisdiction, and a considerable authority in Admiralty law, subject only (though this is a considerable admission) to any statutory

[1] *Ante*, pp. 74, 75.

alterations, and to any decisions of the King's Courts from time to time issued or delivered. But the Canon Law was subjected to somewhat remarkable treatment at the time of the Reformation. As it then stood, it received express Parliamentary sanction, so far as matters properly within its scope were concerned, and so far as it was not inconsistent with the 'Laws, Statutes, and Customs of this Realm, (n)or to the Damage or Hurt of the King's Prerogative Royal,' by the so-called Act for the Submission of the Clergy;[1] and, therefore, the Canon Law as it existed in 1533, is binding, within its proper sphere, and subject to the exceptions just mentioned, both on clergy and laity. On the other hand, no additions subsequently made by Papal or other Roman authority are of any validity in English courts, ecclesiastical or civil; while additions made by the English Convocations under Royal license, though they bind the clergy of their respective provinces, do not bind the laity, because they have not received Parliamentary sanction.[2]

Canon Law

It is sometimes said that, even so late as the period now under discussion, the text-books of certain very eminent writers have been treated as authorities by English Courts, and should therefore be regarded as sources of modern English Law. But this is true only in a modified sense. Doubtless such works as Blackstone's *Commentaries*, Dalton's *Country Justice*, and Hawkins' *Pleas of the Crown*, may be fairly treated by the historian as statements, *primâ facie* correct, of the law at the time when they were written. It may even be that, having regard to the great reputation of such writers, English judges will allow advocates to quote from them, and will even themselves, in delivering judgments, allude with respect and approval to these works. But it cannot be seriously contended, that these works are authorities in the sense in which Bracton, Littleton, and even Coke, are authorities for the law of their respective periods. The difference between the weightiest passage of a modern text-book writer and the most ordinary judgment of a Court of First Instance, or an unimportant

Text-Book Writers

[1] 25 Hen. VIII (1533) c. 19, s. 7. This arrangement was intended to last only until a contemplated revision had taken place (*ibid.*, s. 2 and see 35 Hen. VIII (1543) c. 16). But the revision has never been effected.

[2] See the position learnedly discussed by Lord Hardwicke, C. J., in the case of *Middleton v. Crofts* (1736) 2 Atk. 650.

section of an Act of Parliament, is quite clear. The advocate may show that the passage in question is inconsistent with statute or judicial decision; and, if he succeeds, its so-called 'authority' is at once gone. He may attempt to show the unwisdom, absurdity, or inconsistency, of the judicial decision or the section of the Act of Parliament; but, until these have been overruled by a later statute, or (in the case of the judicial decision) by a superior tribunal, they remain binding *in pari materiâ,* and, even if the advocate is not pulled up for irrelevance, his argument will be of no avail. Even Blackstone, one of the greatest of text-book writers, admits freely the truth of this view.[1] Text-book writers, whatever they once were, are now guides only, and not authorities, for English Law.

Practice Books

The only exception from this last rule is more apparent than real. It consists of the various volumes of precedents which, without any formal official sanction, are compiled by private authors, and accepted by the profession as guides in practice. These fall, generally speaking, into two classes. The first, formerly known as *Entries,* or *Books of Entries,*[2] but latterly as *Precedents of Pleading,*[3] contain specimens or forms of the various documents used in the conduct of litigation. In a very real sense, they are 'authorities' for the law of the period under discussion; but that is because, with barely an exception, all the precedents given are copied from documents which have actually been used in legal proceedings, and have thus passed through the fire of judicial criticism. In other words, such works are really judicial decisions in a somewhat unusual form. The second class of Precedent Books are those concerned with non-litigious business, commonly called 'conveyancing.' By their very nature, they cannot claim the direct authority which belongs to forms which have been treated by the Courts as sufficient for their purposes. But the known unwillingness of the Courts to disturb the public confidence in forms which have been made the vehicles for transferring interests of, perhaps, great value, or to unsettle titles based upon that confidence, tends to give these forms,

[1] *Comm.* I, 72–73.

[2] Among these may be quoted, more or less in chronological order, the works of Aston (1661), Brown (1670), Winch (1680), Robinson and Vidian (1684), Hansard (1685), Levinz (1702), Clift (1703), Lilly (1723), Mallory (1734).

[3] Examples are the works of Chitty, Mitford, Daniell, and Bullen and Leake.

when they have been extensively used, something like a negative judicial authority. Obviously, however, a tribunal cannot refuse to condemn a conveyancing precedent which has never really received judicial or parliamentary approval; if it considers it to be in fact insufficient, or based on a misconception of the law. Such precedents are not, therefore, 'authorities' in the strict sense.

Legal Profession

Though strictly irrelevant to the main subject of the present chapter, it may be convenient to say here a few words about the organization of the legal profession. As we have seen, the earliest lawsuit was a fight; and, in primitive times, deputies or agents are not at first allowed in a fight, for obvious reasons. Even in Trial by Battle, however, the 'champion,' or professional pugilist, appears in English legal history at an early date,[1] at any rate in civil causes; and he may be said to combine in himself the functions of counsel, attorney, and witness, possibly even of the jury, of later times. At any rate, he may fairly be claimed as one of the direct ancestors of the legal profession. No sooner, however, is the system of the common law, with its regular courts and procedure, fairly under way, than we note a specialization of functions which has continued to the present day. The champion gradually disappeared, with the disappearance of Trial by Battle;[2] and his place was filled by the serjeant at law (*serviens ad legem*) and apprentice, and by the *responsalis* or attorney. All these were under official license; indeed, in one well-known instance, the law of supply and demand having failed, the royal justices were bidden (in 1292) to scour the the country for persons suitable for enrolment as attorneys and apprentices.[3] The serjeants were a close Order by the end of the thirteenth century, and received their patents direct from the Crown — in later days with much ceremony. They had their own Inns or colleges.[4] Till 1834, they had exclusive audience in the chief civil court, the Court of Common Bench; and

Serjeants

[1] See, for examples, the cases transcribed into *Bracton's Note Book*, Vol. II, cases 116 (1220), 164 (1222), 243 (1227), 328 (1229), &c.

[2] *Ante*, pp. 42, 43.

[3] Rot. Par. I, 84. (The early Parliament Rolls are full of the privileges and sins of attorneys.)

[4] The names at least of two survive; one behind Chancery Lane, the other behind Fleet Street, in London.

though, in that year, their monopoly was formally abolished by royal warrant directed to the Chancellor,[1] yet, in 1840, this warrant was declared by the Chief Justice of the Court to be invalid, and the Order was only finally shorn of its forensic monopoly by the slow process of extinction. Its still greater judicial monopoly lasted, in theory, till 1875;[2] though in recent years it had become a mere formality, the judge designate being made a serjeant as a preliminary to being sworn into his judicial office. But for centuries it was the firmly established tradition, that all the Justices of both Benches and all Commissioners of Assise[3] should be chosen from among the serjeants; the serjeants sat within the 'bar' or boundary of the Court, and were addressed by the judges as 'brothers.' In the eighteenth century, their place in the legal world began to be taken by the King's Counsel Extraordinary, or, simply, 'King's Counsel,' *i.e.* the officially retained representatives of the Crown other than the Law Officers.[4]

King's Counsel

These new 'patent counsel' were, however, though entitled to precedence over their undistinguished brethren of the Outer Bar,[5] and to seats within that magic boundary, not, like the Serjeants, of a different Order from them. They mingled freely in the society of the 'apprentices' or, as they were later called, 'students'; especially in those great colleges of legal learning, the Inns of Court, which, founded in antiquity, reached their zenith at the end of the sixteenth century. These represented, as has been said,[6] the revolt against Romanism and the triumph of the common law in the thirteenth century, and the consequent severance from

Inns of Court

[1] A full copy is given in Pulling's *Order of the Coif*, p. 100.

[2] Judicature Act, 1873, s. 8.

[3] The author cannot trace Mr. Pulling's reference (*op. cit.*, p. 4, n.) to the statute '4 Edw. III, c. 16,' which he quotes for a statutory monopoly.

[4] Of course there were earlier examples, of whom Bacon at the beginning, and Francis North at the end, of the seventeenth century, are well known. The King's Counsel have disabilities, as well as privileges. Thus they cannot appear for a prisoner against the Crown without royal permission, which, at one time, was only obtainable on payment of a fee. It must be remembered, however, that, when King's Counsel were first created, prisoners had no right to be defended by counsel, except on points of law.

[5] This, and its analogue, the Inner Bar, are orthodox but curious expressions. There is but one bar in each Court; and some advocates are entitled to plead within it, whilst the rest must plead from without. But such inaccuracies are common in every professional language; and the attempts to justify them are often more amusing than the inaccuracies themselves.

[6] *Ante*, p. 20.

the classical learning of the universities. At an unknown date, they seem to have acquired a monopoly of that privilege of 'calling to the Bar,' *i.e.* of licensing 'apprentices' to pursue their calling, which, as we have seen, was entrusted by Edward I to his Justices; but the right of appeal from their decisions to the assembled judges, which still survives, and is occasionally exercised, marks the privilege of the Inns of Court as a delegation, not as an original authority. Each Inn of Court has long had its own internal organization of Benchers (or ruling body), in whose 'Parliaments' the affairs of the Inn are managed, ordinary barristers (for inside the Inns King's Counsel have, as such, no official rank) and students,[1] *i.e.* those who are qualifying for call to the Bar, but are not yet entitled to audience in the Courts. The glorious buildings and gardens of the Inns of Court, their libraries, pictures, and plate, testify to their ancient wealth and importance; and Coke's enthusiastic account of them is well known.[2] In the eighteenth century, they seemed to have fallen into sloth and decay. Their buildings became ruinous, their readerships and exercises mere formalities,[3] their libraries dispersed or deserted, their accounts often confused, or worse. But at length the spirit of reform reached them. Though changes in social conditions, especially the outward march of the suburbs, have almost deprived them of their residential character, they have re-constituted themselves as the professional centres of forensic life, and, though hardly yet to an extent commensurate with their resources and opportunities, as centres of legal study. The establishment, in the year 1852, of the Council of Legal Education, consisting of representatives of the Benches of the Four Inns, marked a great step in advance; and the formation, in the year 1894, of the General Council of the Bar, charged with the guardianship of professional etiquette, though in itself somewhat of a reflection on the activity of the Benches, has provided a wholesome criticism and incentive of the bodies with whom the executive authority still rests. In addition to its purely critical functions, the General Council of the Bar appoints representatives on various important bodies,

[1] The reader must remember that, in the sixteenth century, the term 'student' or 'apprentice' still included members of the Outer Bar, who were entitled, or at least permitted, to speak in Court. The change to modern usage seems to have taken place about the time of the Civil War.

[2] 3 Rep. pref. pp. xxxv–xxxviii.

[3] Blackstone, *Comm.* Vol. I, p. 25.

e.g. the Rule-making committees under the Judicature Acts, the Land Transfer Acts, and the Criminal Appeal Act, and to the Council of Law Reporting.

Attorneys and Solicitors

The earliest attorneys were, in all probability, simple non-professional agents, whose duty it was to represent their employers in legal proceedings. Such persons would be very necessary in days when litigation was rapidly increasing; but when facilities for travel were in an elementary stage.[1] We must, however, again remember how primitive tribunals cling to the view that no proceedings can be taken in the absence of the parties; this will account for the reluctance shown by early law to recognize the existence of agency or attorneyship. It is not till 1235 that 'suitors' (who would probably include both plaintiffs and persons bound to attend the Court as part of the homage) were allowed generally to be represented by attorneys; and then only in the local courts.[2] In 1278, by the Statute of Gloucester,[3] the privilege was extended to defendants, in cases which could not lead to battle. After the great diminution in the prosecutions by way of appeal had taken place, as previously explained,[4] even appeals of homicide could be presented and defended by attorney; if, for any reason, trial by battle could not follow.[5]

The professional character of attorneys begins to make itself felt in the statute of 1402,[6] which speaks with regret of the number of attorneys 'ignorant and not learned in the law,' and requires all candidates for admission to the roll ('*en rolle*')[7] to be examined by the Justices; and a statute of James I [8] repeats this requirement in other terms. Meanwhile, the new jurisdiction of the Court of Chancery had produced another similar body of practitioners. At first, apparently, the Masters in Chancery were supposed to look after the Equity suitors' interests; but the natural desire of litigants to have agents specially charged with furthering or 'soliciting' their causes, led to the recognition of a special body of semi-attached officials, known as 'solicitors,' who are treated by the statute of 1605 as on the same footing with

[1] This is specially mentioned as a ground for appointing an attorney in the so-called Ordinance of Liberties, printed as 27 Edw. I (1299) c. 5.

[2] Statute of Merton (20 Hen. III) c. 10.

[3] 6 Edw. I, c. 8.

[4] *Ante*, pp. 155, 156.

[5] 3 Hen. VII (1486) c. 1, s. 91.

[6] 4 Hen. IV, c. 18.

[7] This must mean 'the rolls' (*i.e.* of the various Courts). It was not until the passing of the Solicitors Act, 1843, that a single Roll of Solicitors came into existence.

[8] 3 Jac. I (1605) c. 7.

attorneys. A third class of non-forensic practitioners who made their appearance before the end of the sixteenth century were the 'scriveners,' [1] who concerned themselves only with chamber or non-litigious business, chiefly borrowing and lending of money. Milton's father was a scrivener; and the Scriveners' Company or Gild, which received a charter from James I, survives, in a somewhat attenuated form, to the present day.[2]

So far as the social and educational side of the non-forensic branch of the profession was concerned, attorneys and solicitors appear, until the close of the sixteenth century at least, to have been, in many cases, members of the Inns of Court, above alluded to. But the overflow of these foundations, in the days of their strength, seems to have resulted in the formation of a number of minor or preparatory Inns, known as Inns of Chancery, in the neighbourhood of the greater foundations. Some of these, such as Thavie's Inn and Barnard's Inn, suggest, by their titles, that they were originally founded by private proprietors; but there is a well-established tradition to the effect that each was affiliated to one or other of the Inns of Court; [3] and the tradition has been acted upon at least in one modern case.[4] Apparently, it was to these Inns of Chancery that attorneys and solicitors chiefly resorted; and though, again and again, in the latter part of the seventeenth century, it was laid down by judicial Order,[5] that all attorneys of the Common Pleas should join some Inn of Court or of Chancery, it is evident, from the wording of the later Orders,[6] that some opposition to the injunction was being experienced from the

Inns of Chancery

[1] These had probably originated in the humble guise of writers of court hand in very early times (Freshfield, *Records of the Society of Gentlemen Practisers*, Introduction, p. xii).

[2] The ancient monopoly of the Scriveners' Company, at any rate in the City of London, was finally defeated, after lengthy ligitation, by the decision in *Harrison v. Smith*, in the year 1760 (Freshfield, *Records*, Introd., p. lxvi). Since that date, conveyancing has been recognized as a proper part of the solicitor's professional work. Of course members of the Bar are entitled also to draw and settle conveyancing documents; and, at one time, there was a middle rank of 'conveyancer under the bar,' now practically extinct.

[3] See the preface to Coke's 3d volume of Reports, p. xxxvi, before alluded to.

[4] In the division of the large sum of money obtained by the sale of the site and buildings of New Inn, in the year 1901, a substantial portion was allotted to the Middle Temple in respect of its overlordship.

[5] Orders of Michaelmas 1654, Trinity 1677, Michaelmas 1684, and Michaelmas 1705, in Cooke's *Rules, Orders, and Notices*.

[6] See Orders of 1684 and 1705, *ubi sup.* ('if those Honorable Societies shall please to admit them').

larger foundations. Ultimately, at some uncertain date, probably at the beginning of the eighteenth century, the Inns of Court succeeded in excluding from their membership all attorneys and solicitors, who thereupon seem to have retired to the Inns of Chancery; thus establishing, in addition to the division of functions between the two branches of the profession, which, as we have seen, existed in the thirteenth century, a division of education and discipline, which was no part of the original system.[1] It is worthy of notice that, according to Roger North,[2] personal intercourse with the lay client, which had formerly been shared between both branches of the profession, became confined to the non-forensic branch in the last half of the seventeenth century, *i.e.* at the very time when the completion of the severance between the two branches was becoming imminent. The natural consequence of the change was, that the business and reputation of individual barristers came to depend largely on the favour of attorneys and solicitors.

The decay which characterized the Inns of Court in the eighteenth century was shared to the full by the Inns of Chancery.

Decay of Inns of Chancery

Already in the Order of 1705 [3] we find the judges of the Common Pleas lamenting the intermission of 'commons,' or social gatherings, in the Chancery Inns, with the consequent decay and detriment of those societies, and attempting to revive them. It was, however, too late to save the Inns of Chancery, which gradually sank into the position of mere dining and perquisite clubs for the benefit of a few 'ancients' or benchers, recruited on a closely co-optative principle. The lowest stage of degradation was reached when, in the nineteenth century, the ancient sites and buildings of the Inns of Chancery were taken for public purposes; and the large sums paid by way of compensation were pocketed by the members of their governing bodies. This scandalous procedure, after prevailing in several cases, was at length put a stop to by the decision of Mr. Justice Cozens-Hardy (now Master of the Rolls) in the case of Clifford's Inn;[4] and the considerable amount realized by the sale of the property of that Inn and New Inn was ear-marked for the

[1] See further on this point L.Q.R. XXVI, pp. 137–145, by H. H. L. Bellot.

[2] *Lives of the Norths* (Bohn) III, par. 175.

[3] Cooke, *Rules, Orders, and Notices*. (The only drawback of this deeply interesting and well-printed volume is, that it is not paged.)

[4] *Smith v. Kerr* [1900] 2 Ch. 511; confirmed [1902] 1 Ch. 774.

purposes of legal education. A bold and comprehensive scheme for the utilization of this and other funds, a scheme in some degree worthy of the capital of the greatest Empire in the world, was presented by the Attorney-General of the day (Sir Robert Finlay), in his capacity of official guardian of charitable funds, but was blocked, temporarily at least, by the refusal of the Benchers of the Inner Temple to concur.

Meanwhile, the status of attorneys and solicitors, as officers of the Courts, had been regulated by more than one statute of the eighteenth century, of which perhaps the most important is that of 1729,[1] which introduced the requirement of five years' apprenticeship, under written articles, to a practising solicitor, as a condition precedent of being admitted to the rolls, and virtually abolished the distinction between attorneys and solicitors, by allowing any duly qualified attorney to be sworn also as a solicitor.[2] But by far the most important step in the interests of the profession was taken, in the year 1739, by the formation, on a purely voluntary basis, of the Society of Gentlemen Practisers in the Courts of Law and Equity.[3] Though the records of this Society are not complete, there is every reason to believe that it continued to flourish, as a private society, until the year 1831, when, with other societies having a briefer history, it was merged in the chartered body known from 1831 to 1903 as 'The Incorporated Law Society,'[4] and from 1903 onwards as 'The Law Society.'

Voluntary Association

One of the most striking features of this body is its dual character — public and private. Membership of the Society (now amounting to about 9000) is purely voluntary; and the voluntary subscriptions of members go towards the social side of the Society's activity, its public rooms, library, and entertainments, and the expenses incurred in the protection of the professional interests of solicitors. But, in its public capacity, the Society acts as the registrar, educator,

The Law Society

[1] 2 Geo. II, c. 23, ss. 5 (attorneys), 7 (solicitors).

[2] *Ibid.*, s. 20. Reciprocity was established in 1750 (23 Geo. II, c. 26, s. 15).

[3] See the Records of this Society, published by The (Incorporated) Law Society in 1897, with Introduction by Dr. Edwin Freshfield.

[4] This was not its official title, which was 'The Society of Attorneys, Solicitors, Proctors, and others, not being Barristers, practising in the Courts of Law and Equity of the United Kingdom.' (See the charters at length in the *Handbook of The Law Society*, pp. 32–41.) Proctors were ecclesiastical agents. They were abolished as a distinct body in 1857, when the Courts of Probate and Divorce were established.

examiner, and discipliner, of present and future solicitors; either as delegate of the State, or as an authority recognized by the State. In the year 1843, though the admission of solicitors to the Roll is still the exclusive prerogative of the Master of the Rolls, the custody of the official Roll, containing the names of solicitors entitled to practise, was entrusted to the Law Society.[1] In the year 1877, the sole control of the examinations qualifying for admission to practise was entrusted to the Society,[2] which was already charged with the education of articled clerks in the theory of their intended profession.[3] From the year 1833 onwards, this function had been more or less completely performed by the holding of lectures and classes; but, in the year 1903, a new and comprehensive system was instituted, which not only provides for articled clerks' complete legal education in London, but substantially assists similar efforts made by provincial Law Societies in large towns, in many cases in conjunction with the newly founded universities and colleges, which sprang up in the latter half of the nineteenth century. The administration of this scheme, subject to the general control of the Council of the Society, is vested in a mixed Committee, annually appointed by the Council, and consisting of a majority of representatives of that body, of representatives of provincial Law Societies, and of two solicitors nominated by the members of students' societies. The examinations are conducted by an ordinary committee of the Council, annually appointed by that body.

Finally, the disciplinary functions of the Law Society, formerly of a purely critical character, assumed a new and important phase when, in the year 1888, the preliminary investigation of charges of professional misconduct against solicitors was entrusted to a committee of the Council of the Society (known as the 'Discipline Committee'), appointed by the Master of the Rolls.[4] This committee, sitting as a court of discipline, but in private, hears charges, and reports to the Court thereon; whereupon the Court, with which executive action still exclusively remains, makes such order as it considers to be just; either dismissing the complaint as unfounded, or suspending the solicitor inculpated from practice for a longer or shorter time,

[1] Solicitors Act, 1843, s. 21. The process was not completed till 1888 (Solicitors Act, 1888, ss. 5–6).

[2] Solicitors Act, 1877.

[3] *Ibid.*, 1877, s. 8.

[4] *Ibid.*, 1888, s. 13.

or, in grave cases, striking his name off the Roll. The statute expressly reserves[1] to any complainant the right to proceed by direct application to the Court; and, presumably, the right to bring a civil action against a solicitor for negligence, and, certainly, the power of the Crown to prosecute for criminal offences, are not affected by its provisions. But the advantage to the Court of being relieved of long and wearisome enquiries into details, and the obvious gain to justice, by allowing charges, which may be reckless or unfounded, to be investigated without the odium necessarily attendant on a public enquiry, are abundant justification of the policy of the Act.

[1] S. 13, *ad fin.*

CHAPTER XIV

REFORM BY EQUITY

IT has often been remarked, that the history of English legislation during the eighteenth century, at least so far as private law is concerned, is almost a blank. If we put aside the Act for the Amendment of the Law passed in 1705,[1] the Diplomatic Privileges Act of 1708, the Land Registry Acts of 1706 and 1708, the Landlord and Tenant Acts of 1709 and 1730, the Charitable Uses Act of 1735, the Distress for Rent Act, 1737, the Inclosure Act of 1773, and the Life Assurance Act of 1774 (none of which measures are really of first-class importance), we shall hardly find a single Act of Parliament of those momentous years, from 1700 to 1800, which has left a permanent mark on the body of English civil law. Apparently, the reaction which followed upon the agitation of the Civil War, combined with the feeling of uncertainty produced by a disputed succession to the Crown, rendered the nation unwilling to allow the laborious and disturbing machinery of Parliamentary reform to tamper with the ancient institutions of the country. At any rate, the striking fact remains, that the century which witnessed the passing of the Statute of Monopolies,[2] the Limitation Act,[3] the Petition of Right,[4] the Star Chamber and Habeas Corpus Acts,[5] the Act for the Abolition of Feudal Tenures,[6] the Navigation Acts,[7] the Act for abolishing Arrest on Mesne Process,[8] the Statute of Frauds,[9] the Statutes of Distribution,[10] the Bill of Rights,[11] the Statute of Fraudulent Devises,[12] the Treason Act,[13] the Bond Execution Act,[14] and the Act of Settle-

Legislative Stagnation

[1] 4 & 5 Anne, c. 3 (or 16). It seems a little strange, that this useful statute, much of which is still live law, should not have an official short title.

[2] 21 Jac. I (1623) c. 3. [3] *Ibid.*, c. 16. [4] 3 Car. I (1627) c. 1.

[5] 16 Car. I (1640) c. 10, and 31 Car. II (1679) c. 2.

[6] 12 Car. II (1660) c. 24. [7] *Ibid.*, c. 18, &c.

[8] 13 Car. II, st. II (1661) c. 2. [9] 29 Car. II (1677) c. 3.

[10] 22 & 23 Car. II (1670) c. 10; 1 Jac. II (1685) c. 17.

[11] 1 W. & M. st. II (1689) c. 2. [12] 3 W. & M. (1691) c. 14.

[13] 7 & 8 W. III (1695) c. 3.

[14] 8 & 9 W. III (1696) c. 11. (This statute also ought to have an official short title.)

ment,[1] was followed by the century whose chief legislative output was the meagre crop of statutes mentioned above. And from this fact it might be hastily concluded, that the eighteenth century was a stagnant period in the history of English Law. In fact it can hardly be described as revolutionary; but it would be a great mistake to suppose that it witnessed no legal reform. The explanation is, that the chief engine of law reform during that century was the judicial action of the Courts, proceeding chiefly under the guise of Equity, and chiefly, though by no means exclusively, in the Court of Chancery.

The successive watchwords of the Chancellor's equitable jurisdiction will give us the best key to the historical explanation of the notion of 'Equity,' as understood by English lawyers. At first the Chancellor's equitable jurisdiction was confined to matters of 'grace,' *i.e.* matters requiring special indulgence or provision. It was thought suitable in the fourteenth century (the exact dates are still obscure) to entrust the exercise of this branch of the prerogative to one who, as the Custodian of the Great Seal, was already a great administrative official, charged with the custody of the Register of Writs, and having also some rather undefined Common Law, or 'Latin' jurisdiction[2] in matters of *sci. fa.* and other strictly legal proceedings. It was, doubtless, the 'grace' foundation of Chancery jurisdiction which gave rise to the popular idea expressed in Selden's *Table Talk*,[3] that 'Equity is a roguish thing,' for that it varies as the length of the Chancellor's foot. Nor can it be denied, that this original characteristic long served the Chancellor in good stead; when he desired to depart somewhat widely from tradition.

'Grace'

Nevertheless, long before Selden's day, 'conscience' had almost superseded 'grace' as the working foundation of the Chancellor's equitable jurisdiction. This was but a natural consequence of entrusting the Great Seal to ecclesiastics, whose leanings towards casuistry, and peculiar means of probing the minds of their penitents, caused them to lean heavily on the inward intent of the parties, rather than on those external forms beloved of the Common Law. The contrast between the two principles is, as we have seen,[4] strongly brought

'Conscience'

[1] 12 & 13 W. III (1700) c. 2.
[2] So called, to distinguish it from the jurisdiction by 'English Bill' in Equity.
[3] Ed. Reynolds, xxxvii, 2.
[4] *Ante*, pp. 139, 140.

out in the *Dialogues of Doctor and Student*, in the middle of the sixteenth century. To the application of the doctrine of 'conscience' the Court owed its vast jurisdiction in Trusts and Fraud.

But now, before the period we are approaching, the long line of ecclesiastical chancellors had ended with Wolsey and Stephen Gardiner,[1] and had been replaced, for a short period, by a line of statesmen of the type of More, Nicolas, and Francis Bacon, men more familiar perhaps with the Council Board than the judgment seat. They it was, doubtless, who had given to Chancery that forcible character *in personam*, which was so powerful a weapon in its armory. It was natural that the direct wielders of the royal prerogative, men who sat in the Star Chamber and the Privy Council, who knew the secrets of State and the necessity for prompt action, should despise the merely declaratory character of a good deal of Common Law process. To them we doubtless owe those four great pillars of Chancery jurisdiction, the injunction, the decree, the sequestration,[2] and the commission of rebellion. The first of these forbade the defendant, on pain of imprisonment, to continue his existing or contemplated course of action; and we have seen how,[3] under a thin disguise, the Chancellor, by means of this process, had, in the year 1618, won a decisive victory over the Common Law courts, and practically enabled the Chancery to control their proceedings. The decree, or positive order, bidding the defendant do some act, was not confined to the mere carrying out, or 'specific performance,' of contracts; though that was its commonest application. As is well known, it was used, though sparingly, to remedy that serious defect in Common Law procedure, which permitted a defeated defendant in Detinue or Trover, to retain the subject matter of the action, on paying its value.[4] It was, probably,

[1] Of course even Gardiner was not absolutely the last ecclesiastical chancellor. He was succeeded by Archbishop Heath of York; and Bishop Williams of Lincoln was Lord Keeper from 1621 to 1625. But these two were of little note.

[2] Roger North, in his amusing but inaccurate work, *Lives of the Norths* (Vol. I, p. 295), attributes the invention of the sequestration to Lord Keeper Coventry (1625–1640). But it is certainly much older. It was, for example, applied for in *Awtry v. George* (1600) *Acta Cancellariae*, 757–759; and, though the Court was reluctant to grant the application, it did not regard it as unprecedented.

[3] *Ante*, p. 166.

[4] See this point discussed, *ante*, p. 59. (The leading cases on the equitable jurisdiction are *Pusey v. Pusey* (1684) 1 Vern. 273; *D. of Somerset v. Cookson* (1735) 3 P. Wms. 390.)

also the origin of the Chancery jurisdiction in partition; for the award of the Court could not convey the legal estate, it merely directed the parties to make mutual conveyances. The sequestration was a far superior process of Distress, which enabled a plaintiff whose opponent refused to appear or to obey a decree, to seize the latter's property, and pay himself out of the proceeds; instead of proceeding laboriously to outlawry, or, through the sheriff, by *Fi. Fa.* or *Elegit.*[1] The commission of rebellion enabled him to supersede the somewhat dilatory officers of the Marshalsea and other civil prisons, by the prompter methods of the Tower.[2] With these weapons in his hands, the Chancery suitor was in a position far superior to that of his brother at Common Law; at least until the cumbrous processes of Attachment and Distress had been superseded by the fictions which enabled a *Capias* to be employed to arrest the defendant in almost all Common Law cases.[3]

'Equity'

But, with the commencement of the seventeenth century, the statesmen Chancellors begun to be superseded by a more specialist class — men like Pickering, Egerton (afterwards Lord Ellesmere) and Coventry, who were lawyers first and last; and, after the retirement of Lord Clarendon in 1667, the change became practically permanent. It is marked by frequent variations of title, which seem to indicate that the Crown was hardly yet prepared to endow the new type of custodian of the Great Seal with all the powers of his medieval predecessors. The title of 'Lord Keeper' appears frequently in the place of that of 'Lord Chancellor'; and in 1562 it was deemed necessary to enact,[4] that the Lord Keeper had, 'and of right ought to have, the same and like Place, Authority, Preheminence, Jurisdiction . . . Commodities, and Advantages' as a Lord Chancellor. The chief difference between a Lord Keeper and a Lord Chancellor was, in fact, that the former was seldom, or at least not necessarily, made a peer, and was, therefore, not a member of, though he pre-

[1] There seems to have been some little doubt whether a sequestration could be issued of any property other than that in dispute in the cause (see *Practice of the High Court of Chancery*, 1672, p. 26).

[2] The form of a Commission of Rebellion is given in *The Clerk's Tutor in Chancery* by W. Brown, 2d edition, 1694, at p. 276. The practice goes back at least to 1594 (see the form of that year given in Crompton's *Authoritie et Jurisdiction des Courts* (ed. 1637, fo. 47)).

[3] See this development explained, *ante*, pp. 170–172.

[4] 5 Eliz. c. 18.

sided over, the House of Lords.[1] Later still, the even more cautious title of Lord Commissioner (or Commissioners) of the Great Seal was frequently employed; and again, in 1688, it was found necessary to define by statute[2] the powers of these officers. Finally, these latter officials must be distinguished from the less important 'Lords Commissioners to Hear Causes,' who appeared during the Commonwealth and after; for these last had no power to affix the Great Seal, which, during their tenure of office, was usually retained by the monarch himself.

But these makeshifts gradually gave way before the long succession of distinguished Equity judges who adorned the Court of Chancery during the century which followed the Restoration. Clarendon's immediate successor, Sir Orlando Bridgman, was, perhaps, more famous as a common lawyer and a conveyancer, than as an exponent of equity. Most of the royalist estates which escaped confiscation during the Civil War had owed their escape to his ingenious drafting of family settlements. But he was followed by Lord Nottingham, one of those 'black, funereal Finches,' who had played a somewhat doubtful part in the troubled years of Charles I; and Lord Nottingham's well-known title, 'Father of Equity,' indicates the respect which his decisions inspired. Among the Chancellors of the period were men of high birth, like Simon, Earl Harcourt, who traced descent from a companion of the conqueror of Normandy, and from a cadet of that house who had accompanied the conqueror's descendant in 1066, and like Talbot, whose family had given warriors, statesmen, and bishops, to his country. But there were also, no less famous and upright, men of humbler birth, like Somers, the great lawyer of the Revolution, and Philip Yorke, afterwards the great Earl of Hardwicke. It is to the work of these men that the term 'equity' is peculiarly appropriate. For, while they did not renounce the ideals of their predecessors — either that 'grace' which enabled them to insist that all their remedies were discretionary, not of strict right, or that 'conscience' which enabled them to administer, and justified them in administering, the severest of interrogatories — they added a new ideal, of equality. For,

[1] The writer believes it to be still the technical rule, that the woolsack, on which the President sits, is not within the sacred limits of the House of Lords.

[2] 1 W. & M. st. I, c. 21, s. 2.

of course, in its origin 'equity' is simply equality or likeness; and the maxim 'equality is equity,' if it is not a mere identical proposition, reads just as well either way. Particularly in the great new department of Equity, which was concerned with the administration of the assets of deceased persons, did the Chancellors apply this new ideal of equality.

Other Chancery Officials

But, before proceeding to sketch the developments of equitable doctrine which took place between the Restoration and the end of the eighteenth century, it may be well to realize that this task was not effected by the occupants of the woolsack alone. Long before the end of the sixteenth century, the Chancery had gathered to itself a vast staff of administrative officials; some, like the Cursitors and the Clerks of the Hanaper and Petty Bag, concerned more with the common law and revenue, than the equitable side of the Chancery jurisdiction, others, like the Masters, the Registrars, and the Six Clerks (the latter of whom were actually made a corporation in 1635[1]) occupied mainly with equity business. The great growth of the latter class (the Six Clerks are said to have had sixty clerks under them[2]) was due to the development of the administrative, as opposed to the litigious side of the equitable jurisdiction; to the taking of accounts, the execution of commissions for partition, the guardianship of infants, and, most of all, to the management of the estates of deceased persons. It was in connection with the high officials known as Masters,[3] that there occurred the second great judicial scandal within a century.[4] In accordance with a practice eminently characteristic of the period, administration suits were treated as the private property of the Masters to whom they were allotted; and, as these suits often lasted for many years, the Masters had, in effect, the custody of the whole of the funds involved during that period, and made large profits by investment of them. The inevitable result followed. At the time of the South Sea Bubble, in 1720, the Masters speculated heavily in South Sea Stock; and, when the crash came, there was a huge

[1] *Ex parte the Six Clerks* (1798) 3 Ves. 589. (But the validity of the incorporation was disputed.)

[2] Scargill-Bird, *Guide to the Documents in the Public Record Office*, p. 8.

[3] Specimens of the early work of the Masters in Chancery may be seen in the *Acta Cancellariae*, by Cecil Munro (1847).

[4] The first was, of course, the impeachment of Francis Bacon for corruption in 1621.

deficit. The chief odium fell upon the Chancellor, Lord Macclesfield. He was impeached, and made to pay a heavy fine, which went in partial reparation of the suitors' wrongs. It fell to Lord King, Lord Macclesfield's successor, to make provision against the recurrence of such a scandal; and the measures which he took to originate the office of Accountant-General in Chancery, produced so much friction in the purlieus of the Court, that from the heated atmosphere sprang the most interesting, if not the most picturesque quarrel in the judicial history of the eighteenth century. An added flavour is given to the affair by the fact that the gladiators in the struggle concealed their identity under a veil of anonymity which has at least succeeded in puzzling posterity.

In the year 1726, less than two years after the fall of Lord Macclesfield, appeared a small anonymous *History of the Chancery*,[1] which made certain reflections on pretentions alleged to have been put forward by the most important of all the Chancery officials, the Master of the Rolls, to a share in the judicial authority of the Court of Chancery. The whole subject bristled with delightful possibilities. On the one hand, it was undeniable, that the Master of the Rolls, who, by virtue of his duties as custodian of the priceless records of the Chancery, was certainly at the head of its administrative staff, had in fact exercised, for at least a century, judicial duties, though of a subordinate kind. Masters of the Rolls had, in quite recent years, been appointed Commissioners to Hear Cases in Chancery;[2] and, in days further back, had even been given temporary custody of the Great Seal.[3] Further, and this was the strongest practical argument of all, it was manifestly impossible for the Chancellor, with his multifarious duties, to get through the whole judicial work of Chancery unaided. These facts were duly pointed out in the anonymous answer to the *History of the Chancery*, viz. the *Discourse of the Judicial Authority of the Master of the Rolls*,[4] which quickly followed, and which is attributed to the pen of the witty and accomplished Sir Joseph Jekyll, then Master of the Rolls. But it was argued, with

Master of the Rolls

[1] London of that date. Published by Walthoe.
[2] *E.g.* Sir Julius Caesar in 1621, and Sir Joseph Jekyll himself in 1725.
[3] *E.g.* John de Waltham in 1383, Simon Gaunstede in 1422, and Robert Kirkham in 1463.
[4] London (Williamson), 1728 (2d edition).

great force, in a really learned reply, *The Legal Judicature in Chancery Stated*, which appeared in 1727,[1] and, like its predecessor, the *History of the Chancery*, was attributed to Sir Philip Yorke, afterwards Lord Hardwicke,[2] that the desirability of a state of things does not prove that such a state exists, that all the alleged instances of the exercise of supreme judicial authority by Masters of the Rolls were to be accounted for by the fact that, at the times in question, the Masters had been enjoying special privileges by virtue of their custody of the Great Seal or their special Commissions, and that, in law, the whole executive power of the Chancery lay in the Great Seal, which, save in the exceptional cases noted above, was the sole possession of the Chancellor or Keeper.

Whatever may have been the historical merits of the quarrel, the obvious result was to demonstrate the necessity for regularizing the position of the Master of the Rolls, and to afford judicial assistance to the Chancellor. Accordingly, in the year 1730, a statute was passed giving formal authority to the Orders and Decrees, past and future, of the Rolls, to the extent warranted by practice;[3] but with a proviso that they should not be enrolled of record before being signed by the custodian of the Great Seal, by whom they could, accordingly, be reversed or amended without formal appeal.[4] Even, however, when the new office of Vice-Chancellor was created in 1813,[5] the judicial position of the Master of the Rolls was still left in its anomalous position; and, though his jurisdiction was extended by the Chancery Reform Act of 1833 to the hearing of motions, pleas, and demurrers,[6] he still remained, until the establishment of the Court of Appeal in Chancery in the year 1851,[7] not merely a subordinate judge, but, in theory, a

Statute of 1730

[1] London of that date. Published by Walthoe.

[2] A curious legend persists in attributing the authorship of the *Legal Judicature* to Sir Joseph Jekyll, and the *Judicial Discourse* to Sir Philip Yorke. Sir Joseph was a noted wag; but he would hardly have written a book to belittle the office which he held for 21 years.

[3] The Act does not specify what this extent was; but, apparently, little difficulty was felt on the point.

[4] When once enrolled, a decree could not be altered without an appeal to the House of Lords.

[5] 53 Geo. III, c. 24.

[6] 3 & 4 Will. IV, c. s. 94, 24.

[7] 14 & 15 Vic. c. 83. Inasmuch as that statute (s. 5) invested the new Lords Justices with all the jurisdiction of the Chancellor, it might be argued that it still left the Master of the Rolls and Vice-Chancellors in the unstable position of mere reporters. But the Judicature Acts definitely placed these officers and their suc-

mere preliminary hearer, whose orders were of no judicial authority till confirmed by the Chancellor. As a matter of fact, his house on the east side of Chancery or Chancellor's Lane, the ancient foundation for converted Jews, which had been confirmed to his great predecessor John de Waltham in 1383,[1] had become the centre of Chancery business; and though the 'Rolls Court' was moved, on the opening of the new Royal Courts of Justice, to that building, the stately pile of the Record Office, rising on the site of the ancient garden of the Masters of the Rolls, preserves the historic continuity of the scene.

We pass now to a sketch of some of the leading equitable doctrines established in the last half of the seventeenth and the eighteenth centuries; and this process will illustrate, better than any other means, that peculiar attitude of Equity towards Common Law which is, juristically speaking, at once the great mystery and the great interest of reform by equity.

We begin, then, by remembering, that this is not the creative, but the developing period of equitable doctrine. As has been pointed out, the new type of Chancellor was essentially a lawyer, with all a lawyer's caution and respect for precedent. One great exception there is, no doubt, from this principle; and to that exception attention will be paid later. But for the most part, in the period now under review, it is not the extension, but the intension of jurisdiction, which is the striking feature of the history of Equity.

Mortgages

No better illustration of this cautious attitude can be chosen, than the subject of mortgages. In 1681 Lord Nottingham, in the leading case of *Harris v. Harris*,[2] firmly laid down the principle: 'once a mortgage, always a mortgage'; a doctrine which not only rendered all agreements in a mortgage for forfeiture of the right to redeem invalid, but also rendered invalid all incumbrances of or dealings with the property by the mortgagee, as against a mortgagor coming to redeem. In some respects, this doctrine was pushed to an

cessors in the rank of judges of First Instance; though the Master of the Rolls has since become a member of the Court of Appeal exclusively.

[1] *Calendar of Patent Rolls* (1897) p. 269.

[2] (1681) 1 Vern. 33. The earliest case known to the writer as illustrating the doctrine, is *Courtman v. Conyers* (1600) *Acta Cancellariae*, 764. And there the mortgagee was alleged to have purposely absented himself on the day fixed for redemption, in order to avoid receiving payment. In other words, it was a case of fraud.

extreme length; with the result, that both parties were prejudiced by the inability of either to make binding dispositions of the property as a whole. But the principle has been productive of fruit even in recent years; and the recent applications of the doctrine of 'clogging the equity'[1] will be familiar to modern lawyers.

On the other hand, Equity in this period laid down rules in favour of the mortgagee, or owner of the legal estate, which show, in the opinion of modern legislators, an almost excessive respect for legal doctrine. Thus in *Hedworth v. Primate,*[2] in 1662, and *March v. Lee,*[3] in 1670, Equity tribunals established the rule of **Tacking**, by which the owner of a second or later equitable charge, who buys up the legal mortgage of the first mortgagee, may squeeze out any intervening (equitable) incumbrancer, of whose existence he had no notice when he lent his money on the equitable charge.[4] Again, in *Shuttleworth v. Laycock,*[5] in 1684, and *Pope v. Onslow,*[6] in 1692, Courts of Equity formulated the doctrine of **Consolidation**; by which a mortgagor who has mortgaged two estates to the same mortgagee cannot, after the day fixed for re-payment has gone by, compel the mortgagee to allow one mortgage to be redeemed without the other.[7] It is, however, quite worthy of note, that both these rules were founded by judges who, though they were then sitting in Equity tribunals, were, in fact, rather common lawyers than equity judges.[8]

Again, in the attitude of Equity towards the law of contract, we notice a profound respect for the Common Law, tempered by equitable considerations. Not only did Equity refuse to enforce contracts invalid at Common Law; but, in one case, in its dislike of mere formalities, it went beyond the strictness of the Common Law. Thus, a contract under seal, in fact made without consideration, could be enforced by an action at law, for historical reasons; but

Specific Performance

[1] *Noakes v. Rice* [1902] A.C. 24; *Bradley v. Carritt* [1903] A.C. 253.

[2] Hardres, 318.

[3] 2 Ventr. 337.

[4] The rule of tacking was abolished in 1874 by the Vendor and Purchaser Act of that year (s. 7), but revived by the Land Transfer Act of 1875 (s. 129).

[5] 1 Vern. 244.

[6] 2 Vern. 286.

[7] The doctrine of consolidation is now applicable only where it has been expressly reserved (Conveyancing Act, 1881, s. 17). It has been extended far beyond its primitive simplicity (*Pledge v. White* [1896] A.C. 197).

[8] The rule of tacking was laid down by Chief Baron Hale, Lord Keeper Bridgman, and Baron Rainsford; the rule of consolidation by Lord Keeper Bridgman.

Equity would not aid it by a decree of specific performance. And though Equity admitted that 'any bond was good enough against an executor,'[1] yet it would not allow a voluntary bond to be paid out of assets until all creditors for value had been satisfied.[2] Moreover, courts of Equity early adopted the principle, that specific performance would not be ordered where damages were an adequate remedy; and Lord Macclesfield carried this restraint so far as to refuse a decree for transfer of South Sea Stock, though at the time only a limited quantity was procurable.[3] Once more, the 'conscience' element in Equity refused to enforce the performance of an 'unreasonable,' though not, technically, an illegal or oppressive contract;[4] and the later developments of the doctrine of 'equitable fraud,' as applied to contracts, are well known.[5] But the most valuable of all the remedies of Equity, in such cases, was, not the mere refusal to assist in oppression, but the active assistance afforded to the oppressed by compelling the holder of an oppressive document to deliver it up to be cancelled. This remedy was applied by Lord Nottingham in 1680.[6] Only in one respect did Equity relax the law of contract. Generally speaking, though professing themselves not to be strictly bound by the words of the Statute of Frauds, equitable tribunals refused to enforce contracts for which the statutory evidence of writing, required by that statute,[7] was not forthcoming. But if the defendant had fraudulently prevented the proper evidence being used,[8] or had admitted in his pleadings the terms of the contract,[9] or if, in reliance on the contract, the plaintiff had incurred loss or liability in part performance of it,[10] then a Court of Equity would decree specific performance; even though no action lay at law. It will be observed, however, that even the

[1] *Edwards v. Countess of Warwick* (1723) 2 P. Wms., at 176.

[2] *Jones v. Powell* (1712) 1 Eq. Ca. Ab. 84 (Lord Harcourt).

[3] *Cud. v. Rutter* (1719) 1 P. Wms. 569.

[4] *Philips v. D. of Bucks* (1683) 1 Vern. 227 (Lord Keeper Guilford).

[5] Notwithstanding *Derry v. Peek* (1889) L.R. 14 App. Ca. 337, the doctrine of 'equitable fraud' is still law. By virtue of it, the Court constantly refuses to decree specific performance, and even orders the contract to be cancelled, where there has been innocent misrepresentation (*Redgrave v. Hurd* (1881) 20 Ch. D. 1). All that *Derry v. Peek* decided was, that no action of Tort could be based on 'equitable fraud.'

[6] *Skapholme v. Hart*, Ca. *temp.* Finch, 477.

[7] 29 Car. II (1677) c. 3, s. 4.

[8] *Maxwell v. Mountacute* (1719) Pre. Cha. 526 (Lord Macclesfield).

[9] *Croyston v. Banes* (1702) Pre. Cha. 208 (Sir John Trevor, M.R.).

[10] *Butcher v. Stapley* (1685) 1 Vern. 364 (Lord Guildford).

Statute of Frauds does not in such cases make void the contract; it merely renders it unenforceable, *i.e.* creates a procedural, not a substantial difficulty.

We have seen,[1] in dealing with the preceding period, that the Court of Chancery had succeeded, without much trouble, in escaping the threatened extinction of its important jurisdiction in trusts. By common consent, as has been pointed out, three classes of 'uses,' viz. (*a*) active uses, (*b*) uses of leaseholds, and (*c*) 'uses upon uses,' had escaped the meshes of the Statute of Uses, and, under the popular name of 'trusts' (though there is no technical value in the word) had completely re-established the doctrine of equitable interests, which indeed, so far as 'pure' personalty was concerned, had never been touched by the statute. It remained only for the Chancellors of the Restoration and the eighteenth century to fill up the outline sketched by their predecessors.

Trusts

This task they performed by the application of several principles which were, indeed, not new, but had not previously been carried out to their logical consequences.

The first of these was the protection of the trustee's estate against claims, founded on his delinquencies or acts, which would have been inconsistent with protection of the beneficiaries. Obviously this doctrine could not be pushed too far, if the whole system of tenures were not to go by the board; the lord must have his rents, reliefs, and other ordinary 'incidents.' But there were other liabilities of the legal estate which stood on a different footing; liabilities in which the claimant occupied more or less the position of a volunteer, or at any rate of a person seeking an unexpected benefit. Thus, for example, it seemed hard that the *cestui que trust* should lose his interest through the escheat or forfeiture of the trustee's estate by the failure of the latter's heirs, or his conviction or attainder for treason or felony. So far as escheat was concerned, Chief Justice Bridgman was, indeed, though on rather doubtful evidence, reported to have said, in *Geary v. Bearcroft*,[2] that the trust would be enforced against the lord taking by escheat; and this view was repeated by Sir John Trevor, M.R., in *Eales v. England*.[3] But these were mere

Protection of Trustee's Estate

[1] *Ante*, pp. 100, 101. [2] (1666) Cart. 67 (felony).
[3] (1702) Pre. Cha., at p. 202 (failure of heirs).

dicta, and were opposed by *dicta* of equally eminent judges, especially in the famous case of *Burgess v. Wheate,*[1] afterwards to be referred to; and eminent text-book writers, who were also judges,[2] also expressed a contrary opinion. With regard to forfeiture for treason, though Sir Matthew Hale gave relief to a mortgagor in 1667, yet he guarded himself carefully against being assumed to rule that the relief would be given in the case of trusts;[3] and Sanders,[4] though he inclines in favour of relief, can give no authority for his view. In fact it was not settled until 1834,[5] that neither the crime nor the failure of heirs of the trustee should endanger the interest of the *cestui que trust.*

With regard to the claims of a trustee's widow to dower. the action of the Courts was more prompt, though, perhaps, less logical. For, though it has always been recognized that a wife is a purchaser for value, Lord Nottingham said, as early as 1678,[6] that it was the constant practice to relieve against such claims; and the rule was extended to claims of freebench by the widows of copyhold trustees in 1681.[7] Until quite recently, women were so rarely made trustees, that the question of claims to curtesy of trust estates does not appear to have arisen.

An even more important protection for the interest of the *cestui que trust* was gained when Lord Keeper Finch (afterwards Lord Nottingham) in 1670,[8] clearly enunciated the principle that the debts of the owner of the legal estate cannot be enforced against the interest of the beneficiary; and this rule was definitely applied to trust estates by Lord Cowper, in 1715.[9] But the safety of the beneficiary from this danger was not complete, until it had been ruled, that even the bankruptcy of the trustee did not affect the *cestui que trust's* interests. This protection was, however, definitely secured in the year 1725, by the case of *Bennet v. Davis.*[10]

[1] (1759) 1 Ed. 177.

[2] *E.g.* Gilbert, C. B., *Law of Uses and Trusts* (2d. edition), p. 10, followed by Lord St. Leonards (Sugden) in the 3d. edition. (1811).

[3] *Pawlett v. A. G.*, Hardres, 465. (It must be recollected, that, even in the case of treason, copyholds were forfeited to the lord of the manor, not to the Crown (*Cornwall's Case* (1683) 2 Ventr. 38).)

[4] *Essay on Uses and Trusts,* 253.

[5] 4 & 5 Will. IV, c. 23.

[6] *Noel v. Jevon,* Freem. Cha. Ca. 43.

[7] *Bevant v. Pope, ibid.,* 71.

[8] *Burgh v. Francis,* 1 Eq. Ca. Ab. 321.

[9] *Finch v. E. of Winchilsea,* 1 P. Wms. 277.

[10] 2 P. Wms. 316 (Jekyll, M. R.).

A second principle, early adopted by Chancery, consisted of applying the rules of the legal estate, so far as possible, to equitable interests; with the result of making the resemblance between the two so close, as sometimes to deceive the superficial observer. Whether the adoption of this principle did not destroy an opportunity of introducing desirable reforms into land law, may well be doubted; but it would, perhaps, have been unreasonable to expect that even Courts of Equity in the eighteenth century should show much boldness in that direction. Thus, though a widow was not allowed until 1833 to claim dower out of her late husband's equitable interest of inheritance,[1] yet a husband was held entitled to curtesy in the equitable interests of his wife;[2] and, generally speaking, all rules as to inheritance,[3] quantity of interest, limitation, and rights of limited owners,[4] which applied to legal estates, except in so far as these depended directly on the maintenance of seisin or possession of the land,[5] were applied by analogy to equitable interests. It was, however, laid down, in the well-known case of *Burgess v. Wheate*,[6] that there could be no escheat of an equitable interest; but that, on failure of the heirs of the owner of an equitable fee simple, who had died intestate, his interest should not be enforceable against the owner of the legal estate.

Statute of Frauds

No account of the law of trusts in this period would, of course, be adequate without a reference to the Statute of Frauds; and this reference is not so irrelevant as it might appear in this chapter, for it is generally agreed that the framing of the statute was left in judicial hands.[7]

[1] It appears that at one time there was considerable doubt on this point. In *Bodmin v. Vandependy* (1685) 1 Vern. 356; Shower, P. C. 69, it was held that a widow could not enforce her claim against the inheritance, when an active term was outstanding; but, where the term was satisfied, it was held (*Dudley v. Dudley* (1705) Pre. Cha. 241) that relief would be granted to her. These were, however, legal claims; and though it was held by Sir Joseph Jekyll, M.R., in 1732 (*Banks v. Sutton*, 2 P. Wms. 700), that a widow might be endowed out of an equity of redemption, this decision was overruled in the following year by Lord Talbot, in the case of *Chaplin v. Chaplin* (3 P. Wms. 229). The reasons are explained by Lord Redesdale in *D'Arcy v. Blake* (1805) 2 Sch. & Lef. 387.

[2] *Sweetapple v. Bindon* (1705) 2 Vern. 536; *Casborne v. Scarfe* (1737) 1 Atk. 603.

[3] *Blackburn v. Graves* (1675) 1 Mod. 102; *Edwin v. Thomas* (1687) 1 Vern. 489.

[4] See the general principle laid down by Lord Cowper in *Watts v. Ball* (1709) 1 P. Wms. 108.

[5] *E.g.* failure of contingent remainders.

[6] (1759) 1 Ed. 177.

[7] The credit is diversely and variously attributed to Lord Nottingham, Sir Matthew Hale, and Sir Leoline Jenkins.

The Statute of Frauds had two substantial effects on the law of trusts. In the first place, by requiring all creations of trusts of lands to be evidenced by writing,[1] and all assignments of trusts whatsoever to be in writing,[2] the statute practically elevated the creation and transfer of trusts to the dignity of professional conveyancing, and, incidentally, dispelled the last lingering doubt, which had even survived the statute of Richard III,[3] as to the assignability of trust interests. In the second, by making equitable interests in land available for payment of the debts both of living and deceased *cestuis que trustent,*[4] it fostered the view that such assets were ordinary property. Incidentally, by excepting from the requirement of written evidence all trusts arising, 'by the implication or construction of law,'[5] the statute revived a vexed question as to the proper inference to be drawn from a voluntary conveyance of land, in which no use was expressed. The Court of Chancery had been strongly inclined to hold, that such a conveyance, where the donee was not *in loco filii* to the donor, raised an implied use in the donor's favour; and this tendency, which was wholly opposed to common law principles, was rather favoured by the words of the statute. But by two useful decisions given by Lord Hardwicke in 1740 and the following year,[6] it was at length established, that a voluntary conveyance, even to a stranger, does not of itself import a secret trust for the donor. The rule is, of course, quite different where there is a purchase in the name of a stranger. In that case, there is clearly a presumption of a trust for the person who actually finds the money.[7]

Finally in connection with the subject of trusts, it may be mentioned that it was Lord King, not otherwise very eminent as an Equity judge, who laid down, in the leading case of *Keech v. Sandford,*[8] decided in 1726, the great principle, that any profit, direct or indirect, made by a trustee out of his position as trustee, should be held by him on behalf of his *cestuis que trustent.* In that case, the lord of a market refused to renew an expired lease, which had been held on trust, either to the trustee as such or to the beneficiaries. He was willing, however,

[1] Statute of Frauds (1677) s. 7. [2] *Ibid.*, s. 9. [3] 1 Ric. III (1483) c. 1.
[4] Statute of Frauds (1677) s. 10. [5] *Ibid.*, s. 8.
[6] *Lloyd v. Spillet* (1740) 2 Atk. 148; *Young v. Peachy* (1741) *ibid.*, 254.
[7] *Dyer v. Dyer* (1788) Cox, 92. [8] 2 Eq. Ca. Ab. 741.

to grant a renewal to the trustee personally. It was held that the renewed lease formed part of the trust estate.

No account of Equity in this period would be in the least adequate, which did not refer, however briefly, to the action of Chancery in building up the doctrine of the separate estate of a married woman. For, though the reports show that, even before the Civil War, the doctrine was recognized,[1] yet it was the Civil War itself, with its attendant cloud of family settlements, which inevitably left to the Restoration Chancellors the task of elaborating the system.

Married Women's Property

At the common law, a wife's corporeal chattels passed to her husband absolutely. He could, if he pleased, enforce, or reduce into possession, her choses in action; but, if he did not do so, and predeceased her, they survived to her. By virtue of this doctrine, he could also collect the rents of her lands from the day of the marriage; but he did not obtain a 'real' interest, or estate, in her lands of inheritance, until the birth of issue by her capable of inheriting. On the birth of such issue, however, if the wife were actually seised of a present estate of inheritance, the seisin passed to the husband for his life, under the name of 'tenant by the curtesy.' The wife, from the day of the marriage, ceased to have any contracting power; her contracts, if they were valid at all, were only valid as the contracts of her husband, and he alone (if any one) was liable on them. He was also liable for her ante-nuptial debts, whether he received any property with her, or not;[2] and for her torts committed before or during the marriage. In a word, her legal personality (but not that of her heirs) was merged in his; to such an extent that, though the husband could not affect the inheritance of her land, yet the wife could not dispose of it otherwise than by Fine. She had no power at all to make a will without his consent; and he could not even authorize her to make a will of land.[3]

Common Law Rules

It was against the common law doctrine which gave all the

[1] *Gorge v. Chansey* (1639) 1 Rep. in Cha. 67 (Lord Coventry).

[2] It was ruled, even in Equity, after some doubt, that the husband's liability did not continue after the wife's death; even though he had received a large property with her (*Reard v. Stanford* (1735) Ca. temp. Talbot, 173).

[3] 34 & 35 Hen. VIII (1542) c. 5, s. 14.

wife's personalty to her husband absolutely, that the first revolt occurred. The case before the Civil War,[1] above alluded to, was that of a married woman separated from her husband, and may, on that account, be regarded as exceptional. Moreover, it only affected personalty. But from the Restoration onwards, it is clear that Chancery would protect any gift to a married woman for her 'separate use,' or 'sole and separate use,' and would, to carry out the donor's intention, effectually protect such gift from the debts, control, or engagements of the husband.[2] For some time there lingered a doubt whether the gift could be made before marriage;[3] and, for some less time, whether it could be made without the intervention of trustees.[4] But these two doubts were ultimately settled in the affirmative; though, as the story of Roger North's brother Dudley's marriage shows,[5] a direct gift of chattels to a married woman for her separate use is of little value. By the time of Addison, the practice of limiting a separate estate had grown so far as to call for protest.

'Separate Use'

But Equity did not content itself with merely protecting property settled upon a married woman; in certain cases it interfered to procure a settlement of her property. The converse of the husband's right to his wife's personalty was his liability to maintain her; and, if he had manifestly shown himself incapable of performing this liability, or been guilty of misconduct, Equity would not allow him or his creditors to claim property coming to the wife, without making some provision for her. The first instance of the exercise of this jurisdiction appears to have been in the case of *Packer v. Wyndham*,[6] where a man had clandestinely married a wealthy lunatic. The ecclesiastical court pronounced in favour of the marriage; but Chancery refused to allow the wife's fortune, which, happily, was in its possession, to be paid to the husband, until he had made a suitable settlement on his wife. This

Equity to a Settlement

[1] *Gorge v. Chansey* (1639) 1 Rep. in Cha. 67.

[2] Early examples are *Darcy v. Chute* (1663) 1 Cha. Ca. 21 (showing the limits of the doctrine); *Haymer v. Haymer* (1678) 2 Vent. 343; *Cotton v. Cotton* (1693) 2 Vern. 290.

[3] Finally set at rest by the leading decision in *Tullett v. Armstrong* (1838) 1 Beav. 1.

[4] *Bennet v. Davis* (1725) 2 P. Wms. 315.

[5] *Lives of the Norths*, II, par. 185. (The lady was the daughter of the great Sir Robert Cann, of Bristol.)

[6] (1715) Pre. Cha. 412. The date of the order decreeing a settlement is not given; but it must have been a good deal before 1715.

'equity to a settlement' soon became a settled doctrine of the Court, and was enforced not only against the husband himself, but his creditors claiming through him;[1] though, somewhat narrowly, the Court refused to extend the equity in favour of children, after the death of their mother.[2] It is to be observed, that the doctrine was, in a sense, negative. Where the husband's title was legal, the Court could not interfere; it was only where he was obliged to resort to a Court of Equity (including an ecclesiastical court)[3] that the opportunity for imposing terms arose.

Wife's Powers of Disposition

Naturally, there was some little doubt as to the wife's powers of dealing with this new kind of property. The Common Law was so unfamiliar with the notion of alienation by a married woman, except through the formality of a Fine, that it fell to Equity to build up the new doctrine. From the earliest cases, it appears that, with regard to pure personalty, a married woman's right to dispose of her separate estate, even by will, was unquestioned; in the middle of the eighteenth century, Lord Hardwicke laid it down, that she might 'dispose of it by an act in her life or will,' without taking the trouble to quote an authority.[4] But, with regard to land, there was more hesitation. In the case last referred to, Lord Hardwicke, though he inclined to think that the married woman might dispose of separate real estate by the medium of a power of appointment,[5] or, of course, by a Fine, thought that she could not defeat the expectations of her heirs by an ordinary will. Again, it had been held as early as 1723, by Sir Joseph Jekyll, M.R., that the bond debt of a married woman was payable out of her separate personalty;[6] but it was not until 1778, in the well-known case of *Hulme v. Tenant*,[7] that the liability was extended to her separate land. When this point was reached, however, the alienability of the separate estate had proceeded

[1] *Jacobson v. Williams* (1717) 2 P. Wms. 382 (Lord Cowper).

[2] *Scriven v. Tapley* (1764) Ambl. 509 (Lord Northington).

[3] *Nicholas v. Nicholas* (1720) Pre. Cha., at p. 548. There is a note in Tothill's Reports of a case of *Tanfield v. Davenport* (1638) p. 114, which, if correct, would make the doctrine of 'equity to a settlement' date back to Charles I's time. But it is too vague to be trustworthy.

[4] *Peacock v. Monk* (1750) 2 Ves. Sr., at p. 191. Perhaps Lord Hardwicke forgot the exception of reversionary personalty.

[5] This had been previously admitted in *Bertie v. Lord Chesterfield* (1723) 9 Mod. 31.

[6] *Norton v. Turvil*, 2 P. Wms. 144.

[7] Bro. C.C. 16 (Lord Thurlow).

so far, that there was danger lest the whole elaborate structure reared for the protection of the married woman should fall by its own weight.

For it is not difficult to see that, to place a married woman in the legal position of a man, as regards her separate property, is to afford her very little real protection. A married woman needs to be protected, not only against her husband, but against herself. It is idle to secure to her separate property; if the first use she makes of her security is to alienate the property. Accordingly, but not until the limits of Equity reform had been nearly reached, Lord Thurlow, the last of the reforming Chancellors, made an attempt to save the situation, by inserting the 'restraint on anticipation' clause, *i.e.* the provision in a settlement which makes the separate estate (either capital, or income, or both) of a married woman, incapable of alienation or anticipation, direct or indirect, so long as she remains a married woman. Those readers who have followed the history of the earlier periods of English law, will readily realize how strongly the new clause was opposed to the current of judicial decisions, which had been all for breaking down restraints on alienation. More than that. Just at the very time when the Court of Chancery was adopting the 'restraint on anticipation,' it was actually formulating the Rule against Perpetuities,[1] designed to prevent the tying up of property. It is not to be wondered at, therefore, if Lord Thurlow's project should at first have met with little sympathy in the Courts. Even Lord Thurlow himself, in *Pybus v. Smith*,[2] was compelled to uphold the alienation of settled property by a wife 'while the wax was yet warm upon the deed.' But the evils revealed by that case set the Chancellor upon devising an improved clause; and at length, in 1817,[3] even the cautious Lord Eldon admitted the validity of the restraint. Whether such very exceptional treatment of the property of a married woman can be justified at the present day, is an open question; and modern legislation has allowed the restraint to be removed

Restraint on Anticipation

[1] *E.g. Stanley v. Leigh* (1732) 2 P. Wms., at p. 689 (Jekyll, M.R.); *Stephens v. Stephens* (1736) Ca. temp. Talbot, 228; *Heath v. Heath* (1781) 1 Bro. C.C. 147 (Lord Thurlow); *Jee v. Audley* (1787) 1 Cox, 324 (Kenyon, M.R.); finally settled in *Cadell v. Palmer* (1833) 1 Cl. & F. 372.

[2] (1791) 3 Bro. C.C. 340.

[3] *Jackson v. Hobhouse*, 2 Mer. 483. Perhaps the credit of the first actual decision is due to Lord Alvanley (*Socket v. Wray* (1793) 4 Bro. C.C. 483).

in certain cases.[1] But it is indubitable, that the original introduction of the clause is one of the most striking efforts of judicial law reform in the eighteenth century.

Administration of Assets

We come lastly to the greatest of all the achievements of Equity in this period, viz., the acquisition of that jurisdiction in the ministration of the estates of deceased persons, which has brought so much grist to the mills of Chancery. The history of that acquisition has, perhaps, never been adequately told; certainly it is instructive and interesting.

At the end of the sixteenth century, the jurisdiction in matters of the estates of deceased persons was in a thoroughly unsatisfactory state. Owing to the jealousy with which the King's Courts had for centuries excluded the ordinary testamentary tribunals from any question concerning land, all disputes concerning the validity and construction of devises, and all questions of inheritance, had to be decided in the courts of Common Law. Similarly, to the very limited extent to which the creditor of a deceased person could enforce payment of his debt out of the real estate of his debtor, he had to sue the heir in a Common Law tribunal. In the same way, the recovery of debts by and against personal representatives could, in effect, only be carried on in the Common Law courts; for, if the Church courts had ever afforded adequate process in such cases, the contempt into which they had fallen since the Reformation, and the increasing efficiency of Common Law remedies, had virtually robbed them of their jurisdiction. To this necessity of resorting to the formal tribunals of the Common Law, the administration of assets owes two at least of its most marked and unsatisfactory features at the present day, viz., the rights of **Retainer** and **Preference**. Inasmuch as an executor could not sue himself in a Common Law court, he was allowed to retain any debt due to him from the testator, in priority to all other creditors of the same degree; the argument being, that he ought not to be in a worse position than a stranger, who could have sued the executor at once and compelled him to pay.[2] The last consideration gave rise to the equally un-

[1] Conveyancing Act, 1881, s. 39; Married Women's Property Act, 1893, s. 2; Trustee Act, 1893, s. 45.

[2] In the case of administrators, the Courts of Probate (not very effectively) framed their bond of security in such a way, that it prevented, or was supposed to prevent, the operation of these technical rules.

satisfactory right which the personal representative still has, of paying one creditor before others of the same, or (now) even of a higher degree.[1] For, if the executor had been sued by the creditor, his only defence would have been '*plene administravit*'; and this defence he could not, obviously, support, as long as assets remained.

On the other hand, for authority to deal with the personal property of his testator or intestate, the personal representative was obliged, as we have seen,[2] to resort to the ecclesiastical tribunal, which still retained all probate and administrative jurisdiction. In such a tribunal alone could the personal representative be compelled to account to the beneficiaries for his administration; and in it alone lay any process to compel the payment of a legacy, or share of an intestate's estate.

Finally, in the event of any creditor or beneficiary requiring the aid of any extraordinary help in securing payment of his debt or legacy, he had to resort to an Equity tribunal for assistance. Particularly, if he wished to enforce payment out of the real estate of the deceased. According to Common Law rules, the simple-contract creditor and the legatee had no claim against the land of their deceased debtor; while the Statute of Wills of 1540, by enabling the debtor to devise the bulk of his lands, had enabled him also to defeat his specialty creditors, by devising away his land to strangers.[3] For, until the passing of the Statute of Fraudulent Devises, in 1691,[4] no action lay by the creditor against the devisee. But, since the passing of the Statute of Wills, it had become increasingly common for testators to charge their real estate, directly or indirectly, with the payment of debts and legacies; and as neither the Common Law nor the ecclesiastical tribunals had any adequate machinery for enforcing such charges,[5] the claimant naturally resorted to Chan-

[1] *Re Samson* [1906] 2 Ch. 584.

[2] *Ante*, p. 62. An attempt to invoke the jurisdiction of Chancery to decide as to the validity of a will seems to have been made, with some success, as early as 1574 (*Mayor of Faversham v. Parke, Acta Cancellariæ*, 410). But perhaps this was a will of lands.

[3] Note that a devise to the heir would not be effective for this purpose. For, by Common Law rules, a devise to an heir is nugatory.

[4] 3 W. & M. c. 14.

[5] Of course there was also the objection, that ecclesiastical courts could not touch land. It is interesting to note, that for some time after the passing of the Statute of Wills it was regarded as doubtful whether there could be a suit in the Church courts for a legacy charged on land (cf. *Paschall v. Keterich* (1557) Dyer, 151b, with an anonymous case of 1567 (*ibid.*, 264b)).

cery, which, with its elaborate organization of Masters, Clerks, Registrars, and the like, would proceed to take the accounts of the deceased's property, and, if necessary, direct a sale of his land, and payment out of the proceeds. Thus arose, in distinction from **Legal Assets**, or estate for which an executor would have to account in a common law action by the creditor, before he could secure a verdict of *plene administravit*, a new category of **Equitable Assets,** or property which could only be reached through the medium of a Court of Equity; and, even though statutes like the Statute of Frauds occasionally removed items from the latter to the former category,[1] sufficient of the latter remains to the present day to preserve the distinction. To these 'equitable assets' the Court of Chancery applied equitable, not legal principles; and, so far as they were concerned, the doctrines of retainer and preference, and the elaborate degrees of priority of different classes of debts, had simply no existence.

Competition for the Jurisdiction

With the commencement of the seventeenth century, we notice a change, which may fairly be described as a movement towards unity of jurisdiction. Though, as has been pointed out,[2] the Reformation did not deprive the Church courts of their testamentary jurisdiction, it had undoubtedly lowered their prestige; and we find attempts, in the early years of the seventeenth century, to bring before lay tribunals matters which at one time unquestionably belonged to the Church courts. The tendency was not confined to matters like defamation and perjury. Thus, in 1611, a plaintiff sued for a legacy in the King's Bench;[3] and, though he was unsuccessful, no objection was raised to the jurisdiction. It is interesting to note, that the form of action was Assumpsit; on the (fictitious) promise to pay, alleged to have been given in consideration that the plaintiff would forbear to sue. This ingenious device was pushed forward during the period of the Commonwealth, when, of course, the Church courts were suspended;[4] and, after the Restoration, it made good its footing,[5] though there was a serious objection to the form of the action in the possible plea of want of consideration for the alleged promise to pay. Of course there

[1] *E.g.* by making trust estates in fee simple assets for payment of debts (29 Car. II (1677) c. 3, ss. 10–11).

[2] *Ante*, pp. 74, 75.

[3] *Smith v. Johns*, Cro. Jac. 257.

[4] The critical moment may be seen in *Tooke v. Fitz-John* (1657) Hardres, 96.

[5] *Nicholson v. Shirman* (1661) 1 Sid. 45.

was no real consideration; and, though Lord Mansfield, with his usual breadth of view, refused to allow the technical objection to prevail,[1] Lord Kenyon, a quarter of a century later,[2] closed the doors of the Common Law courts against such actions.

Long before that time, however, the superior machinery of Chancery had practically succeeded, not only in depriving the ecclesiastical courts of their monopoly, but in preventing actions for legacies becoming really frequent in the Common Law courts. Lord Mansfield, frankly, though with regret, in the case of *Atkins v. Hill*,[3] explains the position. It was at least doubtful if the Common Law court could make an executor account; for the common law Writ of Account only lay, properly speaking, against bailees, and the legatee had not bailed the goods to the executor.[4] Again, the weapon of 'discovery,' or interrogatories, peculiar to Chancery, was especially valuable in such cases.[5] Again, by the use of injunctions, vexatious suits against personal representatives could be stopped, and the assets administered properly and leisurely.[6] It is, in fact, abundantly clear, that, by means of these and other attractions, the Court of Chancery had, not merely acquired a share of administrative jurisdiction before the end of the seventeenth century,[7] but had, by the end of the eighteenth century, practically secured the lion's share of that jurisdiction.[8] In this somewhat invidious position, it at first maintained a delicate affectation of respect for the ecclesiastical tribunals which it had plundered;[9] but, inasmuch as this profession was accompanied by the inconsistent practice of entertaining suits even when proceedings had already been commenced in the Church courts,[10] and, finally, of actually pronouncing on the validity of a will

[1] *Hawkes v. Saunders* (1775) Cowp. 289.

[2] *Deeks v. Strutt* (1794) 5 T. R. 690.

[3] (1775) Cowp., at p. 288. (The writer has traced back the Chancery jurisdiction in actions for legacies to the year 1600 (*Awbry v. George, Acta Cancellariæ*, 757; *Browne v. Ricards*, *ibid.*, 761). But in the second of these cases, the Court admitted that questions as to the validity of wills were for the ecclesiastical tribunal.)

[4] This objection was taken as early as 1557 (*Paschall v. Keterich*, Dyer, 151b, note).

[5] *Morrice v. B. of England* (1736) Ca. temp. Talbot, 217. (In this case the Chancellor fully admits the concurrent jurisdiction of the Common Law courts.)

[6] *Robinson v. Bell* (1690) 2 Vern. 146.

[7] *Noel v. Robinson* (1682) 1 Vern. 93; *Jenks v. Holford* (1682) 1 Vern. 61 (Lord Nottingham).

[8] *Atkins v. Hill* (1775) Cowp., at p. 288 (Lord Mansfield).

[9] *Nicholas v. Nicholas* (1720) Pre. Cha. 546.

[10] *Wright v. Black* (1682) 1 Vern. 106.

itself,[1] it is probable that the judges and officials of the ecclesiastical tribunals derived scant satisfaction from the lip reverence of their successful rivals.

So far as the new jurisdiction of Chancery involved the decision of purely testamentary questions, it took over the existing ecclesiastical law, which was, in effect, Roman Law.[2] The attitude of the Court towards the doctrines of the Common Law has partly appeared from the account already given of the growth of the new jurisdiction; but a better idea of it will be gained by a brief statement of the four great and novel principles evolved by the Chancellors of this period in dealing with the administration of assets.

The doctrine of **marshalling**, which is really an application of the great Roman principle of **subrogation**, was not confined in its scope to the assets of deceased persons; but it is in that connection that its chief importance lies. As we have said, the Common Law recognized different classes of debts, having various priorities. Broadly speaking, simple-contract creditors could only claim to be paid out of personalty; creditors by specialty in which the heirs were bound could *also* claim to be paid out of real estate descended (and, after 1691, devised). If a specialty creditor chose to sue the executor and get paid out of personalty, Chancery could not, or would not, prevent him; but if he failed to get payment in full out of the personalty, and then came to Chancery for help in making the realty liable, the Court would not help him until he had allowed the simple-contract creditors to take out of the land an amount equal to that which he (the specialty creditor) had taken out of the personalty.[3] Or again, in the above circumstances, if,

Marshalling

[1] *Goss v. Tracy* (1715) 1 P. Wms. 287. It is true that this was a will of lands, with which the ecclesiastical court could not concern itself, and that, for some time, it was held that, in a case of pure personalty, Chancery could not pronounce on the validity of the will (*Archer v. Morse* (1686) 2 Vern. 8; *Kerrich v. Bransby* (1727) 7 Bro. P.C. 437). But, ultimately, under cover of deciding on the validity of particular provisions in a will, Chancery acquired the power of pronouncing on the will as a whole (*Marriott v. Marriott* (1725) 1 Stra. 666). In *Barnsley v. Powel* (1748) 1 Ves. 119, Lord Hardwicke took the bold course of decreeing the executors under a will actually admitted to probate, to consent to a revocation of probate in the next term. After this, it would have been idle to deny the practical power of Chancery to decide on the validity of wills; though Lord Mansfield could still deny it in theory (*Atkins v. Hill* (1775) Cowp., at p. 287).

[2] *Atkins v. Hill, ubi sup.*, at p. 287 (Lord Mansfield).

[3] Of course, if the specialty creditor had a legal claim against the devisees (*e.g.* after 1691), he could satisfy it by an action at law; and the Chancery doctrine would not apply.

after all debts paid, there was a balance of personalty, this would go, not to the legatees, but to the devisees of the real estate; for, in view of Equity, which in this respect agreed with the Common Law, the real estate ought not, as between the beneficiaries, to have been resorted to for payments of debts, until the personalty was exhausted. The former was a case of 'marshalling' as between creditors; the latter a case as between beneficiaries. Owing to recent changes in the law,[1] marshalling between creditors is now virtually extinct;[2] but marshalling as between beneficiaries is still quite common. It is, therefore, interesting to note that this doctrine, though foreshadowed in a case of 1664, decided by Lord Clarendon,[3] is virtually the creature of Lord Nottingham.[4] It is obvious that it involves an elaborate foundation of rules as to the 'order of resort,' *i.e.* of the order in which, apart from any intention of the deceased, the different classes of his assets shall be made available for payment of debts, or, which amounts to the same thing, the order of priority in which the different classes of beneficiaries may claim. These rules were also the work, mainly, of the Chancellors of this period; but to go into details would make this chapter too long. Briefly, they depend on three principles — (*a*) that personalty is the primary fund for payment of debts, (*b*) that the devisee or legatee of a specific thing is preferred (*quoad* that thing) to a general legatee, (*c*) that any express beneficiary is preferred to the heir or next-of-kin, who only take in default of disposition.

The second of the peculiar doctrines of Equity evolved in connection with the administration of assets in this period, is the doctrine of **conversion**, which must, of course, be carefully distinguished from the Common Law tort of that name.[5] By the equitable doctrine of Conversion, land directed by its owner to be sold, *i.e.* directed in a binding settlement which duly takes effect, will be regarded as personalty, not as realty, from the delivery of the settlement; whilst, on the other hand, money or other personalty directed to be invested in the purchase of freehold or copyhold lands, will be regarded as real estate from the date of the direction. To the

Conversion

[1] *E.g.* Administration of Estates Act, 1869.

[2] *I.e.* in administration of assets. It can easily arise *inter vivos*.

[3] *Armitage v. Metcalf*, 1 Ch. Ca. 74.

[4] *Anon.* (1679) 2 Ch. Ca. 4. The leading case is *Clifton v. Burt* (1720) 1 P. Wms. 679.

[5] *Ante*, p. 142.

layman, the doctrine appears to be highly artificial and academic. Its practical result, in the cases put, is to cause the property to pass under the will (or intestacy, as the case may be) of the beneficiary for whom it is destined, as personalty, or as realty, whether the direction of the settlor has actually been carried out, or not. Obviously, so long as the distinction between realty and personalty is recognized by English law, it is of great importance to know into which category a particular fund falls; and it would hardly be fair, that the beneficial destination of a fund should depend upon whether third parties, usually trustees, had or had not promptly carried out the settlor's directions. It was, undoubtedly, this last consideration which led Lords Harcourt and Cowper, in the leading case of *Lingen v. Savray*, in 1711,[1] to accept the doctrine, which had previously been hinted at by Lord Guilford[2] and Lord Jeffreys.[3] But it must be confessed that a somewhat doubtful qualification was added by Lord Thurlow in the famous case of *Ackroyd v. Smithson*, in 1780,[4] when the Chancellor decreed that conversion directed by a will was 'for the purposes of the will only.' In that case John Scott, afterwards Lord Eldon, acquired fame by persuading the Court that, notwithstanding a direction in a will to sell the whole of the testator's real estate, and notwithstanding an actual realization, any surplus remaining after the performance of the purposes for which realization was directed, would go, not to the residuary legatees or next-of-kin, but to the residuary devisee or heir.

The third of the special equitable doctrines we are now considering is that known as **satisfaction** or **performance**. It proceeds on the assumption, that if a man has entered into an obligation to perform a certain act, or, in one case, has expressed an intention to confer a benefit, any subsequent benefit conferred by him on the obligee or intended beneficiary, which substantially, though not technically, fulfils the obligation, or may be regarded as an execution of the intended benefit, will have that effect. But there is, of course, this difference between the two cases. If a man enters into a legal obligation, the obligee or creditor is entitled to say that he will take nothing less than literal performance. Therefore, in such a case, all that Equity can do, is to prevent him claiming the

Satisfaction

[1] 1 P. Wms. 172.
[2] *Kettleby v. Atwood* (1684) 1 Vern. 298.
[3] *Knights v. Atkyns* (1686) 2 Vern. 20.
[4] 1 Bro. C.C. 503.

substitute as well, if he insists on his legal right to exact fulfilment. Where the intended benefit is a pure gift, which, being executory, can be revoked, *e.g.* a legacy, the latter provision will, if considered by the Court to be intended as a substitute, actually 'adeem,' or take away, the first.

It is in connection with legacies that we trace the beginnings of the doctrine of satisfaction at the commencement of the eighteenth century. In the case of *Herne v. Herne,* decided in 1706 by Lord Cowper, a husband had, in his marriage articles, agreed that his wife should, at his death, over and above her 'widow's third,' have a legacy of £800 and certain furniture and jewels, and that such provision should not debar her from anything which he should give her 'by will or writing.' The husband died, having bequeathed his wife a legacy of £1000; which she claimed in addition to the £800. But the Court held, that the legacy was a 'satisfaction' of the articles; and compelled the widow to choose between them. Similar cases, of ordinary debts satisfied by legacies, appear immediately in the books;[1] and though there is, in some directions, an apparent reluctance to accept the rule, yet, after the decision by Lord Talbot, in 1735, of the leading case of *Lechmere v. Lechmere,*[2] in which the property agreed to be settled was merely left to descend to an heir of the beneficiary, there could be no question as to its orthodoxy. It is, however, an important qualification to bear in mind, that it is much easier to raise a case of satisfaction against a person *in loco filii* to the person from whom the benefit proceeds, than against a stranger. For Equity 'leans against double portions'; though it will only allow the other persons *in loco filiorum* to object to them.

The fourth and last of the great doctrines of Equity on the subject of the administration of assets is the doctrine of **election.** It grows naturally out of the doctrine of satisfaction; and is, indeed, foreshadowed in the early case of *Herne v. Herne,* before alluded to.[3] As was said above, Equity has no power, as a general rule, to compel a man to forego a legal right; it can only refuse to help him if he claims the equitable substitute for it.

[1] *E.g. Talbot v. D. of Shrewsbury* (1714) Pre. Cha. 394 (Lord Harcourt); *Chancey's Case* (1717) 1 P. Wms. 408.

[2] Ca. temp. Talb. 80.

[3] (1706) 2 Vern., at p. 556. 'If she will take the benefit of the will, she must suffer the will to be performed throughout.'

In other words, he is entitled to choose whether he will abide by his legal right, or take the benefit offered in exchange.

Election

The same principle governs the later and more familiar application of the doctrine of 'election.' If a settlor professes to give A's property to B, and to give some of his own (the settlor's) property to A, A can, of course, refuse to part with his property to B. But, on the other hand, if he refuses to carry out the settlor's intention with regard to B, at least to the extent of compensating him out of his own (A's) property, he cannot claim the benefit proffered by the settlor. He cannot 'approbate and reprobate'; he must 'elect for or against the settlement.' As has been said, the first application of the doctrine is clearly foreshadowed in *Herne v. Herne;*[1] the second is explicitly adopted in another case of the same year, viz. *Noys v. Mordaunt.*[2] In the last case, Lord Cowper seems to restrict the doctrine to the case of rivalries between brothers and sisters; and there can be little doubt that the Roman doctrine of *collatio bonorum* (known in the vernacular as 'hotchpot') had a good deal to do with originating the doctrines of Satisfaction and Performance. But in the slightly later case of *Streatfield v. Streatfield,* decided in 1735,[3] Lord Talbot stated the principle in perfectly general terms; and it is now generally admitted to apply in all cases.

It is not, of course, pretended for a moment, that the whole of the work of judicial reform, in the century following the Restoration, was effected by the Court of Chancery. That the largest share is to the credit of the Chancellors and Master of the Rolls, can hardly be denied; and therefore the bulk of this chapter has been devoted to their achievements. But, as is well known, the jurisdiction by 'English Bill' was exercised by the Court of Exchequer from early times until 1841; and, in the hands of men like Sir Matthew Hale, the Atkins', Eyre, and Gilbert, that jurisdiction was not likely to be unproductive.

Other Sources of Equity

Nor should the splendid services of Lord Mansfield, in a slightly later period, be forgotten. Not only did he and Lord Camden vigorously uphold the liberty of the subject in days

[1] (1706) 2 Vern. 555. [2] (1706) *ibid.*, 581.
[3] Ca. temp. Talb. 176.

when that liberty was only too likely to suffer;[1] but he widened the jurisdiction of the King's Courts by adopting the principles of the Law Merchant into the Common Law, and thus rendering it suitable to deal with the great commercial expansion which was taking place. Finally, by his well-known decision in *Moses v. Macferlan*,[2] delivered when he had been only four years upon the Bench, Lord Mansfield laid down the great and truly equitable principle which is the parent of the whole modern doctrine of Quasi-contract: that where the defendant is 'obliged by the ties of natural justice and equity,'[3] to pay or repay money, no technical objections as to the form of action, or the absence of consideration, will be allowed to defeat the plaintiff's claim. But if this chapter has not succeeded in proving the thesis with which it started: that to judicial reform was due whatever of legal progress there was in the century following the Restoration, it is already too long, and must now close.

Only, in conclusion, the reader can hardly spare a regret, that this beneficent process of adjusting the law to the development of social needs, should have come to an abrupt termination in the last quarter of the eighteenth century. But, with Lord Eldon on the woolsack and Lord Kenyon on the King's Bench, the channels of Equity became choked with the stones of precedent and the weeds of form; and the fountains of justice ran slowly and painfully, till the sweeping hand of Parliamentary Reform released the flow again. Lest it should be said that this criticism is vague and unfounded, the writer may be permitted to mention two obvious and gross evils, which the legislature could hardly have been expected to anticipate, but which a free application of judicial discretion might have nipped in the bud. One is the evil of 'tied' public-houses, under which brewers, publicans, and the public alike groan, but which could have been stopped at once by a liberal interpretation of the established principle of 'restraint of trade,' exercised by the Court of Chancery in its mortgage jurisdiction. Had the Courts boldly declared, that the liquor license was a monopoly supposed to be conferred for the public good, and, therefore, not capable of being restricted by private contract, the 'tied house' system could never

[1] *Wilkes v. Wood* (1763) 19 St. Tr. 1153; *Entick v. Carrington* (1765) *ibid.*, 1030; *Leach v. Money* (1765) *ibid.*, 1001.

[2] (1760) 2 Burr. 1005.

[3] *Ibid.*, at p. 1030.

have come into existence. The second example is that of the company promoter or director, who shields himself from liability towards his real beneficiaries, the shareholders, behind the artificial protection of that purely legal entity,[1] the company. With a reasonable application of equitable principles, the monstrous doctrine: that 'the directors of a company are not trustees for individual shareholders,' would never have been adopted; and directors who are secretly negotiating a profitable sale of their company's assets would not be allowed to go about buying up shares with a view to profiting at the expense of their own shareholders.[2] The Court which decided *Keech v. Sandford* would have made short work of a claim such as that.

[1] The writer has no wish to fall foul of recent theories on the nature of a corporation. Whatever may be the position as regards the outside world, it is tolerably clear that, as regards its own members, a corporation is a very artificial conception.

[2] *Percival v. Wright* [1902] 2 Ch. 421.

CHAPTER XV

CHANGES IN LAND LAW

THE structure of English land law has been compared in these pages[1] with a medieval building, of which the original idea has been transformed, and to which additions have, from time to time, been made, with a view of adapting it to modern requirements, but which, in spite of all, retains its medieval outlines and many of its medieval features. The Civil War, as has been hinted, made a severe breach in the medieval scheme; and, indeed, it may be said to have destroyed, not merely a wing, but the very centre and *omphalos* of the ancient fabric, the nucleus from which all the rest has sprung. So that the modern student of English land law has to begin by grasping a medieval principle, which (he is told) is the basis of the present scheme; only to learn, somewhat later, that the principle itself has ceased to have much practical application. Is it surprising that modern English land law should resemble a chaos rather than a system?

Abolition of Military Tenures

The breach effected by the Civil War is, of course, embodied in the Act for the Abolition of Military Tenures,[2] passed by the first Restoration Parliament in its first session. But, equally of course, that statute, though it formally embodied the change effected, did not of itself effect the change. The military system intended to be maintained by knight-service tenure had long passed away; the mailed knight, with his esquires or men-at-arms, had disappeared before the battles of Crecy and Agincourt, and, with him, the last real justification of military tenure. Since his disappearance, that tenure had been used mainly as an engine of oppressive taxation by the Crown. The Court of Augmentations,[3] and the Court of Wards and

[1] *Ante*, p. 83.
[2] 12 Car. II. (1660) c. 24.
[3] Set up by 27 Hen. VIII (1535) cc. 27 and 28; re-instituted by 7 Edw. VI (1553) c. 2; abolished by 1 Mary, st. II (1553) c. 10.

Liveries,[1] had been set up by the Tudor monarchs to keep the system alive for financial purposes. So searching was their machinery, that the great bulk of the landed gentry, who, owing to the operation of Quia Emptores,[2] had ceased to share in the plunder of infant heirs, endeavoured, on the accession of the Stuarts, to buy up the Crown's rights. But the Great Contract of 1610 had failed, because of the greed of James; and James' son, in his desperate attempt to govern without a Parliament, had revived the oppressions of the Tudor monarchs.

It is not, therefore, surprising to find that, during the Civil War, in February 1646, the two Houses had passed a sweeping Ordinance[3] abolishing the oppressive feudal incidents, and even the military tenures themselves, or that this Ordinance was confirmed and enlarged by a second Ordinance of the Protector and his Parliament, in the autumn of 1656.[4] Although the validity of these Ordinances could not be admitted by a Restoration Parliament which dated the accession of Charles II from the execution of his father, there was not the least desire, even on the part of the enthusiastic royalists of the Restoration, to revive the feudal claims of the Crown; and, as has been said, one of their first works was to pass the statute of 1660.[5] The wording of that enactment is peculiar; but its meaning is tolerably clear. Not only are all military tenures swept away, and the estates held by them converted into estates held by 'free and common socage';[6] but even the distinctively feudal incidents of the last-named tenure (*e.g.* 'aids') are abolished, as well as the peculiar features, *e.g.* fines for license to alienate[7] and payments for 'ousterlemain,' which still distinguished estates held direct from the Crown, or *in capite*, from estates held of mesne lords,[8] and the other prerogative claims of 'purveyance' and 'pre-emption.'[9] On the other hand, the purely financial items of rents, heriots, and reliefs, are expressly saved;[10] as are also the non-military tenures of frankalmoign and copyhold.[11] Finally, with characteristic Stuart notions of justice, the loss to the Crown entailed

[1] Set up by 32 Hen. VIII. (1540) c. 46; abolished by 12 Car. II (1660) c. 24, s. 3.
[2] 18 Edw. I. (1290) c. 1. See *ante*, pp. 102, 103.
[3] *Acts and Ordinances of the Commonwealth*, I, 833.
[4] *Ibid.*, II., 1043. [5] 12 Car. II (1660) c. 24. [6] Ss. 1, 2.
[7] For the nature of these liabilities, see *ante*, p. 103.
[8] 12 Car. II (1660) c. 24, ss. 1, 4. [9] *Ibid.*, ss. 12–14. [10] *Ibid.*, s. 5.
[11] 12 Car. II (1660) c. 24, s. 7.

by this statute was compensated for by an hereditary annual payment, or excise, on beer, ale, spirits, and other strong liquors, as well as on coffee, chocolate, sherbet, and tea.[1] In other words, the royalist landowners of the Restoration Parliament gaily lifted the burden from their own shoulders, and laid it on those of the general public. This part of the measure was entirely their own; but the origin of the reforming part of the statute is placed beyond doubt by the fact, that the statute is expressly made[2] to operate retrospectively from 24th February, 1646, the day of the passing of the Ordinance of the Long Parliament.

The Statute of Frauds

Closely following upon the Act for the Abolition of Military Tenures, came the Statute of Frauds,[3] which, though it was not entirely concerned with land law, contained, as is well known, several provisions relating to that subject. As has already been pointed out,[4] it imposed the requirement of writing on the creation of trusts of lands, and the assignment of all trusts, and made a trust estate in fee simple assets for payment of its owner's debts, both in his lifetime and after his decease. But, in addition to these provisions, the statute dealt a further blow at the principles of medieval conveyancing, by requiring[5] the ceremony of writing for the creation and transfer of all legal estates (including estates for years) save the smallest, and, in the case of devises, the additional ceremony of the presence of three witnesses. Moreover, it must be observed, those requirements, unlike those affecting contracts in the same statute, which will be hereafter referred to,[6] were not evidentiary only, but essential; *i.e.* the statute declared that, in their absence, nothing should pass but, at the most, a mere estate at will. Further, the statute dealt[7] with the tricky 'estate *pur autre vie*' (*i.e.* an estate held for the life of a person other than the tenant) by making it liable for the payment of its owner's debts, and, subject thereto, giving him liberty to dispose of it by his will.

From the passing of the Statute of Frauds, in 1677, to the assembling of the first Reformed Parliament in 1832, we have, as has been previously pointed out,[8] hardly a single statute of first-class importance dealing with land law. If we except such minor enactments as the *Cestui Que Vie* Acts,[9] the Landlord and Tenant

[1] *Ibid.*, ss. 15–27. [2] *Ibid.*, s. 1 (5). [3] 29 Car. II (1677) c. 3.
[4] *Ante*, p. 221. [5] Ss. 1–3, 5. [6] *Post*, pp. 298, 299. [7] S. 12.
[8] *Ante*, pp. 207, 208. [9] 18 & 19 Car. II (1667) c. 6; 6 Anne (1707) c. 18 (or 72).

Acts,[1] and the Statute of Fraudulent Devises,[2] the legislative history of the period is almost a blank; for the development of land law in that period, we must look to the work of the Courts of Equity, of which the last chapter endeavoured to give some account. But with the passing of the Reform Act, the flood-gates were opened; and the rush of waters which followed renders it necessary, in order to make the picture clear, to abandon the purely chronological for a partially analytical method. What have been the achievements of the nineteenth century and its successor in the reform of land law?

Complete Freedom of Alienation

First we may note the complete realization of a tendency which had long been manifest, and which had, in substance, successfully established itself by the close of the preceding period. It has been explained[3] how freedom of alienation, especially of alienation of land, is abhorrent to early stages of law; while as the social organism casts its patriarchal and military sloughs, and emerges into the commercial stage of development, impatience of all restraints on alienation manifests itself, and, ultimately, achieves the victory.

Incidentally, the Act of 1660, which abolished Military Tenures,[4] gave an impetus in this direction; for, the Statute of Wills in 1540,[5] which introduced freedom of testation, so far as land was concerned, expressly restricted that freedom as two thirds of the landowner's knight-service estates. The abolition of knight-service tenure, then, completed the work of the statute of 1540. But there had always been considerable doubt whether that statute applied to copyholds; or, rather, according to the doctrine of *Heydon's Case*,[6] it was assumed that the statute, which clearly derogated from the rights of lords, but did not expressly mention copyholds, did not apply to the latter tenure. It is true, that, by the somewhat clumsy machinery of a 'surrender to the use of the will,' a custom to devise established itself, doubtless in imitation of the statute, in many manors;[7] but when the necessity

[1] 4 Geo. II (1730) c. 28; 11 Geo. II (1737) c. 19.

[2] 3 & 4 W. & M. (1091) c. 14.

[3] *Ante*, pp. 36–38.

[4] 12 Car. II, c. 24.

[5] 32 Hen. VIII, c. 1.

[6] (1584) 3 Rep. 18.

[7] There is also some trace, during that period, of Courts of Equity allowing the equitable fee simple of a copyhold to be devised, even when the custom did not authorize a surrender of the legal estate to the use of the tenant's will (*Smith v. Baker* (1737) 1 Atk. 385).

for this device was abolished in 1815,[1] the statute abolishing it was careful to except all cases in which copyhold tenements were not devisable at all by custom. The Wills Act of 1837, however, completely swept away any doubts existing on the subject, and made all copyhold interests of a heritable nature devisable; while at the same time it authorized the devise of all contingent, executory, and future interests in land, about which there had also been some uncertainty.[2] In fact, so sweeping are the words of the Act, that a literal acceptance of them would even bestow the power of devise on a tenant in tail;[3] but it is unquestioned law, that an estate tail cannot be affected, though one can be created, by devise.

There remains, in truth, only one interest in land, as to the transferability of which there can be any real doubt. This is the possibility or chance of recovering an estate owing to the breach of a condition by the tenant. The Common Law disliked all traffic in such contingencies, fearing lest it should provoke 'maintenance,' or stirring-up of strife. So the benefit of conditions was, at common law, inalienable by act of the parties.[4] At the time of the Reformation, this restriction was broken down, so far as conditions in leases only were concerned, by the statute[5] which permitted the benefit of them to be assigned with the land or the reversion. The rule, however, still applied to conveyances of the inheritance, and to conditions of forfeiture of the inheritance. But the Wills Act of 1837 expressly extends[6] the power of devise to 'all rights of entry for condition broken'; and the Real Property Act, 1845,[7] contains a similar or even more sweeping provision[8] with regard to alienation by deed. Nevertheless, in spite of the express words of these statutes, it seems to be the better opinion, that a right of forfeiture arising from the actual breach of a condition is not

Rights of Forfeiture

[1] 55 Geo. III, c. 192, s. 3. (Before this time, however, some of the more progressive judges had suggested that a custom which made copyholds not devisable would be bad, as 'unreasonable.')

[2] Wills Act, 1837, s. 3.

[3] 'All real estate . . . which, if not so devised, . . . would devolve upon the heir at law or customary heir' (of the testator or his ancestor).

[4] *I.e.* by act *in pais*. In all probability, such rights could pass by Fine, with the approval of the Court. In the case of land, dealing in such rights was expressly forbidden by statute (32 Hen. VIII (1540) c. 9), which has only recently been repealed (Land Transfer Act, 1897, s. 11).

[5] 32 Hen. VIII (1540) c. 28. [6] S. 3, *ad fin.* [7] 8 & 9 Vict. c. 106 s. 6.

[8] 'A right of entry, whether immediate or future, and whether vested or contingent.'

transferable.[1] And a mere *spes successionis* is not assignable at law; though an assignment of it may be enforced in Equity, if made for valuable consideration.[2] But the power of assigning the benefit of future breaches of conditions in a lease has been rendered yet more effectual by the Law of Property Amendment Act, 1859,[3] which allows 'severance' of a condition of re-entry on non-payment of rent, and by the Conveyancing Act, 1881,[4] which allows severance of all conditions in leases, made for the benefit of the lessor.

Relief against Forfeiture of Leases

The relief against forfeitures incurred by breach of condition is, perhaps, only indirectly concerned with freedom of alienation; and yet the possibility of obtaining such relief certainly tends to make property more freely alienable. Accordingly it may be noted, that Equity had quite early, as a branch of its doctrine of relief against penalties, assumed the practice of restraining landlords from ejecting their tenants for breach of conditions in their leases, when such breaches had merely consisted in failure to make punctual payments of money, *e.g.* rent, and had not inflicted irreparable injury on the landlord. In such cases, Equity would decree restitution to the tenant on payment of arrears and interest. To such an extent had this practice been carried, that, in the Landlord and Tenant Act of 1730,[5] the power of Equity to relieve, in such cases, was restricted to a period of six months after the landlord had recovered the premises in ejectment; and this provision, being incorporated into the Common Law Procedure Act of 1852,[6] is the basis of the law on the subject of relief against non-payment of rent at the present day. The Law of Property Amendment Act of 1859[7] allowed a Court of Equity to relieve once against failure to insure; provided that no injury by fire had actually happened. But by far the most sweeping change was effected by the Conveyancing Act, 1881,[8] which, as amended by

[1] *Hunt v. Bishop* (1853) 8 Exch., at p. 680 *per* Pollock, C. B.; *Cohen v. Tannar* [1900] 2 Ch. 609. The Conveyancing Act, 1911, s. 2, has made an alteration as regards conditions in leases.

[2] *Re Ellenborough* [1903] 1 Ch. 699.

[3] 22 & 23 Vict. c. 35, s. 3. (By 'severance' is meant the dividing of the reversion between two or more owners. At the Common Law, the benefit of conditions was indivisible by act of the parties.)

[4] Ss. 10–12. It will be observed that the Act says nothing about severance of conditions for the benefit of the lessee.

[5] 4 Geo. II, c. 28, s. 2.

[6] 15 & 16 Vict. c. 76, s. 210.

[7] 22 & 23 Vict. c. 35, ss. 4–9.

[8] 44 & 45 Vict. c. 41, s. 14.

the Act of 1892,[1] substantially allows relief to be given against breach of any condition in a lease (except one against alienation) in the case of the lessee himself, and in all cases of an under-lessee who has been reasonably diligent. Moreover, the Act of 1881[2] forbids an action of ejectment for breach of a lessee's condition even to be commenced before the service of a notice, giving particulars of the breach complained of, and allowing opportunity for reparation.

It had, however, early been observed, that the full benefits of free alienation of land could not be obtained; unless, in some cases at least, a landowner were able to alienate, not merely his own interest, but those of other persons. At first this may sound to be a somewhat revolutionary doctrine; but the apparent injustice of it disappears when it is understood, that all such suggestions imply the fundamental condition, that in any such disposition, a 'limited owner,' *i.e.* an owner of anything less than the interest sought to be disposed of, must act honestly for the benefit of all parties concerned in that interest. The matter then becomes, simply, one of safeguards.

Limited Owners

The first step taken in the direction of entrusting powers of disposition to limited owners was by a statute of the year 1540.[3] By that time, as we have seen,[4] it had become clearly established, that a tenant in tail could alienate the estate in fee simple, by merely observing the proper formalities. It was not, therefore, a very revolutionary step to provide, as the statute of 1540 did, that leases for twenty-one years or three lives by a tenant in tail, to take effect in immediate possession, with due safeguards against waste by the lessees, and reservation of at least the existing rent, should be binding on the lessor's successors in the entail, notwithstanding the Statute *De Donis*. The real enterprise of the Act is, that it gives the same powers to a husband seised of lands in right of his wife, *i.e.* to a person whose interest was really only a life estate.[5] A less comprehensive alternative provision, affecting tenants in tail only, was contained in the Fines and Recoveries Act, 1833,[6] of which

Tenants in Tail

[1] 55 & 56 Vict. c. 13, ss. 2–4.
[2] S. 14.
[3] 32 Hen. VIII, c. 28, s. 1.
[4] *Ante*, pp. 113, 114.
[5] Doubtless the statute uses the expression 'having an estate of inheritance.' But the context makes it clear, that if the wife had an estate of inheritance, the husband, tenant by the curtesy, might exercise the statutory power.
[6] 3 & 4 Will. IV, c. 74, s. 41.

some explanation will shortly be given; but the powers of the statute of Henry VIII remained legally unaffected, until the passing of the Settled Estates Act, 1856,[1] to which reference must now be made.

'Family Settlements'

The more complicated forms of family settlement introduced by the conveyancers of the Civil War, soon rendered the simple provisions of the statute of 1540 inadequate. For the dangers of forfeiture, and other evils of disturbed times, could not have been avoided by the simple process of entailing the family estate. Not merely would the tenant in tail, in a fit of enthusiastic loyalty, have been able to bar the entail, and pour the purchase money into the royal coffers; but, after the establishment of the Commonwealth, he would have been liable to forfeit the whole estate for engaging in correspondence with the exiled Pretender.[2] So it was necessary, that the head of the family should be sternly restricted by settlement to a life interest in the family land, followed by an estate for protection of his wife's pin-money and jointure, and another for the portions of younger children, before the first estate tail was limited to his eldest unborn son. By this means there would, in most cases, be, for at least twenty-one years after the marriage, no persons able, even by united action, to make a binding lease of any of the land, much less dispose of it entirely.

The latter result was, no doubt, exactly what the framers of the settlement desired; but it was a result wholly inconsistent with that freedom of alienation which the Common Law courts of the preceding period had striven to uphold. Nevertheless, the tribunals of the Restoration period seem to have accepted it with equanimity; doubtless relying upon the liability of the 'contingent remainders'[3] of the sons of the marriage to failure as safeguarding the limitations of the settlement from the dangers of a 'perpetuity.' Further than this, the Chancellors of the seventeenth and eighteenth centuries, in framing the Rule against Perpetuities to restrict those interests which did not come under the risk of failure attaching to contingent remainders (such, for

[1] 19 & 20 Vict. c. 120.

[2] It was for some time an open question whether entailed estates were forfeitable for treason, beyond the life of the actual traitor. But the better opinion was, that the right of the Crown prevailed under 5 & 6 Edw. VI (1552) c. 11, s. 9. And it was tolerably certain that the Long Parliament would not be more merciful to 'delinquents' or 'malignants' than the Crown officials had been to traitors.

[3] *Ante*, pp. 85, 86.

example, as the future uses, or executory interests, now become legal estates by virtue of the Statutes of Uses and Wills, and limitations of personalty), actually adopted the principle of the family settlement, by restricting all such limitations to a life or lives in being at the date of the settlement (father and mother) and twenty-one years afterwards (majority of any child).[1]

But the evils of the system, in tying up land, soon made themselves felt; and some attempt to relieve against them was found in the practice of conferring upon the trustees of settlements express powers of leasing and sale, as well as ordinary powers of management.[2] Unfortunately, these powers were nearly always very restrictively worded, often confided to trustees, and generally hedged about with consents; with the result, that they were only to a limited extent effective. At last the legislature took up the matter, in the Leases and Sales of Settled Estates Act, 1856, which gave power to the Court of Chancery to authorize leases for occupation, mining, or building purposes,[3] and even to delegate similar power to the trustees of the settlement,[4] and to sell the settled estate out and out; the proceeds arising from any disposition to be settled upon the same limitations as the property sold.[5] But the provisions of the Act are timid. They require for their exercise the consent of all persons beneficially interested in the estate up to the first tenant in tail of full age; if there is no such person, then the consent of *all* persons beneficially interested, including trustees for unborn children.[6] Apparently, they can only be exercised on the petition of the first life tenant;[7] and, worst of all, they can be excluded from the settlement by express provision.[8] In other words, the Act only operated to avoid the necessity of inserting express provisions in a settlement intended to be liberally drawn; it did nothing to override the conservatism of settlors. But it is only fair to say, that one section[9] (which had, however, no retrospective effect) enabled a tenant for life in possession (unless forbidden by the settlement) to make an ordinary lease for twenty-one years, without any one's consent; though this

Express Powers

Act of 1856

[1] See the cases quoted, *ante*, p. 225, n. 1.
[2] See forms in Barton, *Modern Precedents in Conveyancing* (3d edition, 1824) pp. 248, 351 *et seq.*, 462 *et seq.*
[3] 19 & 20 Vict. c. 120, s. 2. [4] S. 7. [5] S. 23. [6] S. 17. [7] S. 16.
[8] S. 26 (even 'manifest intention' to exclude is enough). [9] S. 32.

power did not extend to authorize a lease of the mansion house or demesne.

The Act of 1856 was followed by a series of 'Public Money Drainage Acts,' by which limited owners were authorized, subject to restrictions, to pledge the inheritance of their lands to repay by instalments monies borrowed for the purpose of effecting permanent improvements; and these spasmodic efforts culminated in the Improvement of Land Act, 1864, and its various amendments, by which this policy is made permanent. Broadly speaking, a limited owner in possession is entitled, with the approval of the Board of Agriculture, to borrow money for various kinds of permanent improvements,[1] and secure it on the *corpus* of his estate by a terminable rent-charge extending over twenty-five years. Such a rent-charge even takes priority of ordinary incumbrances of earlier date.[2] A useful provision of the later Settled Land Act of 1882,[3] also authorizes the improvements sanctioned by the Improvement of Land Act and the Settled Land Acts to be paid for out of capital arising under the latter Acts; and similar provisions are contained in one or two other modern statutes.[4] But a 'tenant for life' under the Settled Land Acts cannot mortgage under these Acts for the purpose of effecting improvements.

Improvement of Land Act

The Settled Estates Act of 1856 was superseded in 1877 by another Act with a similar title and scope, which seems to have been very little improvement on its predecessor. It is true that it dispenses, for the exercise of its statutory powers, with the consent of persons subsequent to the infant tenant in tail, and some other persons with very remote interests;[5] but it adopts the radical defects of the older measure in making the consent of the Court essential to the exercise of the statutory powers, and entrusting the exercise of them chiefly to the trustees of the settlement — persons naturally and proverbially disinclined to undertake responsibility. It is, in fact, not easy to see how the Act of 1877, which is still in force, is

Act of 1877

[1] These will be found enumerated in s. 9 of the Improvement of Land Act, 1864, and in s. 30 of the Settled Land Act, 1882.

[2] Improvement of Land Act, 1864, s. 63.

[3] S. 21 (iii).

[4] *E.g.* the Housing of the Working Classes Act, 1890, s. 74, and the Agricultural Holdings Act, 1908, s. 20.

[5] Settled Estates Act, 1877, s. 25, 27.

any improvement on its predecessor. But it is occasionally resorted to for special purposes, *e.g.* when a dowress, who is not a 'tenant for life' under the Settled Land Act, 1882,[1] desires to make a lease.[2]

A sweeping change was, however, brought about by the policy of the Settled Land Act, 1882,[3] and its various amendments.

The Settled Land Acts

The great statute is conceived on bold and successful lines. Treating all limited owners in possession as virtually entitled to control, not merely the management and administration of the land, but the form which the investment of the settled capital shall take, the statute, and its amendments,[4] in effect empower any such person to sell, exchange, enfranchise, partition, lease, or effect permanent improvements in any part of the settled land, by dispositions which will bind, not merely the person making them, but all the interests comprised in the settlement.[5] Moreover, the exercise of these powers is in the absolute discretion of the 'tenant for life'; except in certain special cases, such as the disposal of the mansion house and demesnes, or the heirlooms, or the cutting of timber. In such cases, the consent of the Court or the trustees is required.[6] Further still, no alienation of his own personal interest is to deprive the 'tenant for life' of his statutory powers;[7] except to the extent to which it is necessary to protect a purchaser for value from him. Most important of all, no expression or device in the settlement, direct or indirect, can deprive the tenant for life of his statutory powers, or even restrict him in the exercise of them;[8] though, needless to say, the 'tenant for life' is bound, as between himself and the other persons interested, to act in a quasi-fiduciary manner, for the benefit of all parties concerned.[9] Not only, however, may the 'tenant for life' convert the estate or any part of it into money; he has within the provisions of the Acts, control over the re-investment of the money produced by

[1] See enumeration in s. 58 of that Act.
[2] Which she can do under s. 46 of the Act of 1877.
[3] 45 & 46 Vict. c. 38, s. 1.
[4] Amending statutes were passed in 1884, 1887, 1889, and 1890.
[5] Act of 1882, s. 2 (2), s. 3.
[6] Act of 1882, ss. 35, 37; Act of 1890, s. 10. (The consent of the Court is essential to the sale of heirlooms.)
[7] Act of 1882, s. 50.
[8] *Re Richardson* [1904] 2 Ch. 777.
[9] Act of 1882, s. 53. This section actually invests him with the 'duties and liabilities of a trustee.' But, in spite of these express words, it is doubtful whether the 'tenant for life' is, technically, a 'trustee.'

such a conversion,[1] and may employ it in effecting improvements, paying-off incumbrances, or converting copyholds or leaseholds into freeholds.[2] He may even mortgage for the two latter purposes [3] though not for the former. But the actual custody of capital monies arising under a settlement is with the trustees or the Court, not with the tenant for life ;[4] and the trustees are bound to look after the interests of all parties concerned.

Such vigorous action has been taken under the Settled Land Acts, and this action has been so beneficial, that it seems almost ungracious to point out that time has revealed at least three ways in which the policy of the Acts can be substantially evaded. In the first place, it is possible for a settlor to vest the immediate income of the land in trustees, with a purely discretionary trust to make an allowance to the person who would otherwise be tenant in possession, and even to allow such person, if they think fit, to occupy the mansion house. There will then be no 'tenant for life' for the purposes of the Acts; for the trustees are not 'beneficially entitled' to the income, and the beneficiary is not 'entitled.' [5] Second, though the circumstance that in fact (owing to the existence of incumbrances or other causes) the first life tenant under the settlement receives no income, will not prevent him exercising the statutory powers; [6] yet, a person whose interest is actually postponed during the operation of a trust for accumulation, is not a 'tenant for life' under the Acts, and so cannot exercise the powers.[7] Finally, by the device of an assignment for value, a tenant for life can always, in effect, deprive himself of the right to exercise at least some of his statutory powers without the consent of his purchaser,[8] which cannot be compelled.

Flaws in the the Acts

A few words, but they must be few, should be said about the analogous case of mortgagee and mortgagor. The persistent efforts of Equity, previously described,[9] to protect the interest of the mortgagor against the unfair exercise by the mortgagee of his legal powers, had in effect, by the end of the eighteenth century, produced a deadlock almost equivalent to that of the settlement sys-

Statutory Powers of Mortgagees and Mortgagors

[1] Act of 1882, ss. 21, 22 (2).
[2] *Re Bruce* [1905] 2 Ch. 372.
[3] Act of 1882, s. 18; Act of 1890, s. 11.
[4] Act of 1882, s. 22.
[5] *Jemmett's and Guest's Contract* [1907] 1 Ch. 629.
[6] *Re Pollock* [1906] 1 Ch. 146.
[7] *Re Strangways* (1886) 34 Ch. D. 423 (*Non obstante Re Llewellyn* [911] 1 Ch. 451).
[8] Act of 1882, s. 50 (3). (But see Act of 1890, s. 4.)
[9] *Ante*, pp. 215, 216.

tem. No third party could safely deal with the mortgagee; because such dealing might be set aside by Equity after redemption. The mortgagor, of course, had no legal powers; his alienees could be treated by the mortgagee as mere tenants at will. Unless mortgagee and mortgagor could agree (which was but seldom) nothing could be done. The property was under a curse.

It is true, that many mortgagees endeavoured to get over the difficulty by reserving in the mortgage deeds express powers of sale, leasing, and management, exerciseable without the mortgagor's consent; but there was always the fear lest Chancery should quash these powers as oppressive, or as attempts to 'clog the equity.' It was a case for the legislature; and at last the legislature intervened, and by the Law of Property Amendment Act of 1860 (commonly known as Lord Cranworth's Act)[1] conferred upon every mortgagee, after default in payment of principal or interest, the power to sell the mortgaged land and pay himself out of the proceeds, and to insure any insurable property, and to appoint a receiver of the rents and profits. But these powers did not include any power to lease; and they could all be excluded by the express terms of the mortgage.[2]

More drastic was the policy of the Conveyancing Act, 1881, which not only re-enacted the powers of sale, insurance, and appointing a receiver,[3] but conferred upon either mortgagee or mortgagor, when in possession, power to make binding leases,[4] substantially of the same nature as those subsequently authorized by the Settled Land Act for the tenant for life, and also conferred upon the mortagor the valuable rights of demanding, on redemption of the mortgage, a transfer thereof instead of a reconveyance,[5] and, even before redemption, of inspecting and taking copies of the title-deeds.[6] It also entitles a mortgagee in possession to cut ordinary timber (of course subject to account), and even to make a binding twelve-months' contract for such cutting.[7] It is noteworthy that, while the powers of the mortgagee may be waived by express provision in the mortgage,[8] those inserted for the special benefit of the mortgagor cannot be restricted.[9] It is noteworthy also that, by empowering the Court to order

[1] 23 & 24 Vict. c. 145, ss. 11-24. [2] S. 32. [3] Act of 1881, s. 19.
[4] S. 18. (But there is no provision for anything in the way of a mining lease.)
[5] S. 15. (This power cannot be exercised if the mortgagee has been in possession.)
[6] S. 16. [7] S. 16 (iv). [8] *Ibid.*, (3). [9] Ss. 15 (3), 16 (2.)

a sale, instead of a foreclosure or reconveyance, in any action for foreclosure or redemption,[1] and by providing that all mortgage estates, even though of a freehold nature, shall pass to the mortgagee's personal representatives on his death,[2] the Act alleviated many of the difficulties and hardships formerly attendant upon the realization of mortgages.

Liability of Land to satisfy Debts

In one other direction the same tendency towards freedom of alienation may be observed; though, again perhaps, working indirectly. As has been previously pointed out,[3] feudal principles were opposed to making land liable to seizure for the debts of its owner. True that one of the great thirteenth century statutes[4] had allowed the judgment creditor to 'extend' one half his debtor's lands, in lieu of taking his body and goods, and that the specialty debts of a deceased landowner were enforceable against his heirs. Early in the present period, also, as we have seen, trust estates of inheritance were added to the list of 'real assets,' and the remedy of specialty creditors was extended from heirs to devisees.[5] But it was not until 1807[6] that simple contract creditors, and then only when the debtor was a trader, were entitled to be paid out of the land of a deceased debtor. In 1833, however,[7] this liability was extended to the lands (including copyholds) of all debtors; and in 1838,[8] all the lands of a living debtor (also including copyholds) were made available to satisfy the claims of his judgment creditors. Improved remedies were added in 1864[9] for the purpose of giving effect to these claims; and a statute of 1869,[10] commonly known as 'Hinde Palmer's Act,' by abolishing the priority of specialty debts, greatly simplified the distribution of the assets of a deceased person amongst his creditors. Finally, the earlier sections of the Land Transfer Act, 1897,[11] by vesting the real estate of a deceased person (other than legal copyholds) in his personal representatives, the ordinary distributors of his property, greatly facilitated the machinery for obtaining payment of debts out of such property.

[1] S. 25. [2] S. 30. [3] *Ante*, pp. 36, 37.
[4] Statute of Westminster II (13 Edw. I, 1285) c. 18.
[5] *Ante*, pp. 220, 221. [6] 47 Geo. III, st. II, c. 74.
[7] Administration of Estates Act (3 & 4 Will. IV, c. 104).
[8] Judgments Act (1 & 2 Vict. c. 110, s. 11).
[9] Judgments Act (27 & 28 Vict. c. 112, ss. 4–6).
[10] Administration of Estates Act (32 & 33 Vict. c. 46).
[11] 60 & 61 Vict. c. 65 ss. 1–4.

The Act to Amend the Law of Inheritance, passed in the year 1833,[1] though it cannot be overlooked entirely, in any work professing to deal with the history of English law, is hardly a matter of first-rate importance. Owing to the fact that a landowner rarely dies without leaving a will, its provisions are but seldom resorted to. Moreover, unlike the Wills Act of four years later, it is not a code, but merely, as its title implies, a statute designed to remedy certain defects in the Common Law. That law had, as we have seen,[2] become fixed in outline by the end of the thirteenth century. But in one important respect the later Common Law had departed from fundamental principles. By those principles, no one could inherit a fief unless he was descended from, or at least of the blood of, the first acquirer, or 'purchaser' of the fief. But the great importance attached by medieval law to 'seisin,' or corporal possession of the land, had virtually substituted the 'person last seised' for the original donee of the fief, except in the case of estates tail; though the rule that the heir must be 'of the blood' of the first purchaser was in theory preserved.[3] The Act of 1833 restored the ancient rule; dispensing with the requirement of seisin in the stock of descent, and making descent in every case traceable from the last purchaser,[4] *i.e.* the person who last acquired the estate otherwise than by inheritance. Further, the Act made a substantial change[5] by admitting, next after the issue of the purchaser, his nearest ancestor to succeed, and collaterals only through ancestors, and by allowing the claim of the half-blood collaterals to prevail, next after the claims of collaterals of the whole blood of the same degree, and their issue.[6] The preferences given by the common law to males over females and to an elder male over a younger in the same degree, were not, however, altered; and the peculiar local customs of copyhold and gavelkind were, save as to the rule of descent from the purchaser, also left untouched.

Rules of Inheritance

Far more important, really, in the law of succession than the Inheritance Act, has been the series of short statutes known as 'Locke King's Acts,'[7] designed to mitigate the preference given

[1] 3 & 4 Will. IV, c. 106. [2] *Ante*, pp. 34–36. [3] Blackstone, *Comm.*, II, 221.
[4] Inheritance Act, 1833, s. 2. (An amendment of 1859 admitted the heirs of the person last entitled, (not, necessarily, 'seized'), after failure of the heirs of the purchaser.) [5] Ss. 5, 6. [6] S. 9.
[7] Officially styled the 'Real Estates Charges Acts, 1854, 1867, and 1877.'

both by Law and Equity to beneficiaries interested in land over those having claims only on personalty. By the older law, if a testator had mortgaged his freehold estate, and then died, leaving a will under which his real estate went to A and his personalty to B, A would have been entitled to demand that the mortgage debt should be paid off out of the testator's personalty, for the purpose of clearing the real estate; and a similar principle applied if the owner of the estate had died intestate, leaving A as his heir and B as his next-of-kin. If the testator or intestate had, in fact, used the mortgage money to pay his general debts, there was little hardship in this rule.[1] But if, as commonly happened, the mortgage money had been actually borrowed to enable the deceased to purchase the real estate, the hardship was obvious. Accordingly, in 1854, it was enacted,[2] that in such a case, neither devisee nor heir should be entitled to claim payment out of the personal estate; but that, as between the different beneficiaries, each estate should bear its own burdens. And, by later statutes,[3] the new rule has been extended to liens for unpaid purchase-money and to leasehold interests. It does not, however, apply to pure personalty; a specific legatee of which is still entitled to have any incumbrance cleared out of the general personal estate.[4] Of course both old and new rules are subject to any expression of intention by the deceased, contained in his will or other document; but a mere general direction for payment of debts out of personal estate is not such an expression.[5] Finally, it may be mentioned that the old rule of preference for the beneficiaries of the real estate never applied where that estate was already mortgaged before it was acquired by the deceased ('mortgage ancestral').[6] Needless to say, Locke King's Acts in no way affect the right of a mortgagee to resort to his mortgagor's personal estate, either before or after exhausting his security. The matter is put right between the beneficiaries by the process of 'marshalling,' previously described.[7]

Locke King's Acts

[1] Except that, in case of an intestacy, the result might be to favour a very distant heir at the expense of much nearer next-of-kin.

[2] 17 & 18 Vict. c. 113.

[3] 30 & 31 Vict. (1867) c. 69; 40 & 41 Vict. (1877) c. 34.

[4] *Bothamley v. Sherson* (1875) L. R. 20 Eq. 304.

[5] 30 & 31 Vict. c. 69, s. 1.

[6] *Evelyn v. Evelyn* (1728) 2 P. Wms. 659 (Lord King); *Parsons v. Freeman* (1751) Ambl. 115 (Lord Hardwicke).

[7] *Ante*, pp. 230, 231.

Attention should also be given to the extremely important Real Property Act of 1845,[1] which, though its efforts were mainly directed to sweeping away the technicalities of medieval conveyancing, also made one important change in substantive law. A statute of the preceding year [2] had endeavoured to abolish altogether contingent remainders; but this somewhat extreme step was recalled in 1845, and a provision enacted which prevented the 'failure' or destruction of the interests of remaindermen by collusion of other parties to the settlement. Owing to the rule, previously alluded to,[3] that if a contingent remainder was not ready to take effect in possession on the expiry of the preceding estate, it 'failed,' or disappeared entirely, it was possible for the tenant for life under a settlement, prior to the birth or conception of the first remainderman in tail, by procuring a forfeiture of his estate, or a surrender of it to the next vested remainderman, to destroy his (the tenant for life's) estate, and thus, with it, the contingent remainders dependent upon it. This practice, which was the more reprehensible that the persons for whom the contingent remainders were intended were usually the tenant for life's own children, was largely resorted to; and the only way by which it could be prevented was by the rather clumsy device of appointing 'trustees to preserve contingent remainders,' *i.e.* to hold for the residue of the natural life of the tenant in possession.[4] But the Act of 1845[5] rendered this device unnecessary, by providing that the contingent remainder should be capable of taking effect in due course; notwithstanding such prior artificial destruction of the preceding estate. The year 1877[6] saw an extension of this policy, in the Act which rendered contingent remainders indestructible, notwithstanding the natural expiry of the preceding estate; provided that they did not violate the Rule against Perpetuities.[7] This provision, which is, however, only applicable to settlements made after the passing of the Act, virtually assimilated Common Law remainders to the newer executory interests limited by way of use, and operating under the Statute of Uses.[8]

Contingent Remainders

[1] 8 & 9 Vict. c. 106. [2] 7 & 8 Vict. c. 76. [3] *Ante*, p. 85.
[4] *Mansell v. Mansell* (1732) 2 P. Wms. 678. [5] S. 8.
[6] Contingent Remainders Act (40 & 41 Vict. c. 33). [7] *Ante*, pp. 244, 245.
[8] 27 Hen. VIII (1535) c. 10.

But a few words must also be said about the changes in the methods of conveyancing introduced during this period.

Abolition of Fines and Recoveries

One of the early efforts of the reformed Parliament was directed towards doing away with the necessity for resorting to the cumbrous conveyances known as Fines and Recoveries. It has been previously explained[1] how, in early times, these costly fictions performed the useful task of covering the introduction of reforms which could not be openly effected. But these times were long past; and now Fines and Recoveries were merely means of exacting fees from persons dealing in land. In the year 1833, accordingly, they were entirely superseded by simple conveyances enrolled in Chancery;[2] the additional ceremony of examination by the Court or independent commissioners being imposed in the case of married women who were disposed to alienate their lands.

Secret Conveyances

It will be remembered that,[3] soon after the passing of the Statute of Uses, the ingenuity of conveyancers had at last overcome the medieval principle that freehold estates in possession could only be created or transferred by livery of corporal seisin, or 'feoffment.' The common law principle had never been applied to equitable interests, which were merely subject to the formality of writing, prescribed by the Statute of Frauds.[4] But, until nearly the middle of the nineteenth century, the common law rule prevailed, in theory, for legal estates; and was only evaded by the clumsy device of the Lease and Release.[5] In 1845, however, the Real Property Act,[6] by providing that 'all corporeal tenements and hereditaments shall, as regards the conveyance of the immediate freehold thereof, be deemed to lie in grant as well as in livery,' virtually made a simple deed of grant effectual to convey any interest in land *inter vivos*, and thus at last formally recognize the validity of secret conveyances of corporeal hereditaments. Furthermore, the statute made a complete destruction of the medieval theory, by providing, not merely that a deed should be effective for all purposes without a livery, but by enacting,[7] that livery without a deed or writing should not be effective at all; and by abolishing all those peculiar

[1] *Ante*, pp. 112–118.

[2] Fines and Recoveries Act (3 & 4 Will. IV, c. 74).

[3] *Ante*, pp. 121, 122.

[4] 29 Car. II (1677) c. 3, ss. 7–9.

[5] *Ante*, pp. 121, 122.

[6] S. 2. The amendment had, in substance, been made by an Act of the previous year (7 & 8 Vict. c. 76, s. 2).

[7] S. 3.

virtues of a feoffment which depended upon its 'tortious' operation.[1] Naturally the medieval feoffment, now a mere superfluous luxury, has disappeared from modern conveyancing; save in those rare cases in which a person, though incapable of making a binding deed, is, by local custom, able to convey by feoffment.[2] The statute further emphasizes the importance of deeds, in modern conveyancing, by enacting[3] that all transfers required by the Statute of Frauds to be in writing must be made by deed, in order to pass the legal estate. This provision, however, does not affect the passing of equitable interests, nor the conveyance of copyholds by surrender and admittance.[4] A little noticed, but really important section of the statute,[5] to which effect has recently been given by a decision of the House of Lords,[6] abolished the former technical rule that a man could not acquire an immediate interest, or take the benefit of a covenant or condition, under an indenture to which he was not a party.

The scope of this work does not permit of reference in detail to the important provisons of the Vendor and Purchaser Act, 1874,[7] and the Conveyancing Act, 1881,[8] which aim at reducing the expense of conveyancing by limiting the rights of a purchaser under an open contract in the matter of demanding evidence of the vendor's title, and at diminishing the risk of mistakes, by shortening the forms of deeds and allowing alternatives in the use of technical words to pass heritable estates.[9] Space remains only for a very brief sketch of the history of the attempts made to realize that cherished dream of law-reformers, which, as we have seen,[10] haunted the minds even of the members of the Little Parliament, viz. the registration, in a public and accessible form, of all dealings with land.

With the exception of the experiment tried at the passing, in 1663, of the Act for regulating the affairs of the great 'Bedford Level' of the eastern fen country,[11] then recently reclaimed,

[1] S. 4. Certain other changes of minor importance were made by this section. (As to the 'tortious operation' of a feoffment, see *ante*, pp. 107–109.)

[2] *E.g.* an infant holding land subject to the custom of gavelkind. But the only case of recent years reported on this point shows the danger of relying on such a feoffment (*Maskell's and Goldfinch's Contract* [1895] 2 Ch. 525).

[3] S. 3.

[4] *Ibid.*

[5] S. 5.

[6] *Dyson v. Forster* [1909] A.C. 98.

[7] 37 & 38 Vict. c. 78, ss. 1, 2.

[8] 44 & 45 Vict. c. 41, ss. 3–9, 51, &c.

[9] Conveyancing Act, 1881, ss. 6–9, and 51. The case of *Re Ethel, &c.* [1901] 1 Ch. 945, shows, however, that the new words of inheritance are just as technical as the old.

[10] *Ante*, pp. 178–182.

[11] 15 Car. II, c. xvii.

after many unsuccessful attempts, by the Earl of Bedford, it was not until the beginning of the eighteenth century that any definite step was taken to carry out the suggestions of the Little Parliament. In the first decade of that century, however, the West and East Ridings of Yorkshire, and the County of Middlesex, as the result of genuine popular movements, adopted schemes of registration; and the North Riding of Yorkshire followed suit in 1735.[1] But the reader should be cautioned against assuming that the Yorkshire and Middlesex schemes are of the same character as the Torrens system of the British colonies, or the English experiments of the latter half of the nineteenth century. The Yorkshire and Middlesex schemes aimed only at the registration of documents; *i.e.* they were simply directed against the evils arising from the existence of concealed conveyances. All that they did was to protect a purchaser from being deprived of his purchase through the effect of some secret document, of the existence of which he was unaware when he paid his money. They did not pretend to guarantee the positive validity of the title on the faith of which he bought. Thus, to take a very simple example, if B professed, as devisee of A, to sell land in Yorkshire to X, and X duly searched the registry of the appropriate Riding and found everything apparently in order, he would be protected against a claim by a previous purchaser from B, who had not registered his conveyance. But he would lose his land if A's alleged will turned out to be a forged document, or if B, the supposed devisee under it, were not really the devisee, but a person passing himself off as the devisee. Still less would he be protected, if A's title (for any cause other than a concealed document) was defective. Thus, though the protection afforded by the acts was considerable, it was not sufficient to arouse enthusiasm; and, in fact, no serious steps were taken to extend it, or any other system of registration, to the rest of England, until the middle of the nineteenth century. Moreover, it was held that, notwithstanding the unqualified words of the old Middlesex Registry Act, the City of London (which, so far as the value of land is concerned, is probably equal

Land Registration

[1] The statutes are, 2 & 3 Anne (1703) c. 4 (West Riding), 6 Anne (1707) c. 35 (East Riding), 7 Anne (1708) c. 20 (Middlesex), 8 Geo, II (1735) c. 6 (North Riding). These have been superseded by the Yorkshire Registries Act, 1884, and the Middlesex Registry Act, 1891, in their respective spheres.

to the whole of the rest of the county) was excluded from the provisions of the Act.

But, soon after the middle of the nineteenth century, the wave of legislative reform, which, as we have seen, had been busy on questions of land law, reached the subject of registration of title; and two statutes, generally associated with the name of Lord Westbury, were passed in 1862 to deal with it. By the former of these, the Land Registry Act, 1862,[1] provision was made for the establishment of a Registry, applicable to the whole kingdom, which should not merely profess to give a purchaser notice of documents affecting his title, but should actually provide a State guarantee of the validity of all titles appearing on the register. Naturally, however, the State declined to assume this very serious liability in the case of any title which had not been carefully investigated, before registration, by its own officials; and, as this process involved considerable expense, and might have the very serious result to the landowner of advertising the defects of his title, it is not surprising, perhaps, that few landowners consented to submit to it. As a matter of fact, there were, in the 'sixties, probably very few important estates in England the titles to which were technically perfect; and so notorious was this fact,[2] that the average purchaser and his legal advisers allowed their rights of investigation to be cut down in their contracts of purchase, and, unless they wished to be off their bargain, deliberately shut their eyes to remote contingencies. Landowners were, in a vague way, aware of this; and, not unnaturally, refused to incur the expense and risk of a scientific investigation of their titles, for the problematic advantage of obtaining a slightly higher price when they desired to sell. A little use was made of the Act in the earlier years of its existence; but very soon the Registry Act itself, as well as the Declaration of Title Act passed in the same year,[3] became a dead letter.

Lord Westbury's Acts

In the year 1875, however, the matter was again taken up by Lord Cairns; and the Land Transfer Act of that year came into existence. In some ways it was a great improvement upon its predecessor. It no longer,

Lord Cairns' Act

1 25 & 26 Vict. c. 53. (The Act is still in force for the few titles remaining registered under it.)

2 See the remarks of Lord Hatherley on this point, and the rule with regard to damages for breach of a contract to sell land deduced therefrom, in *Bain v. Fothergill* (1874) L.R. 7 H.L. 158.

3 25 & 26 Vict. c. 67.

required all applicants for registration to submit to the costly and embarrassing enquiry necessary to establish an 'absolute' title. It allowed any applicant to register with a 'possessory' title only, *i.e.* a title which merely asserted that the registered proprietor was in fact in possession of the land on the day of registration, under a title *primâ facie* valid.[1] Naturally, in such cases, the State took no reponsibility in respect of the past history of the title; but it did guarantee to a purchaser that, in respect of subsequent transactions, the title appearing on the Register should be unimpeachable.[2] Thus, as time went on, even a merely 'possessory' title would acquire a tolerable security; for the operation of the Statutes of Limitation would gradually eliminate the possibility, or at least the probability, of any claims arising prior to registration being really enforced. Moreover, even if the applicant for registration with 'absolute' title could not show a theoretically perfect title, it was made possible for the Registry to accept his title as 'qualified,' *i.e.* subject only to one or more specified blots, as to the importance of which a purchaser could judge for himself.[3]

In other respects, however, the Act of 1875 was as unsatisfactory as its predecessor. It left it optional with the existing owner or future purchaser of land to register or not, as he pleased; and, though a few landowners were attracted by the more elastic provisions of the statute, yet, after the first few years of existence, very little use was made of it. Moreover, the scheme suffered from one great blot, in that it made no effort to compensate innocent sufferers who might, by reason of abuse of the register, or inaccuracies or omissions in or from it, incur loss. It might, perhaps, have been thought that this defect would not have weighed much with persons acute enough to secure the protection of the Act for doubtful titles; but in fact it tended to make the scheme unpopular.

Accordingly, registration of title once more languished; until a vigorous reform of the scheme of 1875 was set on foot and carried out, mainly through the efforts of Lord Halsbury, the third Conservative Lord Chancellor to champion the system.

By Lord Halsbury's Land Transfer Act of 1897, or rather by the Rules made under the almost unprecedented power con-

[1] Act of 1875, s. 6, and Land Transfer Rule, 1908, Part II.
[2] Act of 1875, s. 8.
[3] *Ibid.*, s. 9.

ferred upon the Lord Chancellor and his advisers by the provisions of the two statutes,[1] yet a fourth kind of title may now be registered, viz. a 'good leasehold' title.[2] A 'good leasehold' title is, in effect, an absolute title to the interest professed to have been created by a lease, if and so far as that interest was validly created. In other words, such a title only guarantees the purchaser of a registered lease against defects in the title to the lease itself, not against defects in the title of the lessor.[3] The Act of 1897 also provides[4] a fund for compensating persons who may have suffered from any omission or error in the register, or from the procurement of any registration by fraud or mistake; and, if the only reported decision[5] on that section is not very favourable to such claimants, still the compensation provisions of the Act are manifestly necessary to prevent injustice.

Lord Halsbury's Act

But by far the most radical change effected by the Act of 1897, so far as registration of title is concerned, is contained in the section[6] which provides for compulsory registration. This change, however, which takes the form of enacting that, on the occasion of any future transfer *by way of sale*, the title to the land shall be registered, only affects certain special areas; and the provisions on this point are remarkable. The Act itself does not create any 'compulsory area'; but gives the Crown, by Order in Council, power to do so, under certain conditions. In the first instance, the power of the Crown was limited only by the fact, that the provisions of the first Order to be made should not include more than one administrative county, and by the fact that the County Council of the area proposed to be affected might, by a majority of at least two-thirds of its members, veto its coming into operation. After the making of the first Order under the Act, however, no further Order was to be made for at least three years after the date of the first Order, and, even then, not until the County Council of the area contemplated should express a wish for the introduction of the compulsory system. No such wish has been expressed by any County Council; and, therefore, outside the County of London, which has been prescribed as a compulsory

Compulsory Registration

[1] Act of 1875, s. 111; Act of 1897, s. 22.
[2] Land Transfer Rules, 1903, No. 52.
[3] *Ibid.*, No. 56.
[4] Ss. 7, 21.
[5] *A. G. v. Odell* [1906] 2 Ch. 47.
[6] S. 20.

area by Orders dated between 1897 and 1903,[1] registration of title is still purely voluntary, and is, in fact, seldom resorted to.

It should be mentioned, of course, that the avowed objects of the Land Transfer Acts include, not merely the guarantee or security of titles, but the diminution of the expense and complexity of conveyancing, and the improvement of the remedies of creditors. With the former object in view, the Acts provide that no 'abstract of title,' other than the land certificate and liberty to inspect the register, can be demanded by a purchaser in respect of title guaranteed by the State;[2] with an eye to the latter, the Act of 1897, by vesting all the heritable freeholds of a deceased person in his personal representatives,[3] and causing all dealings between them and the beneficiaries, so far as relates to registered land, to be entered in the register, aims at providing simple and speedy remedies for the recovery of their claims by creditors.

It is notorious that the policy of land registration has given rise to acute differences of opinion in England, and that the system is still on its trial. On the one hand, it is said that the slight increased security afforded by the State guarantee is more than outweighed by the limited operation of the scheme, and by the fact that, as the beneficial interest in registered land, even in 'compulsory areas,' can be conveyed by unregistered instruments,[4] the Acts have practically substituted a double for the previous single title to each ownership within those areas. On the other, it is urged, that there is a systematic conspiracy of interests to stifle and misrepresent the scheme, and to throw difficulties in the way of its execution, and that, as 'possessory' titles virtually become, by lapse of time, absolute, and it becomes possible to relax the severity of the conditions of registration with 'absolute' title, the drawbacks inevitably attendant upon the introduction of a new scheme of conveyancing will disappear. The subject has recently been under the consideration of a Royal Commission, whose report was published only in 1911;[5] and the

[1] The first Order (18th July, 1908) covered the whole County of London; but made the Order applicable to different parts at different dates. These dates were subsequently altered.

[2] Act of 1897, s. 16.

[3] Act of 1897, ss. 1–4.

[4] The only legal penalty for non-registration in a compulsory area is that the legal estate does not pass (Act of 1897, s. 20 (1)). As to the effect of unregistered dealings with registered land, see *Capital and Counties Bank v. Rhodes* [1903] 1 Ch. 631.

[5] P.P. 1911, Cd. 5483.

author must, therefore, leave the question, with the bare historical observation that, but for the passing of the Statute of Uses, it would have been comparatively easy, at any time in the sixteenth or seventeenth centuries, to substitute for the somewhat complicated scheme of registration of title, a much simpler, but sufficiently effective scheme of a Register of Sasines, or seisins, *i.e.* a bare register of the changes of the legal estate. It may be that the solution of the problem will be found in that direction, as it has been in Scotland.

Registration of Hostile Claims

In dismissing the subject of registration, a mere reference is all that can be allowed for that branch of it which relates to the registration of certain adverse claims, such as judgments, recognizances, annuities or rent-charges, deeds of arrangement with creditors, and other possible flaws in title. These registries are, of course, on the lines of the old Yorkshire and Middlesex Registries, with which they are, in fact, incorporated in those counties. They merely aim at warning the purchaser of dangers, without in any way guaranteeing their extent or probability. The practice commenced with the Statute of Frauds, in 1677,[1] and was embodied in numerous statutes of the next two centuries.[2] It is now governed by the Land Registration and Searches Act, 1888,[3] and the Land Charges Act, 1900;[4] the chief recent change being the provision[5] that no judgment can in the future be registered without leave of the Court, or have any effect as regards the land of the debtor, until a writ of execution upon it has been delivered or put in force, and duly registered. This provision has, perhaps inadvertently, reopened a serious question. By the common law, a personal representative was deemed to have notice of all unsatisfied judgments obtained against his deceased; and if he paid lower claims without making provision for them, he did so at his own peril. It was to remedy this danger, among others, that the statutory provisions for the registration of judgments were introduced. Now that judgments can no longer be registered without special leave, will the judgment creditor's preference still remain? And, if it does, how is the personal representative to protect himself?

[1] 29 Car. II, c. 3, s. 18.

[2] *E.g.* 4 & 5 W. & M. (1692) c. 20; Judgments Act, 1838, s. 19; Judgments Act 1864, ss. 1–3.

[3] 51 & 52 Vict. c. 51, ss. 5, 6.

[4] 63 & 64 Vict. c. 26.

[5] *Ibid.*, s. 2.

This chapter cannot conclude without at least a brief reference to one of the most important reforms in land law effected during the latter half of the nineteenth century, viz. the restriction of the right to enclose common fields and manorial wastes. In form this was a change in procedure; in substance it effected a profound revolution in the powers of landowners.

Enclosures

It has been pointed out, in an earlier chapter,[1] that the typical manor of the later Middle Ages was formed by the super-position of a 'lord' holding by feudal tenure upon a village which cultivated its lands under a communal system of immemorial antiquity. To this communal system the feudal principle of tenure was also applied, though with indifferent success, by the Norman lawyers; so that, in theory, the villagers, whose names and holdings were recorded on the manorial rolls, were technically described as 'holding of' the lord, though 'according to the custom of the manor.'

It was natural that, as population increased, and tenants became more plentiful, the manorial lords should desire the power of taking in more land from the waste which was a normal feature of every village; and equally natural that the villagers, who had, from time immemorial, treated the waste as a treasure-house from which valuable stores of grass, faggots, acorns, gravel, peat, water, and the like, could be drawn to supplement their holdings, should resent any claim which threatened to trench upon their store. Traces of the struggle are visible as early as the thirteenth century; when, by the Statute of Merton,[2] 'magnates' who had 'enfeoffed their knights and freeholders of small tenements in their great manors' were exonerated from actions brought by such tenants against them (the magnates) for 'making their profit of the residue of their manors, to wit of wastes, woods, and pastures'; provided that the complainants were left 'so much pasture as should suffice for their tenements.'

Statute of Merton

This provision, which was extended by the Statute of Westminster the Second[3] to cover the case of persons claiming common of pasture by express grant, seems to have been the foundation of the common law rule, that, in the absence of proof to the contrary, the soil of the manorial waste, or 'common,' is vested in the lord. The immense importance of this rule will appear later;

[1] *Ante*, pp. 27, 28. [2] 20 Hen. III (1235) c. 4. [3] 13 Edw. I (1285) c. 46.

here it is sufficient to point out that there is nothing in the words of the statutes to justify it, and that nothing is said in either statute about the rights of copyholders, which depend, and have all along depended, not on feoffment or grant, but on immemorial custom.

After the thirteenth century, the question seems to have slept until the sixteenth, when the growth of a reform movement in favour of 'several' or enclosed husbandry, as opposed to common, open-field, or 'champaign' farming,[1] resulted in the wholesale enclosure of common fields, especially in the West of England, and to the consequent riots in the time of the Protector Somerset. This movement, it will be noticed, was concerned mainly, if not solely, with the methods, not with the matter, of agriculture; and the manorial 'waste,' or common, continued to be a normal feature of the English countryside for two centuries more.

First Enclosure Movement

Then, indeed, with the genuine prosperity of agriculture in the eighteenth century and the artificial prosperity produced by the French wars and the Corn Laws in the early nineteenth, the 'enclosure movement' took on a new and acuter phase. This time the manorial lords aimed, not merely at securing a free hand for their improvements in the soil already under the plough, but a largely increased area of private land, which they could either use for agriculture, or sell or lease for building or mining purposes. Then was seen the enormous importance of the rule deduced from the Statute of Merton. For, with mineral discoveries and the rapid growth of manufacturing towns, the value of some of the manorial wastes rose to fabulous heights; and, after the commoners or tenants had been compensated on the basis of the value of their ancient rights, the whole of the residue went into the pockets of the lords.

Second Enclosure Movement

One circumstance alone rendered this process of appropriation difficult. Owing to the immutable character of manorial custom, and the certainty that, among the many persons claiming common rights in a waste, there would be some whose title was imperfect or doubtful, it was practically necessary, in almost every case, to obtain a private Act of Parlia-

Inclosure Acts

[1] The academic champion of the movement was Thomas Tusser, whose rhymed tract *Five Hundred Points of Husbandry* (ed. Mavor, 1812) is an amusing and racy, but somewhat one-sided, picture of the agricultural life of his day.

ment to effect a safe enclosure. But Parliament, in the eighteenth century largely composed of landowners, was anxious to facilitate the process; and Inclosure Acts passed with extreme rapidity. Moreover, in the year 1801, a statute known as the Inclosure (Consolidation) Act[1] established a common form which could be incorporated by reference into any private Inclosure Act, and thus still further simplified the process. Finally, in the year 1845, Parliament determined to dispense with the necessity of special legislation altogether. By the Inclosure Act of that year[2] was set up a Board of Inclosure Commissioners, who were entitled to issue provisional schemes for the carrying out of enclosures. These schemes were then to be embodied in Provisional Orders, which, in the form of a Schedule to a short annual Act, should go, more or less automatically, through Parliament.

Inclosure Commissioners

Such vigorous progress was made under these encouraging auspices, that in the early 'sixties, England suddenly awoke to the fact that she was being deprived of one of her chief national assets and threatened with asphyxiation in her rapidly growing towns. The Commons Preservation Society was formed in the year 1865; and one of the first fruits of its vigorous propaganda was the Metropolis (Commons) Act of the following year,[3] which virtually put an end to enclosures within the metropolitan area, and, incidentally, saved for London such priceless possessions as Wimbledon Common and Hampstead Heath. The policy of that Act was to favour dedication to public uses at the expense of enclosure. It did not, in form, repudiate the historical claim of the manorial lords; but it facilitated a compromise for the benefit of the public.

Commons Preservation Society

Encouraged by the success of its first attempt, the Commons Preservation Society pushed its campaign into the country; and, ten years later, secured the passing of the Commons Act, 1876,[4] which virtually did for the provinces what the Act of 1866 had done for London. A most important clause[5] declared any encroachment on a defined village green to be a public nuisance, and authorized proceedings to be taken in respect of it, not merely before the magistrates, who were supposed to

[1] 41 Geo. III, c. 109. [2] 8 & 9 Vict. c. 118. [3] 29 & 30 Vict. c. 122.
[4] 39 & 40 Vict. c. 56. [5] S. 29.

be far too lenient towards offences of that kind, but before a county court judge.[1] Even the individual right of isolated enclosure cannot now be exercised without the approval of the Board of Agriculture;[2] and enclosure schemes have virtually ceased to be practicable. On the other hand, considerable progress has been made with the principle of securing open spaces for the purposes of public recreation;[3] and the latest general enactment on the subject, the Commons Act, 1899, practically authorizes any District Council, urban or rural, with the approval of the Board of Agriculture, to make a scheme for regulating and managing any common within its district.[4]

[1] S. 30. [2] Law of Commons Amendment Act, 1893, s. 2.

[3] The story of these successful efforts may be read in the volume recently published by Lord Eversley, entitled *Commons, Forests, and Footpaths* (Cassell, 1910).

[4] 62 & 63 Vict. c. 30, s. 1.

CHAPTER XVI

NEW FORMS OF PERSONAL PROPERTY

IT has been previously remarked[1] that, owing to the apparently arbitrary decision of the old Common Law Courts not to allow a 'real' or proprietary action for the recovery of chattels, there has never been very much of what may be called 'objective' law of chattels corporeal in England. Whether the apparently arbitrary refusal to which allusion has been made was really due to a belief in the relative unimportance of chattels as compared with land, or to that excessive respect for possession which almost refused a recognition to property unaccompanied by possession, or to the existence of ancient remedies deemed to be adequate for the protection of chattel interests,[2] or to some other cause, is a fascinating problem; but it cannot be further pursued here. It is sufficient to say that, historically speaking, the law of chattels corporeal in England was developed first through the Law of Theft, later, as we have seen,[3] through the Law of Tort, and, finally, as will be explained in the succeeding chapter,[4] through the Law of Contract. Such slender traces of a Law of Chattels Corporeal as remain after these large branches have been shorn away, will be found in connection with the Law of Succession, and the small if important part of the law which deals with 'reputed ownership,' *i.e.* ownership severed from possession. A few words on these two heads must suffice for the subject of chattels corporeal in this period; and we must then turn to the striking development of the law of chattels incorporeal, or 'choses in action.'

Intestate Succession

The subject of succession on intestacy was the first aspect of the Law of Succession to receive attention during the period now under review. As we have seen,[5] it was in an anomalous position. Properly speaking, the ecclesiastical courts ought to have followed the clearly defined

[1] *Ante*, p. 123. [2] See, for suggestions on this point, *ante*, p. 59.
[3] *Ante*, pp. 141, 142. [4] *Post*, pp. 300–303. [5] *Ante*, pp. 60, 61.

rules of Roman Law on the subject. As a matter of fact, they largely followed vague and fragmentary local customs; with the inevitable result, that a good deal of irregularity and plundering went on. Where the case was one of pure intestacy, the administrator was, no doubt, compelled by the ecclesiastical court to enter into a bond to distribute the estate among the next of kin.[1] But there was very grave doubt whether such a bond was valid when the administrator claimed the grant by virtue of a statutory right,[2] as, for example, under the 21 Hen. VIII (1529) c. 5, which[3] compelled the Ordinary to grant administration to the widow or next of kin of a deceased who left no will, or whose executors renounced. And when it was merely a question of intestacy as to a residue, it is to be feared that the all-powerful executor generally obtained the lion's share of it.

Very soon after the Restoration, however, an important statute was passed with the object of controlling the action of administrators, and settling the law of intestate succession. This was the Statute of Distribution of 1670,[4] which required all administrators to enter into bonds before taking up their duties, and subjected them to a process of account in the ecclesiastical courts.[5] It then settled the order of succession,[6] by providing that the widow of the intestate should be entitled, after payment of the intestate's debts, to one-third of the surplus, if the intestate left children or remoter issue; to one-half, if no issue survived the intestate. After the widow is provided for, the residue (or the whole estate, if there is no widow) is to be divided equally among the intestate's children; the representatives of deceased children standing in their parents' shoes, but all issue (except the heir-at-law in respect of land) bringing into 'hotchpot,' or account, all advances made to them by the intestate during his lifetime.[7] If there are no issue who survive the intestate, then the whole estate (or the half if there is a widow) is to be divided equally among the blood relations of the intestate in the nearest degree;

Statutes of Distribution

[1] Godolphin, *Orphan's Legacy* (ed. 1685) 255.

[2] *Davis v. Matthews* (1655) Styles, 455.

[3] S. 3 (6).

[4] 22 & 23 Car. II, c. 10.

[5] *Ibid.*, ss. 2–4.

[6] *Ibid.*, ss. 5–7.

[7] Though the wording of the section (3) is quite general, it is probable that the 'hotchpot' clause only applies to the distribution of the estate of a father.

deceased brothers and sisters, but no other collaterals, being represented by their surviving issue. Finally,[1] the Act lays it down that, for the protection of creditors, no distribution is to be made for at least a year after the intestate's death; and, even then, that the beneficiaries receiving shares shall give bonds to refund in the event of new debts appearing.[2]

The Act of 1670, which was at first only temporary, was made perpetual in 1685,[3] in which same year, however, it was amended by a provision[4] that, in the event of no issue of the deceased surviving him, his personalty, subject to the claims of his widow,[5] if any, should be shared equally between his surviving mother and his brother and sisters (including their representatives); though, of course, the mother is in a nearer degree to the intestate than the brothers and sisters.[6] Thus amended, the statute of 1670 has settled the modern law of intestate succession; but it is noteworthy that it did not come into universal operation throughout England for nearly two hundred years. For the Act itself expressly disclaimed[7] all interference with the special customs of London and the Province of York. It was accordingly deemed necessary, in 1692, to pass a special statute[8] enabling the inhabitants of the Province of York (other than freemen of York and Chester), and in 1696 another enabling the inhabitants of Wales,[9] to dispose of their personalty freely by will, notwithstanding local claims of legitim; and this liberty was extended in 1703,[10] at their own request, to the freemen of York. Finally, by two sections of an Act dealing with the general government of London, passed in the year 1724,[11] free liberty of testation was given to the citizens of the capital. But, so far as intestate succession was concerned, the City of London and the Province of York remained governed

[1] 22 & 23 Car. II, c. 10, s. 8.

[2] Presumably also the next of kin would have to refund in the event of a will being discovered.

[3] 1 Jac. II, c. 17, s. 5.

[4] *Ibid.*, s. 7.

[5] It was expressly ruled in *Keylway v. Keylway* (1726) 2 P. Wms. 344, that the section held good for the residue, even if the intestate left a widow.

[6] It seems clear from the wording of s. 7 of the Act of 1685, that the widow of a deceased child can claim her part of her deceased husband's share in the intestate's personalty.

[7] S. 4.

[8] 4 W. & M. c. 2.

[9] 8 & 9 Will. III, c. 38.

[10] 2 & 3 Anne, c. 5.

[11] 11 Geo. I, c. 18, ss. 17–18. (The restriction had only applied to 'freemen,' not to mere residents.)

by their own local rules until the year 1856,[1] the eve of the transfer of testamentary jurisdiction to the new Court of Probate. Moreover, a statute of the year 1890[2] gives a preferential and additional claim of £500, payable rateably out of realty and personalty, to the widow of an intestate who leaves no issue.

Wills of Personalty

On the other side of succession, viz. the making of wills, the period of the Restoration was also important. For the ecclesiastical courts, though again they should have followed the severe rules of Roman Law, made, apparently, no stipulations whatever on the subject of the form of wills;[3] the only formal requirement being that of writing introduced by the Wills Act of 1540,[4] which only applied to devises of land. But the Statute of Frauds, which, as has already been mentioned,[5] added, for wills of land, the further requirement of three witnesses, did something, though not much, to amend the scandalous laxity permitted by the ecclesiastical courts in cases of personalty. Parliament, unfortunately, did not venture to abolish entirely the 'nuncupative,' or verbal will; but, if the value of the estate exceeded £30, it required that it should be attested by three witnesses, whose testimony could not be received after six months from the making of the will, unless it had been committed to writing within six days from that event.[6] Moreover, the statute provided that no written will of personalty should be revoked or altered by word of mouth; unless the words were committed to writing in the testator's lifetime, and approved by him in the presence of three witnesses.[7]

Exclusion of Testimony

On the other hand, though the Church courts were criminally lax in the matter of testamentary forms, they positively discouraged the employment of witnesses, by laying down all sorts of restrictions with regard to their impartiality, or 'interest.' The ecclesiastical tribunals refused to accept, in proof of a will, the testimony of any person who might be interested, directly or indirectly, in its establishment. Thus no executor, legatee, or even creditor of the deceased,[8]

[1] 19 & 20 Vict. c. 94.

[2] 53 & 54 Vict. c. 29 (Intestates' Estates Act, 1890).

[3] Godolphin, *Orphan's Legacy*, p. 9, *ad fin.*

[4] 32 Hen. VIII, c. 1, s. 1.

[5] *Ante*, p. 239.

[6] 29 Car. II, c. 3, ss. 19, 20.

[7] *Ibid.*, s. 22.

[8] The objection to creditors only applied where the testator had, by his will, charged his lands with payment of their debts, and thus improved their position.

could be admitted as a witness of his will; and, unfortunately, these absurd exclusions were expressly made to apply to the witnesses required by the Statute of Frauds for the proof of a nuncupative will.[1] A useful statute of the year 1752,[2] however, did much towards the alleviation of the position, by admitting the testimony of a creditor, even though the will contained a charge of debts on land, and of all beneficiaries; with a proviso that no beneficiary who was also a witness should be able to take any benefit under the will, except that legatees who had actually been paid their legacies, should not be deprived of them, even though called upon to give evidence, in the event of the will being upset. But the common sense rule, that all testimony shall be admitted for what it is worth, was not finally adopted till the passing of the Wills Act of 1837.[3]

Wills Act, 1837

This last statute, in addition to requiring all wills (other than those of soldiers and sailors on active service)[4] to be made in writing signed by the testator in the presence of two witnesses,[5] expressly enacted that no will should be invalidated on the ground of incompetency of any witness, and that beneficiaries, creditors, and executors should be admitted to prove the execution of a will;[6] the penalty imposed by the statute of 1752, however, remaining upon the beneficiaries, including the husband or wife of any witness.[7] The Wills Act of 1837 also formulated the rules as to the revocation [8] and revival [9] of wills; provided that a general devise or bequest, if otherwise appropriately worded, should pass not merely property belonging to the testator at his decease, but property over which he has a general power of appointment;[10] and abolished the old perverse rule, that a gift over after the death of a person 'without issue' must be construed, in the absence of counter-expressions, as applying to an indefinite failure of issue, not merely a failure at the death of the person named.[11] Finally, the Act prevents a 'lapse' or failure of a gift, whether of real or personal estate, by the death of the beneficiary in the lifetime of the testator, if the intended beneficiary is a descendant of the

[1] 4 Anne (1705) c. 16, s. 14 ('Act for the Amendment of the Law').

[2] 25 Geo. II, c. 6.

[3] 7 Will. IV & 1 Vict. c. 26.

[4] Ss. 11, 12. Wills of these persons are now regulated by a statute of the year 1865, the Navy and Marines (Wills) Act (28 & 29 Vict. c. 72).

[5] S. 9. (The requirement attaches also to the exercise of a testamentary power of appointment — s. 10.)

[6] Ss. 14–17.

[7] S. 15.

[8] Ss. 18–21.

[9] S. 22.

[10] S. 27.

[11] S. 29.

testator and has left issue who have in fact survived the testator.[1] In such a case, the gift goes as though the beneficiary had survived the testator, and died immediately after.

The Wills Act of 1837 has been explained in one particular (the position of the testator's signature) by a statute of the year 1852;[2] in other respects it is practically intact. But an important statute of the year 1861,[3] commonly known as Lord Kingsdown's Act, has mitigated the harshness of the rule of private international law which requires wills of movables to be executed in accordance with the formalities prescribed by the law of the testator's domicile at the time of his death.[4] Most of this Act only applies to British subjects. An attempt was made in the same year to establish with foreign States reciprocal agreements as to the requisites of domicile for testamentary purposes; but the Act embodying this attempt[5] has remained a dead letter, no convention under it having been made.

The other change in the law of chattels corporeal which deserves a word of notice, is concerned with '**reputed ownership.**' In spite of the fact that bailments of all kinds were well known in the Middle Ages, and, as we have seen,[6] were early recognized by English law, that law always looked with suspicion upon any attempt to separate possession and ownership. Thus, soon after the famous statute of 1571[7] had been passed to invalidate dispositions made with intent to defraud creditors, it was laid down, in *Twyne's Case*,[8] that retaining of possession by a person who conveyed away the property in goods was one of the 'badges of fraud' which would go far to upset the disposition. In 1623, one of the earliest Bankruptcy Acts[9] laid it down, that goods in the pos-

Transfer without Possession

[1] S. 33. (S. 32 makes a corresponding provision in the case of any devise of an estate tail, where the issue in tail survive the testator.)

[2] 15 & 16 Vict. c. 24 ('Wills Act Amendment Act').

[3] 24 & 25 Vict. c. 114 ('Wills Act, 1861').

[4] The will of a British subject is good as to form, if it is made according to the forms of the law of the place (a) where it is made, or (b) of the testator's domicile at the time of making the will, or (c) of the testator's domicile of origin, being in the British Dominions (s. 1). If the will is made in the United Kingdom, it may be made according to the law of the place where it is made (s. 2). And no subsequent change of domicile by the testator affects a will (s. 3).

[5] 24 & 25 Vict. c. 121.

[6] *Ante*, p. 134.

[7] 13 Eliz. c. 5.

[8] (1601) 3 Rep.

[9] 21 Jac. I, c. 19, s. 11. (According to Lord Hardwicke in *Bourne v. Dodson* (1740) 1 Atk., at p. 157, this section was not acted upon until the unreported case of *Stephens v. Sole* in 1736.)

session, order, and disposition of the bankrupt, as reputed owner, with the consent of the true owner thereof, at the time of the adjudication in bankruptcy, should pass to the bankrupt's creditors; and this provision, in a slightly modified form,[1] has appeared in every succeeding Bankruptcy Act.

Bills of Sale

But the most striking development of the principle: *en fait de meubles, possession vaut titre,* appears in the successive Bills of Sale Acts passed since the middle of the nineteenth century. In spite of the fact that delivery, or transfer of possession, was long considered by the common law as the only satisfactory evidence of transfer of chattels corporeal, the doctrine was admitted in theory, before the end of the sixteenth century,[2] that the property in goods would pass by assignment under seal, without delivery. Here again, the transaction was, after 1571, always subject to impeachment under the statute of that year;[3] but if in fact it was made *bonâ fide,* either as an absolute transfer or as a mortgage, it would be good, at any rate as against individual creditors.

In the year 1854, however, the evils attendant on this state of the law evoked a statute[4] designed, somewhat on the lines of the earlier Land Registry Acts, to enable any person who might be thinking of giving credit to another, to ascertain whether the latter was really owner of his stock-in-trade of furniture. This statute provided,[5] that every bill of sale or document (other than marriage settlements and ordinary commercial documents of title) transferring the property in, or authorizing a stranger to take possession of, goods in the 'possession or apparent possession'[6] of the transferor or licensor as security for debt, should be void against the assignees in bankruptcy and the execution creditors of the apparent owner of the goods, unless it, or a true copy of it, with an affidavit as to the time of its execution, were filed with an official of the Court of Queen's Bench, within twenty-one days after the

[1] The later provisions, *e.g.* Acts of 1869 (s. 15 (5)) and 1883 (s. 44 (iii)) are confined to goods apparently owned by the bankrupt in the way of his trade.

[2] See *Butler's and Baker's Case* (1591) 3 Rep., at 26b (2d resolution of the Court).

[3] 13 Eliz. c. 5. Apparently, it was immaterial whether or not the transaction was for value.

[4] 17 & 18 Vict. c. 36.

[5] S. 1.

[6] The writer has been unable to discover what 'apparent possession' may be. 'Apparent ownership' has a meaning; but what is 'apparent possession,' as distinct from any other 'possession'?

making. The officer of the Court was to keep a book [1] in which particulars of all such documents were to be entered; and this book was to be open to inspection at any time, on payment of a small fee.

Modern Bills of Sale Acts

The Act of 1854 was considerably amended in detail, and rendered more efficacious, by a statute of the year 1866,[2] which, among other things, required renewal of registration every five years. But both statutes were repealed and replaced by the Bills of Sale Act, 1878,[3] which has itself been severely amended by the Bills of Sale Act (1878) Amendment Act, 1882.[4] The relations to one another of these last two statutes are not very clear; but the short result appears to be, that bills of sale given by way of absolute transfer are governed only by the provisions of the former; [5] whilst bills of sale given by way of security are governed mainly by the latter, but also by such provisions of the Act of 1878 as have not, in the case of bills given by way of security, been repealed by the later statute.

The chief differences between the two classes of documents are as follows. While each must contain a true statement of the consideration, and be registered within seven days of execution, and re-registered every five years,[6] the attestation of an absolute bill of sale must be by a solicitor, who must state that he has explained the effect to his client,[7] but the bill of sale by way of security need only be attested by one credible witness, not a party.[8] On the other hand, the security bill must be in the precise form prescribed in the Act of 1882, which comprises a schedule of the goods included in it; [9] and, in the case of the security bill, also, the creditor can only seize the goods on the happening of one of the five events specified in the Act of 1882.[10] Finally, the security bill is totally void as a bill of sale if it is given in consideration of less than £30, or if it fails to comply with the requirements of the Act of 1882 [11] (except in the matter of the schedule[12]); and in any case it does

[1] S. 3. [2] 29 & 30 Vict. c. 96. [3] 41 & 42 Vict. c. 31.
[4] 45 & 46 Vict. c. 43. [5] *Swift v. Pannell* (1883) 24 Ch. D. 210.
[6] Act of 1878, ss. 8, 10, 11. (In the case of the security bill, it is sufficient if it is registered within seven clear days after the earliest time at which it could arrive in England. Act of 1882, s. 8.)
[7] Act of 1878, s. 10 (1). [8] Act of 1882, s. 10.
[9] Act of 1882, s. 9. [10] Act of 1882, s. 7. [11] *Ibid.*, ss. 4, 8, 9, 12.
[12] Here it is only void as regards the omitted goods (*ibid.*, s. 4).

not protect the grantee against the grantor's trustee in bankruptcy.[1] While an absolute bill, if properly registered, and correct in form, is a complete protection against all creditors except the landlord; [2] and an informality only lets in the trustee in bankruptcy and execution creditors, *i.e.* as between the parties, it is good.[3]

But it is in that great and growing domain of personal property which consists of choses in action, that the great revolution of the latest period in the history of English law has taken place; and to that revolution we must now turn our attention.

'Choses in Action'

As its name implies, a chose in action was, originally, a claim which could only be enforced by legal proceedings, as contrasted with a right or interest which could be enforced by actual seizure or possession of a tangible object. In early days, the precise situation of the border line between a chose in possession and a chose in action evidently depended on the extent to which self-help was permitted. And, though the rules on the subject of 'forcible entry' of lands have long been severe,[4] there is warrant for saying that the law on the subject of the seizure of chattels is deplorably lax.[5] Thus, in cases like bailment, delicate questions might easily arise. Say that I pawn a watch with C. Whilst it is still unredeemed, is it, as regards me, a chose in possession, or in action? Obviously, I have no right to take it from C; but it has been held[6] that I can sell it to B, not as a chose in action, but as an ordinary chattel corporeal. And yet, the execution creditor of the pawnbroker can seize it for his debt,[7] whilst my creditor cannot seize it for his.[8] On the other hand, if the bailment be merely of a permissory character, terminable at the option of the bailor, it seems but reasonable to treat him as still in possession of the chattel; and he is so treated.[9] For, probably, he would be

[1] Act of 1878, ss. 8, 20; repealed, as to security bills, by Act of 1882, s. 15.

[2] Act of 1878, ss. 8, 20. [3] *Ibid.*

[4] Statutes of Forcible Entry (5 Ric. II, st. 1 (1381) c. 4; 15 Ric. II (1391) c. 2 — both still in force).

[5] *Cf. Blades v. Higgs* (1861) 10 C. B. (N.S.) 713, where the bailiff of a landowner was allowed to seize rabbits shot by a poacher on his employer's land, and found at a railway station.

[6] *Franklin v. Neate* (1844) 13 M. & W. 481 (but against the opinion of that very learned judge, Baron Parke). [7] *Rollason v. Rollason* (1887) 34 Ch. D. 495.

[8] *Rogers v. Kennay* (1846) 15 L. J. Q. B. 381.

[9] *Manders v. Williams* (1849) 18 L. J. Ch. 437.

allowed to seize the chattel by force. But, obviously, there are difficulties.

It is not, in fact, till we depart still further from the notions both of a mere right of action, and of a concrete object to be reached by means of it, that we arrive at the most important classes of modern choses in action. Doubtless the bills of exchange which, as we have seen,[1] were familiar to English eyes before the end of the sixteenth century, were popularly regarded as 'property' from an early date; but the Common Law persisted in treating them as mere rights of action, alienable only by reason of their inheritance from the Law Merchant. It was not till the advent of patents, copyright, stock, and shares, that the true importance of choses in action appeared. For these interests could not possibly be regarded as mere rights of action; they were far too positive and comprehensive, though the French term for a share ('*action*') suggests that in one country, at least, the idea of procedural rights clung tenaciously. To take a juristic test, these interests are clearly *jura in rem*, rights enforceable against all and sundry; while bills of exchange, and rights of action generally, are, as a rule, only *jura in personam*, *i.e.* rights enforceable against specific persons. And we remember the ancient rule of English law: that chattels personal cannot be recovered by any form of real action.

On the other hand, these new interests were certainly incapable of possession; nobody could bring the action of Trespass for injury to them. And so they fell, almost inevitably, by reason of their 'incorporeal' character, into the class of 'choses in action.' But it is obvious that there is a wide difference between such interests, and, say, the right to recover damages for a breach of contract or a tort; and a statute which lumps them all together, or, at least, uses the phrase 'legal chose in action,' or 'things in action,' without explanation, will need a deal of interpretation.[2]

With these preliminary remarks, we turn to examine the history of four leading groups of choses in action of the modern type, viz. copyright, patents, stock and shares, and interests in ships.

It has been already pointed out,[3] that the disciplinary action

[1] *Ante*, pp. 126–128.

[2] Judicature Act, 1873, s. 25 (6); Bankruptcy Act, 1883, s. 44 (iii). (For a discussion of the scope of 'choses in action' see L. Q. R. Vol. ix, pp. 311–315; x, 143–157; xi, 223–240.)

[3] *Ante*, pp. 129, 130.

of the Court of Star Chamber, combined with the express grants of patents or monopolies by the Crown, had, in effect, created a literary property in published works long before the end of the last period. But the point is so interesting, and has been so much debated, that a brief summary of its history will not be out of place here.

Copyright

The alarm created by the introduction of the art of printing was immediately reflected on the Statute Book. So early as the year 1483,[1] the protectionist statute of Richard III had expressly exempted printed books from its general exclusion of foreign merchandise; but this clause was repealed by a statute of 1533,[2] which totally forbade the sale of books imported from beyond the seas, while at the same time empowering the Lord Chancellor, Treasurer, and two Chief Justices, to abate the 'enhanced' prices of native works.

As has been said before, the control of the press, from the time of its invention, was exercised by the Privy Council, working through the Star Chamber. The Star Chamber, again, used as its agent the Stationers' Company, which is said[3] to have received its first charter from Philip and Mary in 1556, and a confirmation from Elizabeth two years later. No one was entitled to exercise the art of printing unless he was a member of this company; and the company was vested with the usual disciplinary powers of craft gilds, for the double purpose of preventing any infringement of its monopoly and controlling its own members. Further than that, no book could be published without an express license of some high State official. It is obvious, therefore, that any infringement of the monopoly *de facto* created by the grant of a license to publish, could only be effected with the collusion of the government; even though no express grant of a monopoly were made. And it is said, that this fact was explicitly recognized by a decree of the Star Chamber in 1637.[4]

The Stationers' Company

It might have been supposed that the withdrawal of the Crown from Parliamentary proceedings at the outbreak of the Civil War, would have led to a relaxation of this rigid system. But the Long Parliament proved to be no more liberal on this point than the statesmen of Eliza-

Commonwealth Ordinance

[1] 1 Ric. III, c. 9, s. 12.
[2] 25 Hen. VIII, c. 15.
[3] *Donaldson v. Beckett* (1764) 2 Bro. P. C. 136.
[4] *Ibid., ubi sup.*, at p. 136.

beth and James; and, by an Ordinance of the year 1643,[1] the system was substantially confirmed, with the necessary adaptations. No books were to be printed without license of the Parliamentary Commissioners, and entry in the Stationers' Register 'according to ancient custom.' Moreover, no unauthorized person was to print or import copies of books licensed and duly registered as belonging to a member of the company;[2] and the most drastic powers of search and seizure, extending even to arrest of the person, were given to the company.

In spite of the indignant protest of Milton, before referred to, this system appears to have continued during the rest of the Interregnum. Immediately after the Restoration, it was revived and intensified by the **Licensing Act** of 1662,[3] which not only confirmed the monopoly of the Stationers' Company and its drastic powers[4] as well as the rule against unlicensed printing,[5] but extended the right of search to King's Messengers, armed with warrants of a Secretary of State, who 'for the better discovering of printing in corners without license,' are empowered to take with them constables or such other assistance as they shall see fit, and, at any time they shall think fit, to search all houses and shops where they shall know, or on some probable reason suspect, any unlicensed printing to be going on.[6] This drastic clause was probably the origin of those 'general warrants' which played such a conspicuous part a century later; but the Act of 1662 is also important as introducing the rule,[7] that free copies of all published works are to be sent to the King's Library and the two older English universities, whose peculiar privileges are expressly preserved.[8]

Licensing Act

It is again obvious, that the Licensing Act, though not in form creating any positive copyright, in effect would make it impossible, without a breach of law or the connivance of the State, for any unauthorized person to infringe the negative monopoly conferred by the licensing system on the printer of a duly licensed and registered book. And, in fact, there are substantial traces, so early as the year 1679, of the recognition

[1] *Acts and Ordinances of the Commonwealth*, I, 184–7.

[2] This is a clear recognition of copyright, though rather in the printer than the author.

[3] 13 & 14 Car. II, c. 33.

[4] Ss. 3, 10 (the number of printers was also severely restricted).

[5] S. 3.

[6] S. 15.

[7] S. 17.

[8] S. 18.

of a right of action, a variety of the Action of Case, for such infringement;[1] while, from the year 1681 onwards, Chancery seems to have granted injunctions to prohibit similar offences.[2]

But, as is well known, the Licensing Act, which was from the first treated as temporary, was, after various short renewals, finally cast out by Parliament in the year 1695;[3] and thereupon the whole licensing system, together with a large part of the monopoly of the Stationers' Company, fell to the ground. Unfortunately, the indirect protection afforded to authors by the system fell with it; and, though Chancery seems to have continued to give them some trifling assistance,[4] it is doubtful whether this assistance extended to any but 'prerogative' rights, such as those connected with the sale of Bibles and almanacs. It was, of course, difficult, if not impossible, in face of the Statute of Monopolies, to revive the practice of granting patent rights.

First Copyright Act

At length, however, in the year 1709,[5] the first direct statutory creation of copyright took place. By the statute of Anne, the exclusive right of publishing was conferred upon the author and his assigns for a period of fourteen years from publication; provided that the work in question were registered before publication at Stationers' Hall.[6] The period of fourteen years was probably due to the reflex action of the Statute of Monopolies of 1623; but a relaxation of it was found in a clause giving the author an extension to another period of fourteen years, if he should be living at the expiry of the first period.[7] The former licensing authorities were still allowed to regulate, to a certain extent, the prices of books;[8]

[1] Lilly, *Modern Entries* (ed. 1723) p. 67, where the Declaration in *Ponder v. Braddell* for the unauthorized printing of Bunyan's *Pilgrim's Progress*, is given; but the fate of the action is not stated. The plaintiff is described as 'proprietor of the copy of a certain book.' Needless to say, the plaintiff was not the author.

[2] Particulars are given in the report of *Donaldson v. Beckett* (1774) 2 Bro. P. C., at pp. 137–8.

[3] This fact is not so obvious as it might be; owing to the peculiar history of the Licensing Act. The statute was renewed in 1692 by the Expiring Laws Continuance Act (4 W. & M. c. 24, s. 14) for one year from 13th February, 1692, and thence until the end of the next session of Parliament. The next session after 13th February, 1693, began on 12th November, 1694, and ended on 3d May, 1695. By that time the Commons had definitely refused to include the statute in the Expiring Laws Continuance Act of the year 1695 (6 & 7 Will. III, c. 14). The Licensing Act, therefore, ceased to be in force on 3d May, 1695. (I owe these facts to the kindness of Master Romer.)

[4] See particulars in *Donaldson v. Beckett*, *ubi sup.*, at p. 137.

[5] 8 Anne, c. 19 (or 21).

[6] Ss. 1, 2.

[7] S. 11.

[8] S. 4.

and the policy of prohibiting the importation of English books printed abroad was continued, doubtless in the supposed interests of authors themselves.[1] The list of free copies was extended to nine; for the purpose of including the Scottish universities, Sion College, and the Faculty of Advocates.[2]

So far as literary copyright is concerned, the period between the passing of the Act of Anne and the Copyright Act of 1842, was marked chiefly[3] by the settlement of two important questions. One of these was precisely that which has presented itself in these pages. Was there or not, apart from the Act of Anne, any 'common law' copyright in published works? This question was decided, for legal purposes, in the negative, by the House of Lords, in the famous case of *Donaldson v. Beckett,* in the year 1774.[4] The case is interesting, for literary as well as for legal reasons; for it was concerned with the proprietorship of Thomson's charming poem *The Seasons,* and his much less valuable tragedy *Sophonisba.*[5] The other question related to the property in unpublished writings, such as letters and diaries. Could any person into whose hands such documents lawfully came print and publish them for profit? This question was answered in the negative by Lord Hardwicke, in the case of *Pope v. Curl,* decided in 1741,[6] in which, it is interesting to note, the author of the letters in question was himself plaintiff. Lord Hardwicke's Order lays it down, that the fact that letters are written to A, does not make them the property of A, in the sense that he may publish them. They are his to read, not to publish.

Copyright Act, 1842

In the year 1842, the second great Copyright Act[7] made a liberal extension of the period of copyright, by providing that it should continue for forty-two years from publication, or, if the author were then living, till the expiry of seven years from his death; and this extension applied to works then in existence of which the copyright had

[1] S. 7. (This policy was not abandoned till 1801 (41 Geo. III, c. 107, s. 7).)

[2] S. 5. (It will be remembered that the Union with Scotland had taken place two years before the passing of the Act of 1709. On the Union with Ireland in 1801, an Act (41 Geo. III, c. 107) was passed to extend the rules of the Act of 1709 to that country.)

[3] There was a statute in 1814 (54 Geo. III, c. 156) which extended the author's copyright to the period of his life, when that exceeded 28 years from publication (s. 4).

[4] 2 Bro. P. C. 129.

[5] Again, it is perhaps needless to say, the author was not the plaintiff.

[6] 2 Atk. 342.

[7] 5 & 6 Vict. c. 45.

not expired, and was still vested in the author or his family.[1] The Act settled a somewhat burning question, by providing[2] that the contributions to encyclopædias and periodical works or works published in series, should belong to the proprietor who had commissioned and paid for them; but, in the case of a contribution to a periodical, the Act provided[3] that the contributor might republish after twenty-eight years, during which time the proprietor of the periodical should not be entitled to publish in separate form without the author's consent. The right to forbid reproduction of their work in dramatic form, which had been conferred upon authors for a period of twenty-eight years or life by a statute of the year 1833,[4] was, by the Act of 1842,[5] placed on the same footing as to duration as literary copyright, and extended to musical works.

International Copyright

Meanwhile, an attempt had been made[6] to extend the protection afforded by the copyright law to the works of English authors in foreign countries, on terms of reciprocity which should equally protect the works of foreign authors here; and this attempt was repeated in a statute of the year 1844,[7] which empowered the Crown, by Order in Council, to grant protection to foreign authors in whose countries English authors received similar consideration. Obviously, however, such an attempt, in the absence of international co-operation, was not likely to go very far, or be very satisfactory; and accordingly, the friends of literature bent their efforts to secure such co-operation. At length, in the year 1885, a conference took place, which produced a document known as the 'Berne Convention,' setting forth a basis of an international copyright code for the civilized world. Obviously, this document is of no legal validity in any country which has not accepted it. But Great Britain immediately gave in her adhesion; and, in the year 1886, the Imperial Parliament passed a short Act[8] to enable the Crown, and all persons interested, to give its provisions the force, not merely of international, but of national law.

[1] Ss. 3, 4. [2] S. 18. [3] *Ibid.*

[4] 3 & 4 Will. IV, c. 15, s. 1. (It is to be observed, that the period of protection given to dramatic works by this Act, and to dramatic and musical works by the Act of 1842 (s. 20) ran from publication (or representation), and that it obviously only applied to dramatic and musical works composed as such, *i.e.* not to the right of adaptation.) [5] S. 20. [6] By 1 & 2 Vict. c. 59.

[7] International Copyright Act (7 & 8 Vict. c. 12).

[8] International Copyright Act (49 & 50 Vict. c. 33).

One other point remains to be noticed, before we proceed to a brief summary of the statute which, just as this book goes to press, has remodelled English copyright law.

Colonial Copyright

Acts of the Imperial Parliament do not affect the colonies; unless 'either by express words or necessary implication (they) extend to the colonies.'[1] No such expression or implication is to be found in the early copyright statutes, as regards the general purview of copyright; but in those statutes, and especially in the Act of 1842, will be found certain provisions[2] prohibiting the import into any part of the British Dominions of copies of British copyright works printed abroad, *e.g.* the well-known 'Tauchnitz' editions. And so, until the passing of the Colonial Copyright Act, 1847,[3] there appears to have been no prohibition (other than the expense involved) against the printing and selling in the British colonies of British copyright books; even against the wishes of the proprietors of the British copyright. By that statute, however, the Crown was empowered, on the passing in any colony of a proper copyright statute, affording due protection to British authors, to exempt that colony from the operation of the prohibitory clauses of the Acts of 1842 and 1845; and, though this does not seem to be a great inducement, in fact the good sense and loyalty of the great self-governing colonies, have caused them, in most cases, to enact proper copyright legislation. Accordingly, after an Act relating specially to Canada had been in operation for eleven years, the Imperial Parliament, in the International Copyright Act, 1886,[4] boldly extended the law (with certain slight exceptions) both of national and international copyright, to the whole of the British dominions.

Act of 1911

The Copyright Act, 1911, deals with all aspects of the question — national, colonial, and international; also, in addition to books and other printed matter, with dramatic work, artistic work (pictures, sculptures, and architectural drawings),[5] engravings, and photographs.[6] The chief

[1] *New Zealand Loan, &c. Co. v. Morrison* [1898] A. C., at p. 357, *per* Lord Davey.

[2] Copyright Act. 1842, s. 7; 8 & 9 Vict. (1845) c. 93, s. 9.

[3] 10 & 11 Vict. c. 95.

[4] S. 8.

[5] The protection extends, not merely to the reproduction of the drawings, in similar form, but to application of the 'character or design' on other buildings (s. 35).

[6] The Act does not, however, give protection to industrial designs intended to be multiplied by industrial process (s. 22). These may be protected under the Patent Act.

changes introduced by it are, to fix a uniform period for copyright of the author's life, and fifty years further,[1] or, where the work is posthumously published, of fifty years from publication.[2] In the case of photographs, however, the protection only runs for fifty years from the making of the original negative from which the photograph is taken;[3] and, in the case of gramophone and similar records, for a like period from the making of the original plate.[4] But, though copyright remains generally assignable, no assignment (otherwise than by will) by an author, who is also the first owner of any copyright, will operate to pass any copyright beyond twenty-five years from his death; on the expiration of which period the copyright will pass to the author's personal representatives.[5] There are, however, important provisions in the Act to prohibit the suppression of an author's works after his death.[6]

The practice of requiring delivery of free copies to public institutions, which began, as we have seen,[7] in 1662, and has since undergone so many fluctuations, is now settled by requiring the publisher to deliver one copy of the best and most complete form of every book published by him to the British Museum, and entitling five other libraries, those of Bodley, Cambridge University, the Faculty of Advocates at Edinburgh, Trinity College, Dublin, and the National Library of Wales (the latter with certain reservations) to claim copies of the most numerous edition.[8]

A somewhat startling feature of the Act is, that it professes[9] to abolish entirely the so-called 'common law' or proprietary rights of an author or any one else, in both published and unpublished material; but this apparent revolution in the law affecting unpublished material is substantially explained by the fact that, under the new statute, copyright in literary, dramatic, musical, and artistic work will run, not from the date of publication, but from that of creation.[10] The change will, however, doubtless affect the date of publication of political memoirs and the like; though, presumably, so long as these remain

[1] S. 3. (Generally speaking, the extension applies to existing copyright (s. 24) in the manner specified in Sched. I of the new Act.)
[2] S. 17.
[3] S. 21 } In these cases, the owner of the original negative or plate is deemed to
[4] S. 19 } be the author of the work.
[5] S. 5 (2).
[6] S. 4. The Act retains the generally discredited 'compulsory license' system.
[7] *Ante*, p. 277.
[8] S. 15.
[9] S. 31.
[10] Ss. 1 (1), 3. (This fact is not made so clear as it might be.)

in the actual custody of the persons entitled to publish them, the ownership of the material will be protected by the ordinary law of property. With regard to copyright in work which first appears in an oral form, the Act in effect gives no exclusive right to the reproduction of political speeches;[1] but, as respects other oral deliveries, such as lectures, addresses, non-political speeches, and sermons, it treats the first authorized delivery in public as the creation, and gives the authors the general period of life and fifty years as the period of copyright.[2]

Finally, the new statute substantially incorporates the provisions of the existing International Copyright Acts, by empowering the Crown[3] to extend their operation to such countries as shall have made due provision for reciprocal treatment of British authors; but the operation of such an Order will not extend to a self-governing colony, unless that colony voluntarily adopts it.[4] Similarly, the Copyright Act itself, though generally operative throughout the Empire, will not apply to a self-governing colony; unless either such colony has enacted satisfactory provisions for the protection of British authors within its boundaries, or unless the legislature of such colony has expressly adopted it.[5] But, until the new Act does apply to a self-governing colony, the previous law will be in force there;[6] although, for most purposes, the Act of 1911 has superseded all previous legislation on the subject of copyright.[7]

Patents

The modern system of monopoly rights in the reproduction and distribution of newly invented articles of manufacture, commonly known as 'patents,' had also, as we have seen,[8] established itself during the preceding period, under the exempting clause of the Statute of Monopolies, passed in 1623.[9] Apparently, this simple provision served the needs of the country for more than two hundred years; except that the so-called 'copyright in designs,' *i.e.* the exclusive right to reproduce articles of a particular design, was acquired by those interested in the Manchester soft-goods trade in the eighteenth century.[10] But in the year 1835, the Crown was empowered, in special cases, to extend the duration of a patent

[1] S. 20. Apparently, only a newspaper may publish unauthorized reports (Qu. any time limit?).
[2] Ss. 1 (3), 35 (1). [3] S. 29. [4] S. 30. [5] S. 25 (1).
[6] S. 26 (2). [7] S. 36. [8] *Ante*, pp. 128, 129. [9] 21 Jac. I, c. 3, s. 6.
[10] 27 Geo. III (1787) c. 38; 34 Geo. III (1794) c. 23.

for seven years; and the unauthorized use of the name of a holder of a patent was prohibited under penalties.[1] In the year 1839, 'copyright in design' was made applicable generally to all manufactures, or, at least, widely extended to include, not merely printed patterns, but models of solid fabrics, and the shape of any article of manufacture not included in the statutes, previously alluded to, of the eighteenth century.[2] The protection given by this statute was brief, covering only a period of twelve months;[3] but this period was extended to three years, and the scheme considerably amended, by statutes of the years 1842 and 1843.[4]

The great increase of inventiveness in mechanical processes which attended the industrial revolution of the first half of the nineteenth century, soon outgrew the primitive machinery by which the Statute of Monopolies had been worked. Accordingly, in the year 1852,[5] the present Patent Office was established by Act of Parliament; and a regular process of application, with provisional and complete specifications, reference to Law Officer, advertisement, and objections, much as it now exists,[6] was set up. This Act also introduced the system of periodical payment of stamp duties, first fixed at the amounts of £50 and £100, payable at the end of the seventh and tenth years respectively of the currency of the patent.[7] The Act also provided for the establishment of a Patent Register, in which inventors desirous of ascertaining whether their ideas had been anticipated might make effective search.[8]

For some time prior to the year 1875, Courts of Equity, in the exercise of their jurisdiction in the matter of fraud, had been in the habit of issuing injunctions[9] against the false use of trade names, practised for the purpose of 'passing off' goods as those of some well-known firm of high reputation. Not unnaturally, this protection had greatly added to the value of a 'trade name'; and, in spite of the protests of some distinguished judges, it was at length too plain to be ignored, that a new form of property had in fact arisen. Accordingly, it was determined to put this

[1] 5 & 6 Will. IV, c. 83, ss. 4, 7. [2] 2 & 3 Vict. c. 17, s. 1. [3] *Ibid.*
[4] 5 & 6 Vict. c. 100; 6 & 7 Vict. c. 65. [5] 15 & 16 Vict. c. 83.
[6] Ss. 6, 13. [7] S. 17. [8] S. 34.
[9] Well-known cases are *Millington v. Fox* (1838) 3 M. & Cr. 338; *Croft v. Day* (1844) 7 Beav. 43; *Burgess v. Burgess* (1853) 3 De G. M. & G. 896 (where the injunction was refused). The Common Law Courts also recognized the right to relief (*Sykes v. Sykes* (1824) 3 B. & C. 541).

new property on a statutory footing; and, by the Trade Marks Registration Act of 1875,[1] a person who claimed that a certain name or style (not necessarily his own) had become so closely associated in the public mind with a particular class of goods sold by him, that it would, in effect, be fraudulent in any rival to sell other goods under it, was authorized to register his claim in a public register.[2] At first, this registration was only to be *primâ facie* evidence of title; [3] but if, after a period of five years' registration, no one had succeeded in procuring its removal from the register, the registered proprietor's title would become absolute, and would be assignable and transmissible with the good-will of his business,[4] while, in any case, he would be unable to take proceedings for an alleged infringement, until his claim was registered.[5] Apparently, once his title completed, the proprietor would be able to hold or transmit it in perpetuity.

Trade Marks Registration Act

An important statute of the year 1883, the Patents, Designs, and Trade Marks Act,[6] introduced several alterations into the law. It allowed the fees due to the Crown to be paid by yearly instalments,[7] extended the maximum period of duration of a patent to twenty-eight years,[8] made patents bind the Crown (with due safeguards for the right of Government departments to use them on payment of compensation),[9] provided for the issue of compulsory licenses where the patent was not being adequately worked in the United Kingdom,[10] and even made some attempt towards establishing Imperial and international patent rights.[11] Moreover, it extended the so-called 'copyright in designs' from three to five years; [12] and provided for the re-registration of a trade-mark at the end of fourteen years from its first registration.[13]

Patents Act of 1883

Statutory amendments of minor importance followed in the years 1885, 1886, and 1888; [14] and, in the year 1905, the subject of trade-marks was definitely severed from Patent Law (with which it has, really, little in common) by the consolidating Trade Marks Act of 1905.[15] A far more im-

Acts of 1907

[1] 38 & 39 Vict. c, 91.
[2] S. 1
[3] S. 3.
[4] S. 2.
[5] S. 1.
[6] 46 & 47 Vict. c. 57.
[7] Sched. II.
[8] S. 25.
[9] S. 27.
[10] S. 22.
[11] Ss. 103, 104.
[12] S. 50.
[13] S. 79.
[14] 48 & 49 Vict. c. 63; 49 & 50 Vict. c. 37; 51 & 52 Vict. c. 50.
[15] 5 Edw. VII, c. 15.

portant statute was that of the year 1907, which contains [1] the famous clause authorizing the Comptroller of Patents [2] (subject to any appeal to the Court) to revoke any patent after the expiration of four years from its issue, on the ground that it is being worked wholly or mainly outside the United Kingdom. The same Act [3] contains a provision to the effect that the unintentional infringer of a patent shall not be liable to damages, but only to an injunction, and another making a renewal of the copyright in a design obtainable as of course for a period of five years, with a discretionary renewal of a second similar period, or a maximum of fifteen years.[4] One of the most useful amendments introduced by this Act is that [5] which substitutes the High Court for the Privy Council as the tribunal concerned with petitions for extension of patents; the substitution of a petition to the Court for the ancient process of *Sci. Fa.*, in the matter of the revocation of a patent, having been effected by the Act of 1883.[6] Finally, the whole law on the subject of Patents and Designs was consolidated by a statute of the year 1907.[7]

Stock and Shares

A third and even more important new form of 'incorporeal' personal property, which acquired definite recognition in this period, is that which consists of stock, shares, and debentures in or of various forms of joint enterprise. Some day, it is to be hoped, the History of Association in England will be adequately written; certainly it is well worth writing. Meanwhile, we can only here give a brief sketch of the legal aspect of the subject.

The medieval forms of co-operation, such, especially, as the village-community, the trade and craft gild, and the 'regulated' company,[8] had virtually done their work by the end of the sixteenth century; though some of the gilds survived, and some of the companies actually did business for some time after. These associations had left as a heritage to modern English law the various forms of co-ownership (joint tenancy, tenancy in common, and parcenary) still recognized by that law, and, above all, the

[1] Patents and Designs Amendment Act (7 Edw. VII, c. 28) s. 15.

[2] This official of the Board of Trade had been substituted in 1883 (Act of 1883, s. 83 (1)) for the Patent Commissioners set up by the Act of 1852.

[3] S. 27. [4] S. 31. [5] S. 17. [6] S. 26.

[7] 7 Edw. VII, c. 29. The amending Act of that year (c. 28) was thus really stifled at its birth; but its provisions were, of course, incorporated into the consolidating Act.

[8] See *ante*, p. 129.

priceless conception of the 'corporation,' or juristic person. But co-ownership, as understood by English law, is far too limited in its scope, and crude in its rules, to afford a satisfactory basis for great commercial enterprises; and the corporation was still in an undeveloped condition, which required much care to render it a really flexible instrument of economics.

The practice of creating chartered joint-stock companies of a modern type seems to have begun at the commencement of the seventeenth century; and the formation of the East India Company is one of the earliest, if not the very earliest, examples. At first, it appears, the 'joint stock' of the company was separately made up for each ship; perhaps for each voyage. But, in the year 1612,[1] the Company made the momentous resolve to have one joint stock for the whole of its affairs, and thus inaugurated a new epoch. The East India Company, or Companies, (for there were two of them), were followed by the Hudson's Bay Company (1670), the existence of which was recognized by statute in 1707,[2] and by the Bank of England and the notorious South Sea Company. Owing to the practice which had hitherto connected such companies with the monopoly of a particular trade, there were grave doubts whether, after the passing of the Statute of Monopolies in 1623,[3] the Crown had power to create any such companies; and it is said,[4] that it was through fear of this statute that the Royal African (or 'Guinea') Company abandoned its monopoly. The Bank of England and the South Sea Company were, of course, established by Act of Parliament;[5] but a simpler solution of the difficulty was found by omitting from charters of incorporation all grants of monopoly rights. It was under this new practice, presumably, that the numerous 'bubble' companies which precipitated the disaster of 1720 were formed. Still, however, when any enterprise of great magnitude was to be undertaken on a 'joint stock,' it was the practice to procure incorporation under powers conferred by Act of Parliament. A notable example occurs in the statute of 1719,[6] under which the London Assurance and the

Joint Stock Companies

[1] Cunningham, *Growth of English Industry and Commerce,* II, 27.
[2] 6 Anne, c. 37, s. 23. [3] 21 Jac. I, c. 3.
[4] Cunningham, *op. cit.* II, 125.
[5] Bank of England Act, 1694 (5 & 6 W. & M. c. 20); 5 Geo. I (1718) c. 19, s. 31.
[6] 6 Geo. I, c. 18. The two corporations were amalgamated for borrowing purposes in 1831, and consolidated in 1853. (See *Eloe v. Boyton* [1891] 1 Ch. 501.)

London Fire Assurance Corporations were founded. By an important section of that Act,[1] all unauthorized joint undertakings formed since 1718 were declared illegal; but not to the prohibition of any legitimate partnership 'in such manner as hath been hitherto usually.'[2]

The passing of Sir John Barnard's Act of 1733 against stock-jobbing,[3] and of the statute of the year 1767,[4] which forbade a stockholder to vote at any meeting unless he had held his stock for at least six months, shows that the practice of dealing in stocks and shares was growing; but it was, apparently, not till the year 1825, that a new departure of first-rate importance was made. In that year, however, Parliament completely reversed the policy of 1719, by abolishing all restrictions on joint-stock trading,[5] and authorizing the Crown, in grants of future charters, to provide that the members of the corporation should be 'individually liable, in their persons and property, for the debts, contracts and engagements of the corporation, to such extent, and subject to such regulations and restrictions, as His Majesty . . . may deem fit and proper' (to be expressed in the charter).[6] This clause virtually gave the Crown power to establish the principle of 'limited liability'; but it is not quite clear whether in favour of shareholders or creditors. The old rule: *quod ab universitate debetur, ab omnibus non debetur*, would have relieved shareholders of all liability. On the other hand, doubtless, the members of an unincorporated association would have been each individually liable to the full extent of the association's engagements.

Limited Liability

A distinct advance towards modern conditions is seen in the Act of 1837[7] which (repealing and substantially re-enacting a slightly earlier statute of 1834[8]) definitely authorizes the Crown to restrict the liability of members of even an unincorporated association, to a fixed maximum for each share.[9] But the Act provides,[10] that every association to which this privilege is granted must have a registered deed of partner-

Act of 1837

[1] S. 18.

[2] S. 25. (The framers of the section made no attempt to distinguish legally between such a partnership and an unauthorized association. Probably any such attempt would have failed.)

[3] 7 Geo. II, c. 8.

[4] 7 Geo. III, c. 48.

[5] 6 Geo. IV, c. 91, s. 1.

[6] S. 2.

[7] 7 Will. IV & 1 Vict. c. 73.

[8] 4 & 5 Will. IV, c. 94.

[9] 7 Will. IV & 1 Vict. c. 73, s. 4.

[10] S. 5.

ship, in which the capital is divided into 'a certain number of shares'; and members are to remain liable until transfers of their shares are registered.[1] This important statute, which, apparently, started the Register of Joint Stock Companies,[2] also provided for the incorporation of companies for a limited period;[3] but its chief curiosity is the machinery provided for enabling creditors to assert their rights, and for liabilities to be apportioned among shareholders. The association, in its deed of partnership, names two or more officers by whom it may sue and be sued;[4] but, in the latter case, the judgment creditor may, apparently,[5] issue execution against any shareholder up to the amount of his liability. The latter must pay; but he may then claim repayment from the association.[6]

The year 1844–5 may, however, with justice be regarded as laying the foundation of the modern company system. No less than six great statutes[7] were passed within that period for the purpose; and these establish certain fundamental principles of classification. In the first place, they distinguish between what may be called 'public companies' in a special sense (*i.e.* companies formed to execute undertakings of a public nature under special Parliamentary sanction) and ordinary commercial companies, formed simply for profit. The former, though usually incorporated by special Act of Parliament, are governed, in the absence of legislation to the contrary, by the Companies Clauses Act of 1845.[8] The latter are, practically, incorporated as of course,[9] on fulfilment of the statutory requirements, by registration under the Companies Acts, and are governed by their Memorandum and Articles of Association. Again, these latter companies are now, for the first time, definitely distinguished from unincorporated enterprises, by the provision that no association of more than six persons may carry on the business of banking,[10] and (with cer-

Legislation of 1844–5

[1] S. 21. [2] S 16.

[3] S. 29. This clause is probably due to the survival of the medieval idea that a corporation is a body 'having a perpetual existence.'

[4] S. 5. [5] S. 24. [6] Ss. 11, 12.

[7] These are the Railway Regulation Act, 1844 (7 & 8 Vict. c. 85), the Joint Stock Companies Act, 1844 (7 & 8 Vict. c. 110), the Winding Up Act, 1844 (7 & 8 Vict. c. 111), the Joint Stock Banks Act, 1844 (7 & 8 Vict. c. 113), the Companies Clauses Act, 1845 (8 & 9 Vict. c. 16), and the Railways Clauses Act, 1845 (8 & 9 Vict. c. 20).

[8] See preamble of the Act. [9] Ss. 7, 25.

[10] Joint Stock Banks Act, 1844, s. 1.

tain exceptions) not more than twenty-five any other business, except as a duly incorporated company under the Acts.[1] The Companies Act of 1844 also introduced the familiar scheme of directors, general and extraordinary meetings of shareholders, production of balance sheet, audit and other features of the present day.[2]

Apparently, the principle of limited liability was not made a matter of general right until the year 1855, when a statute[3] (repealed but substantially re-enacted by a statute of the following year[4]) definitely adopted it as part of the normal system, except for insurance companies and banks. The Act of 1856 reduced the maximum limit of non-incorporated partnerships to twenty,[5] made calls upon shareholders recoverable as debts due to the company,[6] and drew the present well-known distinction between compulsory and voluntary winding-up.[7] In the following year,[8] a limited company was empowered to convert its fully paid shares into unnumbered stock; and, a year later still,[9] the principle of limited liability was extended, for the first time and with special precautions, to banks.

In the year 1862, was passed the great consolidating statute,[10] which for so long served as the basis of company law. Incidentally, it introduced[11] an alternative method of limitation of liability, viz. limitation by guarantee, and defined the liability of past shareholders in the event of a winding-up, by providing[12] that they should be liable to contribute towards payment of the company's debts only for one year after the transfer of their shares, and, even within that period, only for debts contracted before the registration of the transfer, and in default of shareholders existing at the commencement of the winding-up.

Companies Act, 1862

Apparently, the power to issue debentures and debenture stock is part of the general borrowing power conferred upon most commercial companies by their Memorandum or Articles of Association, and did not, originally, spring from special leg-

[1] Companies Act, 1844, s. 1. (The section is involved; but that, apparently, is its meaning.)

[2] Ss. 21, 27, 29, 35, 36, 39, and Sched. A.

[3] 18 & 19 Vict. c. 133.

[4] 19 & 20 Vict. c. 47, s. 3.

[5] S. 4.

[6] S. 22.

[7] Ss. 67, 102.

[8] 20 & 21 Vict. (1857) c. 14, ss. 5–9.

[9] 21 & 22. Vict. (1858) c 91.

[10] 25 & 26 Vict. c. 89.

[11] S. 9.

[12] S. 38.

islation.[1] But the Companies Act, 1865,[2] authorized the creation of a special class of 'mortgage debentures,' *i.e.* debentures charged on certain specific assets of the company, as opposed to a mere floating charge on the assets for the time being created by an ordinary debenture. The provisions of the Act of 1865, which are only applicable to companies entitled to lend money on land, and only to certain registered securities, were substantially modified by an Act of the year 1870.[3]

Various other amendments of company law followed, in the years 1867, 1870, 1877, 1879, 1880, and 1883; but the next year of great importance in this connection is 1890, which witnessed the passing of three company statutes. The first of these, the Companies (Memorandum of Association) Act, 1890,[4] enabled a company, with the leave of the Court, and after a special resolution of its shareholders, to alter the provisions of its fundamental document of incorporation, viz. its Memorandum of Association or Deed of Settlement. The second, the Companies (Winding Up) Act, 1890,[5] made considerable alterations in the procedure of winding up a company then in existence. The third, the Directors Liability Act, 1890,[6] passed in consequence of the decision in *Derry v. Peek*,[7] rendered directors of a company or prospective company issuing a prospectus containing untrue statements, responsible, in certain circumstances, to persons applying for shares on the strength of them; even though they (the directors) were ignorant of the untruth of their statements, or even of their issue.

The year 1900 also witnessed the passing of an important statute [8] dealing with the formation of companies,[9] and prescribing certain strict conditions with regard to the first or 'statutory' meeting of a new company,[10] the registration of mortgages affecting the assets of a company,[11] and the audit of companies' accounts; [12] and, in the year 1908, these and all other legislative provisions at present affecting ordinary commercial companies, were consolidated in the Companies (Consolidation) Act, 1908,[13] which at present comprises the law on the subject. Insurance

[1] Lindley, *Companies*, I, 300. [2] 28 & 29 Vict. c. 78.
[3] 33 & 34 Vict. c. 20. (These provisions are not affected by the Act of 1908.)
[4] 53 & 54 Vict. c. 62. [5] *Ibid.*, 63. [6] *Ibid.*, 64.
[7] (1889) L.R. 14 App. Ca. 337.
[8] Companies Act, 1900 (63 & 64 Vict. c. 48).
[9] Ss. 1–11. [10] S. 12. [11] S. 14. [12] Ss. 21–23. [13] 8 Edw. VII, c. 69.

companies, however, are the subject of a separate consolidating statute passed in the following year, the Assurance Companies Act, 1909;[1] and banks, and companies specially incorporated by Act of Parliament for carrying out public undertakings, do not fall within the scope of either of these Acts.

Consolidating Act of 1908

The fourth and last kind of personal property to which reference can here be made, is property in ships. Ships, in the widest sense of the term, including both ocean-going and coastal or inland vessels, were, of course, familiar to the Courts, as chattels corporeal, long before the close of the previous period. The facts that a ship on a distant ocean can hardly be said to be under the direct control of her home-sitting owner, and that, in a storm, even the master may be said to be controlled by, rather than in control of, his ship, did not deter the Courts from applying to ships the ordinary possessory remedies; for are not cattle and sheep, the oldest kind of 'chattels,' liable to similar accidents? But the system of registration and partition of ships introduced by the Navigation Acts of Charles II and his successors,[2] combined with the later enormous increase in the cost of ships, did undoubtedly change the character of ship-owning to such an extent as to give to it much of the character of that 'ideal property' which is usually classed as a chose in action. As such, a word must be said about it, regarded as a product of the period now under review.

Ships

Navigation Acts

The Navigation Act of 1660,[3] as incidental to its policy of requiring all non-European goods to be imported in English ships, and especially of keeping the colonial carrying trade as a close preserve, required all foreign-built ships, claimed as the property of Englishmen, to be registered in an English or Irish port, with oath as to true ownership, before being allowed to ply between the mother-country and her colonies. The amending Act of 1696[4] extended this provision to all vessels taking part in British or inter-colonial trade, and required[5] that whenever

[1] 9 Edw. VII, c. 49.

[2] These were, like so much of the Restoration policy, a legacy from the Commonwealth. The principles of the Navigation policy are clearly laid down in an Ordinance of the 9th October, 1651. (*Acts and Ordinances of the Commonwealth*, II, 559-562.) [3] Car. II, c. 18. [4] 7 & 8 Will. III, c. 22, s. 17. [5] S. 22.

any alteration of property should take place 'by the sale of one or more shares in any ship after registering thereof, such sale shall always be acknowledged by indorsement on the Certificate of the Register.' A slight relaxation took place in 1773, by a statute [1] which, by implication, allowed a foreigner to acquire a share in a registered British ship with the consent of the owners of three-fourths of the shares, indorsed on the Register. But this concession was probably due to the exigencies of the American War; and, on the reconstruction of national policy which took place after the loss of the American colonies, the old rule was renewed in full vigour by a drastic Act of the year 1786.[2] That statute lays it down, that no foreign-built ship (except a prize) may be registered as a British ship; [3] that every British ship having a deck or being of fifteen tons burden, must be registered in Great Britain, the Channel Islands, or a British colony, at the port to which she belongs; [4] that no ship may be registered as a British ship unless an affidavit is made that all her owners are British, even British subjects resident abroad (other than members of 'factories') being excluded; [5] and, finally, that, whenever property in a British ship is transferred, the certificate of registry must be 'truly and accurately recited . . . . in the bill or other instrument of sale thereof.' [6]

Act of 1786

A new code of shipping law was contained in an Act of 1823,[7] which, besides making the system of registration universal and compulsory, as a condition of claiming privileges as a British ship,[8] introduced one or two new legal features. The customary division of the property in a ship into sixty-four shares was made statutory, with a provision that no more than thirty-two owners should be registered; [9] while it was also provided,[10] that transfer of a share in a British ship should only take place by bill of sale or other instrument in writing entered on the Registry, the transfer, in the event of a later sale to a *bonâ fide* purchaser, dating from the endorsement on the certificate of registry. On the gigantic overhauling of the Customs Laws which took place in 1825,[11] a new Registry Act,[12] repealing but virtually re-enacting the statute of 1823, was passed.

The year 1845 witnessed the passing of the first of the great

[1] 13 Geo. III, c. 26. [2] 26 Geo. III, c. 60. [3] S. 1. [4] Ss. 3, 4.
[5] S. 10. [6] S. 17. [7] 4 Geo. IV, c. 41. [8] S. 1. [9] S. 30. [10] Ss. 29, 35.
[11] The 6 Geo. IV, c. 105, repealed no less than 119 statutes.
[12] 6 Geo. IV, c. 110.

modern Merchant Shipping Acts,[1] which deal, not merely with the ownership and transfer of British keels, but with the many other interests of the mercantile marine. It would be impossible, in the limits of space at our disposal, to attempt a summary of the legislation on this subject. But it may be pointed out, that the Merchant Shipping Act of 1854[2] definitely abandoned the policy of compulsory British building, which had been part of British navigation policy for so long;[3] and, by allowing[4] five persons to be registered as undivided owners of a share in a British ship, and requiring a special form of transfer to be used and registered,[5] practically put the law with regard to the ownership of British vessels on its present footing. After many amendments, the Act of 1854 was repealed, and the whole law of merchant shipping re-stated in the great Merchant Shipping Act of 1894,[6] which has itself been frequently amended.

Merchant Shipping Acts

Finally, a word must be said about the transferability of this new kind of property, and of choses in action generally; for, with regard to the latter subject, there has been a misunderstanding which ought never to have arisen.

It has been, on more than one occasion,[7] previously pointed out, that the medieval common law had the greatest dislike to the assignment of rights which could only be enforced by legal proceedings; the Courts taking the view that such a transaction was, in effect, transferring a lawsuit, and thus encouraging maintenance, barratry, and other evils. This dislike extended to the attempted assignment of possibilities, or even future interests of any kind; which were looked upon in much the same light as choses in action. The attitude of the Common Law Courts is well summed up in the leading *Lampet's Case*, decided by the full Court of Common Pleas in the year 1612,[8] which was not definitely overruled until the decision of the House of Lords in *Theobalds v. Duffry*, in 1724.[9]

Transfer of Choses in Action

Meanwhile, however, the completeness of the common law

[1] 8 & 9 Vict. c. 116.
[2] 17 & 18 Vict. c. 120.
[3] S. 18.
[4] S. 37.
[5] S. 55.
[6] 57 & 58 Vict. c. 60.
[7] *Ante*, pp. 175, 176, 240, 241, 275.
[8] 10 Rep. 46b.
[9] 9 Mod. 102.

rule had been broken down in more than one direction. It is clear, for example, that choses in action were recognized as being devisable by will early in the seventeenth century; for, in the case of *Gorge v. Chancey*,[1] decided in the year 1639, it was freely admitted, that even a married woman could bequeath a chose in action which formed part of her separate estate. Obviously, in such a case, for reasons previously given, the Common Law courts would have very little opportunity of interposing their veto; for, if they refused to recognize the title of the legatee, the Court of Chancery could be appealed to.

Break-down of Common Law Rule

Again, the strictness of the common law rule had been circumvented by the practice of appointing the intended assignee of a chose in action the attorney of the assignor, and thus enabling him to sue the debtor in the assignor's name. That this device was known as early as 1641, is shown by the judgment of the Lords Commissioners in *E. of Suffolk v. Greenvil*,[2] decided in that year. But the drawback to it was, that the death of the assignor revoked the power of attorney, and destroyed the assignee's title, at least at law.[3]

But the most hopeful way of escape was through the doors of a Court of Equity; and, soon after the middle of the seventeenth century, it becomes clear that the common law rule prohibiting alienation is being set at nought by Chancery. The case of *Hurst v. Goddard*[4] shows a slight inclination to restrict the help of the Court to cases in which the alleged assignment was really made to complete an informal title; as where a husband sued as his wife's administrator, or where the alleged chose in action was in fact a trust. But the passing of the Statute of Frauds, which clearly recognized the assignability of trusts,[5] must have rendered the Court's assistance of little value in such cases; and, in fact, it becomes clear, as early as 1680, that Chancery will recognize even verbal assignments of legal choses in action, such as bond debts,[6] or, at length, even simple contract debts,[7] and that it will treat such assign-

Equitable Assignments

[1] 1 Rep. in Cha. 67. [2] 3 Rep. Cha. 50.

[3] *Mitchell v. Eades* (1700) Pre. Cha. 125. (The report in 2 Vern. 391 is defective on this point.)

[4] (1670) 1 Cha. Ca. 169. [5] 29 Car. II (1677) c. 3, s. 9.

[6] *Fashion v. Atwood* (1680) 2 Cha. Ca. 6, 38. (Lord Nottingham.)

[7] *Mitchell v. Eades* (1700) Pre. Cha. 125.

ments as binding, even on the creditors in the subsequent bankruptcy of the assignor.[1] At the same time, Chancery is fully alive to the risks of the proceeding, and lays it down repeatedly,[2] that the assignee takes subject to all 'equities,' *i.e.* claims by the party liable against the assignor, arising before notice of the assignment was received by the debtor. Subject, however, to this reservation, Equity will, if the chose in action is enforceable in Chancery, allow the assignee to sue as plaintiff there; or, if it is 'legal,' *i.e.* enforceable only in a Common Law court, compel the assignor to allow the assignee to sue in his (the assignor's) name, on proper indemnity for costs.

Valuable Consideration

But the equitable doctrine of the assignability of choses in action was at one time subject to the alleged limitation, that it was only effectual, even in Equity, when made for valuable consideration. The limitation is stated by the Lords Commissioners, in *E. of Suffolk v. Greenvil,*[3] and repeated by Lord Keeper Bridgman in an anonymous case of 1675.[4] The argument in favour of the limitation seems to have been, that a so-called assignment in equity operated only as an agreement to assign, and that, according to its well-known doctrine, Equity would not enforce a voluntary agreement, even under seal.[5] But the fallacy of this reasoning at least as pretending to general application, was soon apparent. Where the assignment was of a contingency or possibility, then, no doubt, according to current ideas, there could be nothing more than an agreement to assign, and the doctrine of valuable consideration applied.[6] But where the debt or other liability was actually due, the reasoning did not apply; and it is doubtful if the requirement of valuable consideration was ever enforced in such a case. At any rate, if it was, it soon ceased to be; for in *Atkins v. Daubeny,* decided in 1714,[7] the voluntary assignment of a bond was supported, and in *Carteret v. Paschal,*[8] it was admitted by all parties, though it was vital to the decree, that 'if a man in his own right

[1] *Peters v. Soame* (1701) 2 Vern. 438.

[2] *Ashcomb's Case* (1674) 1 Cha. Ca. 232; *Coles v, Jones* (1715) 2 Vern. 692. (For this reason it was usual, in Equity, to make the assignor a party, in case questions between him and the debtor should arise.)

[3] (1641) 3 Rep. Cha. 50.

[4] 2 Freem. Cha. 145.

[5] *Ante,* p. 217.

[6] *D. of Chandos v. Talbot* (1731) 2 P. Wms., at p. 610. (This was the whole point in *Tailby v. Official Receiver* (1888) L.R. 13 App. Ca. 523, sometimes quoted in support of the exploded doctrine.)

[7] 1 Eq. Ca. Ab. 45.

[8] (1733) 3 P. Wms. 198.

be entitled to a bond, or other *chose en action*, he may assign it without any consideration.' At length, in *Bates v. Dandy*,[1] Lord Hardwicke gave the finishing stroke to the doubt by laying it down, that, though a husband may not dispose of his wife's chose in action without a valuable consideration (because his right is only a possibility) 'yet he may release the wife's bond without receiving any part of the money.' A similar doubt arose later on the subject of 'imperfect declarations of trust';[2] but it should have been seen that the same distinction applied there, viz. that such a disposition can only be enforced as an agreement to make a proper settlement, and, as such, it requires a valuable consideration. Thus the framers of the Judicature Act,[3] in making debts and other legal choses in action assignable at law, without requiring a valuable consideration, were following sound historical precedent. Had they adopted the opposite course, and required a valuable consideration, it would have been impossible to make a valid legal gift *inter vivos* of any chose in action for which a special form of transfer had not been provided.

This last exception is, no doubt, a wide one; for, in fact, many of the most important choses in action are subject to special rules in this respect. Thus, negotiable instruments are transferable, according to the rules of the Law Merchant, adopted into English Law, by delivery or indorsement.[4] Copyrights, patents, shares and stock, were at early dates made transferable at law by special statutory forms. Probably, however, they are all (with the exception of negotiable instruments) assignable in Equity (*i.e.* as against all persons but purchasers for value without notice) by mere word of mouth.[5]

[1] (1741) 2 Atk., at p. 208.

[2] *Ellison v. Ellison* (1802) 6 Ves., at p. 662, *per* Lord Eldon; *Kekewich v. Manning* (1851) 1 De G. M. & G., at p. 187, *per* Knight Bruce, L.J.

[3] Judicature Act, 1873, s. 25 (6).

[4] It seems to have been Lord Somers, in an anonymous case of 1697 (Comyns, 43) who refused to disturb the mercantile rule of negotiability, as distinct from mere assignability, by issuing an injunction against a *bonâ fide* holder for value.

[5] *Brandt v. Dunlop* [1905] A.C., at p. 462, expressions of Lord Macnaghten.

CHAPTER XVII

CONTRACT AND TORT IN MODERN LAW

THE decision in *Slade's Case*, explained in a previous chapter,[1] to the effect that 'every contract executory imports in itself an assumpsit,' seemed to have put the coping stone on the edifice of the law of simple contract, which, as we have seen, had been reared with so much pains in the fifteenth and sixteenth centuries. Now it appeared to be beyond question, that every promise of a lawful character, given in exchange for a valuable consideration, by a person of full legal capacity, amounted to a legally enforceable contract. Whatever view may be taken of the suitability of 'consideration' as the test of simple contract, it cannot be denied that it has the singular merit of appealing to the average man, and, further, of being remarkably easy for a Court mainly concerned with material interests to apply. It avoids all difficult and unsatisfactory enquiries about intention and other mental elements; and substitutes a broad external standard of the kind beloved by the Common Law. There was at one time a theory, that valuable consideration owed its origin to the influence of Equity. Anything more unlike an equitable doctrine it would be impossible to conceive; although, as we have also seen,[2] Equity did not refuse to adopt it in cases to which it had already been applied by the courts of Common Law. To have done otherwise would have been to open a feud between the two jurisdictions upon a fundamental principle of wide application.

It was, doubtless, the rapid increase in the popularity of the action of Assumpsit, following upon the decision in *Slade's Case*, that led to the enactment of the celebrated provisions with regard to the evidence for simple contracts contained in the Statute of Frauds. By the terms of that statute, no action is to be brought on any contract or promise falling under

Statute of Frauds

[1] (1603) 4 Rep. 92b. *Ante*, p. 140. [2] *Ante*, pp. 216, 217.

any one of five important classes of transactions; unless such transaction has been embodied (not necessarily at the time of entering into it) in some writing signed by the party sought to be charged, or his agent. These five classes of transactions are — (1) promises by executors or administrators to be personally responsible for the obligations of their deceased, (2) promises in the nature of guarantees, (3) agreements made in consideration of marriage, (4) contracts 'or sales' of land, tenements, or hereditaments or any interest in or concerning them, and (5) agreements not to be performed within the space of one year from the making thereof.[1] Further, in a later section,[2] the Act laid it down, that no contract for the sale of any goods, wares, or merchandizes for the price of £10 sterling [3] or upwards should be 'allowed to be good,' unless there should be acceptance and receipt of at least part of the goods, or giving of earnest or part payment by the buyer, or some memorandum in writing of the kind just described. Owing to the difference in the wording of the two sections, it was at one time thought that the later (s. 16) actually nullified contracts not conforming to its provisions; while it has always been admitted that the earlier (s. 4) is procedural only, *i.e.* that a contract not conforming to it is merely unenforceable by action, and not invalid altogether.[4] But this doubt has been finally resolved by the substituted section 4 of the Sale of Goods Act, 1893,[5] which, in repealing section 16 of the Statute of Frauds, adopts the wording of section 4 of that statute. In order to comply with the requirements of the sections, all the essential features of the contract must be expressed in the writing;[6] except that, (1) by virtue of the Mercantile Law Amendment Act, 1856,[7] the consideration for a contract of guarantee need not be embodied in it (though of course there must be a consideration unless the contract is under seal), and (2) the price need not

[1] 29 Car. II, c. 3, s. 4. [2] *Ibid.*, s. 16.

[3] By the Statute of Frauds (Amendment) Act, 1828, s. 7 (9 Geo. IV, c. 14) value was substituted for price, and the section made to apply to 'future goods,' *i.e.* goods not in existence, or not ready for delivery, when the contract of sale was made. It had formerly been suggested, that such a contract was a contract of employment, not of sale. These alterations are now embodied in the Sale of Goods Act, 1893, s. 4.

[4] *E.g.* it may cause the property in goods to pass, or be used as a defence or set-off.

[5] 56 & 57 Vict. c. 71.

[6] *Wain v. Warlters* (1804) 5 East, 10.

[7] 19 & 20 Vict. c. 97, s. 3.

appear in the note of a contract of sale, unless it was actually expressed in making the contract.[1]

The provisions of ss. 4 and 16 of the Statute of Frauds have been the subject of much litigation; but the story of that litigation, which is mainly concerned with pure details, cannot find a place in a condensed history like the present. A far more interesting, if less easily intelligible chapter in the development of the simple contract, now demands some attention; for, with its conclusion, the theory of the simple contract may be said to have become virtually complete.

A substantive reform which has, like so many legal reforms, been accomplished by the indirect machinery of legal procedure, is always liable to the danger of being defeated by some slight imperfection of that machinery, or some trifling defect in the logic of technical process. This danger threatened the law of simple contract when it was turned on to the subject of **bailments,** one of the very oldest and most important branches of the Common Law.

Bailments

The word 'bailment' is one of the numerous words which, originally used in a wide and general sense, have gradually acquired a special technical meaning. Originally, a 'bailment' was simply a delivery or handing over of any kind (*bailler*, whence our word 'bail'), whether of body, land, or goods. In connection with land, it retains its significance in the country of its birth, where the *bail à cens* is a common interest at the present day. In England, for reasons alluded to elsewhere,[2] it had first been confined to the subject of movables, and then to a particular kind of delivery of movables, viz. the delivery on condition of return. As we have seen,[3] it was, in this capacity, fully recognized as an important legal transaction in the fourteenth century; when the remedies of Detinue and Trover were invented to protect it.

The late Professor Ames, in those articles of his to which we owe so much, insisted[4] that Detinue was really a contractual action; because it was brought on the promise to return the goods. Now, apart from the fact that the remedy of Detinue is far older than the recognition of simple contract by the King's

[1] *Hoadly v. McLaine* (1834) 10 Bing. 482.
[2] *Ante*, pp. 123–126. [3] *Ante*, pp. 134, 141.
[4] Select Essays in Anglo-American Legal History, III, 433, &c.

Courts, and that its connection, through the action of Debt, with the real action to recover land, can easily be traced,[1] it seems difficult, in the face of the controversy now to be described, to hold the view that, even in the seventeenth century, Detinue was regarded as an action of contract. It was, in fact, simply an action to recover the goods of the plaintiff in the hands of the defendant, who refused to give them up.

Southcote's Case

The truth of this view appears nowhere more clearly than in the famous case of *Southcote v. Venner*,[2] decided in 1601. In that case, the plaintiff brought Detinue for goods delivered to the plaintiff to keep safely. The defendant pleaded that he had been robbed of them by J. S. But the Court set aside the plea as irrelevant to a claim in Detinue; 'for he (the defendant) hath his remedy over, by Trespass, or Appeal, to have them again.' In other words, the action was not on an implied promise of a modified nature (or, as the Court put it, 'a special bailment'); it was a strict action of right.

Southcote's Case, which was in the highest degree favourable to bailors, would, it may be imagined, have definitely consecrated the action of Detinue as the proper remedy in bailment. But in fact, there were weighty counter-reasons why plaintiffs, despite its apparent attractions, should turn from it to the newer remedy of Assumpsit, if the latter could possibly be moulded to meet the facts. For, at this time, Detinue was looked upon as an action of Tort; and the maxim *actio pœnalis moritur cum personâ* would rule it out in many cases.[3] More serious still, the defence of 'wager of law' was, as we have seen,[4] open to the defendant in Detinue; and that defence was rapidly becoming a farce. In fact, Detinue was a discredited form of action by the end of the sixteenth century.

It is hardly surprising, therefore, to find a distinct effort on the part of bailors, at the very commencement of the eighteenth century, to seek a remedy by the new and highly popular action of Assumpsit. The form did not, at first sight, present any serious difficulty. It was easy to allege an imaginary promise by the bailee to return the goods; a promise which a

[1] *Ante*, pp. 55–57. [2] 4 Rep. 83; Cro. Eliz. 815.
[3] Of course the statute of 1330 (4 Edw. III, c. 7) would not help the bailor's executor in the event of the bailor's death; because that only referred to Trespasses.
[4] *Ante*, p. 141.

jury could imply from the mere fact of the bailment. The difficulty came in when the question arose as to the precise nature of the implied promise. Had the bailee promised to return in all events: *i.e.* to insure? Or had he merely promised to do his best, to avoid negligence, or what? And, finally, how was the new doctrine of 'valuable consideration' to be applied to this imaginary promise? In some kinds of bailments, *e.g.* bailments in fact made for the benefit of the bailee, it might not be difficult to imply a promise for valuable consideration. But what if the bailment were solely for the benefit of the bailor?

It was precisely these questions which gave rise to the well-known judgments in the leading case of *Coggs v. Bernard*, decided in 1703,[1] which was an action of Assumpsit, not of Detinue; and, though Lord Holt's laudable effort to dispose of them all at once was hardly successful, yet the case is memorable as establishing two points. In the first place, it clearly adopts the doctrine of the implied promise, based (if on nothing else) on the detriment suffered by the plaintiff in parting with his goods. In the second, it decides that the extreme rule of liability laid down in *Southcote's Case* cannot be imported into the new doctrine of contractual bailment. The first conclusion has since been decisively affirmed in the case of *Bainbridge v. Firmstone*[2] and other decisions. The latter is being slowly applied by the numerous decisions which, from time to time, settle the various rules of a bailee's liability in differing circumstances;[3] thus fulfilling Lord Holt's modest suggestion, that he had 'stirred these points, which wiser heads in time may settle.'[4] And thus, in effect, the action on the simple contract once more enlarged its boundaries, by incorporating the important subject of bailments. But it is worthy of notice that, even so late as 1781, Sir William Jones, in his famous *Essay on the Law of Bailment*, could define[5] a bailment as a 'delivery of goods,' not on a promise, but 'on a condition.' The difference between a promise and a condition is, of course, familiar to all lawyers.

Coggs v. Bernard

But, though the theory of the simple contract may be said to

[1] 2 Ld. Raymond, 909. [2] (1838) 8 A. & E. 743.

[3] These, so far as they have at present gone, will be found set out in the *Digest of English Civil Law*, edited by the author; see Bk. II, Pt. II (by R. W. Lee, §§ 434, 439, 449, 550–554, 562).

[4] 2 Ld. Raymond, at p. 920. [5] 1st edition, p. 1.

have been now complete, another enlargement of the practical scope of the doctrine was effected by the adoption of the action for breach of promise of marriage. This, again, was, virtually, an incursion into the province of the ecclesiastical courts. Even after the Reformation, the proper remedy for the aggrieved swain was a suit in the spiritual court, *causâ matrimonii prœlocuti.* Upon satisfactory proof of the facts, the spiritual tribunal would order the defendant to celebrate the marriage in the face of the Church, and even, if necessary, dissolve a marriage with another person contracted subsequently to the promise. But, in the fatal epoch of the Interregnum, when the Church courts were closed, and the ecclesiastical remedy thereby suspended, disappointed plaintiffs began to resort to the secular tribunals, and to bring the action of Assumpsit, as on an ordinary contract. At the Restoration, there was some little hesitation on the part of the Common Law judges about recognizing the new action; but at length, in *Dickison v. Holcroft,*[1] decided in 1674, the Court of King's Bench, despite the strenuous opposition of Chief Justice Vaughan, held the action, even when founded merely on mutual promises, to be good.

'Breach of Promise'

Almost immediately after this decision, the new action was threatened from two quarters by the provisions of the Statute of Frauds. Was it founded on an 'agreement made upon consideration of marriage,' or was it an 'agreement that is not to be performed within the space of one year from the making thereof'?[2] In either case, it was not actionable unless written evidence was forthcoming. The last alternative was not seriously discussed; but it seemed at first a strong thing to say that an action on a breach of promise to marry was not an 'agreement made upon consideration of marriage.' Lord Holt, however, appears to have taken a decided view, that the statute only 'intended agreements to pay marriage portions';[3] and, in effect, after a little hesitation, it was clearly decided that its provisions did not apply to mutual promises to marry.[4] The passing of Lord Hardwicke's Marriage Act of 1753, which, as part of its policy of insisting on the validity only of formal marriages, expressly abolished the ecclesiastical suit *causâ matrimonii prœlocuti,*[5] rendered the civil remedy of

[1] 3 Keb. 148. [2] 29 Car. II (1677) c. 3, s. 4.
[3] *Harrison v. Cage* (1698) 1 Ld. Raym. 386.
[4] *Cork v. Baker* (1725) 1 Stra. 34; *Horam v. Humfreys* (1771) Lofft, 80.
[5] 26 Geo. II, c. 33, s. 13.

Assumpsit still more popular; and to the present day it plays a large part in the business of the courts. Among its other peculiarities may be noticed the requirement of Lord Denman's Evidence Act, 1869,[1] that an oral proof of the promise to marry given by the plaintiff, must be supported by independent evidence.

The passing of the Infants Relief Act, in 1874[2] may perhaps be said to have restricted, to a certain extent, the scope of simple contract. By the common law, the contracts of an infant were, generally speaking, voidable by him, *i.e.* he could himself sue on them, but they could not be enforced against him.[3] He could even repudiate, on coming of age, contracts of a 'continuing nature,' such as tenancies and partnerships, entered into by him during infancy; but if he wished to do so, he must exercise his right within a reasonable time after attaining his majority.[4] On the other hand, there were some contracts, such as contracts to pay a reasonable price for necessaries, and contracts clearly beneficial to his interests, which were binding on an infant, in spite of his nonage;[5] and a statute of the year 1855, the Infants Settlements Act,[6] had enabled male and female infants to make valid settlements, with the approval of the Court, on their marriage.

Contracts of Infants

The Infants Relief Act, 1874, however, makes absolutely void all contracts by an infant for repayment of money lent or to be lent, or for goods supplied (other than necessaries), and all accounts stated with infants.[7] Presumably, therefore, neither the infant nor the other party can sue on such contracts; and their effect in passing property is *nil*. But the Act goes further, and makes it impossible for a person to be sued on any ratification made after he comes of age, of a promise given or debt incurred by him while an infant; even though there is new consideration for the ratification.[8] At the same time, the statute is careful not to invalidate such contracts as by the common law were binding on an infant, *e.g.* contracts for necessaries;[9] and it has, apparently, no effect on the position of contracts voidable at common law, but not expressly made void by the statute,

[1] 32 & 33 Vict. c. 68, s. 2. [2] 37 & 38 Vict. c. 62.

[3] *Warwick v. Bruce* (1813) 2 M. & S. 205 (affd. in Exch. Ch.). This rule applied even to contracts to marry (*Holt v. Ward* (1732) 2 Stra. 937).

[4] *Edwards v. Carter* [1893] A.C. 360.

[5] *Walter v. Everard* [1891] 2 Q.B. 369.

[6] 18 & 19 Vict. c. 43. [7] S. 1. [8] S. 2. [9] S. 1.

except that no alleged ratification of them after majority will have any operation. If the contract would have been binding without ratification, it will still be valid, despite the Act; if not, no ratification will affect it. It may be noted that, although a loan to an infant to purchase necessaries would be void under the express terms of the Act of 1874, there seems no reason to doubt that the lender, according to the equitable doctrine of subrogation, recognized to apply to such a case as early as 1719,[1] would still be able to stand in the shoes of the person supplying the necessaries, and sue the infant for so much of the loan as had been actually expended in necessaries.

Finally on the subject of the scope of simple contract, it may be mentioned that, during the nineteenth century, the courts and the legislature between them completed that emancipation of married women from the medieval theory of contractual incapacity, which, as we have seen,[2] had already been broken in upon by the Chancellors of the preceding century. Thus, the cautious doctrine of *Hulme v. Tenant*,[3] which made the bonds or other solemn engagements of a married woman enforceable in Equity against her actual separate estate, was extended, by the middle of the nineteenth century, to her general engagements;[4] though the Court still refused to apply it to property over which she had merely a general power of appointment.[5] And in 1866, a married woman's separate property was made liable for calls on shares held by her.[6] Obviously, after this, the medieval theory had become untenable; but, on the passing of the first Married Women's Property Act, in 1870,[7] the only change effected in this direction was to make the separate property of a married woman liable for her ante-nuptial debts, thus relieving her husband from liability on that head. This Act, which greatly extended the separate property of married women, secured to them their separate earnings,[8] all personal property coming to them under intestacy and all sums not exceeding £200 by deed or will[9] and the rents and profits of inherited land,[10] and allowed them to hold, as their separate estate, deposits in savings banks, stock in the funds, shares and other

Married Women

[1] *Marlow v. Pitfield*, 1 P. Wms. 558. [2] *Ante*, p. 224.
[3] (1778) 1 Bro. C.C. 16. [4] *Murray v. Barlee* (1834) 3 My. & K. 209.
[5] *Vaughan v. Vanderstegen* (1853) 2 Drew. 165.
[6] *Matthewman's Case* (1866) L.R. 3 Eq. 781.
[7] 33 & 34 Vict. c. 93, s. 12. [8] S. 1. [9] S. 7. [10] S. 8.

benefits in companies and benefit societies, and policies of insurance.[1] It was slightly amended by a statute passed in the year 1874,[2] which re-imposed on the husband a modified liability for both the ante-nuptial contracts and torts of his wife, to the extent of any property which he might have acquired through her.

But these cautious advances were quite overshadowed by the passing, in the year 1882, of the present Married Women's Property Act.[3] That statute not merely makes all the property of a woman married after 31st December 1882,[4] and the property of a woman previously married accruing to her after that date,[5] her separate property; but it completely emancipates her from her medieval incapacities with regard to alienation and contract,[6] and gives her all legal remedies for the protection of her rights.[7] It is true, that her contractual and tortious liabilities can only be enforced against her to the extent of her separate estate;[8] and only to that extent in so far as such estate is not 'restrained from anticipation,'[9] in manner previously explained.[10] But her personal capacity is complete; and a narrow construction which restricted it to cases in which she had separate estate at the time of incurring the liability,[11] has been definitely overruled by an amending statute.[12] On the other hand, her husband still remains liable, to the extent of property which he may have acquired through her, for his wife's ante-nuptial liabilities (contractual and tortious);[13] and his medieval liability for the torts of his wife committed during marriage, has not been removed by the Acts.[14] Apparently, however, his former personal liability for her ante-nuptial torts is abolished by the express provisions on that subject of the principal Act.[15] As for a husband's liability for his wife's contracts entered into during marriage, that stands where it did, viz. on the footing of agency. And so a tradesman who in fact gives credit to the husband or the wife, may find himself unable to recover from either.[16]

[1] Ss. 2–5, 10. [2] 37 & 38 Vict. c. 50. [3] 45 & 46 Vict. c. 75.
[4] S. 2. [5] S. 5. [6] S. 1. [7] Ss. 1 (2), 12.
[8] *Scott v. Morley* (1887) 20 Q.B.D. 120. [9] S. 19. [10] *Ante*, p. 225.
[11] *Palliser v. Gurney* (1887) 19 Q.B.D. 519.
[12] Married Women's Property Act, 1893 (56 & 57 Vict. c. 63) s. 1.
[13] M.W.P. Act, 1882, s. 14.
[14] *Seroka v. Kattenburg* (1886) 17 Q.B.D. 177; *Earl v. Kingscote* [1900] 2 Ch. 585. But the liability only continues during the marriage, and is even discharged by a judicial separation (*Cuenod v. Leslie* [1900] 1 K.B. 880). [15] S. 14.
[16] *Paquin v. Beauclerk* [1906] A.C. 148. (This case went even to the length of deciding that the knowledge of the tradesman is immaterial. Thus, if a tradesman

Apart from the important subject reserved for the end of this chapter, there is not much to record of the Law of Tort during the period under review. The general scope of the action was enlarged by the provision of the Civil Procedure Act of 1833,[1] which enabled the personal representatives of a deceased person to sue in Trespass or Case for any injury committed against the deceased in respect of his real estate within six months before his death, and a similar action to be brought against them in respect of any wrong committed by their deceased against the plaintiff in respect of the latter's property, real or personal. And it was still further extended by the provisions

Fatal Accidents Act

of the Fatal Accidents Act, 1846,[2] commonly known as Lord Campbell's Act, which, for the first time in English legal history, allowed a civil action to be brought for the death of a human being. The statute declares that the death of the party injured through the act or default of another shall not exonerate that other from any liability which would have rested on him for such act or default had the victim lived; and the statute applies even to felonious injuries. It is further noteworthy for the fact, that the damages recovered do not form part of the deceased's estate (which would make them liable to his debts), but are to be divided, according to the decision of the jury trying the case, among his nearest relatives, regardless whether such relatives were in fact dependent upon the deceased's exertions, or not.[3] But only one action will lie in respect of the same subject-matter; and it must be brought within a year of the deceased's death.[4]

Only one really new action of Tort, viz. the action of **Deceit**, made its appearance in this period; if we except the development of Civil Conspiracy, to be afterwards dealt with.

Deceit

The action of Deceit is an example, like Maintenance and Malicious Prosecution, of the extension to ordinary persons

gives credit to Mrs. X believing either (1) that she is a single woman, or (2) that she is acting as her husband's agent, he cannot recover from either husband or wife, if, in fact, Mrs. X intended to contract as her husband's agent, but had no authority to do so.)

[1] 3 & 4 Will. IV, c. 42, s. 2. (The action by the representatives must be brought within one year of their deceased's death; the action against the representatives within six months from their having taken up the administration.)

[2] 9 & 10 Vict. c. 93. (There was a procedural amendment in 1864.)

[3] S. 2.

[4] S. 3. (It was in connection with the difficulties caused by this rule, that the amending statute of 1864 was passed.)

of a remedy originally devised for the benefit of the Crown. There was a very old Writ of Deceit at the common law;[1] but it was confined, in substance, to acts amounting to personation or trickery in legal proceedings. It is clear, however, that liability for deceit, or fraud, was making its way into purely civil actions in the fifteenth century; for, as we have seen,[2] it was frequently alleged, as was also negligence, in early actions of Assumpsit. When the necessity for such allegations disappeared with the definite recognition of 'consideration' as sufficient ground for Assumpsit, the action of Deceit still lingered on in connection with warranties, which it seemed difficult to class as 'contracts executory' within the meaning of *Slade's Case*.[3] Even so late as 1778, it could be doubted whether Assumpsit lay for breach of warranty.[4] Ultimately, however, these scruples disappeared, and with them the action of Deceit; until it was revived, with great effect, as a purely tortious action, in the case of *Pasley v. Freeman*, in 1789.[5] In that case, the defendant appears (for his actual words are not given, the case being decided on the pleadings) to have assured the plaintiff, that one Falch was a person who could be trusted to pay for certain goods which the plaintiff was asked to deliver to him on credit. This was, of course, very like a guarantee; but the plaintiffs, unfortunately, could not sue on contract, as they had no written evidence to satisfy the Statute of Frauds.[6] So they framed their action in pure tort; alleging that the defendant 'falsely, deceitfully, and fraudulently' asserted and affirmed the solvency of Falch, knowing him to be untrustworthy; that he thereby caused the plaintiffs to give credit to Falch; that Falch had failed to pay; and that the plaintiffs had thereby lost their money. The Court, after much hesitation, allowed the validity of the action, which immediately became immensely popular as a means of evading the Statute of Frauds. In the year 1828, however, the statute known as Lord Tenterden's Act[7] restrained its activities in that direction, by imposing the requirement of written evidence on alleged statements of credit used to found

[1] Old *Natura Brevium*, ff. 50–52.

[2] *Ante*, pp. 137–138.

[3] *Ante*, p. 140. If I warrant a horse as sound at the time of sale, I really promise to pay damages if he turns out to have been unsound at that time. But in form I merely make an assertion.

[4] *Stuart v. Wilkins*, Doug. 18.

[5] 3 T. R. 51.

[6] 29 Car. II (1677) c. 3, s. 4.

[7] Statute of Frauds (Amendment) Act, s. 6. (The wording of the section is notoriously peculiar.)

actions; and in *Derry v. Peek*,[1] before alluded to, the House of Lords further clipped its wings by refusing to allow it to be applied to a mere innocent, though untrue, misrepresentation, or, as it was often absurdly called, 'equitable fraud.' Still, despite these limitations, the action of Deceit can still be brought to recover damages suffered as the result of credence placed in a written statement deliberately false and fraudulent, made with intent that the plaintiff should act upon it.

Defamation

The action of Defamation, which, as we have seen,[2] had definitely become a branch of the Law of Torts at the end of the preceding period, has undergone considerable modification in the eighteenth and nineteenth centuries. Towards the close of the former was passed, after much agitation, the famous Libel Act[3] connected with the name of Fox; and, though the statute itself is confined to criminal proceedings, it appears to have been extended by analogy to civil actions for defamation.[4] As is well known, the dispute was, whether a jury, in a criminal prosecution for libel, was entitled to consider, not merely the question of publication, but the question of the libellous character of the document on which the prosecution was based. The judges stoutly contended that this last was a question of law, not of fact. Their opponents urged that, apart from statements obviously defamatory, it was impossible to say, without knowledge of the surrounding facts, whether a particular statement suggested a particular *innuendo*, or whether such *innuendo*, if really suggested, was defamatory. The Libel Act of 1792[5] definitely gave the jury power to find a general verdict of 'guilty' or 'not guilty,' which would, in effect, entitle them to acquit the accused, even though he had clearly published the document upon which the prosecution was based.

In the year 1840, in consequence of the well-known proceedings connected with the case of *Stockdale v. Hansard*,[6] was passed the Parliamentary Papers Act,[7] exempting absolutely from all proceedings for defamation the publishers of any reports, papers, votes, or proceedings ordered by either House of Parliament to be published; and, in 1868, a decision of the Court[8] extended a

[1] (1889) L.R. 14 App. Ca. 337.
[2] *Ante*, pp. 144–147.
[3] 32 Geo. III, c. 60.
[4] *Parmiter v. Coupland* (1838) 6 M. & W., at p. 108.
[5] S. 1.
[6] (1839) 9 A. & E. 1.
[7] 3 & 4 Vict. c. 9.
[8] *Wason v. Walter* (1868) L.R. 4 Q.B. 73.

qualified [1] privilege to independent reports of Parliamentary proceedings. Lord Campbell's Act of 1843 [2] allowed an apology to be pleaded by way of mitigation of damages in any action of defamation; and statutes of the years 1881 and 1888 did a good deal to mitigate the hardships caused to the newly developing energies of the newspaper press by the survival of medieval rules on the subject of responsibility for defamatory statements. The former of these statutes, the Newspaper Libel Act, 1881,[3] though mainly dealing with criminal prosecutions, provided that a fair, accurate, and unmalicious newspaper report of the proceedings at a lawfully convened public meeting should be privileged, notwithstanding that it contained defamatory reflections, unless the editor refused to insert, in his next issue, a reasonable explanation by the party reflected upon. The latter statute, the Law of Libel Amendment Act, 1888,[4] goes considerably further. It gives absolute protection [5] to fair and accurate reports of judicial proceedings, and qualified privilege, on conditions similar to those of the Act of 1881, to similar reports of any meeting of a local government body which is open to press or public,[6] or of proceedings before Justices at Quarter Sessions, and to publications of notices and reports issued by Government departments, and published at the request of such departments. But in neither case does the statute authorize the publication of blasphemous or indecent matter.

Finally, a statute of the year 1891, the Slander of Women Act,[7] enables a woman to recover damages for spoken words imputing to her unchastity, without proof of 'special' damage. This statute points, of course, to one of the great differences between libel (written or printed defamation) and slander (oral defamation). The former always carries a right to damages; whether the plaintiff can prove actual loss or not. Slander (except where it imports certain specific accusations) does not; unless actual loss can be proved. This proof is, by the nature of things, sometimes very hard to come by; especially where the accusation is against moral, rather than material, character.

[1] The difference between an 'absolute' privilege (such as that given by the Act of 1840) and a 'qualified' privilege, is, that the former is complete bar to proceedings, while the latter is only a bar if the plaintiff cannot prove (or, in some rare cases, the defendant cannot disprove) actual malice in fact in the publication of the defamatory statement.

[2] 6 & 7 Vict. c. 96. [3] 44 & 45 Vict. c. 60. [4] 51 & 52 Vict. c. 64.

[5] S. 3. [6] S. 4. [7] 54 & 55 Vict. c. 51.

The Act of 1891, then, simply places an accusation, made against a woman, of unchastity, in the list of slanders 'actionable *per se*,' *i.e.* without proof of special damage. The statute has redressed a grievance peculiarly hard. Before the virtual suppression of the Church courts such actions as those contemplated by the statute could be brought there; and the Church would not demand proof of special damage, because an accusation of incontinence was an accusation of sin, which was punishable with penance and fine.[1] But incontinence is not a civil offence; and, when the Common Law courts robbed the Church courts of their jurisdiction in defamation, they virtually left women without a remedy for this kind of slander. In theory, such suits could be maintained in the ecclesiastical courts until the year 1855, when they were expressly abolished by statute.[2] In practice, they ceased to be common after the beginning of the nineteenth century.[3]

Negligence

A few very simple words must here be said about the much-disputed subject of the alleged 'Action of Negligence.' With the exception of the action for 'negligently guarding of his fire,'[4] there never has, in form, been such an action in English Law; and the fact is significant. The individualism or the cautiousness of the Courts in early times declined to admit that one person could be legally liable to another for mere omissions; unless he had expressly or by implication 'undertaken' to do the omitted acts. We have seen[5] how this latter exception was, ultimately, made the basis of the law of simple contract. About the same time, the Court of Chancery, especially in the matter of trusts, acted on the higher standard of morality which requires, in certain cases, the performance of positive duties, independently of express contract; though, of

[1] The ordinary remedies in an ecclesiastical court for defamation were (1) public retractation, (2) penance (usually remitted), and (3) payment of costs. For the general doctrine of jurisdiction, see *Harris v. Buller* (1798) 1 Hagg. 463 n.

[2] Ecclesiastical Courts Act (18 & 19 Vict. c. 41).

[3] The last case known to the author is *Collis v. Bate* (1846) 4 Thornton, *Notes of Cases*, 540 (in the Arches Court). They were more numerous in the country districts than in London (*Report on Ecclesiastical Courts*, 1831, Appx. D, p. 596).

[4] This was a very striking exception; for, by the common law, a man was liable for all damage done by fire which spread from his premises; whether he caused it to be lit, or it had come from other sources (*Tubervil v. Stamp* (1697) 1 Salk. 13). But a statute of 1774 (14 Geo. III, c. 78, s. 86), still in force, exempts from liability the person on whose premises a fire may 'accidentally begin.' Blackstone gives a curious version of the statute (*Comm.* I, 419).

[5] *Ante*, pp. 137, 138.

course, a trust, voluntarily undertaken, is not unlike a contract. Once more, criminal law, slowly and cautiously, began to hold people responsible, in certain exceptional cases, for mere non-feasance.[1] But the Common Law courts remained content with repressing active wrong-doing; and, in all their long record, there is hardly a single case of Tort founded on mere omissions, before the end of the eighteenth century,[2] unless we count the well known, but really unimportant, decision in *Ashby v. White*,[3] as an exception. That decision, which was certainly not free from party prejudice,[4] laid it down, that when an individual was entitled, by statute or common law, to demand of a public official the performance of a ministerial duty, wilful refusal by the official to perform the duty is a ground of action by the individual, though no special damage is proved. Apparently very sweeping in its scope, the decision has really been barren of results; only some eight subsequent decisions involving the principle laid down being reported.[5]

With the appearance of the nineteenth century, however, the introduction of new methods of transit, new methods of manufacture, and other novel conditions, compelled a revision of the *laissez-faire* attitude of the Courts; and gradually they began to hold people responsible in Tort for mere omissions, where such persons had placed themselves in positions inviting confidence, or induced others to handle dangerous materials, or take part in dangerous processes. But the limits of tortious responsibility for mere omissions are still extremely narrow;[6] and by far the greater part of the vast number of cases under the head of 'negligence' in textbooks and Digests, will be found to be cases of contract and trust.

Beyond all question, however, the most important development of the Law of Tort in this period is connected with the

[1] Examples are to be found in the early Poor Law statutes; and the Courts, independently of statute, began to hold 'wilful neglect' as equivalent to act in homicide cases.

[2] L.Q.R. xxix, pp. 159–166, by the author.

[3] (1703) 2 Ld. Raym. 938.

[4] The facts were, that a returning officer wrongfully refused to record the plaintiff's properly tendered vote at a Parliamentary election.

[5] These are collected in *Digest of English Civil Law*, § 1019. For actions in respect of special damage caused by failure to perform statutory duties, see § 726 of the same work.

[6] They are set out, with tolerable completeness, in the *Digest of English Civil Law*, §§ 727–734 (by J. C. Miles). At the end of Bk. II will be found a brief *Excursus* on the subject.

attitude of the State, especially as represented by the Courts, towards artizans and labour organizations during the last century. For reasons which will shortly appear, it is impossible, in dealing with such a subject, to avoid including, not merely the Law of Contract and Tort, but Criminal Law; for the three branches are inextricably mixed up together. Unhappily, the subject is one which has aroused much feeling; and nothing beyond a bare statement of the facts would be advisable.

Labour Organizations and the Law

The system of servile or forced labour which had existed in England from the time of the Norman Conquest until the middle of the fourteenth century, was definitely broken up by the occurrence of that cardinal event in medieval history, the visitations of the plague known as the 'Black Death,' followed as they were, throughout almost the whole of Western Europe, by armed risings of the peasantry. The latter, whose value had risen to a premium, owing to the frightful ravages of the Plague, burst the bonds of the manorial system, and refused to work except for high wages.

The Statutes of Labourers

In England, the answer of the State to what was, in effect, a social and political revolution of the first magnitude, was comprised in a series of ordinances known as the Statutes of Labourers.[1] These, in effect, set up what may be called a system of State Regulation, to replace the old customary system of feudal lordship. The chief features of the new system were — (1) the fixing of the wages of each class of servant by statute,[2] (2) the compulsion of every able-bodied man and woman under the age of sixty, not being a merchant or skilled artificer,[3] nor living on his own land, to serve any one who might require his or her services at the accustomed or statutory rate of wages,[4] (3) the placing of the enforcement of these provisions, with all their attendant regulations, in the hands of the Justices of the Peace,[5] thus making

[1] 23 Edw. III (1349) cc. 1–8; 25 Edw. III (1351) st. II; 34 Edw. III (1360) cc. 9–11.

[2] 25 Edw. III (1351) st. II, c. 1; 11 Hen. VII (1494) c. 22, ss. 1–4; 6 Hen. VIII (1514) c. 3, ss. 1–3.

[3] The language of the statute of 1351 shows that this exception must have been very strictly construed. Probably only master-craftsmen were exempted. At any rate, carpenters, masons, tilers, and plasterers were included in the system of statutory wages. (25 Edw. III (1351) st. II, c. 3.)

[4] 23 Edw. III (1349) c. 1.

[5] 25 Edw. III (1351) st. II, c. 7.

the law of master and servant, in effect, a branch of the criminal law as summarily administered. This system was substantially modified in the middle of the sixteenth century, by the Elizabethan statute which replaced the statutory regulation of wages by a periodical assessment by the Justices in Quarter Sessions,[1] and introduced a carefully regulated system of apprenticeship for skilled trades.[2] But the essential features of the system were not altered; and it was actually a criminal offence under the statute of Elizabeth,[3] as it had been under the statute of Edward III,[4] for a master to give, or a servant to receive, more than the statutory or assessed rate of wage.

There seems little reason to suppose that, after the first excitement of a depleted labour market had passed away, the system of State Regulation was, as a whole, unpopular with masters or servants. It comprised provisions regarding prices[5] which, if they gave more protection to the rich than the poor, were not without benefit to the poor, and rules as to meals and hours of work, which were certainly a substantial protection to the labourer.[6] In the days when the Law of Contract was in its infancy, and when competition was considered to be unfair, it was deemed inevitable that some authority should control the relationship of employer and employed; and, after the breakdown of one status-system, it was natural to set up another. But the regulation of the labour system by the State implied, of course, that any attempt to infringe that system, was an offence against the State; and especially any concerted attempt to throw the system out of gear. Accordingly, we are not surprised to find that, in addition to the penalties prescribed by the earlier statutes for individual offences, a statute of the year 1548 makes it an offence, punishable with much heavier penalties, for the sellers of victuals to 'conspire' to raise prices, or for any artificers, workmen, or labourers to 'conspire, covenant, or promise together, or make any oaths, that they shall not make or do their works but at a certain price or rate, or shall not enterprize or take upon them to finish

[1] 5 Eliz. (1562) c. 4, ss. 14–17. [2] *Ibid.*, ss. 25–37. [3] *Ibid.*, ss. 18–19.

[4] 23 Edw. III (1349) cc. 4, 5, 8.

[5] 23 Edw. III (1349) c. 6 (victuals); 25 Edw. III (1350) c. 4 (shoes, &c.).

[6] 11 Hen. VII (1494) c. 22, s. 4; 6 Hen. VIII (1514) c. 3, s. 4; 5 Eliz. (1562) c. 4, s. 9. (In spite of the fact that these provisions are generally couched in restrictive language.)

what another hath begun, or shall do but a certain work in a day, or shall not work but at certain hours and times.'[1] This statute, however, aims[2] at breaking down the medieval system of close corporate towns, by forbidding any molestation of 'foreign,' *i.e.* outside, labourers.

The Factory System

But the system of State Regulation set up in the fourteenth century, good or bad, broke down hopelessly before the industrial revolution of the later eighteenth century, and the new factory system which it rendered inevitable. Most of the old skilled trades, with their elaborate apprenticeship organizations, rapidly became relics of a bye-gone day, and their organizations mere social clubs or benefit societies. The vast crowds of artizans drawn into the manufacturing towns were, on the other hand, wholly unorganized, and fluctuated between reckless prosperity and sudden destitution. Prices, and, consequently, wages, were continually disturbed by the events of the Napoleonic wars, and by bad harvests. When times were good, the workmen could make their own terms; though most of them were far too unused to town life to make them to advantage. When times were bad, or the labour market overstocked, employers had it their own way, and were not always very scrupulous in turning their advantages to the best account.

Trade Unions

It is by no means certain, that the workmen were not the last of the parties concerned to abandon the old system.[3] But it ultimately became clear that a continuance of it was impossible. Naturally, the workmen, in course of time, were led to form organizations of their own; and thus **Trade Unions**, if they had ever really died out after the passing of the statute of 1548, revived again with great vigour. Equally naturally, the employers, who regarded such organizations as dangerous to their interests, appealed to the State for protection; and the State, scared by the excesses of the French Revolution, replied with a vigorous series of Combination Laws,[4] intended to stamp out the new organizations. It is not neces-

[1] 2 & 3 Edw. VI (1548) c. 15, s. 1.
[2] *Ibid.*, s. 4.
[3] There is a petition of labourers as late as 1796, asking for legislative regulation of wages and prices. (Cunningham, *op. cit.* II, 498.)
[4] The most important were 39 Geo. III (1799) c. 81, repealed and replaced in the following year by the 39 and 40 Geo. III (1800) c. 106. But there had been many earlier.

sary to go into particulars of these statutes, which were of great severity. It is sufficient to say that, instead of allaying, they merely inflamed the passions of masters and servants, who resorted to extreme and even violent measures against one another, and against such of their competitors as disagreed with their methods. In particular, the method of 'boycott' was used, with cruel effect, both by masters and men;[1] and the 'black list' was a familiar document both in employers' counting houses and workmen's clubs.

In the year 1824, chiefly owing to the labours of Joseph Hume and Francis Place, aided by the favourable attitude of Huskisson and Sir Robert Peel, members of Lord Liverpool's Government, but opposed to the repressive policy of Eldon and Sidmouth, a great victory in the cause of labour was achieved by the passing of the Act for repealing the Combination Laws. The statute formally wiped out of existence the repressive code which had grown up since 1548,[2] and expressly enacted,[3] that no workman should be 'subject or liable to any indictment or prosecution for conspiracy, or to any other criminal information or punishment whatever, *under the common or statute law*,' for 'entering into any combination to obtain an advance, or to fix the rate of wages, or to lessen or alter the hours or duration of the time of working, or to decrease the quantity of work, or to induce another to depart from his service before the end of the time or term for which he is hired, or to quit or return to his work before the same shall be finished, or, not being hired, to refuse to enter into work or employment, or to regulate the mode of carrying on any manufacture, trade, or business, or the management thereof.'

Repeal of the Combination Laws

It has been necessary to specify the terms of this enactment at length, partly because they show, beyond question, that the familiar objects and methods of modern Trade Unionism, on its militant side, were equally familiar when the Act of 1824 was passed, and partly because of an event which immediately happened, and which is apt to puzzle the student.

It appears that even such champions of the workmen's cause as Place thought that Trade Unions were simply the reflex

[1] Francis Place, though a thoroughly capable and responsible workman, was boycotted by the master breeches-makers of London for taking part in a strike, and nearly starved in consequence. He was saved by the intercession of his wife (*Life of Francis Place* (Wallas), p. 9). [2] 5 Geo. IV (1824) c. 95, s. 1. [2] *Ibid.*, s. 2.

action of the Combination Laws, and that, with the repeal of those laws, they too would disappear. The event completely falsified their expectations. Times were good in 1824; and the Trade Unions, released from their legal shackles, made use of the fact to claim higher wages. Strikes followed; the manufacturers, and the wealthy classes generally, became alarmed; the Government, divided in opinion, inclined in favour of strong measures. In the session of 1825, a new Bill, to be substituted for the Act of 1824, was introduced, with a view of reviving the old restrictions. But it was fought gallantly by the friends of labour; clause after clause disappeared; the new Bill began to look more and more like the measure it was intended to replace. Finally, it appeared on the statute-book in such a form that no eye but that of an expert could tell wherein it differed from its predecessor. But that difference proved, none the less, vital. For whereas the Act of 1824 not only repealed the Combination statutes, but went on expressly to exempt from punishment, *either under the common or statute law,* all combinations for the purposes named, the Act of 1825,[1] while continuing the repeal of the statute law,[2] followed with the creation of a fresh series of offences for the exercise of force in achieving the objects of combination,[3] and only then provided that, for acts of much less gravity, there should be no prosecution or penalty, 'any law or statute to the contrary notwithstanding.'[4] In spite of this ominous modification, however, there can be little doubt that the legislation of 1824–5 radically altered the position of the labourer, by lifting him from a status to a contract system. But it should be carefully noted, that neither the Act of 1824, nor that of 1825, repealed that part of the old system which referred the decision of all disputes between master and servant, relative to the contract of service, to the Justices of the Peace — in other words, brought them under the criminal law.

Act of 1825

The next event of first-rate importance in the history of our topic, is the appearance and rapid development of the doctrine of 'common employment,' viz. that, in the absence of statutory provision or personal negligence, an employer is not responsible to his workman for injuries caused to him (the workman) by the act or neglect of a fellow-

'Common Employment'

[1] 6 Geo. IV, c. 129. [2] S. 2. [3] S. 3. [4] S. 4.

employee in the course of the employer's business. This doctrine is universally admitted to date from the decision in *Priestly v. Fowler*,[1] in the year 1837. In that case, a butcher's man sought to recover against his employer for injuries caused by the over-loading by a fellow-workman of a van upon which the plaintiff was travelling in the course of his duty. Very wisely, the plaintiff's advisers avoided resting his case on any implied term in the contract of service; fearing that they might be referred by the Court to the magistrates. They laid it as a simple claim in Tort, based on the maxim: *respondeat superior*. There can be no doubt that, had the plaintiff been a mere stranger who had been run over by the negligent driving of the defendant's servant, the defendant would have been liable. But the Court of Exchequer held that he was not liable to the plaintiff, his workman. It is a little difficult to follow Lord Abinger's reasoning; for his lordship rests the decision of the Court[2] on the ground of the inconvenience which would follow if a plaintiff in a similar case were to be able to sue on the negligence of the coach-maker, the harness-maker, the servants at an inn at which the plaintiff might be called upon to stay in the course of his work, the upholsterers who made the bed, etc. The short answer to these objections is, that none of such persons are servants of the employer. But the somewhat later cases which adopted the decision in *Priestly v. Fowler*, confined it strictly to common employment,[3] which, however, included persons in such very different positions as a common labourer and an overseer, or even a mining engineer or manager.[4] The ground usually adopted was that chosen by Alderson, B., in *Hutchinson v. York, &c. Railway*,[5] viz. that the plaintiff must be held to have consented to run the risk of negligence by a fellow-servant. There were certain conditions of exemption, *e.g.* that the employer should have done his best to employ proper servants, and not have exposed the plaintiff to unreasonable risks. Nevertheless, the working of the doctrine of 'common employment' deprived the artizan classes of most of the benefits of the Fatal Accidents Act, 1846,[6] and continued to work great

[1] 3 M. & W. 1.
[2] 3 M. & W., at p. 6.
[3] *Hutchinson v. York, &c., Railway* (1850) 5 Exch. 351; *Bartonshill Coal Co. v. Reid* (1858) 3 Macq. 326 (extending the doctrine to Scotland).
[4] See last case, and *Wilson v. Merry* (1868) L.R. 1 H.L. (Sc.) 326.
[5] *Ubi sup.*,
[6] *Ante*, pp. 307, 308.

hardship, until its partial modification by the passing, by Mr. Gladstone's Government, of the Employers Liability Act, 1880.[1] It still applies to the injury caused by the negligence of an ordinary adult fellow-servant of the plaintiff, not due to the directions of the employer, or to the defective working of a railway. But its importance has been greatly lessened by the passing of the Workmen's Compensation Acts, to be hereafter referred to.[2]

Almost concurrently with the definite adoption of the doctrine of 'common employment,' another danger threatened the aspirations of the working-classes, especially those expressed by the labour organizations. These bodies had prospered greatly since the acquisition of the modified protection given to them by the repeal of the Combination Laws, and were now, in many cases, in a highly flourishing condition. In addition to their earlier objects, they had adopted a system, or, rather, various systems, of provision for old age, sickness, loss of employment, and other contingencies. Sometimes these benefits were secured by the agency of a society exclusively concerned with them, and known, generally, as a 'Friendly Society.' In other cases, the older type of organization, known as a Trade Union, originally formed principally to protect and assist its members in trade disputes, had extended its objects, and included the functions of a Friendly Society. Moreover, about the year 1850, a very formidable movement was started for the federation of the numerous local Trade Unions in a particular trade, which had hitherto existed independently throughout the kingdom. One of the earliest and most important results was the formation of the great Amalgamated Society of Engineers. Thus greatly strengthened, both in funds and membership, the new bodies felt their power, and used it. The capitalist classes, equally naturally, felt alarmed; and prosecutions followed.

'Common Law' Conspiracy

But it was a little difficult for the prosecutors to know how to proceed. It was generally supposed, that the statute of 1825 had repealed all the old laws against labour organizations, and that, so long as Trade Unions kept within the terms of that Act, they were safe. Baron Rolfe, in a case tried in 1847,[3] had actually ruled to that effect. Accordingly, one of

[1] 43 & 44 Vict. c. 42. [2] *Post*, pp. 329–331. [3] *Reg. v. Selsby* (1847) 5 Cox, 495.

the prosecutions of 1851[1] was especially based on the third section of the Act of 1825, which forbade, on pain of three months' hard labour, any attempt to force, by violence, threats, or intimidation, any workman to leave his employment, return his work unfinished, or refuse to enter any employment, or to join or remain a member of any society, or any employer to alter his methods of carrying on his business. But it is to be observed, that the defendants were charged, not with an actual breach of the section, but merely with a conspiracy to cause a breach of it; the Court holding, in spite of an express decision to the contrary by Lord Ellenborough, forty years before,[2] that an agreement or combination to procure the commission of a statutory offence, is itself a criminal conspiracy, punishable by fine and imprisonment, at the common law. The prosecutions of 1851 went further still, and procured the ruling of Mr. Justice Erle,[3] to the effect that, quite independently of statute, or the use of illegal means,[4] a combination of workmen for the purpose of 'obstructing' an employer in his business, and so of forcing him to agree to a certain schedule of prices, by 'persuading' 'free men'[5] to leave the employer's service, would be 'a violation in point of law.' Thus was born the doctrine of 'common law conspiracy' in its criminal aspect. And now the vital importance of the change of language between 1824 and 1825[6] became apparent; for it would have been practically impossible for Mr. Justice Erle to have delivered his celebrated ruling in face of the language of the statute of 1824. That ruling, in effect, declared, that any combination to obtain even a perfectly lawful object, *e.g.* a rise of wages or prices, by means of a strike, was a criminal offence at the common law.

For such a doctrine it is difficult to find historical warrant. Every offence against the State Regulation systems of the fourteenth and sixteenth centuries had been carefully created and defined by statute; and, with the repeal of those statutes,

[1] *R. v. Rowlands.* (This part of the case will be found at pp. 466–495 of 5 Cox.)

[2] *R. v. Turner* (1811) 15 East, 228.

[3] *R. v. Rowlands* (1851) 5 Cox, at p. 462. See also a similar ruling of the same learned judge in *R. v. Duffield* (1851) *ibid.*, at p. 431, where the object was to raise wages.

[4] 'There are no threats or intimidations supposed to have been used towards the workmen' (Erle, J., at p. 431).

[5] By 'free men' the learned judge apparently meant men not under a legally binding engagement (see p. 431).

[6] *Ante*, p. 317.

had fallen to the ground. The common law offence known as Conspiracy (which was itself founded on statute[1]) was directed to a totally different class of offences, viz. the procuring of false indictments. In the Elizabethan books on criminal law, the cases of Conspiracy are entirely confined to this latter type; and there is no suggestion that it includes strikes or boycotts.[2] Indeed, it is a little difficult to see how such a crime could have existed, unless we suppose it to have been reserved exclusively for trial by the King's judges; for the jurisdiction of the Justices of the Peace was entirely statutory. It is true that the English Courts refuse, and have long refused, to enforce contracts made 'in restraint of trade'; but, as Lord Halsbury carefully pointed out in a case to be afterwards more particularly alluded to,[3] such contracts were never 'unlawful,' in the sense that they were 'contrary to law,' *i.e.* punishable either criminally or civilly. It is true also that certain ancient offences against the medieval system of markets, *e.g.* 'forestalling,' 'regrating,' and 'ingrossing' still lingered on the statute book. But from these it was a long step to the formidable doctrine of criminal conspiracy.

Legislation of 1867

As might have been expected, this new doctrine caused great ill-feeling among the working classes; and the next few years after 1851 were filled with strikes. The Trade Unions throve on the resentment thus created; and it is to be feared that the officials of some of them, unduly exalted, were guilty of grave excesses and crimes. But the Royal Commission which sat in 1867, with statutory powers,[4] was totally unable to discover the existence of any general criminal features in Trades Unionism; and the action of Lord Derby's Government, in bringing in a Bill to revive the neglected jurisdiction of the magistrates in dealing with questions arising out of the contract of service, was deeply resented. Nevertheless, it passed into law as the Master and Servant Act, 1867,[5] and remained in force till 1875.[6] The net result of it was, that breaches of contract, which, by anyone but a workman, would have been matter for a civil action, were punishable by

[1] 28 Edw. I (1300) c. 10; 33 Edw. I (1304) st. II.
[2] See Fitzherbert, *L'Office*, &c.: Lambarde, *Eirenarcha*, sub tit. 'Conspiracy.'
[3] *Mogul Steamship Co. v. M'Gregor* [1892] A.C., at p. 39.
[4] 30 & 31 Vict. cc. 8, 74.
[5] *Ibid.*, c. 141.
[6] Conspiracy and Protection of Property Act, 1875, s. 17.

fine and imprisonment. It is true that the civil rights of the parties were not taken away,[1] and that the section empowering the magistrates to inflict fine and imprisonment might conceivably have been applied to an employer; [2] but it was so worded as to render it doubtful if that was the intention of its framers, and, in any case, the alternative of a fine (limited to £20) always afforded a door of escape to the capitalist. Meanwhile, the new doctrine of 'common law conspiracy' had been quietly incorporated into statute law by that section of the great Offences against the Person Act of 1861,[3] which speaks of 'any unlawful combination or conspiracy to raise the rate of wages.'

The Trade Union Acts

But the tide soon turned in favour of the workmen. In the year 1871, Mr. Gladstone's Government introduced and passed the first Trade Union Act, by far the most important victory up to that time achieved by the champions of labour organizations. By that statute,[4] it was expressly provided, that the purposes of a Trade Union should not, merely because they were 'in restraint of trade,' be deemed criminal, nor should they render void any agreement or trust. But the Act went further; and provided that any Trade Union which chose to register itself might vest its property in trustees,[5] who should be capable of suing and being sued on all matters touching the 'property, right, or claim to property,' of the Union. Moreover, the treasurer and other officials of a registered Trade Union were compelled to account; [6] and persons embezzling or improperly obtaining possession of the funds or other movable property of a registered Union, were made liable to criminal prosecution.[7] This was an enormous benefit to the Unions, which, hitherto,[8] as bodies not recognized, or even suspect, by law, had no remedy for crimes committed at their expense. On the other hand, the Act of 1871 is careful to deny a legal personality to Trade Unions, by enacting that no Union may register as a company under the Companies Acts,[9] and that no legal proceeding may be instituted to enforce any agreement entered into for the direct pur-

[1] Master and Servant Act, 1867, s. 18. [2] *Ibid.*, 9.
[3] 24 & 25 Vict. c. 100, s. 41.
[4] 34 & 35 Vict. c. 31, ss. 2, 3. [5] S. 8. [6] S. 11. [7] S. 12.
[8] A very partial and inadequate protection had been given by the Trades Unions Funds Protection Act, of the year 1869 (32 & 33 Vict. c. 61).
[9] S. 5 (3).

pose of carrying out any of the objects of the Union, or any bond for securing performance of such agreement.[1]

It may seem a little surprising, that the passing of such a statute as that of 1871 should have been almost immediately followed by a fresh appearance of the doctrine of 'common law conspiracy'; but such in fact was the case. For, in the celebrated trial of *R. v. Bunn*,[2] Mr. Justice Brett (afterwards Lord Esher) directed the jury that (1) an agreement of workmen to 'control the will' of masters, and (2) an agreement to induce men to break their contracts with a view to secure the re-instatement of a fellow-workman, were common law criminal conspiracies, even though no violence was used, and, further, that the former, at least, was 'molestation and obstruction' within the meaning of the Criminal Law Amendment Act, 1871,[3] passed concurrently with the Trade Union Act. This construction seemed to the workmen to be simple defiance of the plain intention of the legislature; and they did not rest till they had persuaded Mr. Disraeli's Government to pass the Conspiracy and Protection of Property Act, 1875. That important statute, repealing the Master and Servant Act, 1867, the Criminal Law Amendment Act, 1871, and the whole of the old legislation 'making breaches of contract criminal,'[4] expressly enacted that 'an agreement or combination by two or more persons to do or procure to be done any act in contemplation or furtherance of a trade dispute' should 'not be indictable as a conspiracy if such act committed by one person would not be punishable as a crime'; unless such combination were expressly made a conspiracy by statute.[5] Moreover, to restrain still further the doctrine of 'conspiracy to commit a crime,' the Act provided,[6] that nothing in this connection should be deemed a 'crime' which was not punishable, at least as an alternative, with imprisonment, and that when the 'crime' was only punishable on summary conviction, the maximum sentence on the conspirator should be three months' imprisonment. Finally, and this was, perhaps, the most highly-prized victory of all, the statute, though making such acts as the use of force or

Conspiracy and Protection of Property Act

[1] S. 4. [2] (1872) 12 Cox, 316. [3] 34 & 35 Vict. c. 32, s. 1 (3).
[4] The few breaches, involving danger to life or property, which are still criminal, were provided for by new legislation in ss. 4–7 of the Act.
[5] S. 3. [6] *Ibid.*

threats, 'shadowing,' 'rattening,' 'watching and besetting.' and bullying, punishable on summary conviction, expressly provides[1] that 'attending at or near a house where a person resides, or works, or carries on business, or happens to be . . . in order merely to obtain or communicate imformation, shall not be deemed a watching or besetting within the meaning of the section.' Thus the right of '**peaceful picketing**' was definitely established by statute.

After 1875 we hear nothing more of the 'criminal conspiracy at the common law'; but the workmen were much mistaken if they thought that the right of combination was threatened with no further dangers. The next development seems to have been suggested by the words of Mr. Justice Erle, in the case of *Reg. v. Rowlands*,[2] previously referred to; and it is decidedly interesting.

It appears that, even by the common law, there was a very ancient action for depriving a master of his servant. This was natural in days when a servant was regarded as his master's property. Moreover, the Statutes of Labourers would, obviously, have been rendered futile, if employers, in the fierce competition for labourers produced by the ravages of the Plague, had been allowed to draw away their neighbour's servants. This fact was fully recognized; and Fitzherbert, in his well-known book, gives[3] the form of writ devised as a remedy for employers whose servants were 'seduced,' or enticed away, by rivals, or even merely 'retained' by third parties after unlawfully leaving their former masters.

This writ was not highly popular for the purposes for which it was immediately invented; but it became the parent of other more or less remotely analogous actions. From it are derived the action for debauching a woman, now technically known as the 'action for seduction,'[4] the action for 'stealing a wife,' or for 'loss of *consortium*,'[5] and the action

Deprivation of Services

[1] S. 7 *ad fin.*

[2] (1851) 5 Cox, at p. 462.

[3] *Natura Brevium*, ff. 167 B–168 B.

[4] This application of the writ is as old as 1704 (*Russell v. Corne*, 2 Ld. Raymond, 1031); and to the form of action the remedy for seduction owes most of its unfortunate peculiarities.

[5] *Winsmore v. Greenbank* (1745) Willes, 547. It is probable, regard being had to the decision in *R. v. Jackson* [1891] 1 Q.B. 671, that this action now only lies where the wife has been involuntarily injured by the defendant, *e.g.* by negligent driving. But, in such cases, it is common enough.

for harbouring a servant who has improperly left his employer's service.[1] But, so far as the writer is aware, it was never used by an employer against workmen before the middle of the nineteenth century.

It so happened, however, that, in the year 1853, attention had been called to the existence of the old remedy by the well-known case of *Lumley v. Gye*,[2] in which an opera impresario had successfully maintained an action against a rival who had knowingly engaged a singer while she was under exclusive engagement to sing for the plaintiff. The decision provoked much difference of opinion; and it obviously extended the action for deprivation of services beyond the scope originally contemplated. Nevertheless, it was followed in the year 1881 in the case of *Bowen v. Hall;*[3] and still more recent decisions have shown a tendency to extend it to wilful procurement of breaches of all kinds of contracts.[4] This is really a wide departure from the older theory of contract, which strictly confined actions on a contract to the parties themselves.[5] But that objection is met by the argument that the new action is not for breach of the contract, but for procuring a breach of contract — *i.e.* an independent tort, which treats the contract, not as the cause, but as the mere subject-matter of the offence.

Of the boundless horizon opened up by this new kind of action, it is not possible here to speak. The point in the narrative is, that it was taken up by the employers as yet another weapon against the claims of labour organizations.

'Civil Conspiracy'

Accordingly, in the case of *Temperton v. Russell*,[6] the plaintiff, a builder at Hull, sued the members of the joint committee of three Trade Unions for damages for inducing, under threat of a strike, various tradesmen, who had contracted to supply him with goods, to break their contracts, and, further, for damages for inducing such persons not to enter into contracts with him (the plaintiff). The cause of the dispute was the alleged non-observance by the plaintiff of certain trade rules laid down by the Unions for their members.

With regard to the first claim, there was, after the recent decisions in *Lumley v. Gye* and *Bowen v. Hall*,[7] very little hope

[1] *Blake v. Lanyon* (1795) 6 T.R. 221. [2] 2 E. & B. 224. [3] 6 Q. B. D. 333.
[4] *National Phonograph Co. v. Ball* [1908] 1 Ch. 335.
[5] *Tweddle v. Atkinson* (1861) 1 B. & S. 393.
[6] [1893] 1 Q.B. 715 (C.A.). [7] *Ubi sup.*

of resistance. But in the way of the second, there was a peculiarly awkward obstacle. For, no later than the previous year, the House of Lords had solemnly decided in *Mogul Steamship Co. v. McGregor*,[1] that a ring of shipowners, who, in order to secure a monopoly of a certain trade, had not merely combined to underbid all rivals in the matter of freights, and offered a rebate of 5 *per cent.* to all shippers who should ship only with members of the ring, but actually threatened with dismissal agents of members who should act for such rivals, had committed no breach of the law. What they had done was in the pursuit of legitimate trade competition.

But, in the case of *Temperton v. Russell*, the Court of Appeal, in spite of the decision of the House of Lords in the previous year, boldly adopted the doctrine, hitherto unknown to English tribunals,[2] that a combination of persons, if not a single person, who knowingly induced others not to enter into contracts with A, would be liable to an action by A, if the latter actually suffered loss in consequence of the defendants' conduct. Instead of explaining away the *Mogul Case*, the Court of Appeal used expressions of the learned Lords in that case as the justification of its conclusion; despite the fact that, as the *Mogul Case* was decided in favour of the defendants, these expressions must have been mere *obiter dicta*.[3]

Nevertheless, both branches of the decision in *Temperton v. Russell* were fully acted upon by the Courts. Though the case of *Allen v. Flood*[4] failed, on the ground that there was no evidence of actual breach of contract by the employers, the principle that the inducing either of masters or workmen to break existing contracts is actionable, either by the workmen discharged or the master deprived of his servant, has been upheld in *Reed v. Operative Stonemasons*,[5] *Giblan v. National Labourers' Union*,[6] *Glamorgan Coal Co. v. S. W. Miners*[7] and other cases. And the doctrine, that a combination to induce third persons

[1] [1892] A.C. 25.

[2] There was a faint authority claimed for the thoroughly untrustworthy case of *Gregory v. D. of Brunswick* (1843) 6 M. & G. 205, 953. In this case, though actual violence was alleged against the defendants, they obtained a verdict; and the question of law was never really discussed.

[3] It is a little difficult to trace the passages to which Lord Esher, in [1893] 1 Q.B., at p. 729 refers.

[4] [1898] A.C. 1.

[5] [1902] 2 K.B. 732. (Here the action was by the dismissed workman.)

[6] [1903] 2 K.B. 600.

[7] [1905] A.C. 239.

not to enter into the employ of, or supply goods to, the plaintiff, though no actual breach of contract occurs, is, if it occasions loss to the plaintiff, a cause of action, is fully upheld by the leading decision of *Quinn v. Leathem*[1] (the 'Belfast Butchers' Case'), in spite of the fact that two of the learned Lords who decided that case had taken part in the unanimous judgment in the *Mogul Case*.[2] Thus came into existence the new doctrine of **civil conspiracy**, to replace the doctrine of 'common law' criminal conspiracy, which had been extinguished by the Act of 1875.[3] It is a far-reaching doctrine, the end of which it is difficult to foresee;[4] despite the fact that it has, by recent legislation, been deprived of its application to industrial disputes.[5] It must be carefully noted that, as explained by Lord Esher in *Temperton v. Russell*,[6] 'civil conspiracy' differs from criminal, in that, in the case of the former, damage to the plaintiff is essential to the action; while, in the case of criminal conspiracy, it is the conspiracy which is the gist of the prosecution. The suggestion that a single person might be held liable for similar conduct has not been adopted.[7]

Trade Unions and Corporations

A far more serious matter, however, even than the development of the doctrine of civil conspiracy, was the decision given by Mr. Justice Farwell in the well-known *Taff Vale Case*,[8] which after being reversed by the Court of Appeal [9] was confirmed by the House of Lords.[10] By this celebrated decision, which really worked a revolution in English law, it was held that a Trade Union, registered under the Act of 1871,[11] might be made a defendant in an action founded

[1] [1901] A.C. 495. [2] *Ante*, p. 326.

[3] *Ante*, pp. 323, 324. (The notion that an action for civil conspiracy, of the kind alleged, was known to the common law, is still more baseless than the view that the common law knew a doctrine of criminal conspiracy. The action of Conspiracy on the old statutes had given birth in the sixteenth century (Fitzherbert, *Natura Brevium*, fo. 116 A) to the action of Malicious Prosecution; and there it had ended. Of course, Malicious Prosecution cannot be brought for inducing people not to enter into contracts.)

[4] There has been some suggestion that the doctrine is confined to cases of injury to the plaintiff's trade, business, or profession. But see *Sweeney v. Coote* [1907] A.C. 221.

[5] Trade Disputes Act, 1906, s. 1. [6] [1893] 1 Q.B., at p. 729.

[7] It was favoured by Lord Lindley in *Quinn v. Leathem* [1901] A.C., at p. 537, and by Romer, L. J., in *Giblan v. National Labourers* [1903] 2 K.B., at pp. 619–20. Obviously, if it were adopted, it would render s. 1 of the Trade Disputes Act inoperative in this important class of cases.

[8] (1900) 70 L.J.K.B. 905. [9] [1901] 1 K.B. 170.

[10] [1901] A.C. 426. [11] *Ibid.*

on torts alleged to have been committed by its officials on its behalf, and the Trade Union funds be made liable to pay the damages awarded. There was no historical authority for such a proposition. As Mr. Justice Farwell admitted,[1] 'a corporation and an individual or individuals' were 'the only entity known to the Common Law who can sue or be sued'; yet he held, and was followed by the House of Lords, that, by implication (for it was common ground that the Acts contained no expressions to that effect) the Trade Union Acts of 1871 and 1876,[2] by conferring upon Trade Unions many valuable rights in connection with the protection of their funds, had rendered them liable to be sued for torts, quite unconnected with property, but alleged to have been committed by their officials acting on their behalf. If the Court had held that the trustees of the Union, in a matter 'concerning the real or personal property of such Trade Union,' could be sued, it would, of course, have been merely following the words of the Act of 1871;[3] but that course would not have suited the plaintiffs, who, probably, could not prove any complicity by the trustees. All the learning and ingenuity of the Court and the House of Lords could not discover more than a dozen quotable precedents; and one of these was so remote from the point as that of *Sevenoaks Ry. Co. v. L. C. & D. Co.*,[4] which merely decided that a statute might, by implication, authorize a lease in perpetuity. Apart from such attenuated analogies, there was no attempt to meet the common sense argument, that the framers of the Trade Union Acts, who expressly gave to the trustees of the registered Unions limited powers of suing and being sued, could not possibly have omitted, by mere forgetfulness, to confer similar powers on the Unions themselves. They did not confer such powers; because they did not think it wise to do so. The decision of the Lords in the *Taff Vale Case* was pure legislation; and it threatened to ruin Trade Unionism, by making huge drafts upon its funds. The House of Lords had first invented a new civil offence ('civil conspiracy'), and had then created a new kind of defendant against whom it could be alleged.

But this decision, combined with certain severe decisions

[1] [1901] A.C., at p. 429.

[2] The Act of 1876 (39 & 40 Vict. c. 22) had amended the Act of 1871 (*ante*, pp. 322) in various minor points.

[3] S. 9.

[4] (1879) 11 Ch. D., at p. 635.

given about the same time in connection with the much-disputed point of 'peaceful picketing,'[1] seems to have convinced the Unions that it was hopeless, in the existing state of the statute law, to attain what they conceived to be their just rights. They accordingly bent their whole energies towards obtaining an alteration of the statute law; and, after the General Election of January 1906, as one of the first measures of the new Parliament, they succeeded in procuring the passing of a short but drastic Act, the Trade Disputes Act, 1906.[2] The first thing to note about this important statute is, that the first three of its four enactments are by express words,[3] and the fourth by judicial interpretation,[4] confined to acts done 'in contemplation or furtherance of a trade dispute.' Subject to this qualification, however, the Act expressly renders non-actionable —

Trade Disputes Act

1. Any act done by a combination of persons which would not be actionable if done without such combination (s. 1).
2. Any act which merely induces a breach of a contract of employment, or interferes with trade, business or employment, or the right of some other person to dispose of his capital or labour as he wills (s. 3).
3. Any alleged responsibility by a Trade Union, as a body, for the tortious acts of its officials or members (s. 4).

And the Act expressly authorizes[5] representatives of a Trade Union or employer to 'attend at or near a house or place where a person resides or works or carries on business or happens to be, . . . merely for the purpose of communicating information, or of peacefully persuading any person to work or abstain from working.' This new definition of 'peaceful picketing' is substituted for the older definition given in the Conspiracy and Protection of Property Act, 1875.[6]

Thus the labour organizations appeared to have suddenly turned the whole fortunes of war in their favour. But their opponents are resourceful; and, even since the passing of the Trade Disputes Act, 1906, have recovered a certain amount of ground. Thus, it has been held

Recent Decisions

[1] *Lyons v. Wilkins* [1899] 1 Ch. 255; *Charnock v. Court* [1899] 2 Ch. 35; *Walters v. Green, ibid.*, 696.

[2] 6 Edw. VII, c. 47.

[3] Ss. 1-3.

[4] *Richards v. Bertram* (1909) 25 T.L.R. 181.

[5] S. 4.

[6] S. 3.

that, though a workman is precluded by the express words of the Trade Union Act, 1871,[1] from bringing an action to recover sick pay alleged to be due to him under the rules of the Union,[2] yet a member of a registered Trade Union may obtain an injunction against the Union, restraining it from applying its funds for purposes beyond the proper objects of the Union,[3] and, further, may secure protection against a Union which threatens to expel him for not subscribing to such funds.[4] Again, while the Court of Appeal has confirmed the jurisdiction of the Court to pronounce, at the instance of a member of a registered Trade Union, upon the validity or invalidity of any rule of the Union,[5] it has, just as this book goes to press, refused to enforce, at the instance of a Union, a bond entered into by one of its members with it for return of a large sum of money paid to him by the Union as sick benefit, upon events which had happened.[6] Obviously, the rights and liabilities of Trade Unions, and, therefore, by analogy, of other unincorporated bodies, are in a somewhat uncertain condition, in which every kind of surprise is possible.

In concluding this long and somewhat painful story, it is pleasant to refer to the beneficent provisions of the Workmen's Compensation Acts 1897, 1900, and 1906,[7] which have enabled a workman who has suffered injury in the course of his employment, or the dependents of a workman who has been killed in such course, to recover compensation from his employers by arbitration proceedings in the County Court, quite apart from any question of negligence by employer or fellow-workman.[8] Doubtless these statutes have given rise to much litigation; and doubtless they are sometimes abused. But the general adoption of the system of insurance against liability had practically deprived the measures of all terrors for ordinarily prudent employers; while the same system has guaranteed compensa-

[1] S. 4 (3).

[2] *Burke v. Amalgamated Society* [1906] 2 K.B. 583; *Russell v. Amalgamated Society* [1910] 1 K.B. 506.

[3] *Amalgamated Society v. Osborne* [1910] A.C. 87.

[4] *Id.*, (No. 2).

[5] *Gozney v. Bristol, &c., Society* [1909] 1 K.B. 901. (This case is valuable as containing a repudiation by Fletcher Moulton, L.J., at p. 919, of the doctrine that every Trade Union is an 'illegal association at the common law.')

[6] *Baker v. Ingall* [1911] 2 K.B. 132.

[7] 60 & 61 Vict. c. 37; 63 & 64 Vict. c. 22; 6 Edw. VII, c. 58.

[8] Thus the Acts have, incidentally, almost abolished the operation of the doctrine of 'common employment' (*ante*, pp. 317–319) so far as 'workmen' are concerned. But in some cases even workmen may have to resort to the common law; and, in the case of other employees, the doctrine is still important.

tion to thousands of deserving workmen who would otherwise have been dependent on charity. Bare allusion may also be made to the Old Age Pensions Act, 1908, and the Insurance Act, 1911, which will, in the future, still further alleviate the hardships of the poorer classes of the community. But these measures hardly come within the scope of the present survey.

CHAPTER XVIII

REFORM IN THE CRIMINAL LAW

WE have seen[1] that, broadly speaking, the Law of Crime had, by the end of the preceding period, definitely separated itself, both from the older procedure by way of revenge (the 'appeal of felony') and from the civil procedure of the King's Courts. This fact, however, only resulted at first in bringing out, more clearly than before, its barbarous character. Not only did it recognize, in theory, but one punishment for all serious offences, viz. death with confiscation of property, but it clung to the original idea that a criminal prosecution did not really begin until the accused had been found suspect by the Grand Jury, and that, therefore, there was very little likelihood of his innocence. Historically speaking, as we have also seen,[2] the petty jury, or Jury of Inquest, was a mere after-thought, designed to fill the gap left by the abolition of the ordeal; and the presumption was heavily against the accused. Naturally, therefore, he was not given much liberty in his defence. He was not allowed to see a copy of the 'indictment' or accusation preferred before the Grand Jury; nor to obtain a list of the Crown's witnesses. It is doubtful whether he could call witnesses on his own behalf. If he could, they were not allowed to testify on oath; and the rules as to 'interested' witnesses excluded, in all probability, the very persons upon whose testimony he most relied. He was not allowed to have counsel to speak for him; unless a point of law arose at the trial. It may be that the requirement of a preliminary approval by the Grand Jury, of all accusations of a serious nature, justified the boast that a man was presumed to be innocent until he was 'found' guilty; but that presumption certainly ceased to have practical application, so soon as the Grand Jury had returned a 'true bill.'

[1] *Ante*, chap. XI.

[2] *Ante*, pp. 50, 52.

Happily, the record of the period now under review, save in the stationary period of the eighteenth century, is one of steady progress towards enlightenment and humanity in the treatment of criminals.

The first great reform was the passing of the statute which guaranteed the citizen against arbitrary arrest on a criminal charge — the Habeas Corpus Act of 1679. The history of the famous remedy of 'Habeas Corpus' is one of the quaintest and most characteristic in English legal literature; but it can only be briefly summarized here.[1] In the thirteenth century, the 'Habeas Corpus' was merely an ordinary judicial writ, the necessary incident of every criminal trial, bidding the sheriff or other person charged with the custody of an accused person, 'have his body' before the Court for the purpose of trial. Such a person might be either in actual custody, in which case the direction was merely formal, or he might be at large 'on bail,' *i.e.* on security to give himself up for trial.[2] In that event, it would be, practically, the duty of the sheriff to see that the accused was available on the day of trial.[3]

Habeas Corpus

But, in the fourteenth and fifteenth centuries, there arose the practice of applying this judicial writ for the purpose of carrying out the objects of another and more comprehensive writ, the Writ of Privilege. This latter remedy was the process by which, in the way so characteristic of the Middle Ages, each tribunal protected its own officials from unfair treatment by jealous rivals. Any official of one Court, who was sued or prosecuted in another, was entitled to a Writ of Privilege to remove him to his own tribunal, where he was supposed to be wanted to carry on official business.[4] If he succeeded in establishing his right to this writ, his own tribunal would send a writ of Habeas Corpus to the rival tribunal by which he was detained, bidding the responsible official of that tribunal 'have the body' (of the privileged person) 'before

Writ of Privilege

[1] It will be found at greater length in Select Essays in Anglo-American Legal History, II, pp. 531–548, by the author.

[2] The right to bail was at this time carefully regulated by the Statute of Westminster I (3 Edw. I (1275) c. 15).

[3] A very late survival, or revival, of this use of the Habeas Corpus is that provided by the statute of 1661 against vexatious arrests (13 Car. II, st. II, c. 2, s. 5), in actions against prisoners in the Fleet prison.

[4] This hypothesis accounts for one of the defects in the process of Habeas Corpus prior to 1679, viz. that the writ could not be obtained in vacation, when the Courts were closed.

us' (on such a day) 'together with the cause' of his detention.[1]

A century later, we find this writ of '*Corpus cum causâ*' used by the old-established 'superior' Courts to test the validity of imprisonment by their newer 'prerogative' rivals, or the exercise of irregular authority by executive officials. The latter was the more serious danger; and the successful claim to the protection afforded by the writ established in two cases of the year 1588,[2] is a landmark in the history of the struggle between liberty and prerogative. In the latter case, the applicant had been arrested by virtue of a warrant signed by a Secretary of State; and the issue of the writ assumed the inadequacy of the authority. On the trial, the Court reluctantly admitted the power of the Privy Council, as a body, to arrest without reason assigned; but, four years later, the judges adopted a famous resolution,[3] to the effect that, even in such cases, the gaoler must produce the prisoners when required to do so by Habeas Corpus. All pretence that the applicant was an official of the tribunal applied to had by this time been abandoned; and there is some little evidence to show that the Court of Chancery had even made use of the remedy in its struggle with the Common Law Courts at the beginning of the seventeenth century.[4]

Corpus cum causâ

But the weakness of a remedy resting on a series of historical fictions appeared in the struggle between Charles I and his Parliament. In the famous *Case of the Five Knights* in 1627,[5] the Court of King's Bench remanded the applicants to the Fleet; and, in spite of the express words of the Petition of Right in 1628,[6] it even refused to order the production of the six members of Parliament arbitrarily imprisoned under royal warrant in 1629.[7]

Charles I and Habeas Corpus

One of the first acts of the Long Parliament, however, on its assembling in November, 1640, was to pass a sweeping statute dealing with the abuses of prerogative jurisdiction; and, in that

[1] Even so recently as the eighteenth century, the great case between the scriveners and the attorneys in London (*ante*, p. 202, n. 2) was fought out on a Writ of Privilege. (See a full account in *Report of the Proceedings*, Williams, 1768.)

[2] *Search's Case*, 1 Leon. 70; *Howell's Case*, *ibid.*, 71.

[3] Anderson's Reports, p. 298.

[4] If the Common Law Court committed a defendant to prison for applying for an injunction to stay proceedings at law, Chancery would get him out by a Habeas Corpus.

[5] 3 St. Tr. pp. 1–235.

[6] 3 Car. I, c. 1, ss. 5, 10.

[7] *Six Members Case*, 3 Str. Tr. pp. 235–294.

statute, it was provided that every person imprisoned by such authority should be entitled as of right to his Habeas Corpus.[1] Unfortunately, in the heat of debate, the clause was badly worded; and, in the later days of Charles II, it was practically set at defiance by venal judges acting in the interest of the Court. At length, however, chiefly as the result of the oppressive proceedings in *Jenks' Case*,[2] tried in 1676, the great statute of the year 1679[3] was passed. Its provisions are well known. It gives every prisoner an absolute right to have the validity of his imprisonment speedily raised and discussed by a superior Court in his presence, whether in Term time or vacation. If the authority under which he is imprisoned is lawful, as in the ordinary case of a prisoner committed for trial, with bail lawfully refused, the applicant will, of course, simply be remanded to prison.[4] But save in the rare case of an absolutely friendless man suddenly carried off to gaol, or an arrest so secretly effected that no one but the prisoner and his custodians are aware of it, it is absolutely impossible for any irregularities in arrest or imprisonment now to take place in this country.[5] The most striking feature of the statute (which has since been amended to include arrest on civil process)[6] is that which imposes a heavy pecuniary penalty[7] on any judge refusing the application for the writ. This statute, re-inforced as it was by the civil remedies applied in the well-known 'General Warrant' cases at the end of the eighteenth century,[8] may be said to have definitely established in England that 'Rule of Law' which is the chief guarantee of English liberty. For both statute and decisions are based upon the principle, that even an official acting under the authority of the Crown must show definite legal authority for any act which interferes with the personal freedom or domestic privacy of the ordinary citizen.

Criminal Informations

One of the first reforms in the criminal law which took place after the Revolution was aimed at the abuse by which the process of criminal information was employed by private plaintiffs in civil cases, to vex and oppress their

[1] 16 Car. I, c. 10, s. 8.
[2] 6 St. Tr. pp. 1189–1208.
[3] 31 Car. II, c. 2.
[4] Ss. 2, 10.
[5] The case of *Ex parte D. F. Marais* [1902] A.C. 109, which is not binding on English courts, makes it doubtful whether this statement is true of the colonies.
[6] 56 Geo. III (1816) c. 100.
[7] 31 Car. II (1679) c. 2, s. 10.
[8] *Wilkes v. Wood* (1766) 19 St. Tr. 1153; *Entick v. Carrington* (1765) 19 St. Tr. 1030; *Leach v. Money* (1765) 19 St. Tr. 1001.

opponents. The criminal information was, in theory, a process by which one of the King's officials, *e.g.* a coroner, informed His Majesty of the existence of claims enforceable by the Crown. It was made through the Master of the Crown Office, the Chief Coroner of the Kingdom; and that official ought not, of course, to have allowed private suits to be converted into criminal prosecutions by this means. Most abuses could be practised for adequate consideration in the reign of Charles II; but the framers of the Bill of Rights determined to suppress this scandal, and, though the clause was struck out of their draft, a statute [1] was devoted to the subject in 1692. By that Act, the Clerk of the Crown in the King's Bench is forbidden to receive any such information; except under an order pronounced in open Court, or on the security by the informer in £20 for prompt prosecution, and payment of costs if unsuccessful. To this statute we probably owe the rule that a common trespass is not now a criminal offence, and that the words so frequently to be seen disfiguring the country-side — 'Trespassers will be prosecuted' — are, as has been wittily said, a 'wooden falsehood.'

Trials for Treason

If William of Orange had no other claim to the gratitude of the Englishman of his day, he would have been entitled to it for assenting to the noble Treason Act of 1695.[2] By that statute, the procedure on trials for that very offence which is most apt to inspire severity in rulers, was brought, almost at one step, to the modern plane of humanity and justice. All persons prosecuted for treason, or misprision (*i.e.* concealment) of treason, are to have a copy of the indictment delivered to them five days, and a copy of the 'panel' or jury list two days,[3] at least, before their trials; they may be represented by counsel at their trials, and may call witnesses who shall give evidence on oath. If the accused is too poor to retain the services of counsel, the Court must assign him two of his own choice, free of expense.[4] No prosecution for treason or misprision committed in England (except a direct design on the life of the King) is to be commenced more than three years after the date

[1] 4 & 5 W. & M. c. 18.

[2] 7 & 8 Will. III, c. 3.

[3] S. 7. The right of a person accused to 'challenge' or reject jurors, was regulated by 33 Hen. VIII (1541) c. 23, s. 3, which forbade 'peremptory' challenges for treason. But the right of the accused to challenge 'for cause' had been also rendered nugatory by the secrecy preserved as to the composition of the list.

[4] S. 1.

of the alleged commission.[1] Finally, by what is, perhaps, the most striking provision of all, no one may be tried for treason or misprision except on the oaths of two witnesses, who, though they need not speak to the same precise act or acts, must testify to the same kind of treason.[2]

The later years of the seventeenth century were also memorable for the introduction of the system of 'transporting' offenders beyond the seas to the newly-acquired possessions of the Crown, where the scarcity of labourers rendered them welcome immigrants. As a stage in the evolution of criminal law, the practice was eminently humane, and beneficial for both the parties to the transaction. But, as it involved compulsory exile, it could at first only be applied to persons who voluntarily accepted it as an alternative of capital punishment. There was no power to transport a convict, if he preferred to be hanged. But, in the year 1717,[3] this scruple was overruled by a statute which allowed sentence of transportation to be passed upon all offenders entitled to 'benefit of clergy,'[4] for a period of seven years, and upon other convicted offenders for twice that period.

Transportation

Again, the thick darkness of the eighteenth century descended upon the criminal law; but at the very end of that century we get an important statute,[5] connected with the immortal name of Fielding, which sets up a small body of skilled and salaried Metropolitan magistrates, in place of the old 'trading justices,' paid only by fees, whose conduct was a disgrace to the administration of the criminal law. These 'trading' Justices, mostly uneducated men, of no morality but considerable natural parts, ignoring the 'watch' or official guardians of the peace, had employed a semi-professional body of 'runners,' devoted to their masters' interests, and entirely unscrupulous in the exercise of their special knowledge. Accordingly, if the prosecutor made it worth while for the Justice to exert his powers, the criminal was speedily brought to book; while, if the latter outbid his adversary, he enjoyed practical immunity. Any prospect of a falling off in the magisterial income had been promptly remedied by a raid among prostitutes,

Stipendiary Magistrates

[1] S. 5.
[2] Ss. 2, 4.
[3] 4 Geo. I, c. 11.
[4] *Ante*, pp. 156–158.
[5] 32 Geo. III, c. 53. (Of course it is not suggested that Henry Fielding lived until 1792. But the suggestion was due to him.)

gamblers, cut-purses, and other habitual offenders; upon whom an extra arrest or two made little impression, but who could be made to yield fines. The new system worked so well, that it was extended to other municipalities, which chose to apply for it, in 1835.[1]

Penal Servitude

Meanwhile, the loss of the American colonies had practically put a stop to the process of transportation, which had grown by leaps and bounds since its legalization in 1717; and the difficulty had been met by the substitution of the new form of punishment known as 'penal servitude,' *i.e.* imprisonment — no longer, as in the old days, mere stupid, aimless confinement, but restriction of liberty accompanied by compulsory labour. At first the process was carried out in ships moored in the Thames and other rivers, known popularly as 'the hulks'; and there can be no doubt that, at first, it was very imperfectly administered. Moreover, the practice of sending convicts to the newly-acquired colonies in Australia for a time rendered its development less urgent. But when the outflux to Australia was also closed,[2] as that to America had been, the 'penal servitude' system, greatly improved by the introduction of 'ticket-of-leave,'[3] good-conduct marks, police supervision, the 'Borstal system' for juvenile offenders,[4] and other modern developments of scientific criminology, has become the chief engine for the enforcement of the criminal law in the more serious classes of cases. The power to add 'hard labour' and solitary confinement to a sentence of imprisonment was conferred in 1827.[5]

Peel's Acts

But it was not sufficient to improve the mere machinery of the criminal law, while the substance of that law remained in its barbarous condition. Accordingly, even before the passing of the Reform Act, a series of statutes, connected with the name of Sir Robert Peel, was passed with the object of moderating that sanguinary code. By the Act of 1827,[6] previously referred to, the tendency which, as we have seen,[7] had formerly manifested itself, to distinguish between

[1] Municipal Corporations Act (5 & 6 Will. IV. c. 76, s. 99).

[2] In the year 1853. The process was prohibited by statute in 1857 (20 & 21 Vict. c. 3, s. 2).

[3] Penal Servitude Act, 1853 (16 & 17 Vict. c. 99) ss. 9–11.

[4] Prevention of Crime Act, 1908 (8 Edw. VII, c. 59) ss. 1–4.

[5] 7 & 8 Geo. IV, c. 28, s. 9.

[6] 7 & 8 Geo. IV, c. 28.

[7] *Ante*, pp. 151–153.

capital and non-capital felonies, was given a wide extension. No longer was the mere declaration by a statute that certain acts should be 'felonious' to render them capital offences; no new offence was to be capital unless expressly declared so to be. And, as a fact, opportunity was taken, in the almost contemporary group of statutes known as 'Peel's Acts,'[1] to remove the death penalty in many cases; though it was still allowed to figure far too frequently in the statute-book.

The passing of the Reform Bill was speedily followed by renewed efforts in this, as in other directions. Spurred on by the energies and reputation of the veteran jurist Jeremy Bentham, and of his enthusiastic disciples, a Royal Commission went thoroughly through the whole of the criminal law, and produced a crop of amending statutes, which passed into law in the year 1837,[2] shortly after the accession of the youthful Queen Victoria. It is impossible to go into details of them; but attention may be especially drawn to the last of the group,[3] which abolished the death penalty in the case of a large number of offences, such as riot, rescue, seducing from allegiance, administering unlawful oaths, prison-breach, slave-trading, and certain forms of smuggling. On the other hand, it should not be forgotten that the system of trained and disciplined police, introduced by Sir Robert Peel into London in the year 1829,[4] was extended to the municipal boroughs by the Reform Act of 1835; and that thus the criminal law, if it had become more lenient, was infinitely better enforced, than in the old days of the watch and parish constable. The system of police in the boroughs, however, and in the counties, where it was introduced in 1839,[5] was not made compulsory till the year 1856.[6] It should, moreover, be remembered in this direction, that, if the skill and certainty of prosecutions had been increased, the chances of a successful defence had also been largely increased by an important statute, the Trials for Felony Act, passed in the year 1836,[7] which extended to the accused in all cases, whether tried by indictment or summarily, the right to be defended by counsel, and gave to all prisoners

[1] The chief subjects affected were — (1) larceny and malicious injuries to property (1827); offences against the person (1828); forgery (1830); the coinage (1832).

[2] The chief are 7 Will. IV & 1 Vict. c. 84 (forgery), c. 85 (offences against the person), c. 86 (burglary), c. 87 (robbery and theft from the person), c. 88 (piracy), c. 89 (arson), c. 90 (transportation), c. 91 (capital punishment).

[3] 7 Will. IV & 1 Vict. c. 91.

[4] 10 Geo. IV, c. 44.

[5] 2 & 3 Vict. c. 93.

[6] 19 & 20 Vict. c. 69.

[7] 6 & 7 Will. IV, c. 114.

the right to have copies of the depositions of the Crown witnesses, or to inspect such depositions at their trial.

The next important year in the history of the Criminal Law is 1848, the year of European revolutions. In that year was passed the important trio of statutes known as 'Sir John Jervis' Acts.' These are concerned with the jurisdiction of the Justices of the Peace, which, with the enormous increase in the population, had become of ever-growing importance. The statutes distinguish clearly between the merely preliminary, and the judicial work of the magistrates. In the former,[1] the sole object of the Justices is to see whether there is such a *primâ facie* case against the accused as will justify them in committing him for trial. But it is recognized, that even mere committal for trial is a heavy blow to an innocent man; and, accordingly, the accused is to have the opportunity, if he desires it, of cross-examining the witnesses for the prosecution, and to be represented by counsel or solicitor.[2] Moreover, to prevent groundless accusations, he may only be arrested, in the first instance, if a sworn information has been laid against him; on a mere summons, he cannot be arrested unless he fails to appear and make his defence.[3] And, all through the preliminary proceedings, the accused is entitled to bail; except on the heavy accusations in which the magistrates are entitled to refuse bail, or even unable to grant it.[4] Moreover, it is expressly provided,[5] that the room in which the preliminary examination takes place, shall not be deemed an open Court, and that the magistrates may exclude the public, if they think that such a course will best serve the ends of justice.

Sir John Jervis' Acts

The second of Sir John Jervis' Acts, the Summary Jurisdiction Act, 1848, deals with the final or judicial work of the Justices. This had also grown enormously in recent years; especially in its 'summary' aspect, *i.e.* when the magistrates sat without a jury to dispose of minor accusations. Here again arose the question which, as we have seen,[6] was left in a somewhat uncertain condition at the close of the preceding period. Technically, all such 'summary jurisdiction' was still exercised 'out

[1] 11 & 12 Vict. c. 42.

[2] 11 & 12 Vict. c. 42, s. 17. The right of the accused to call witnesses at this stage was not conferred till 1867 (Criminal Law Amendment Act, 30 & 31 Vict. c. 35, s. 3).

[3] S. 9. [4] S. 21. [5] S. 19. [6] *Ante*, pp. 151–154.

of sessions,' *i.e.* Quarter Sessions. But more and more it was coming to be regarded as unsuitable work for the Justice's private room; and, though the decisive enactment which made all such business matter only for a Court of two ordinary Justices or one Stipendiary, sitting in an open Court House, was postponed till 1879,[1] yet the Act of 1848, which, moreover, clearly recognizes a right of appeal in every case to Quarter Sessions,[2] goes far in that direction.[3]

Finally, the third of Sir John Jervis' Acts, the 'Justices' Protection Act,'[4] by a very rare exception from the 'Rule of Law,' granted in recognition of the unpaid services of the bulk of the magistracy, mitigates, to a certain extent, the sharpness of the common law rule, that even for a mere technical breach of the law, innocently committed in the exercise of his functions, a magistrate is personally liable to the injured party.

Another Royal Commission on the Criminal Law, which sat for several years prior to 1861, was responsible for an important group of consolidating statutes which, though not in themselves amounting to a Criminal Code, gave fair promise of the appearance of such a code in the future. These are the five great enactments of the year 1861,[5] which deal respectively with larceny, malicious damage to property, forgery, false coinage, and offences against the person. They still regulate, to a great extent, the everyday business of the criminal courts; and, in the opinion of so well-qualified a critic as the late Sir Fitz-James Stephen,[6] have been productive of immense good. An attempt was made to add a Homicide Act in 1874;[7] but the times were not propitious, and the effort was unsuccessful. A very recent enterprise in another direction has been more fortunate; and the value of the consolidating Perjury Act of 1911[8] may be gathered from the suggestive fact, that it repeals, in whole or in part, no less than 131 other statutes, among which the statutory law of perjury had previously been dispersed.

Consolidation of 1861

The remaining events to be recorded in the history of the Criminal Law have been mainly concerned with procedure;

[1] Summary Jurisdiction Act, 1879 (42 & 43 Vict. c. 49) s. 20.
[2] S. 27. [3] S. 12. [4] 11 & 12 Vict. c. 44.
[5] 24 & 25 Vict. c. 96 (larceny), c. 97 (malicious damage), c. 98 (forgery), c. 99 (coinage), and c. 100 (offences against the person).
[6] *Digest of the Criminal Law*, Preface, p. xvi.
[7] *Ibid.*, p. 1. [8] 1 & 2 Geo. V, c. 6.

although, in this branch of the law, the connection between substance and procedure is exceptionally close.

An important statute passed in the year 1865, the Criminal Procedure Act,[1] by avowedly setting up, as a model of a criminal trial the practice followed in civil cases between private persons, gave to English criminal procedure its most striking features. The Crown steps down from its prerogative pedestal, and enters the lists as an ordinary litigant, abandoning the formidable prerogative weapons which, for so long, as the outcome of historical causes, had been at the disposal of its representatives. The speeches of counsel are regulated with strict impartiality, as between prosecution and accused;[2] the prosecution may not discredit its own witnesses if they are favourable to the accused;[3] while all witnesses may be confronted with previous statements made by them relative to the subject-matter,[4] and may even be cross-examined on such of them as are in writing.[5] Moreover, either side is entitled to show that a witness produced by the other has previously been convicted of a criminal offence;[6] though whether this provision, at the present day, works in favour of accused persons, may be considered doubtful. In former times, when the evidence of 'common informers' was much more relied upon than at present, it would have been of great value to them in many cases. The assimilation of a criminal to a civil trial was rendered yet more complete, by the passing of the Costs in Criminal Cases Act, 1908,[7] which enables any Court by which an indictable offence is tried, or proceedings preliminary to the trial of such case conducted, to award costs to the prosecution or the defence. The analogy, however, breaks down in the method of securing fulfilment of the award; for, in cases covered by the statute, the costs are first paid out of public funds, and then recovered (if possible) by the public authority from the unsuccessful party.

The procedural reform of 1865 was rapidly followed by the abolition of public executions for felony,[8] and of the barbarous system of escheat and forfeiture which reduced to beggary the families of men of substance who had strayed from the paths of

[1] 28 & 29 Vict. c. 18.

[2] S. 2. (The privilege of the reply, which can be claimed by the Attorney-General, even when the prisoner calls no evidence, is, however, not abolished.)

[3] S. 3. [4] S. 4. [5] S. 5. [6] S. 6.

[7] 8 Edw. VII, c. 15. [8] 31 & 32 Vict. (1868) c. 24.

virtue.[1] In the year 1879, the ancient connection between private vengeance and public prosecution was finally severed, or, at least, reduced to the slenderest proportions, by the establishment of a Public Prosecutor, or Director of Public Prosecutions, charged with the institution and carrying on of criminal proceedings in the interests of justice, and of giving advice and assistance to police officers, magistrates' clerks, and other persons, official or private, concerned in criminal proceedings.[2] The right of a private person to take up, or insist on continuing, a prosecution, is strictly preserved; [3] but, as the special scandal which the Act was directed to meet was the unwillingness of private prosecutors to undertake costly proceedings, and the consequent immunity of well-known offenders, it may, perhaps, be safely predicted, that this part of the statute is not likely to prove the most valuable in practice. The establishment of the new official, whose functions were, until quite recently, combined with those of the Solicitor to the Treasury and the King's Proctor, of course in no way derogates from the long-established tradition, which makes the Attorney-General the mouthpiece and adviser of the Crown in all criminal matters. In fact, the statute creating the office places it under regulations made by the Attorney-General with the approval of the Lord Chancellor and a Secretary of State.[4] The Director of Public Prosecutions is, however, appointed by the Secretary of State, not by the Attorney-General.[5]

Criminal Evidence

In the year 1898, was passed the important Criminal Evidence Act,[6] which put the crown on the long series of statutes passed in the nineteenth century, with the object of liberalizing the law of evidence. We have seen [7] how this movement began with the subject of testamentary witnesses. In the year 1843, Lord Denman's Act[8] had admitted, generally, the advisability of hearing all witnesses, whether interested or not, in both criminal and civil proceedings; but it had stopped short of the admission of parties, their husbands or wives. In 1851, the second of Lord Brougham's Evidence Acts[9] had departed from

[1] 33 & 34 Vict. (1870) c. 23.
[2] 42 & 43 Vict. c. 22, s. 2.
[3] Ss. 6, 7.
[4] Prosecution of Offences Act, 1879, s. 8.
[5] S. 2.
[6] 61 & 62 Vict. c. 36.
[7] *Ante*, p. 270.
[8] Evidence Act, 1843 (6 & 7 Vict. c. 85, s. 1).
[9] Evidence Act, 1851 (14 & 15 Vict. c. 99, s. 2).

the last exclusion, and admitted the evidence of parties;[1] but, again, it had expressly excluded the evidence of an accused person in a criminal trial, and his or her wife or husband.[2] At length, however, after considerable hesitation, this ancient disability was swept away by the enactment of 1898, which makes the accused, and his or her wife or husband, competent witnesses in a criminal prosecution,[3] and even allows the wife or husband to be summoned in a few special cases without the consent of the accused.[4] But, generally speaking, neither can the accused himself be compelled to give evidence, nor can his or her wife or husband be called, except upon the application of the accused.[5] Moreover, the fact, that the accused has not volunteered testimony, may not be commented on by the prosecution;[6] though, apparently, there is nothing to prevent the Court making such a comment.

A more decided benefit was conferred upon accused persons by the Poor Prisoners' Defence Act of 1903,[7] by which the magistrates committing a prisoner for trial, or the judge before the hearing of the trial, may certify for legal aid; whereupon the prisoner becomes entitled to have solicitor and counsel assigned to him at the public expense.[8] But the most striking evidence of the sensitiveness of the public conscience in the administration of the criminal law was the establishment, in the year 1907, of the Court of Criminal Appeal, consisting of the Lord Chief Justice and eight King's Bench judges, of whom three, or any greater uneven number, constitute a quorum.[9] Under the statute establishing this tribunal, any prisoner, convicted on indictment, may, with the leave, either of the tribunal itself or the Court which tried him, appeal on grounds of fact, or mixed law and fact, or any other ground, against his conviction; while, with the leave of the appellate tribunal, he may even appeal against the amount of his sentence, unless that is fixed by law.[10] The Court of Criminal Appeal, on the hearing of an appeal, may totally quash the conviction, or alter the sentence (not necessarily in the

Poor Prisoners' Defence

Court of Criminal Appeal

[1] Apparently not their husbands or wives. But this omission was rectified (with certain precautions) by the Evidence Amendment Act, 1853 (16 & 17 Vict. c. 83, s. 1).

[2] S. 3.

[3] 61 & 62 Vict. c. 36, s. 1.

[4] S. 4. (But not against the will of the witness.)

[5] S. 1 (*a*) (*c*).

[6] *Ibid.*, (*b*).

[7] 3 Edw. VII, c. 38.

[8] S. 1.

[9] 7 Edw. VII, c. 23, s. 1.

[10] S. 3.

appellant's favour);[1] but, if it thinks the appellant was rightly convicted, it is not bound to decide in his favour on a technical point,[2] and, even though the appellant succeeds in upsetting the conviction on one charge in an indictment, or in showing that he has been found guilty of an offence which he did not commit, he may yet be made to serve a proportionate sentence in respect of a charge on which he was properly found guilty, and be sentenced as for conviction on the offence which he really did commit.[3] The Court of Criminal Appeal has, however, no power to direct a new trial. The statute affects neither the prerogative of mercy[4] nor the former right of the accused to appeal on a point of law.[5] But, in the event of the latter being exercised, the appeal will be heard by the new tribunal, which has taken over the duties of the old Court for Crown Cases Reserved.[6]

[1] S. 4. [2] S. 4.
[3] S. 5. (Of course it must be clear that the jury were satisfied of facts sufficient to justify the amended conviction.)
[4] S. 19. [5] S. 3 (*a*). [6] S. 20 (4).

CHAPTER XIX

MODERN CIVIL PROCEDURE

IMMEDIATELY after the Restoration, steps were taken to modify what, as we have seen in a former chapter,[1] had become the most striking abuse of civil process in personal actions, viz. the power of the plaintiff to arrest the defendant on mesne process, before proving his claim, and either to hold him in prison till the trial of the action, or to compel him to give heavy bail to secure his freedom. We have seen, also, how this abuse had been the means by which the rival Courts of Common Law had stolen one another's jurisdiction, and how, therefore, in spite of the enactment passed in the fifteenth century to modify it,[2] it speedily revived again and flourished with all its old vigour.

Arrest on Mesne Process

It is to be feared, however, that the Restoration attempt at reform was hardly due to the purest of motives. If the testimony of the time can be trusted,[3] it was due to the jealousy of the judges and officials of the Court of Common Pleas, who saw with anger their once flourishing and (as they, not unfairly, alleged) proper business, filched away by the King's Bench, with its cheaper processes of Bills of Middlesex and Latitats.

The first effort made by the Common Pleas was through the Chancellor, Lord Clarendon, who, as will be remembered, in his capacity of Custodian of the Great Seal, was supposed to authorize the issue of all the Writs Original, the proper process with which to commence an ordinary civil action. The Chancellor, accordingly, in his *Orders in Chancelry* of 1660,[4] forbade the Cursitors to issue writs returnable in the King's Bench containing the famous *ac etiam* clause; [5] on the ground that they

[1] *Ante*, pp. 169–174. [2] 23 Hen. VI (1444) c. 9 (5).

[3] See, for example, Hale, *Discourse*, &c., Hargrave's *Law Tracts*, Vol. I, pp. 367–368; North, *Lives of the Norths*, I, par. 146.

[4] Pp. 80–82. [5] *Ante*, pp. 170, 171.

were 'to the great damage of the subject . . . and of His Majesty's Revenue for the casual fines due and payable on the proper Original Writs.' But, in the following year, the Common Pleas achieved a still more striking victory in Parliament, by securing the enactment of a statute[1] which provided, that no one, bailable under the statute of 1444, should be kept in prison, by colour of any writ, bill, or process, issuing out of the King's Bench or Common Pleas, in which the certainty and true cause of action was 'not expressed particularly,' but that any one so arrested should be entitled to his immediate freedom, on giving security in a sum not exceeding £40 for his appearance.

Act of 1661

This statute, though speciously worded to cover both Courts, was thought, at the time, by both to have inflicted a deadly blow upon the Court of King's Bench, whose writs of Latitat and Trespass *quare clausum fregit*, did not specify the precise nature of the cause of action, or the amount of damage claimed by the plaintiff. Indeed, they could not well do so, inasmuch as the trespass in question was wholly fictitious. But the Court of King's Bench quickly recovered from its temporary defeat, by the simple expedient of adding to its formal Latitat or Trespass an amended *ac etiam* clause, in which the cause of action was stated to be a plea of Debt or Case in the sum of £200, or whatever it might be.[2] The object of this change is freely admitted by Sir Matthew Hale,[3] who, with statesman-like impartiality, reviews the whole dispute on the merits, *i.e.* the merits of the Courts, and proposes various compromises. The Court of King's Bench also took care that the new process should not be abused, by forbidding its application to heirs or personal representatives.[4]

But the Court of Common Pleas was in no mood to listen to proposals of compromise; and, under the guidance of its new Chief, Sir Francis North, afterwards Lord Chancellor Guilford, it retorted by once more making use of the Writ of Trespass *quare clausum fregit*, which was, apparently, 'not finable,'[5] and, by another *ac etiam* clause, tacking on to it the true cause of action.[6]

[1] 13 Car. II, st. II, (1661) c. 2, s. 2.

[2] Hale, *op. cit.*, p. 368.

[3] *Ibid.*

[4] *Orders of the King's Bench in* 1663 (ed. 1796, p. 48).

[5] This was, probably, yet another peculiarity of the Writ of Trespass. The King could hardly demand a big fee for enforcing his own peace.

[6] North, *op. cit.*, I. par. 147.

Thus the Common Pleas was able to offer as equally cheap a remedy as the King's Bench, combined with an equally potent power of arrest on special bail. And thus the whole ostensible purpose of the statute of 1661 was apparently defeated; although, owing to the obscurity of the quarrel, we cannot be quite certain what happened.[1] It is, however, satisfactory to find, that repeated attempts were made by the legislature, even in the eighteenth century, to ensure that the power of arrest should not be exercised in trifling cases,[2] that, in others, the plaintiff's cause of action should be genuine,[3] and that the defendant should really understand the matter of the claim made against him.[4] The defendant was also, ultimately, allowed to pay money into Court to abide the trial of the action, instead of giving bail.[5] Nevertheless, in spite of these mitigations, the oppressive power of arrest on mesne process went on, without substantial check, until the year 1838, when it was abolished in all cases,[6] except those in which it appears that the defendant is about to leave the country to avoid meeting the claim against him.[7] Meanwhile, however, the ancient remedy of seizing the debtor's body in satisfaction (*Ca. Sa.*) of a debt actually adjudged to be due, remained untouched; except so far as it was mitigated by alternative remedies against the debtor's property. It was not until the year 1869, that, on the overhauling of the Bankruptcy laws, the power of imprisonment on civil process was entirely swept away; except in cases in which the debtors are deemed to have been 'fraudulent,'[8] or to be contemptuously resisting an order to pay which they can, if they choose, obey.[9]

English in the Courts

Again, amid the thick darkness of the eighteenth century, we see a point of light in the statute of the year 1731,[10] which enacted that the proceedings in all Courts in England should be conducted in English, and such of them as were written should be written in ordinary legible hand, and not in the medieval character known as 'court hand.' Needless to

[1] North (*ibid.*, par. 48) says that his brother left a MS. dealing with the whole subject. So far as the writer knows, it has not been published.

[2] 12 Geo. I (1725) c. 29, s. 1 (amended by 19 Geo. III (1779) c. 70).

[3] *Ibid.*, s. 2.

[4] 5 Geo. II (1732) c. 27, s. 1.

[5] 43 Geo. III (1803) c. 46, s. 2.

[6] Judgments Act, 1838 (1 & 2 Vict. c. 110) s. 1. This section was re-enacted by the Debtors Act, 1869, s. 6.

[7] Judgments Act, 1838, ss. 3, 4.

[8] Debtors Act, 1869 (32 & 33 Vict. c. 62) s. 4.

[9] S. 5. (2). The 'contempt' is too often fictitious.

[10] 4 Geo. II, c. 26, s. 1.

say, there were not wanting in those days great men who foresaw in the change the downfall of all things, including the legal profession; and who brought forward the quaintest arguments in opposition to the proposal, one of the best known being the contention, that the absence from legal documents of the quaint barbarisms of the neo-Latin of the Year Books, would injure the study of classical literature. When such arguments are gravely put forward, one can hardly help indulging in an equally grave doubt, whether those who adopt them have really any acquaintance, either with classical literature or with legal forms.

Once again, and for the last time, we note in our survey of legal history, the almost dead blank of the eighteenth century in the history of civil procedure. Save for the small reforms before noticed, the statute-book from 1710–1830 yields scarcely a grain of harvest; while the Rules and Orders of Court, though they appear with some regularity, are confined to small points of no special importance. A Royal Commission to examine the scandalous abuses of the Court of Chancery was appointed in 1826; but, as it was presided over by Lord Eldon, it is not, perhaps, surprising that it should have developed into something like an apologia for that nest of hoary abuses. Not until the year 1831 was any serious attempt made to reform the Court of Chancery. But it will, perhaps, be well to adhere to the order hitherto followed, and deal first with the important changes in Common Law procedure which took place in the years 1832–3. During those two years, four important statutes dealing with the procedure of the Common Law Courts were passed, and must receive a few words of notice.

Silence of the Eighteenth Century

The first of these, the Uniformity of Process Act, 1832,[1] was aimed at abolishing a very grievous scandal which had grown up from historical causes, but which now remained as a mere oppression of the suitor, and a source of profit to the unscrupulous official and practitioner. As we have seen,[2] the gradual introduction of the various common law remedies, and their distribution among the three Common Law Courts, had given rise to great differences of procedure. Not only had each action its appropriate process; but, where the action might

Uniformity of Process

[1] 2 Will. IV, c. 39.

[2] *Ante*, pp. 169–174.

be commenced in more than one court, this appropriate process might be still further specialized by the Rules of the court actually chosen. The consequence was, that the way of the litigant was beset with various traps; some of them meaning death to his action if he fell into them, others merely involving him in expense to recover his lost ground. At one time, no doubt, these differences had all had meanings; but these meanings had long disappeared and been forgotten, with the result, that the most successful practitioner in the Common Law Courts was not the man with the greatest grasp of principle, or the strongest sense of justice, but the man with the memory for irrelevant details, and the least scruple in making use of them. The practical over-lapping of jurisdictions of these courts, which, as we have also seen,[1] was chiefly brought about by the manipulation of these peculiarities of procedure, made it all the greater scandal that the conduct of a Common Law action should resemble an obscure game of chance, in which the rules were determimed by forgotten authorities.

The Uniformity of Process Act, 1832,[2] then, attempted to provide that, with a few necessary exceptions, every Common Law personal action should follow, *mutatis mutandis*, the same steps, at least in all its initial stages. The first step was to be a simple writ of summons stating briefly the nature of the action, and requiring an appearance to be entered by the defendant within a limited time. This writ was to be served personally on the defendant;[3] but, if personal service could not be effected, the defendant might be distrained by the sheriff to compel his appearance.[4] Then came a momentous change from the old superstitious rule that proceedings could not continue in the defendant's absence. If the sheriff returned *non est inventus* and *nulla bona* to the Distringas, the Court might allow the plaintiff to enter an appearance for the defendant,[5] instead of resorting to the old cumbrous process of outlawry. Thus, the result of the defendant's contumacy would be, that judgment would be given against him in his absence. And thus the process of civil outlawry became reserved, practically, for cases on which the plaintiff was entitled to proceed to arrest the defendant for failure to appear; and, as we have seen,[6] these cases were swept away by

[1] *Ante*, pp. 169–174. [2] 2 Will. IV, c. 39, s. 1. [3] S. 3.
[4] *Ibid.* [5] *Ibid.* [6] *Ante*, p. 348.

the Judgments Act, 1838.[1] The Act of 1832 made special provision[2] for the cases of defendants really (not fictitiously) in custody in the Marshalsea or the Fleet, and for members of Parliament entitled to privilege from arrest on civil process. Various minor regulations connected with writs were added; and, as we have seen,[3] a very useful Rule-making power was conferred on the judges, for the purpose of giving effect to the Act. It should, however, be carefully noted, that the statute makes no attempt to abolish 'forms of action'; *i.e.* as appears by the Schedule of forms annexed to the Act, the plaintiff was still bound to name his proper writ, and, if he chose the wrong one, he was, presumably, non-suited as before.

The reform begun in the year 1832, in the initiatory proceedings at common law, was carried much further with regard to the later stages by the Civil Procedure Act of the following year.[4] Beginning[5] with a frank recognition of the fact that the amendment of a subtle and complicated piece of machinery, like the 'special pleading' system, could not be undertaken by laymen, the legislature empowers and requires the Common Law judges,[6] within five years from the passing of the Act, to produce a set of Rules and Orders, to be approved by Parliament, for regulating common law pleadings, especially with a view to diminishing delay, formalities, and expense. It then proceeds to abolish a number of surviving procedural anomalies, such as 'wager of law,'[7] 'venue,'[8] and close days,[9] or holidays, on which no procedural steps could be taken, to some of which reference has previously been made. It lays down the rule[10] limiting actions on sealed contracts (or 'specialties') to a period of twenty years, penal actions to two years, and several other kinds of claims to six years[11] after the cause of action arises. Finally, various procedural difficulties, which really amounted to deprivation of rights, were specially abolished. Thus, the rule that a right of action in Tort perished with the

Civil Procedure Act, 1833

[1] 1 & 2 Vict. c. 110, s. 1. (Civil outlawry was formally abolished by the Civil Procedure Acts Repeal Act, 1879, s. 3.)
[2] Ss. 8, 9. [3] *Ante*, pp. 189, 190. [4] 3 & 4 Will. IV, c. 42.
[5] S. 1. [6] *Ibid.* [7] S. 13.
[8] S. 22. Before this time, 'a local' action (*i.e.* an action relating to land) could only be tried in the county where the land was situated.
[9] S. 43. [10] Ss. 3–5.
[11] This was the normal time fixed for personal action by the Limitation Act, 1623 (21 Jac. I, c. 16). But the wording of that statute left many loop-holes.

death of either party, was partially modified by the sections allowing executors or administrators to sue[1] in respect of recent damage to the land of their deceased, and to be sued [2] for similar damage done by their deceased or on simple contracts entered into by him. Juries were allowed to award interest, in addition to the principal debt, in certain cases; even where it was not specially stipulated for.[3] The personal representatives of a lessor were empowered to distrain, within six months of the decease, for arrears falling due in the deceased's lifetime.[4]

The judges of the Common Law Courts made some use of the authority conferred on them by the Civil Procedure Act, 1833; and, in the year 1834, produced a set of *General Rules and Orders* for the conduct of pleadings in the superior Courts of Common Law.[5] They contain some reports of importance, of too technical a nature to be dealt with here. But they probably failed to satisfy the ardent hopes of the reformers who framed the Act of 1833; and it is with some suspicion that we read, in the preface to Mr. Joseph Chitty's edition of the following year, the triumphant claim, that the new Rules have 'not occasioned any material alteration either in the principles or the forms of pleading.'[6] A somewhat more drastic method of reform, though, as the author of the book just referred to suggests, it might have been 'annoying to an aged author,'[7] would have been welcome in the interests of justice.

The other two statutes referred to are mainly concerned with a matter which is always of first-rate importance in legal procedure, and which has a direct effect on substantive law, viz. restriction on the pursuit of ancient claims. We have seen already, in this chapter,[8] how the subject had been touched by the Civil Procedure Act, 1833; but the provisions of the Real Property Limitation Act, 1833, and the Prescription Act, 1832, were found more sweeping. We take the former first, as dealing with more familiar topics.

Theoretically, by far the most important clause of the Real Property Limitation Act, 1833, is that which abolishes,[9] at one

[1] S. 2.

[2] S. 14. This was the last surviving shred of the 'tortious' character of Assumpsit. As we have seen (*ante*, p. 140) it had really been abolished by judicial decision.

[3] Ss. 28, 29.

[4] Ss. 37, 38.

[5] Given in the Appendix to *A Concise View . . . of Pleadings* (2d ed. 1835), by Joseph Chitty, pp. 39–58.

[6] P. iii.

[7] *Ibid.*

[8] *Ante*, p. 351.

[9] 3 & 4 Will. IV, c. 27, s. 36.

fell swoop, almost the whole[1] of the 'real' and 'mixed' actions to recover land, which once were the pride and boast of English lawyers. In fact, these actions had almost entirely disappeared, long before 1833;[2] and when, in the period of grace allowed for the taking effect of the Act, an attempt was made to revive them, the most eminent practitioners displayed the grossest ignorance, even of the common terminology of the subject. Their true connection with the main purport of the statute was, that the period within which they could be brought had been limited by all sorts of conditions, not necessarily effluxion of time;[3] while their disappearance left the more modern procedure by Ejectment or Chancery action without fixed limits of time. It is true, that the statute of 1623,[4] formerly referred to, had prohibited any entry upon land after twenty years from the time at which the right accrued; but, as the entry in Ejectment was purely fictitious, it could easily be dated as at any time.

Abolition of 'Real' Actions

The main purport of the Real Property Limitation Act, 1833, is to be found in the second section, which provides that no person shall make an entry or distress, or bring an action, or suit in Equity,[5] to recover any land or rent, after twenty years have elapsed since his right to do so first accrued. Various special provisions are added for special cases; as where the claimant is under disability,[6] or his interest is by way of remainder or reversion,[7] right, and to meet the difficulty occasioned by tenancies of uncertain duration.[8] Even for cases of disability, however, the extreme limit is forty years from the accrual of the right to bring an action;[9] except that patrons or incumbents of ecclesiastical benefices are to have two incumbencies,[10] or sixty years, and that advowsons can be recovered at any time within three incumbencies or sixty years.[11] Two points should, however, be

New Time Limit

[1] The exceptions are the Writs of Right of Dower, Dower *unde nihil habet*, *Quare Impedit*, and Ejectment.

[2] They had been, of course, superseded by the action of Ejectment (*ante*, pp. 173–177).

[3] The most general enactments on the subject appear to have been the 32 Hen. VIII (1540) c. 2, and the 1 Mary, st. II (1553) c. 5. These statutes generally fixed a limit of sixty years.

[4] 21 Jac. I, c. 16, s. 1 (3).

[5] S. 24.

[6] S. 16. If the period has once commenced to run, a supervening disability will not suspend it.

[7] S. 3.

[8] Ss. 7, 8.

[9] S. 17.

[10] S. 29.

[11] S. 36. (There is an extreme limit of 100 years.)

carefully noted on the Act. The first is, that 'rent,' in the main section,[1] does not include the most common rent of all, viz. rent-service; it being the steady doctrine of the Courts that no failure to enforce his rights can bar the right of a landlord during the continuance of a term, or cause the statute to run against him till its expiry.[2] The second is, that though, logically, the Act is purely procedural, yet, in fact, adverse possession of land for twenty years will, save in exceptional cases, confer a positive title on the possessor. This result is due to section 34 of the Act, which provides that, with the expiry of the period during which he has the right to bring an action, the title itself of the claimaint shall be extinguished. For, if the former owner may not disturb the possessor, the latter is, to all intents and purposes, owner; even though the Court may hesitate to force his title on an unwilling purchaser. It should be remembered, however, that, by a well-known decision of the Judicial Committee, though an adverse possessor may hand on his possession, even before maturity, by assignment, devise, or inheritance,[3] yet, if he abandons his possession, the right of the true owner, and, consequently, the period of limitation, begins *de novo*.[4]

The period of limitation laid down by the Act of 1833 has been further cut down by the amending Act of 1874[5] from twenty years to twelve; but the general scheme of the Act of 1833 remains untouched.[6]

Prescription

The Prescription Act, 1832, is concerned with those 'incorporeal hereditaments,'[7] which, not being susceptible of possession, cannot be acquired by entry. For the benefit of persons who had *de facto* exercised such rights without formal evidence of title, the common law had invented the doctrine of 'immemorial user,' *i.e.* it allowed such a claim to be raised either by a plaintiff or a defendant, by an

[1] S. 2.

[2] *Archbold v. Scully* (1861) 9 H. L. C., at p. 375, *per* Lord Cranworth; *Walter v. Yalden* [1902] 2 K.B. 304. (Of course, s. 42 limits recovery of arrears of rent-service.)

[3] *Asher v. Whitlock* (1865) L.R. 1 Q.B. 1; *Perry v. Clissold* [1907] A.C. 73.

[4] *Trustees and Executors Co. v. Short* (1888) L.R. 13 App. Ca. 793.

[5] 37 & 38 Vict. c. 57.

[6] A rather important recent amendment of s. 25 is s. 8 of the Trustee Act, 1888 (51 & 52 Vict. c. 59), which allows even trustees to plead the Statutes of Limitation in certain cases.

[7] *Ante*, pp. 92–95.

allegation that the plaintiff (or defendant) and his ancestors, or 'those whose estate he hath, had openly, peaceably, and of right,' exercised the right claimed 'from the time whereof the memory of man runneth not to the contrary.' But, inasmuch as, by the common law, such an allegation meant, strictly, a claim of continuous user since 1189,[1] and as it became manifestly impossible to bring actual evidence of such user the Courts used to allow a proof of user for twenty years to raise a presumption of title. This presumption was, at different periods, put in different forms; either as that of immemorial user, or that of a 'lost grant.' But, in the former case, it was liable to be defeated by equally artificial evidence, *e.g.* that, at some period after 1189, but more than twenty years before the action, the dominant and servient tenements had been vested in one person, who could not, of course, exercise a true servitude over his own land, while juries sometimes shrank from declaring, on oath, the existence of a grant which they knew did not, in fact, exist.

It was to remedy these defects, and not to do away with common law prescription, that the Prescription Act of 1832[2] was passed. Like another Act associated with the name of Lord Tenterden,[3] it is not free from verbal inaccuracies; but its general scheme is simple. It does not affect tithes, rents, or services,[4] nor (it is believed) franchises or customary rights.[5] Advowsons, too, as we have seen,[6] fall under the Real Property Limitation Acts, and not under the Prescription Act. With these exceptions, however, the Prescription Act deals with easements and profits under three heads, and provides that proof of continuous user for certain periods, in the course of legal proceedings, shall have certain definite legal consequences. Proof of the enjoyment of the access of light to a building for twenty years, gives the claimant an absolute title to the light as against all persons but the Crown; unless the objector can prove that the claimant enjoyed it by virtue of a written agreement.[7] Similar proof as

[1] The date of the accession of Richard I, taken as the 'commencement of legal memory.'

[2] 2 & 3 Will. IV, c. 71.

[3] Statute of Frauds Amendment Act, 1828 (9 Geo. IV, c. 14).

[4] S. 1.

[5] Franchises are not mentioned. It is a little doubtful whether customary rights are included (*Mercer v. Denne* [1905] 2 Ch. at p. 586).

[6] *Ante*, pp. 353-355.

[7] S. 3. (Presumably a written agreement consistent with the claim would not invalidate it.)

to any other easement, raises a presumption of title which cannot be defeated merely by showing a commencement at some prior period since the commencement of legal memory, though it may be defeated in any other way.[1] Proof of similar enjoyment of such a right for forty years, will confer a title as against all persons (including the Crown); unless there is a written agreement against it.[2] As regards profits *à prendre*, these stand on the same footing as easements other than lights; except that the respective periods of enjoyment are thirty and sixty years.[3] The recent decision of the House of Lords in *Home and Colonial Stores v. Colls*,[4] has cut down the 'enjoyment' of light claimable under the statute to the amount necessary for reasonable convenience; though this conclusion is exactly contrary to the words of the section. The Act can only be relied upon in support of enjoyment continued until within one year[5] 'immediately prior to the commencement of the suit or action in which it is questioned'; enjoyment without litigation, therefore, confers no title under the Act. For this, and other reasons stated, 'common law prescription' is by no means extinct; and is, in fact, not infrequently resorted to.[6] Apparently, however, the Act of 1832 has abolished the necessity for suing in the name of the owner of the fee, in all cases.[7]

Chancery Reform

In the year 1830, the very modest result of the Chancery Commission of 1826, appeared in the shape of an Act to deal with commitments for contempt in not answering bills in Equity.[8] The Court of Chancery had had the same difficulty with contumacious defendants as the Courts of Common Law; and, though it had dealt with them in a somewhat more effective way than by the clumsy process of outlawry, it had manifested the same tenderness, amounting almost to timidity, in dealing with absentees. The elaborate provisions of the Contempt of Court Act, 1830, seem really to amount mainly to this: that if the Court is quite satisfied that the defendant has either been served with the subpœna, or is deliberately evading

[1] S. 2. [2] *Ibid.* [3] S. 1.

[4] [1904] A.C. 179. The foundation of the action is declared to be Nuisance, not diminution of actual enjoyment.

[5] S. 4. (Interruption for less than a year does not count.)

[6] *E.g. Hyman v. Van den Bergh* [1908] 1 Ch. 167; *Hulbert v. Dale* (1909) 78 L.J. Ch. 457; *Whitmores v. Stanford* [1909] 1 Ch. 427.

[7] S. 5. [8] 11 Geo. IV & 1 Will. IV, c. 36.

service, and is not labouring under any of the usual disabilities, he may be proceeded against in his absence.[1] There are also elaborate rules for making the process of the Court effectual;[2] and the time for petitioning for a rehearing of a cause is limited to six months.[3] But nowhere in this Act, nor in the Act of twelve years later,[4] whereby, after the transfer to the Court of Chancery of the equity jurisdiction of the Exchequer,[5] certain minor changes in the Chancery offices were made, is there any evidence of a strong reforming hand. In fact, a good deal of these last two statutes is taken up with providing liberal compensation for the few dispossessed officials, and with creating new offices.

The real period of reform in the superior Courts does not begin until the year 1850, when, as the result of two Royal Commissions, serious steps were taken to amend the procedure of the higher tribunals. From that year onwards, we notice two converging streams of statutes, having for their objects, not merely the improvement, on existing lines, of the procedure of the respective Courts, but the breaking down of what was, both theoretically and practically, the greatest blot on the system of English civil procedure, viz. the conflict of, or, at least, the separation between, Law and Equity. We have seen how this conflict arose,[6] and how, after some centuries of cautious preparation for hostilities, Equity won a decisive victory at the commencement of the seventeenth century.[7] After the latter event, there was no substantial doubt that, if the Court of Chancery determined to alter a rule of law, it would succeed in doing so. But the manner of doing it might be grievously slow, and intolerably costly to the suitor.

Broadly speaking, Equity jurisdiction fell under three heads. Under the first, it was '**exclusive**,' *i.e.* Chancery (or the Exchequer on its Equity side) dealt with the matter from beginning to end. This was the least vexatious, though not, perhaps, the least costly form of equity. It covered such cases as trusts and (after the close of the seventeenth century) the administration of the estates of deceased persons. Under the second head, Equity's jurisdiction was '**concurrent**,' *i.e.* the suitor could get one class of remedies in Equity, and an-

'Exclusive' Equity

[1] S. 3. [2] S. 15. [3] S. 6. [4] 5 & 6 Vict. (1842) c. 103.
[5] 5 Vict. (1841) c. 5 [6] *Ante*, pp. 80, 163–166. [7] *Ante*, pp. 165, 166.

other at Common Law; but not both from either. He had, therefore, to bring two processes, if he wished to obtain all his remedies. Or, again, it might be that a defendant, sued at law, would rely on a defence only available in Equity. It would be necessary for him to file a separate bill in Chancery, to restrain the proceedings at Common Law. Obvious examples would be in a case of contract; in which the plaintiff sought both damages (the common law remedy) and a decree of specific performance (the remedy of Equity); or in which a defendant, sued at law, wished to set up the equitable defence of 'undue influence.' Finally, under the third head, Equity jurisdiction was '**auxiliary**,' to that of Common Law; as where a plaintiff, unable to secure the right to inspect his opponent's documents in a common law action, filed a supplementary 'bill of discovery' in Equity. This was, of course, a dilatory and costly process.

'Concurrent' Equity

'Auxiliary' Equity

Thus the two streams of legislation to which reference has been made had for their secondary objects (*a*) the bestowal of equitable powers on the Common Law Courts, (*b*) the bestowal of common law powers on the Court of Chancery; in order to prevent the waste and delay caused by the necessity of recurring to rival jurisdictions. The former stream is represented by the Common Law Procedure Acts of 1852, 1854, and 1860; the latter by the Chancery Amendment Acts of 1852 and 1858. Probably the successful establishment of the County Court system, with its cheap and rapid procedure, in the year 1846,[1] had something to do with the progress of the transformation.

The Common Law Procedure Act, 1852,[2] is an enormously long statute; and only one or two of its leading provisions can be alluded to. But these will serve to show that the spirit of reform had got to work at last. The danger of being defeated by the choice of a wrong 'form of action' was definitely abolished by the clause[3] which provides, that all personal actions shall be commenced by a simple writ of summons, in common form, making no mention in the body of it of any particular cause of action.[4] But, further, where the claim is for a mere debt or 'liquidated' sum of money, the plaintiff, by endorsing 'special' particulars of his claim,

Common Law Procedure Acts

[1] 9 & 10 Vict. c. 95.
[2] 15 & 16 Vict. c. 76.
[3] S. 2.
[4] See form in Sched. A.

may save himself the costs of formal pleadings, by dispensing with further particulars of demand; and may, in the event of the defendant not appearing, obtain summary judgment for the amount of his claim.[1] The power of amendment, all through the proceedings, is to be almost unlimited;[2] and all kinds of venerable technical rules, as to joinder of parties and claims,[3] 'abatement' of writs,[4] fictitious averments in pleadings, formal production of documents (*e.g.* '*profert*' and '*oyer*' of bonds),[5] 'express colour,'[6] form of pleadings in Contract and Tort respectively,[7] pleading of inconsistent pleas,[8] and including several matters in one plea,[9] are abolished. With a view to saving of expense, many unnecessary forms, such as the 'rule to plead,'[10] and the elaborate steps taken to get together a jury,[11] are declared unnecessary, and forbidden. The time for appealing by way of 'error apparent on the record' is reduced to six years.[12] The action of Ejectment, which, as will be remembered,[13] escaped the abolition of the 'real' actions in 1833, is simplified; only such differences from the ordinary personal action being allowed as are rendered necessary by the fact that the proceedings 'savour of the realty.' Finally, with a view to rendering more effectual injunctions and orders to stay proceedings, it is provided[14] that the tribunal in which the proceedings sought to be stopped are pending, shall take direct notice of the injunction or order, by staying all further proceedings; instead of keeping up the fiction that the injunction or order is addressed merely to the plaintiff and not to the court itself.

Contemporaneously with the Common Law Procedure Act, 1852, was passed another statute almost equally important. So long as the Common Law officials were numerous, and paid by fees, it was hopeless to expect that statutes having for their object the simplification and cheapening of Common Law procedure would have a fair field. Accordingly, by the **Common Law Courts Act, 1852,**[15] the whole staffs of the King's Bench, Common Pleas, and Exchequer were reorganized. Useless and hereditary offices, such as those of the Marshals of the Court,[16] the Chief Proclamator of the Common Pleas, and the Usher of the Ex-

[1] Ss. 25, 27. [2] S. 36. [3] Ss. 34–41. [4] Ss. 38–39.
[5] S. 55. [6] S. 64. [7] S. 74. [8] S. 80.
[9] S. 81. [10] Ss. 62, 82. [11] Ss. 104–113. [12] S. 146.
[13] *Ante*, p. 353, n. 1. [14] S. 226. [15] 15 & 16 Vict. c. 73. [16] S. 1.

chequer,[1] with the patronage attaching to them,[2] were abolished, and their nominal duties transferred to working officials.[3] The performance of duties by deputy,[4] except in cases of actual disablement,[5] was forbidden. Payment by fees was suppressed; and fixed salaries substituted for the officials retained.[6] Finally, the bad habit, which had clung like a pestilence to the administration of justice for centuries, whereby officials of the courts acted as the private advisers of litigants, was entirely forbidden;[7] this time, at last, with success. Perhaps the best testimony to the effectiveness of the reforms of 1852 is the fact, that men of a slightly later generation, familiar with the working of the courts half a century after, find it difficult to believe that such abuses as are plainly described by the legislation of that year, should really have existed in the middle of the nineteenth century.

Considerable further progress in the reform of common law procedure was made by the long **Common Law Procedure Act, 1854**;[8] especially in facilitating the conduct of arbitrations under the supervision of the Court,[9] and the drawing up of agreed statements of fact ('special cases') by the parties or by an inferior tribunal, for the opinion of the superior Court on the questions of law involved.[10] But the great merit of the Act of 1854 is, that it makes a decided advance in the direction previously described, of drawing together the jurisdictions in Law and Equity. It will be recollected that, by Lord Brougham's Act of 1851,[11] the parties to an action had recently been rendered competent and compellable witnesses, with certain exceptions. The new statute, accordingly, virtually introduces[12] the machinery of 'discovery' and 'interrogatories' into Common Law procedure, and thus renders the filing of a 'bill of discovery' in Equity unnecessary. The old and rather cumbrous remedy by Mandamus, or positive order for the fulfilment of a quasi-public duty, is extended to ordinary private liabilities;[13] and the historic unwillingness of the Common Law courts to order specific delivery up of a chattel claimed by the plaintiff, instead of merely awarding damages, is at last swept away.[14] The power of the Common Law courts to issue prohibitory injunctions at any

[1] S. 22. [2] S. 23. [3] S. 32. [4] S. 30. [5] S. 6. [6] Ss. 12, 21.
[7] S. 11. [8] 17 & 18 Vict. c. 125. [9] Ss. 3–17. [10] Ss. 4, 5.
[11] 14 & 15 Vict. c. 99, s. 2. [12] Ss. 46–55.
[13] Ss. 68–73. (This reform has not been particularly successful.)
[14] S. 78.

stage of the proceedings is declared in the most general terms;[1] and, perhaps most important of all, the defendant is empowered, subject to the discretion of the Court, to plead, in a Common Law action, any defence which he might have set up in a Court of Equity.[2] Thus, instead of having to resort to a separate suit in Equity to restrain the Common Law action, the defendant in that action gets a decision of the point, at much less expense, in the original proceedings.

The Common Law Procedure Acts of 1852 and 1854 were carried still further by the **Common Law Procedure Act, 1860**;[3] the two most noteworthy provisions of which were, that which extended to the Common Law courts the powers long enjoyed by Equity of giving relief against forfeiture of leases owing to non-payment of rent or insurance premiums,[4] and that which abolished the few remaining 'real actions' of Right of Dower, Dower *unde nihil habet*, and *Quare impedit*,[5] and substituted for them ordinary personal actions commenced by Writ of Summons. But it is time that we turn now to the contemporary reforms in Chancery procedure.

Chancery Amendment Acts

The first of these required the passing of no less than four statutes in the year 1852. By the **Court of Chancery Act**,[6] the venerable office of 'Master in Ordinary' was swept away,[7] and provision made for the speedy winding up of causes which had long slept in the security of the Masters' chambers.[8] Most of the more important duties which had hitherto fallen to the disestablished officials were to be performed by the Chancery judges[9] themselves, sitting in the privacy of 'chambers';[10] and the rest by 'chief' and subordinate clerks attached to each of the Chancery Courts. To the layman, it might seem that this great change merely amounted to the substitution of a Chief Clerk for a Master. In reality, it meant the entire abolition of a subordinate but semi-independent jurisdiction; for the Chief Clerks,[11] though they perform re-

[1] Ss. 79–82. [2] S. 83. [3] 23 & 24 Vict. c. 126. [4] Ss. 1, 2.

[5] S. 26. (The action of *Quare impedit* was brought to try the right to present to a vacant ecclesiastical benefice.)

[6] 15 & 16 Vict. c. 80. [7] S. 1. [8] Ss. 8, 10.

[9] These had been recently increased to five, by the appointment of two additional Vice-Chancellors. [10] Ss. 11–15.

[11] The ancient style of 'Master' has, in quite modern days (22nd February, 1897) been restored to these officials. But the ancient powers of the Masters have not been revived. The title was, apparently, restored by mere administrative direction;

sponsible duties, requiring the exercise of great technical skill, are, avowedly, only the judges' deputies, and will readily give any party desiring it an opportunity of taking the judges' opinion on any point, however trifling. Even the expert opinion of a new class of Chancery officials, the Conveyancing Counsel of the Court, may be questioned by suitors, and referred to the Court itself.[1] Though the conduct of business under the new system is not made the subject of detailed enactment in the statute, the latter contains a section [2] requiring the Chancellor, with the advice of two of the other Chancery judges, to make General Rules and Orders for the conduct of 'chamber' business; and this enactment was carried into effect on the 16th October, 1852.[3]

Meanwhile, however, the practice of the Court had been made the subject of a long statute, the **Chancery Amendment Act**, 1852.[4] Its provisions are too technical to be set out here. The most important changes made by the Act are the substitution of simple service of a copy of the bill, or initiatory complaint, for the elaborate machinery of 'subpœna' and 'claim' which had grown up around it,[5] the abolition of the formal process of 'obtaining leave' to answer a bill,[6] the power given to the plaintiff to move for a summary decree on facts admitted or not denied by the defendant,[7] and the corresponding power given to the defendant to apply to dismiss a bill not duly prosecuted,[8] the introduction of oral testimony at the request of any party, in place of the purely written interrogatories and depositions hitherto used by the Court,[9] the cutting down of objections for 'want of parties,' [10] the power conferred on the Court, in a foreclosure action, to order a sale of the mortgaged property instead of a foreclosure,[11] and generally, to order a sale of any real estate the subject of a suit,[12] and, finally, the abolition of the necessity for sending a case for the opinion of a Common Law court, on a point of common law which has arisen incidentally in the suit.[13]

and, presumably, it will have no effect on the statutory qualifications for the office of Master of the Supreme Court, formerly attached exclusively to the Queen's Bench Division. [1] Ss. 40–41. [2] S. 38.

[3] Order entitled 'Proceedings at Judges' Chambers.' [4] 15 & 16 Vict. c. 86.

[5] Ss. 2–5. [6] S. 13. [7] S. 15. [8] S. 27.

[9] S. 30. (But the evidence is to be taken by 'examiners,' not at the actual hearing of the cause.) [10] S. 42. [11] S. 48. [12] S. 55.

[13] S. 61. (This provision was strengthened and made compulsory by a statute of the year 1862.)

The Chancery reform legislation of 1852, comprised also the **Suitors' Funds Act**,[1] containing elaborate rules for the administration of the vast funds under the control of the Court, and abolishing a host of offices with weird titles; and, in the year following, the legislation of 1852 was supplemented by three additional statutes,[2] only one of which, that which substituted ordinary Commissioners for Oaths for the old Masters Extraordinary in Chancery, is worthy of special reference. But the **Chancery Amendment Act**, 1858,[3] made an important change in the direction of 'fusion' by empowering the Court of Chancery[4] to award damages in any case of contract or tort in which it had power to give an equitable remedy by way of injunction or decree of specific performance,[5] and either in substitution for, or in addition to, those equitable remedies. Inasmuch as practically all civil actions are either actions for breach of contract or actions on torts, and inasmuch as the Court of Chancery had long been able, by virtue of its discretionary power, to grant injunctions and decrees for specific performance, to deal with all actions on contracts and torts, the Act might incautiously be read, or might even, perhaps, have been fairly interpreted, to confer on the Court of Chancery co-ordinate jurisdiction with the Courts of Common Law in all common law actions. In fact, the statute was not so interpreted. The Court of Chancery steadily declined to entertain ordinary actions for damages on the ground that it had the power (if it chose to exercise it) of granting injunctions and decrees of specific performance in such cases. In practice, it continued to entertain only suits substantially brought to obtain equitable remedies; and only in such cases, where the right, or quasi-right, to an equitable remedy was clear, but there was some special inconvenience in granting such remedies, did it fall back on its statutory powers and award damages instead. By a somewhat rash exercise of the revising broom, the statute has been lately repealed;[6] but it has since been judicially held that the powers conferred by it on the Court of Chancery and its successor, the High Court of Justice, still remain.[7] To close

[1] 15 & 16 Vict. c. 87. (The title is not official.)

[2] 16 & 17 Vict. c. 22 (examiners), 78 (Commissioners for Oaths), 98 (Suitors' Funds).

[3] 21 & 22 Vict. c. 27. [4] S. 1. [5] S. 2.

[6] Statute Law Revision Act, 1883, s. 3.

[7] See the position of the statute, and the use to be made of it, elaborately discussed by the learned judges in the case of *Sayers v. Collier* (1884) 28 Ch. D. 103.

this brief account of the reforms of the years 1850–60, it may be mentioned that, in the latter year, an elaborate set of *Consolidated General Orders of the High Court of Chancery,*[1] ranging from 1556 to 1895, was issued by Lord Campbell, with the concurrence of all the other Chancery judges.

The Judicature Acts

Thus, at long last, as a visible emblem of unity was daily growing in the new Palace of Justice then being erected in the Strand, half way between the historic site of Westminster and the historic centre of the commercial capital of the world, there began to grow up, in the minds of reformers, the vision of a great and united Supreme Court of Justice, with uniform principles, uniform law, and uniform procedure. With a curious indifference to the facts of history, some of the most distinguished leaders of the new movement appeared to draw their inspiration from the past, rather than the future. Much was heard of an imaginary *Curia Regis* of ancient times, which was supposed to have been a court of supreme and universal jurisdiction, in which all the grievances of the subject were redressed; and earnest appeals were addressed to the world to return to primitive simplicity and uniformity. Those who have read the earlier chapters of this work will realize that, if those chapters are at all a faithful picture, the facts were the exact opposite of those imagined by the reformers who framed the Judicature Acts; that anomaly, privilege, multiplicity, and narrowness of jurisdiction, not uniformity and simplicity, were the marks of the medieval system of justice. But it is not the first time that the baseless visions of an imaginary Golden Age have worked practical good; and we need not be the less grateful to the reformers of 1870, that their views of legal history were unsound.

The Royal Commission

It was in the year 1867 that a Royal Commission was appointed 'to enquire into the operation and effect of the present constitution of' (the various Superior Courts in England and Wales) . . . 'and into the operation and effect of the present separation and division of jurisdictions between the said several Courts.' The Commission made two reports. The first is dated Lady Day, 1869. It is an admirably clear and concise document, dealing with the organization of business

[1] Published by Stevens & Sons, 1860.

and the procedure of the Superior Courts. The second, dated 3rd July, 1872, made after an enlargement of the scope of the Commission's enquiry, to include the Courts of Quarter Sessions and the inferior courts, is marked by great differences of opinion, whereas the first Report is almost unanimous. The recommendations of the majority in the second Report virtually amounted to a proposal for the incorporation of the County Courts as inferior branches of the High Courts of Justice, the first or lower stage of the proposed Supreme Court, and the consequent virtual suppression of civil business at the local sittings, or Assises, of the Superior Courts. These recommendations have never been acted upon; and need not here be further discussed.

The chief recommendations contained in the first Report of the Royal Commission were five in number; and they have since been substantially carried out by one or more of the numerous Judicature Acts [1] which have since been passed.

The Supreme Court.

The first and most important recommendation was the union of all the existing superior tribunals into one Supreme Court of Judicature, organized into two stages, of first instance and appeal. As we have previously seen, practically the whole of the Superior Courts had become directly royal tribunals; there was, therefore, no question of abolishing independent jurisdictions. But, owing to their history, they had developed different procedures, and, to a substantial extent, actual differences of law, and had, consequently, not infrequently come into conflict with one another. In any case, it was something approaching a scandal, that different tribunals of co-ordinate jurisdiction, professing to administer the same law and to derive their authority from the same source, should thus differ; and the only way to conciliate rivalries was to incorporate them in one body. This plan is actually carried out by sections 3–5 of the Judicature Act, 1873; [2] and the signs and symbols of the union thus effected are to be found in the two cardinal rules of the new system, that no objection for want of jurisdiction can be taken in any branch of the Supreme Court,[3] and that no

[1] Judicature Acts of 1873, 1874, 1875, 1877, 1879, 1881, 1884, 1890, 1891, 1894, 1899, 1902, 1909, 1910.

[2] 36 & 37 Vict. c. 66. The position of the Palatinate Courts of Common Pleas at Lancaster and Durham is a little peculiar. These courts are not incorporated into the Supreme Court (s. 3); but their jurisdictions are transferred to the High Court (s. 16).

[3] S. 16.

injunction or prohibition shall issue from any tribunal of that Court to restrain any proceeding pending in any other.[1] Thus, though, to a superficial observer, the appearance of the names of the old tribunals, as titles of the 'Divisions' of the new High Court of Justice, may appear to indicate a mere change of name, the truth is very different. Though the Chancery Division in practice still retains most of the business which would have fallen to it had it continued to be the High Court of Chancery,[2] it does so only as a matter of convenience. Any branch or tribunal of the High Court can exercise, not merely all the old powers of Chancery, but also all the old powers of all the other tribunals incorporated into the High Court; so that, in words which are the keynote of the statute, 'all matters so in controversy between the said parties respectively may be completely and finally determined, and all multiplicity of legal proceedings concerning any of such matters avoided.'[3]

The House of Lords and the Judicial Committee

With one matter the Royal Commission dealt delicately; the first Judicature Act, boldly. It was not quite clear whether the scope of the Commission's enquiry extended to the highest appellate tribunals, viz. the House of Lords and the Judicial Committee of the Privy Council. The Commission made it fairly clear, however,[4] that it would welcome the abolition of that surviving feature of medievalism which linked legislative and executive bodies to the judicature. The statute of 1873 accordingly provided,[5] that no appeal should in the future be brought from any judgment or order of any of the tribunals incorporated into the Supreme Court, to the House of Lords or the Judicial Committee. But the Judicature Act, 1873, did not take effect till November, 1875.[6] In the interval, a change of Government occurred; and an amending Act of the latter year[7] restored the threatened jurisdictions. The reversal of the policy of 1873 has been productive of important results. Nearly all the decisions which, in recent years, have provoked strong feeling, have been decisions either of the House of Lords or of the Judicial Committee, which latter tribunal is composed, practically, of the same persons as those who

[1] S. 24 (5). [2] S. 34. [3] S. 24 (7). [4] First Report, pp. 20–21. [5] S. 20.

[6] It was intended originally, to take effect in November, 1874 (s. 2); but this clause was repealed by the Supreme Court of Judicature (Commencement) Act, 1874, s. 1.

[7] Judicature Act, 1875 (38 & 39 Vict. c. 77) s. 2.

de facto exercise the appellate jurisdiction of the House of Lords.[1] These persons are not technically 'judges'; but 'lords of appeal' or members of the Judicial Committee, *i.e.* persons whose functions are, at least partially, legislative and executive. It is not known how far their lordships regard themselves as bound by the strict rules of law in dealing with appeals; certainly their position in such matters, inherited as it is from remote history, is nowhere legally defined in documents accessible to the public.

Conflicting Rules of Law

One other important point was involved in the first great proposal of the Royal Commission. Though, doubtless, most of the differences in the rules administered by the different courts incorporated by the Judicature Act had grown out of differences of procedure, some of them had, in effect, hardened into rules of law. Still, if different legal rules are concerned with different subjects, the differences, though 'inelegant' (as a Roman jurist would have said) are not fatal to practical harmony. Different rules of succession to real and personal property have worked for ages in the same country without serious inconvenience. But when different tribunals apply different rules of law to the same subject-matter, then the fate of a litigant obviously depends on his choice of tribunal; and, when all tribunals are fused, there must be some means of deciding which rule is to prevail.

This was the object of the famous section 25 of the first Judicature Act. It dealt with the chief cases in which the rules of the incorporated courts differed on the same subjects; and decided between them. Thus, the rules of the Court of Bankruptcy differed from those of the Court of Chancery in the administration of insolvent estates; the rules of the Court of Bankruptcy were, at least partially, adopted.[2] The rules of the Court of Chancery differed from those of the Common Law Courts in many matters in which there was 'concurrent' jurisdiction; the rules of the Court of Chancery were preferred.[3]

[1] Any member of the House has a right to attend and vote at the hearing of appeal. But appeals may not be 'heard and determined' unless three Lords of Appeals are present at the hearing and determination (Appellate Jurisdiction Act, 1876, s. 5). No lay peer has taken part in an appeal since 1883.

[2] S. 25 (1), amended by s. 10 of the Act of 1875. Strictly speaking, there was no conflict; for the Court of Bankruptcy at that time only dealt with the estates of living debtors, Chancery only with those of deceased debtors. But the differences were a scandal.

[3] S. 25 (2)–(8).

In the principle on which damages for collision between ships were assessed, the rule of the Court of Admiralty differed from that of the Common Law Courts; the rule of Admiralty was adopted.[1] Finally, the section contains a general enactment [2] that, in any conflict between the rules of Equity and those of Common Law, 'with reference to the same matter,' the former shall prevail.

Before leaving this central change of the judicial system, it is necessary, even at the risk of being accused of boredom, for the historian to point out, that the Judicature Acts have not destroyed the distinction between Law and Equity, even in relation to the same matters. For obvious instance, legal estates and equitable interests in the same land can subsist comfortably side by side, and be governed by common law and equitable rules respectively. Legal remedies are still due *ex debito justitiæ*, equitable remedies only *ex gratiâ*. It is even true that, where no considerations of Equity forbid, or, as it is put, 'where the equities are equal,' the strict rule of Law is even superior to the rule of Equity.[3] It is only where, owing to a conflict between the rules of Law and of Equity, in the same matter, it is necessary, if the equitable rule is to prevail, that the common law rule should be set aside, that the concluding clause of section 25 applies.

Law and Equity still distinct

Only a few words can be given to the remaining, and less important, recommendations of the Royal Commission. The second aimed at the shortening of pleadings; and suggested, in effect, that, without the special leave of the Court, these should never exceed three in number, viz. (1) a brief statement of the plaintiff's claim, setting out the material facts, but neither the evidence nor the arguments, (2) a similar brief statement of the facts on which the defendant relies, and (3) a reply, or joinder of issue, by the plaintiff. If the defendant has any ground of action against the plaintiff, this should be made the subject of a counter-claim, delivered with the defence. Thus both claims could be tried in one action.[4] This recommendation was, virtually, adopted by the Act of 1873;[5] and has

Pleading

[1] S. 25 (9). [2] S. 25 (11).

[3] *Pilcher v. Rawlins* (1872) L.R. 7 Ch. App. 260 (land); *Joseph v. Lyons* (1884) 15 Q.B.D. 280 (chattels).

[4] First Report, pp. 11–12. [5] S. 69 and Schedule, 18–24.

since been made the subject of Rules enacted in pursuance of the statutory authority conferred by the Acts themselves.[1]

The third recommendation of the Commission was the abandonment of the jury system as the sole, or, at least, the ideal method of trial of questions of fact. The Report pointed out that, owing to the increasing complexity of legal business, there were many cases in which a decision of fact by a judge, or, in complicated matters of account, by a referee, was far preferable to the verdict of a jury. The Commission proposed, in effect, that the plaintiff should be allowed to choose, among these three, his own method of trial; subject, in the case of objection by the defendant, to the discretion of the Court.[2] This recommendation was substantially adopted by the Act of 1873;[3] and has been the subject of careful consideration by the Rules. But the unfettered choice originally proposed for the plaintiff has been, in effect, substantially restricted by the last named authority.[4] The plaintiff or the defendant may insist on a trial by jury in cases of slander, libel, false imprisonment, 'seduction,' or breach of promise of marriage;[5] but the Court may direct a trial without a jury of any question of fact which, before the Act, could have been tried without a jury, as well as any matter requiring any prolonged examination of documents or accounts, or any scientific or local investigation.[6] As a matter of practice, Chancery, in spite of statutory powers, rarely employed the jury system; and this practice is confirmed by the Rules, which forbid the trial by jury of any matter assigned by the Act of 1873 to the Chancery Division — except upon a judge's order.[7]

Jury System

The fourth recommendation of the Royal Commission contemplated little change in the existing practice. Owing to the enactments previously noticed,[8] almost all testimony (including that in the Probate, Divorce, and Admiralty Courts) was, in 1869, given orally at the trial. Only in Chancery the practice of taking evidence out of Court before 'Examiners' continued. It was proposed to adapt the Equity practice to

Evidence

[1] O. XIX. The Rules have also introduced the practice of obtaining summary judgment without pleadings, on a 'specially endorsed' writ (O. XIV).

[2] Report, pp. 12–13. [3] S. 56. [4] R. S. C. XXXVI. [5] R. 1.

[6] R. 3. These matters are usually tried by the Official Referees attached to the Court under ss. 57 and 83 of the Act of 1875.

[7] R. 3. [8] *Ante*, pp. 343, 344.

that of the other Courts;[1] and this proposal was accepted by Parliament, subject to the reservation, that evidence on interlocutory application might continue to be given by affidavit. The Act of 1873, however, contained a provision that, even on such occasions, a witness might, on the application of either party, be ordered to attend for cross-examination.[2]

The fifth recommendation of the Royal Commission was concerned with the sittings of the Court. Originally these were confined to four short 'Terms,' fixed by the ecclesiastical calendar. But, as legal business grew, more and more cases were disposed of outside these strict limits; and thus the 'sittings' of the Courts became much more extensive than the legal 'Terms.' Moreover, it was one of the few advantages of the cumbrous and antiquated system of Commissions, under which ordinary jury cases were tried, that there were no time limits to these trials; the King, though he was bound by statute to send judges or commissioners on circuit at least so many times a year, could (within wide limits) choose his own time for sending them.

Terms and Sittings

The Royal Commission in effect proposed,[3] that the sittings of the Court should constitute Terms; in other words, that all kinds of legal business should be capable of transaction at any time when the Courts were sitting. Further than that, the Commission made a most important recommendation, to the effect that, as regards the heavy business of the metropolitan area, in place of the existing system by which each of the three Common Law Courts held separate Nisi Prius sittings in London and Middlesex three times a year, there should be a common system of continuous sittings throughout the legal year for the Home Counties, in which all common law actions should be entered on a single list, and disposed of in rotation by as many judges as should be necessary, or could be spared, for the purpose. Even during the holding of the circuits, there were to be at least two Nisi Prius Courts sitting in London. Finally, the Commission recommended that the Home Circuit, as a separate entity, should be abolished altogether; its criminal work being absorbed by the Central Criminal Court established in 1834,[4] and its

[1] Report, p. 14.
[2] Ss. 36, 37.
[3] First Report, pp. 15–16.
[4] By the Central Criminal Court Act, 1834 (4 & 5 Will. IV, c. 36) for a metropolitan area carved out of the Home Counties. It sits twelve times a year for the decision of heavy criminal cases.

civil business being absorbed by the Nisi Prius Courts for Middlesex.

Most of these recommendations were adopted by Parliament, and appear in the Judicature Act, 1873. By that Act, the year is divided into Sittings and Vacations; and, for purposes of Court work, 'Terms' cease to exist.[1] Continuous sittings in London and Middlesex are provided for; and the formerly independent and fleeting Courts created by the opening of circuit commissions are, in effect, made branches of the Supreme Court.[2] But the ancient system of issuing special commissions for each sitting on assise or circuit is not disturbed;[3] and the proposal to abolish the Home Circuit is not adopted. A greater flexibility in the circuit system was rendered possible by the amending Judicature Act of 1875, which[4] empowered Her Majesty, by Order in Council, to fix the dates, seasons, and places for the holding of assise cases. But the somewhat hesitating suggestions of the Commission[5] for a re-arrangement of the basis of the circuit system were not adopted; and the reform of that system remains one of the most pressing needs of the present day.

Mention has, incidentally,[6] been made of the 'County Courts' established in the nineteenth century for the local decision of disputes in small matters. The need for such tribunals had been felt ever since the virtual disappearance of the ancient local courts of the shire and the Hundred, and the Courts Merchant of the chartered boroughs, at the close of the Middle Ages. These ancient courts had, as we have seen, been virtually destroyed by the rivalry of the circuit-system. But the machinery of the circuit-system was altogether too costly for the settlement of small disputes; and, when business of this kind increased, with the increase of wealth and population, in the eighteenth century, the corresponding need for cheap and speedy justice was met by the establishment, as occasion or urgency demanded, of special local tribunals, usually by virtue of private Acts of Parliament.[7] But this system, if system it can be called, was thoroughly bad. In

County Courts

[1] S. 26. (There are still a few dates regulated by the old Terms; and they are enshrined in the prandial arrangements of the Inns of Court.)

[2] S. 29.

[3] *Ibid.*

[4] 38 & 39 Vict. c. 77, s. 23.

[5] First Report, p. 17.

[6] *Ante*, p. 365.

[7] A list of the tribunals will be found in the Schedule to the County Courts Act of 1846.

spite of a hesitating attempt in the year 1754 [1] to introduce something like uniformity, these 'Courts of Request' or 'Conscience,' as they were commonly called, remained, for nearly another century, a mass of anomalous and isolated units, each governed by its own rules, and strictly limited in scope to a particular area.

Act of 1846

In the year 1846, however, a great and successful attempt at reform was made. By a statute of that year,[2] and Orders in Council thereunder, the whole of England and Wales was mapped out into 'circuits,' each provided with one (or, in rare cases, two), professional judges, and subdivided into 'districts,' each provided with a Court for the decision of cases involving limited amounts. Each judge visits the Courts within his circuit at frequent intervals, and disposes of cases awaiting trial, in a summary manner.[3] Generally speaking, though subject to certain exceptions, a case must be tried in the district in which it arises, or in which the defendant lives. The jurisdiction of the County Court, which was limited by the statute of 1846 to £50 for ordinary 'Common Law' business, and £500 in 'Equity' matters, has, by a later statute of 1903,[4] been increased to a limit of £100 in the former class; and there is power in the High Court to remit compulsorily any action within this limit for trial in a County Court, and even, if the plaintiff will not give security for costs, to remit *any* action of Tort where the defendant is prepared to swear that the plaintiff, if defeated, cannot pay costs.[5] Certain special kinds of cases, *e.g.* libel, slander, seduction, and 'breach of promise,' are excluded from the jurisdiction of the County Court.[6] On the other hand, subject to these exceptions, *any* Common Law case, however important, may, by consent of the parties, be tried in a County Court.[7]

[1] 27 Geo. II, c. 16. (The act is an admirable example of the 'omnibus' type of the eighteenth century. It deals with the destruction of turnpikes, the extension of the powers of the Trustees of the British Museum, the fees of Justices' Clerks, the offences of waggoners, and other miscellaneous matters.)

[2] 9 & 10 Vict. c. 95. (It has been repealed, but largely re-enacted, by the County Courts Act, 1888, at present the chief authority on the subject.)

[3] It is possible for the judge to order, either upon or without the request of a party, a trial by jury. But such cases are rare; and, in any event, there are no pleadings.

[4] 3 Edw. VII, c. 42 (County Courts Act, 1903).

[5] Act of 1888, ss. 65, 66.

[6] S. 56.

[7] S. 64.

In addition to its ordinary 'Common Law' and 'Equity' business, a County Court specially selected by Order in Council or Act of Parliament for the purpose, may exercise Admiralty jurisdiction up to £300 (if the claim is for towage, necessaries, or wages, only up to £150),[1] and bankruptcy jurisdiction up to any amount.[2] Moreover, there has been a tendency in recent years to throw upon the County Court judges a large amount of quasi-judicial or administrative business. Thus, they may be called upon to decide disputes under the Friendly Societies Act, and to assess compensation as arbitrators under the Agricultural Holdings Acts and the Workmen's Compensation Act. In the latter respect, their functions are of great and growing importance.

Admiralty and Bankruptcy Jurisdiction

Finally, a few words must be said about the uninteresting but important subject of bankruptcy jurisdiction, or the process by which the property of an insolvent debtor is realized for the benefit of his creditors, in proportion to their proved claims.

Bankruptcy Procedure

Whether or not any informal bankruptcy process existed at the common law, or was practised in any of the old local courts administering the Law Merchant, it seems impossible at present to say; but the former alternative, at least, is unlikely. The essence of bankruptcy proceedings is, that all creditors shall be paid rateably; and, with the machinery for enforcing individual debts which was available in the King's Courts from the thirteenth century onwards, it is unlikely that any customary process would have sufficed to restrain the individual creditor from stealing a march upon his fellows. But the statutory process begins so far back as the year 1542, when an 'Act against such persons as do make Bankrupt' was passed by Henry VIII's Parliament.[3] This statute adopts a sharp way with offenders; empowering a quorum of certain high officials (Chancellor, Treasurer, President of the Council, Privy Seal, and the Chief Justices) to 'take such order' with their bodies and property (lands as well as chattels) as shall be necessary to pay all their debts in full, or, at least, rateably. Of the familiar features of modern bankruptcy process, we notice

Statutes of Henry VIII

[1] County Courts Admiralty Jurisdiction Act, 1868, ss. 2, 3, 5. (By consent the amount may be unlimited.)

[2] Bankruptcy Act, 1883, ss. 92, 95–100.

[3] 34 & 35 Hen. VIII, c. 4.

already, in the Act of Henry VIII, the power to summon and examine persons believed to be concealing property of the bankrupt,[1] to deal with fictitious or collusive claims against the bankrupt,[2] and to punish absconding debtors.[3] But the remedies of the creditor were only to be suspended, not extinguished, by the bankruptcy. The debtor was to remain legally liable, as before, for the unpaid balances of all his debts.[4]

And Elizabeth

The statute of Henry VIII was not, in terms, confined to merchants. But it appears to have been so regarded in practice; for one of the first cares of the statute of Elizabeth is to define the class of merchants capable of being made bankrupt.[5] This statute marks a great advance in the development of bankruptcy procedure. It carefully enumerates[6] 'acts of bankruptcy,' *i.e.* such acts of a debtor as will justify the Court in commencing bankruptcy process against him. It provides[7] that the bankrupt and his property shall be handed over to a body of 'Commissioners' appointed by the Lord Chancellor under the Great Seal, who are to realize the property for the benefit of the creditors, and are, for that purpose, invested with large powers, both over the bankrupt himself, and persons suspected of colluding with him.[8] Property acquired by the bankrupt after the commencement of the bankruptcy is likewise to be made available, through the Commissioners, for the payment of his debts.[9] A bankrupt failing to surrender himself to his Commissioners after due proclamation, is to be deemed an outlaw; and any one sheltering him is to be liable to fine or imprisonment.[10]

An amending statute of the year 1603 introduced[11] the now important feature of the formal 'examination' of the bankrupt as to the conduct of his affairs, and made an important relaxation in the medieval rule against the assignment of choses in action,[12] by allowing debts due to the bankrupt to be sold by his Commissioners.[13] In 1662 it was deemed necessary, in consequence of the decision in *Sir John Wolstenholme's Case,* delivered by the Upper Bench in 1653, to pass a statute[14] declaring that shareholders in the privileged East India and Guinea

[1] 34 & 35 Hen. VIII, c. 4, s. 2. [2] *Ibid.*, ss. 3, 4. [3] *Ibid.*, s. 5. [4] *Ibid.*, s. 6. [5] 13 Eliz. (1570) c. 7, s. 1. [6] *Ibid.* [7] S. 2. [8] Ss. 5, 6. [9] S. 11. [10] S. 9. [11] 1 Jac. I, c. 15, s. 6. [12] *Ante*, p. 294. [13] 1 Jac. I, c. 15, s. 13. [14] 13 & 14 Car. II, c. 24.

joint-stock Companies should not, merely as such, be liable to become bankrupt.

Act of Anne

The early eighteenth century is remarkable for the first sign of any relenting from the pitiless severity of its predecessors towards the unfortunate merchant. A statute of the year 1705 [1] permits an allowance for maintenance to be made to a bankrupt who duly surrenders, and, even more important, grants him his 'discharge' from all debts owing at the commencement of his bankruptcy.[2] A significant provision of the same statute also forbids any allowance for 'eating or drinking' of the Commissioners or other persons at meeting of creditors.[3]

Statute of 1732

Apparently, however, this leniency was not without its dangers; for we notice a distinctly severer tone in the next great bankruptcy statute, passed in 1732.[4] This Act seems even to hint that people deliberately 'brought on' their own bankruptcies for the sake of getting rid of their liabilities; and it both increases the list of bankruptcy offences,[5] and extends the definition of persons liable to be made bankrupt.[6] The bankrupt is not to obtain his discharge, unless a certificate of due compliance with the law is furnished by his Commissioners, with the consent of four-fifths of the creditors, to the Lord Chancellor.[7] The Act of 1732 is also interesting as introducing [8] the institution of the 'assignee,' appointed at first by the Commissioners, afterwards by the creditors, to give closer attention to the affairs of the bankrupt than was possible for the Commissioners.

Act of 1825

The consolidating and amending Bankruptcy Act of 1825 [9] does not contain any features of startling novelty; though mention may be made of the preferential payment of workmen's wages,[10] the power given to the Commissioners to 'bar' the estates tail of the bankrupt,[11] and to nine-tenths in value of the creditors to accept a 'composition' from the debtor in lieu of continuing the bankruptcy proceedings,[12] and the limitation of the landlord's right to distrain on

[1] 4 & 5 Anne, c. 4 (or 4 Anne, c. 17). [2] S. 8. [3] S. 21.
[4] 5 Geo. II, c. 30. [5] S. 1. [6] S. 39 (bankers, brokers, and factors).
[7] S. 10. [8] S. 30. [9] 6 Geo. IV, c. 26. [10] S. 48.
[11] S. 65. The preceding section seems to contain a foreshadowing of the policy afterwards adopted in the Act for the Abolition of Fines and Recoveries.
[12] S. 133.

the bankrupt's goods to one year's arrears of rent.[1] But a radical change in the machinery of bankruptcy administration took place in 1831,[2] when the formerly independent groups of Commissioners gave way to a Court of Bankruptcy with a Chief and three 'puisne' judges, of whom three were to act as a Court of Review or appeal, and a staff of subordinate 'Commissioners' acting under the 'fiat' of the Court.[3] There can be little doubt that the system of independent Commissioners was thoroughly bad; but it may be doubted whether the scheme of 1831 was a great improvement upon it. For the Act of 1831 saddled upon the country not merely the judicial staff of the new Court, and the London and country Commissioners, but a staff (not to exceed thirty) of 'official assignees,'[4] to assist the 'creditors' assignees' appointed under the statute of 1732. However, in 1842,[5] the country Commissioners were abolished, and country bankruptcies removed to the local District Courts set up under the Act. The same statute[6] took away the power of the creditors to veto the grant of the debtor's discharge, and left the latter entirely to the discretion of the Court.

Act of 1847

In the year 1847 came a curious and, apparently, inconsistent statute.[7] On the one hand, it abolished[8] the 'Court of Review' set up in 1825, as well as the office of Chief Judge; transferring its jurisdiction to a Vice-Chancellor to be designated by the Lord Chancellor for the purpose.[9] It also transferred the jurisdiction of the 'District' or local Bankruptcy Courts set up under the Act of 1842 to the newly-established County Courts.[10] On the other hand, it established a new Court for the Relief of Insolvent Debtors,[11] *i.e.* for the benefit of those insolvent non-mercantile persons who, though incapable of being made bankrupt, were yet able, by surrendering their property, to escape imprisonment for debt, under the provisions of an Act of the year 1809.[12]

[1] S. 74.
[2] 1 & 2 Will. IV, c. 56.
[3] 1 & 2 Will. IV, c. 56, s. 1.
[4] S. 22.
[5] 5 & 6 Vict. c. 122, ss. 46, 59.
[6] S. 39.
[7] 10 & 11 Vict. c. 102.
[8] Ss. 1, 2.
[9] On the establishment of the Court of Appeal in Chancery, in the year 1851, the appellate jurisdiction in Bankruptcy was transferred to the Lords Justices then created (14 & 15 Vict. c. 83, s. 7.)
[10] 10 & 11 Vict. c. 102, s. 4.
[11] *Ibid.*
[12] 49 Geo. III, c. 115. The process had been improved by the Judgments Act, 1838.

In 1849 came another great consolidating statute,[1] without substantial change in principle. True that it continues the tendency,[2] previously begun, of eliminating quasi-independent Commissioners. But in other respects it does not seriously depart from the scheme of 1825; though it further enlarges the definition of a 'trader,'[3] adds failure to comply with a (Debtor's) Summons to the list of 'acts of bankruptcy,'[4] and introduces[5] the rule by which the creditors' representative is entitled to 'disclaim' a lease or other continuous obligation of the bankrupt, so as to capitalize at once all claims in respect of it.

Act of 1849

The first of the modern Bankruptcy codes may be said to be that of 1861.[6] It abolished the fundamental distinction, which had existed so long, between the trader and the non-trader, and made every adult person (other than a married woman) liable to be declared bankrupt.[7] As a natural consequence, it also abolished the Court for the Relief of Insolvent Debtors;[8] and put the crown on a tendency, long manifest, by doing away with 'Commissioners' and transferring the control of the creditors' assignees to the Registrars of the Court.[9] It added a further safeguard against abuse of bankruptcy process by placing conditions on the grant of an order of discharge.[10]

Act of 1861

The Bankruptcy Act, 1869, however, manifested a distinct reaction against the tendency to keep a tight official hand on the administration of a bankrupt's estate. The policy of 1869 was to entrust everything to the creditors in the belief that motives of self-interest would produce efficiency. The 'official assignee' of the Court was entirely abolished,[11] in favour of the creditors' assignee, or 'trustee,' who was to be supervised by a Committee of Inspection, elected by the creditors from among their own number.[12] To prevent undue leniency, however, further restrictions and limitations were placed[13] on the grant of the bankrupt's discharge. The Act of 1869 is, further, important as introducing the well-known 'voluntary settlement' clause,[14] by virtue of which voluntary dispositions of property, even though perfectly *bonâ fide*, are set aside as of course, if the settler's bankruptcy follows within a limited time.

Act of 1869

[1] 12 & 13 Vict. c. 106. [2] S. 7. [3] S. 65. [4] S. 78.
[5] S. 145. [6] 24 & 25 Vict. c. 134. [7] S. 69. [8] S. 1. [9] S. 4.
[10] S. 159. [11] 32 & 33 Vict. c. 71, s. 14 (1). [12] *Ibid.* (3). [13] S. 48. [14] S. 91.

In that Act, however, the settlement clause only applied to a trader. The Act also contained [1] an elaborate scheme of voluntary 'liquidation by arrangement,' by which creditors might, if they pleased, dispense entirely with the assistance of the Court, as well as a renewal of the policy of 1825, by which, after the passing of an 'extraordinary' resolution, duly confirmed, the creditors might simply accept a 'composition' offered by the debtor, without further process.[2]

Unfortunately, however, the confidence in enlightened self-interest manifested by the Act of 1869, did not prove to be entirely justified. In fact, the psychology of its framers was at fault. They failed to realize, that a busy tradesman or professional man would far rather 'write off' a moderate loss, and have done with it, than waste time in attending creditors' meetings or investigating his debtor's accounts. The inevitable consequence of this fact was, that, under the Act of 1869, bankruptcy proceedings tended to fall entirely into the hands of lawyers and accountants, whose zeal for despatch and economy was apt to wane, in the face of indifference on the part of those who should have been their constant critics. Accordingly, in the year 1883, Mr. Joseph Chamberlain, then President of the Board of Trade, determined upon a radical change of policy; and the statute of that year is as remarkable for its insistence on State control as was its predecessor of 1869 for its confidence in *laissez-faire*.

Acts of 1883 and 1890

By virtue of the Bankruptcy Act, 1883,[3] and its amendment of 1890,[4] as soon as a bankruptcy petition is presented against a debtor, a 'receiving order' may be made by the Court, which will entitle the Official Receiver of the Board of Trade to assume control, in the interest of the creditors, of all the debtor's property.[5] Of course, if, on the hearing of the petition, it is dismissed, the receiving order will be cancelled; but its value to the creditors, as a precaution, can hardly be over-estimated. On adjudication, the property (present and future) of the bankrupt (as he now is) vests in the Official Receiver,[6] unless and until a trustee is appointed by the

[1] S. 125. [2] S. 126. [3] 46 & 47 Vict. c. 52.
[4] 53 & 54 Vict. c. 71. [5] Act of 1883, s. 5.
[6] Owing to a series of somewhat inconsistent decisions of the Courts, while freehold property coming to the bankrupt (*New Land Development Assocn. v. Gray*

creditors; and the summoning and direction of creditors' meetings, and the conduct of the debtor's examination, are largely in the hands of the same official, acting under the supervision of the Registrar of the Court.[1] Further, the Board of Trade is charged, not only with the appointment and control of Official Receivers, who are its servants, but with the audit of trustees' accounts,[2] the removal of incapable, defaulting, or misbehaving trustees,[3] and the appointment of trustees in those cases in which the creditors fail to appoint.[4] Other noticeable features of the Act of 1883 are, the provision for the expeditious conduct of 'small bankruptcies,'[5] and, of the Act of 1890, that for the actual winding up in bankruptcy of the estates of deceased insolvents,[6] and severe restrictions on the granting and operation of an order of discharge.[7] Notwithstanding all these precautions, the working of bankruptcy procedure still leaves much opening for criticism; and new legislation is believed to be contemplated.

[1892] 2 Ch. 138) vests at once in his trustee, leaseholds and other property do not, until claimed by the trustee, at any rate in favour of *bonâ fide* purchasers for value from the bankrupt (*Cohen v. Mitchell* (1890) 15 Q.B.D. 262).

1 Act of 1883, s. 99. (The old Court of Bankruptcy was, by the Act of 1883 (s. 93 (2)) merged in the Supreme Court of Judicature; and its jurisdiction is exerciseable by a Judge of the High Court 'assigned' for the purpose.)

2 Act of 1883, s. 78.

3 S. 86; Act of 1890, s. 19.

4 Act of 1883, s. 21.

5 S. 121.

6 S. 22. (The rules of administration applicable in bankruptcy had been partly extended to the administration of insolvent estates in Chancery by s. 10 of the Judicature Act, 1875).

7 S. 8.

INDEX